"*Marketing Channel Strategy: An Omni-Channel Approach* is fresh, insightful, a packed with information. The material is easy to read and digest and flows well. Readers will walk away with a clear understanding of the omni-channel ecosystem and how to build effective omni-channel strategies. The role and impact of omni-channels on each sector of the channel landscape is clearly laid out. The book is built on solid theoretical foundation but is very managerial at the same time."—**Rajdeep Grewal, The Townsend Family Distinguished Professor and Area Chair, Marketing Editor-in-Chief,** *Journal of Marketing Research*, **Kenan-Flagler Business School, University of North Carolina-Chapel Hill, USA**

"*Marketing Channel Strategy: An Omni-Channel Approach* is a very readable and updated take on a classic text. Omni-channels are growing in importance, and they fundamentally change the way firms go to market and connect with their customers. Unfortunately, however, there are few available frameworks to guide managerial decision-making in this area. This book draws on current academic research and industry practice to develop a compelling strategic framework that fills this void in the literature. The framework's guiding principle is the idea of an omni-channel 'ecosystem,' and the authors apply it to a variety of different channel contexts, including wholesaling, franchising, and retailing. The book is packed with insights, and the authors do an excellent job of illustrating them with current examples."—**Jan B. Heide, Michael Lehman Distinguished Chair in Business, Wisconsin School of Business, University of Wisconsin-Madison, USA**

"This leading textbook on marketing channels is completely redone and offers a unique take on channel marketing management in the light of the present-day reality. *Marketing Channel Strategy: An Omni-Channel Approach* builds a model that shows students and practicing managers how to engage and make the customer experience seamless across multiple channels. I find the chapter on international channels and base of the pyramid particularly informative, pragmatic, and interesting. The book is modular and can be used in a variety of classes including retailing, international marketing, channels, e-marketing, and marketing strategy."—**Constantine S. Katsikeas, Arnold Ziff Research Chair and Professor of Marketing and International Management, University of Leeds, UK**

"Effective omni-channel management is a critical source of value and an important differential edge in the modern marketplace. Given the trends toward omni-channel ecosystems, it is key that managers and managers-in-training (i.e., students) focus more of their attention on channel management. This cutting-edge text can be a catalyst for renewed interest in channel management; it highlights the need for a greater focus on this element of the go-to-market marketing strategy."—**Dhruv Grewal, Toyota Chair of Commerce and Electronic Business and Professor of Marketing, Babson College, USA**

"*Marketing Channel Strategy: An Omni-Channel Approach* blends theory with practice-oriented examples to clearly enunciate the difference between a multi-channel and omni-channel worldview. The examples and exercises make it easy for managers and students to grasp the challenges involved in developing effective omni-channel strategies. This book can be used as a stand-alone in a distribution or channel strategy class or modules can be used in a variety of marketing classes."—**Robert Dahlstrom, Joseph Siebert Professor, Miami University, USA and Professor of Marketing, BI Norwegian Business School, Norway**

Marketing Channel Strategy

Marketing Channel Strategy: An Omni-Channel Approach is the first book on the market to offer a completely unique, updated approach to channel marketing. Palmatier and Sivadas have adapted this classic text for the modern marketing reality by building a model that shows students how to engage customers across multiple marketing channels simultaneously and seamlessly.

The omni-channel is different from the multi-channel. It recognizes not only that customers access goods and services in multiple ways, but also that they are likely doing this at the same time; comparing prices on multiple websites, and seamlessly switching between mobile and desktop devices. With the strong theoretical foundation that users have come to expect, the book also offers lots of practical exercises and applications to help students understand how to design and implement omni-channel strategies in reality.

Advanced undergraduate and graduate students in marketing channels, distribution channels, B2B marketing, and retailing classes will enjoy acquiring the most cutting-edge marketing skills from this book.

Robert W. Palmatier is Professor of Marketing and John C. Narver Endowed Professor in Business Administration at the Foster School of Business, University of Washington, USA and the Research Director of the Sales and Marketing Strategy Institute.

Eugene Sivadas is Professor of Marketing and Associate Dean at the Milgard School of Business, University of Washington Tacoma, USA.

Louis W. Stern is John D. Gray Distinguished Professor Emeritus of Marketing at the Kellogg School of Management, Northwestern University, USA.

Adel I. El-Ansary is the Donna L. Harper Professor of Marketing at the University of North Florida, USA.

Marketing Channel Strategy

An Omni-Channel Approach

Ninth Edition

Robert W. Palmatier,
Eugene Sivadas, Louis W. Stern, and
Adel I. El-Ansary

NEW YORK AND LONDON

First published 2020
by Routledge
52 Vanderbilt Avenue, New York, NY 10017

and by Routledge
2 Park Square, Milton Park, Abingdon, Oxon, OX14 4RN

Routledge is an imprint of the Taylor & Francis Group, an informa business

Library of Congress Cataloging-in-Publication Data
A catalog record for this title has been requested

ISBN: 978-1-138-59393-0 (hbk)
ISBN: 978-0-367-26209-9 (pbk)
ISBN: 978-0-429-29199-9 (ebk)

Typeset in ITC Stone Serif
by Swales & Willis Ltd, Exeter, Devon, UK

Visit the website: www.routledge.com/cw/marketingchannelstrategy

Brief Contents

Contents

Figures, Tables, Sidebars, and Appendices

FIGURES

TABLES

SIDEBARS

APPENDICES

Preface

NEW TO THIS EDITION

The primary goal for this Ninth Edition, as reflected in the change in the title—from *Marketing Channel Strategy* to *Marketing Channel Strategy: An Omni-Channel Approach*—has been to create a completely repositioned, comprehensive, research-based, readable, action-oriented guide for practicing managers and managers-in-training with an interest in how to adopt and apply real-world omni-channel strategies. This edition of the book is structured to provide background knowledge and process steps for understanding, designing, and implementing high-performing omni-channel strategies.

Many significant changes have been made to the Ninth Edition. A new omni-channel strategy framework, introduced in Chapter 1, defines the structure of the rest of this book, providing an approach that guides managers through the steps necessary for developing and implementing an omni-channel strategy. We offer a distinction between omni-channel and multi-channel strategies in this chapter, outline the tasks and functions of channel members, and provide a snapshot of the various actors involved in a marketing channel ecosystem. This chapter also addresses topics such as going to market with an omni-channel strategy and the five trends driving the growth of omni-channels. To help channel managers design a strategy and manage it over time, Chapter 1 addresses some central omni-channel questions:

- What is an omni-channel strategy?

- What is driving the importance of an omni-channel world?

- How does an omni-channel strategy differ from a traditional and multi-channel strategy?

- What are the key trends in omni-channel strategy and going to market with such a strategy?

In each chapter of the book, we have added several pull-out examples from around the world; we also provide longer sidebars in each chapter in an effort to bring the concepts outlined in the book to life. With a renewed focus on readability, we acknowledge that developing sound channel strategies first requires that managers have a good understanding of channel fundamentals, along with a more detailed understanding of the various intermediaries involved in omni-channel marketing.

The first part of the book (Chapters 1–5) accordingly focuses on channel and omni-channel fundamentals. In Chapter 2, we review omni-channel and channel basics. We discuss the benefits of marketing channels for upstream and downstream channel members, the key functions marketing channels perform, and how to audit marketing channels and omni-channels in particular. Chapter 2 draws from materials that were part of Chapters 3–5 in the Eighth Edition. Chapter 3 details issues of power and dependence; Chapter 4 focuses on channel relationships. Chapter 5 then deals with channel conflict (covered in Chapters 10–12 in the previous edition). These vastly rewritten chapters reflect an omni-channel perspective, replete with current examples. We have moved the discussion of these topics earlier in the book, in the belief that to implement effective channel and omni-channel strategies, we need a good grasp of the issues that channel managers frequently encounter.

Next, the second part comprises Chapters 6–9, with a specific focus on channel participants in retailing, wholesaling, franchising, and international channel domains, respectively. Reflecting our revised perspective on omni-channel considerations, discussions that previously appeared in a separate chapter on e-commerce have been integrated with retailing (Chapter 6). In addition, we integrate substantial discussions of e-commerce in various chapters, to reflect the role of mobile commerce and other emerging technologies. All chapters have been updated with current examples and recognition of modern trends in retailing, wholesaling, and franchising, as well as how the move to omni-channels is affecting these sectors. The new Chapter 9, focused on international channels, describes ways to distribute products overseas and the various methods for doing so, from exporting and export management companies to vast trading companies. We also introduce a section about marketing to channels at the base or bottom of the pyramid and provide more insights about channels as they appear in emerging markets.

The third part deals with omni-channel strategies. Whereas in the Eighth Edition, the end-user analysis appeared in Chapter 2, in the current edition, we shift it to Chapter 10, so that we can better integrate omni-channel perspectives. Thus the revised text outlines the challenges of end-user analysis and segmentation in omni-channel contexts. In Chapter 11, we outline omni-channel strategies and the four pillars on which such strategies should be built.

Some chapters on channel legalities and channel logistics have been removed.

Overall, then, *Marketing Channel Strategy: An Omni-Channel Approach* is designed for an international audience of practicing managers and managers-in-training. The focus is firmly on going to the market with an omni-channel strategy—that is, the set of activities that work seamlessly to design and manage a marketing channel that can enhance the firm's sustainable competitive advantage and financial performance and provide a unified end-user experience. More simply, companies and processes come together to bring products and services from their point of origin to their point of consumption. Through omni-marketing channels, the originator of the products or services gains access to markets and end-users. Channel structures and strategies thus are critical to any firm's long-term success.

The book features examples taken from around the world and from a range of industries and markets. However, the ideas and processes generalize to virtually any context and channel situation. Sidebars appear in every chapter to highlight key channel issues and strategies and provide concrete examples of the theories, processes, and ideas presented in the text.

Each chapter also is designed to stand on its own. The chapters are modular, so they can be combined with other material and used in various classes for which channels are relevant concepts (e.g., service marketing, marketing strategy, business-to-business marketing, Internet marketing, retailing, international marketing). The content of each chapter reflects leading academic research and practice in distinct disciplines (e.g., marketing, strategy, economics, sociology, political science).

The framework that underlies this book also is useful for creating a new omni-channel strategy in previously untapped markets, as well as for critically analyzing and refining existing channel strategies. Various supporting materials for this textbook are available to adopting instructors through our instructors' resource center (IRC) online.

Acknowledgments

Robert Palmatier thanks his colleagues and doctoral students whose insights into sales and marketing have helped inform this book in multiple ways: Denni Arli, Todd Arnold, Joshua T. Beck, Abhishek Borah, Daniel Claro, Andrew Crecelius, Eric Fang, Gabe Gonzalez, Srinath Gopalakrishna, Dhruv Grewal, Rajdeep Grewal, Colleen Harmeling, Conor Henderson, Mark B. Houston, Brett Josephson, Vamsi Kanuri, Frank R. Kardes, Jisu J. Kim, Irina V. Kozlenkova, Justin Lawrence, Ju-Yeon Lee, Kelly Martin, Jordan Moffett, Stephen Samaha, Lisa K. Scheer, Hari Sridhar, Jan-Benedict E.M. Steenkamp, Park Thaichon, George Watson, Scott Weaven, Stefan Worm, and Jonathan Zhang. His debt to past MBA, EMBA, and PhD students is vast; they were key in developing many of the insights in this book. He is also extremely grateful to Charles and Gwen Lillis for their past support of the Foster Business School and his research, which helped make this book possible. All of the authors extend their appreciation to Elisabeth Nevins for editing and often rewriting the chapters to enhance the readability of this book. Finally, Rob acknowledges the support and love of his daughter, Alexandra, which have made this effort worthwhile.

Eugene Sivadas thanks Rob Palmatier for inviting him to join this intellectual journey and also acknowledges the extraordinary contributions of those who contributed to previous editions of this book. He thanks F. Robert Dwyer for introducing him to the world of marketing channels and direct marketing—little realizing that it would become the foundation for an omni-channel worldview. Eugene also thanks Raj Mehta for initiating him into the world of Internet marketing in the mid-1990s. He appreciates the insights of his many coauthors and countless students who have shaped his thinking and thanks his colleagues at the University of Washington Tacoma for their support. Eugene acknowledges the assistance of students Phoebe Stoican, Tina Van, John Bates, Jr., McKenzie Krause, and Kouga Brennan Rollins. Eugene acknowledges the support and love of his parents, wife Amanda, and sons Neal and Jay.

Louis Stern acknowledges the support, encouragement, and friendship of his Northwestern University marketing department colleagues over a long period of time; they have never wavered in their enthusiasm for his work. He is especially grateful to Anne Coughlan, who shouldered a number of revisions of the text, along with his dear, late friend, Erin Anderson of INSEAD. His greatest debt, however, is owed to his doctoral students at Northwestern and Ohio State universities (one of whom, Adel El-Ansary, has been his coauthor on this text for more than 30 years), who kept him current, intellectually stimulated, and enthusiastic throughout his career. And his appreciation of Rob Palmatier and Eugene Sivadas is unbounded, for keeping this text alive for future generations of students who find the study of marketing channels fascinating, challenging, and rewarding.

Adel El-Ansary acknowledges the intellectual exchange and friendship of faculty colleagues of the Inter-organizational and Relationship Marketing Special Interest Groups, Academic Division of the American Marketing Association, and the Board of Governance, Distinguished Fellows, and Leadership Group of the Academy of Marketing Science. His greatest debt is owed to his mentors at Ohio State University: the late William R. Davidson and the late Robert Bartels fueled his interest in the study of marketing; Lou Stern sparked his interest in marketing channels, leading to a lifetime of intellectual inquiry and partnership on this text. Rob Palmatier is a leader in the field. His taking charge, commencing with the Eighth Edition of *Marketing Channel Strategy*, has extended the life of the brand and ensures that future generations of students will be informed of the importance of the role of channels in marketing and society.

Finally, we are indebted to the vast number of authors whose work we cite throughout this text. Without their efforts, we could not have written this book.

Robert W. Palmatier, Seattle, Washington
Eugene Sivadas, Tacoma, Washington
Louis W. Stern, Evanston, Illinois
Adel I. El-Ansary, Jacksonville, Florida

The Omni-Channel Ecosystem

INTRODUCTION

This book examines ways to design, modify, and maintain effective channel strategies and structures, in consumer goods markets and business-to-business markets, for both physical products and services, within nations and across country borders. We take an omni-channel perspective. In this first chapter, we define and elaborate on the concept of omni-channels and discuss the factors driving and shaping their ecosystem. We also contrast an omni-channel approach with a multi-channel approach and provide examples of ways to go to market with an effective omni-channel strategy.

This approach represents an expansion beyond a traditional marketing strategy, which focuses on the four marketing mix elements: product, price, promotion, and channel (or "place," in the popular 4P designation).[1] Marketers devote attention and energy to decisions about the development, branding, promotion, and prices of the products and services they offer; the ability to make products and services available to customers, when and where they want them, is also a critical and indispensable marketing function and the focus of this book. Each firm must make a series of decisions, both strategic and tactical, to determine how to distribute its offerings to ensure they are available to end-customers. These comprehensive, firm-to-end-user links essentially function as the routes a firm uses to get its products and services into the hands of the end-users. Actors within these links together make up a **marketing channel** or **marketing channel system**, composed of inter- and independent organizations that work to go to market with a product or service, so that it is available for use or consumption.

Developing a **go-to-market strategy** that deploys the most optimal combination of actors in an efficient manner, such that the product or service is available and easily accessible for purchase, is indispensable to firm success. Conversely, inadequate distribution is a primary cause of failure.[2] A go-to-market strategy is the blueprint used to deliver the firm's offerings to end-users in a manner that conforms to their preferred mode and method of buying and also is efficient and cost-effective, so that it confers a competitive advantage on the firm.

When developing a go-to-market strategy, the firm must know its consumers' or end-users' buying preferences, including the information and education end-users might need before they can make purchase decisions, the services and after-sales support they seek, their expectations, their willingness to pay for extras, their delivery preferences, their financing needs, and the mode of ordering they like best. As a firm devises its go-to-market approach, it also must be cognizant of the costs and benefits associated with various routes to market and balance them against customers' preferences, as well as with the firm's own desire for market coverage, willingness and ability to invest to acquire this necessary market coverage, and desire for control.

Thus, developing a go-to-market strategy requires three main steps.[3] First, the firm must perform a thorough analysis of industry channel practices to isolate critical successful factors. Second, channel managers should identify areas of improvement in their practices. Third, the firm can develop policies and procedures to incentivize and alter channel partners' behaviors to motivate their efficient execution of channel tasks. That is, most distribution systems rely on independent third parties, whose incentive systems may not align with the seller's, so implementing a go-to-market strategy also entails managing the relationship with partners, to get them to do what the firm wants from them.

Firms have many alternatives when it comes to designing a channel system, each with its own strengths and weaknesses. Consider two massive restaurant chains, McDonald's and Starbucks. Franchising is the preferred route to market for the fast food giant McDonald's, such that 82 percent of its 36,000 outlets are franchised.[4] But Starbucks typically operates company-owned stores and has avoided franchising, at least in the United States, due to fears about diluting the brand and customers' in-store experience.[5] Yet even Starbucks makes some concessions, such that it uses licensing to operate stores in airports and college campuses and has also adopted franchising as a go-to-market strategy in European markets, where the high rents made company-owned stores infeasible.[6]

Some firms take over distribution functions, by building an in-house distribution system over which they maintain complete control, but such a system also requires developing internal expertise and making considerable investments to build company-owned distribution channels—such that this option might not be feasible or desirable in all cases. Furthermore, most products and services need to go through multiple marketing channels before reaching end-users. A direct distribution model, in which items move straight from the manufacturer to the end-user without any intermediaries, is rare, due to the conflicting demands associated with resource availability, cost, coverage, specialization requirements, and end-consumer preferences. Intermediaries can perform many required tasks at lower costs or with greater efficiency and effectiveness, especially when they possess superior operational expertise, better infrastructure (e.g., warehousing facilities), market knowledge, or connections to consumers. It likely would be cost and time prohibitive for manufacturers to acquire such expertise, resources, and connections, so, for example, many firms use Amazon or Alibaba as a key channel to market, granting the massive retail channel partner the responsibility for most channel tasks.

EXAMPLE: FULFILLMENT BY AMAZON (USA)

Amazon is the 237th largest corporation in the world.[7] Among its customer base of about 120 million people, 63 million are Prime members and pay an annual membership fee to receive enhanced services, such as free shipping.[8] Amazon also offers its business clients a service, Fulfillment by Amazon (FBA),[9] that permits them to ship their products in bulk to Amazon. For a fee, it will store the product and then complete individual customer orders as they come in and provide the customer support service. Thus, businesses get access to Amazon's huge customer base and delegate many channel functions to it, all for a relatively small fee.

WHAT IS A MARKETING CHANNEL?

A marketing channel goes by many aliases, including "place" in the 4P framework, distribution channel, route to market, and go to market, or simply channels. We define a **marketing channel** specifically as the set of interdependent but in many cases independent organizations involved in the process of taking a product or service to market and making it available for use or consumption. Unique organizations, each with specific strengths and weaknesses, comprise any marketing channel system: distributors, wholesalers, brokers, franchisees, and retailers. With the participation of these various actors, marketing channels represent a significant portion of the world's business, and an effective marketing channel strategy can be a source of competitive advantage, by delivering superior customer value.

Total sales through such channels represent approximately one-third of the world's annual gross domestic product, so understanding and managing these marketing channels is critical for most businesses.[10] For example, raw material and component product manufacturers often rely on distributors and manufacturer representatives to sell their offerings to original equipment manufacturers (OEMs), so that they can outsource various necessary functions like sales, business development, education (or information), logistics, contracting, and order processing and financing. In addition, these intermediaries may share risk and help manage the customer relationship. Then the end-customer—that is, the OEM—assembles the components into finished products and services, which it sells to wholesalers and retailers, and the retailers ultimately make the products available to consumers. Figure 1.1 outlines some varied channel functions. A marketing channel strategy specifically defines the design and management of a channel structure to ensure that the overall channel system operates efficiently and effectively.

The end goal of any channel system is to make products and services available and easy for users to buy, in accordance with their preferences. Otherwise, the firm's reach and attractiveness to buyers will be limited, with negative effects on firm sales. For example, a movie's success strongly depends on the number of screens on which it is shown, so it is in the interest of movie producers to manage their distribution systems effectively. But any channel system also must be efficient and cost-effective.

The Changing Channel Landscape

Technological advances significantly affect channel landscapes, and as the role of physical stores changes, manufacturers and retailers face new conundrums.

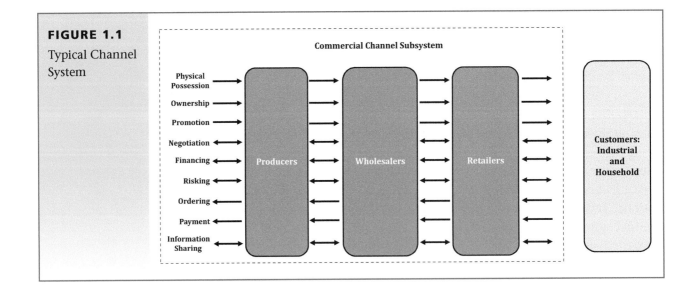

FIGURE 1.1

Typical Channel System

The Internet and e-commerce, smartphones and mobile technologies, and social media all have altered how consumers and end-users buy, with far-reaching implications across the channel landscape. Social media and online review sites present opportunities for brand advocacy but are also taking over information functions traditionally provided by channel partners, leaving them with less control over what information gets spread.[11] Department stores such as Macy's, JCPenney, and Sears are struggling to find their bearings,[12,13] while various specialty stores such as Sports Authority have closed shop.[14]

Managers are vexed by such altered channel landscapes for several reasons. First, building or modifying a channel system involves costly, hard-to-reverse investments. Taking the effort to do it right the first time has great value; making a mistake may put the company at a long-term disadvantage. Second, modifying channels means confronting entrenched interests and the way things have always been done. Channel conflicts intensify and require attention. Third, managers face challenging decisions when devising an optimal channel strategy, including where to devote the considerable financial investments required and how to adjust the roles and compensation of different channel members. The latest frontiers of e-commerce, including automatic replenishment, virtual and augmented reality, and shorter delivery time frames, will continue to vex marketers.

Integrating across channels also remains a challenge. For example, the proliferation of mobile devices makes price and product comparisons easier, so consumers demand greater pricing transparency but also learn about various features available from competitive brands. Price differences across channels can exacerbate channel conflict, but online stores accrue much lower operating costs, because they do not need locations in high-rent districts or expensive salespeople. Thus, whereas in 2015, only 8 percent of consumers bought groceries online, that percentage doubled just one year later.[15]

Showrooming also has grown into a difficult challenge, such that consumers use one retail outlet to touch, feel, and try on products but then buy from a different, e-commerce outlet. In the practice of **pseudoshowrooming**, consumers inspect a product in the store but buy a related but different product online.[16]

EXAMPLE: BEST BUY'S RESPONSE TO ONLINE THREATS (USA)

Even as the wider retail industry confronts store closings on a vast scale, the consumer electronics retailer Best Buy—faced with the threat of becoming a showroom for online retailers such as Amazon—is heading off most challenges. Key elements of its strategy include charging prices comparable to those offered by online vendors, to minimize showrooming tendencies. In addition, with store-within-a-store formats, it partners with key vendors such as Samsung

(continued)

(continued)

that can drive consumers to visit stores, because of their loyalty to the brands or because they want to experience and try items before purchasing them. For example, the recent addition of Dyson products means that consumers can try out innovative hair dryers and vacuum cleaners in Best Buy stores.[17] Furthermore, Best Buy invests heavily in training a knowledgeable, customer-friendly sales force. To establish an omni-channel experience, the retailer lets consumers shop for products across multiple platforms and buy according to their own preferred shopping combination, whether that involves researching in store and buying online, or vice versa, or some other combination of channels.[18]

Marketing Channel Actors

To be straightforward and avoid confusion, we identify and define three key entities involved in every marketing channel: *manufacturers*, *intermediaries* (wholesale, retail, and specialized), and *end-users* (business customers or consumers). The presence or absence of a particular type of channel member is dictated by its ability to perform the necessary channel functions in such a way that it adds value. Sidebar 1.1 details an example from the tea industry in Taiwan that showcases the value that an intermediary can provide.

SIDEBAR 1.1
Tea Selling in Taiwan: The Key Roles of Tea Intermediaries[19]

The Taiwanese tea industry got its start when tea trees imported from China got planted in the Taiwanese hills in the mid-1800s. By the late 1920s, there were about 20,000 tea farmers in Taiwan, who sold their product (so-called *crude tea*) to one of about 60 tea intermediaries, who in turn sold it to 280 tea refineries located in Ta-tao-cheng, on the coast, ready for commercial sale and exportation. The tea intermediaries traversed the hills of Taiwan to search for and buy tea then bring it down to the dock to sell to refineries. But they also suffered a poor reputation among both farmers and refineries. Intermediaries were accused of exploiting the market by buying low and selling high; critics suggested that a simple direct trading system could be instituted to bypass them completely.

Thus in 1923, the Governor-General of Taiwan set up a tea auction house in Ta-tao-cheng. Farmers could ship their tea directly to the auction house, where a first-price, sealed-bid auction would determine the price refineries would pay to obtain their products. The auction house's operating costs were covered by farmers' membership fees, trading charges, and subsidies by the Governor-General, so the tea intermediaries suddenly had to compete with the auction house. Despite this new and well-supported form of competition, the intermediaries not only survived, they ultimately forced the closing of the auction house. But how could this outcome arise if they were just "exploiters" of the buy–sell situation? The answer is that they weren't. They served key functions.

First, the intermediaries *facilitated search* in the marketplace. An intermediary would visit many farms, finding tea to sell, which constituted an upstream search for product supply. With the product supply in hand, the intermediary would take samples to a series of refineries and ask for purchase orders. Visiting multiple refineries was necessary because the same variety and quality of tea could fetch very different prices from different refineries, depending on the uses to which they would put the tea. This search process repeated every season, because each refinery's offer changed from season to season. The intermediaries thus found buyers for the farmers' harvest and tea supplies for the refineries.

Second, tea intermediaries performed various *sorting* functions. Crude tea was highly heterogeneous; even the same species of tea tree, cultivated on different farms, exhibited wide quality variations. Furthermore, 28 different species of tea trees grew in the Taiwanese hills! The appraisal process, at both intermediary and refinery levels, therefore demanded considerable skill. Refineries hired specialists to appraise the tea they received; intermediaries facilitated this process by *accumulating* the tea harvests of multiple farmers into homogeneous lots for sale.

Third, tea intermediaries *minimized the number of contacts* in the channel system. With 20,000 tea farmers and 60 refineries, up to 1,200,000 contacts would be necessary for each farmer to market the product to get the best refinery price (even if each farmer cultivated only one variety of tea tree). Instead, each farmer tended to sell to just one intermediary, such that about 20,000 contacts existed at this first level of the channel. If the average intermediary collected n varieties of tea, and we assume that each of the 280 intermediaries negotiated, on behalf of the farmers, with all 60 refineries, we find $[60 \times 280 \times n]$ negotiations between intermediaries and refineries. The total number of negotiations, throughout the channel, in the presence of intermediaries thus was $[20,000 + 16,800 \times n]$, a value that exceeds 1,200,000 negotiations only if the number of tea varieties exceeded 70. But because there were only about 25 tea varieties in Taiwan at the time, intermediaries reduced the number of contacts from more than 1 million to about 440,000.

Such value-added activities had been completely ignored in the attacks made on the tea intermediaries as "exploiters." The resulting failure of the government-sanctioned and -subsidized auction house suggests that, far from merely exploiting the market, tea intermediaries were efficiency-enhancing market-makers. In this situation, the intermediation of the channel added value and reduced costs at the same time.

In many cases, one channel member serves as the **channel captain**, taking the keenest interest in the workings of the channel for the focal product or service and acting as the prime mover in establishing and maintaining channel links. The channel captain is often the manufacturer; it typically designs the overall go-to-market strategy, particularly for branded products. In the subsequent sections, we thus take the manufacturer's perspective frequently when describing a marketing channel strategy, but we explicitly acknowledge that manufacturers are not the only ones that can function as channel captains.

Manufacturers: Upstream Channel Members

When we refer to **manufacturers**, we mean the producer or originator of the product or service being sold. In the modern retail marketplace, ownership of a brand can belong to the manufacturer (Mercedes-Benz) or a retailer (e.g., Arizona clothing at JCPenney), or the retailer may be the brand (e.g., The Gap). Manufacturers can produce brands, or they can sell private labels, and these two broad categories feature some key distinctions. First, manufacturers that brand their products are known by those names to end-users, even if intermediaries distribute their offerings. Famous examples include Coca-Cola, Budweiser beer (owned by Anheuser-Busch InBev), Mercedes-Benz, and Sony. Second, manufacturers that make products but do not invest in a branded name for them produce **private-label products**, and the downstream buyer (manufacturer or retailer) puts its own name on them. For example, Multibar Foods Inc. makes private-label products for the neutraceutical marketplace (health, diet, and snack bars); its branded clients include Dr. Atkins' Nutritionals and Quaker Oats Co. The company takes care of research and development, so the expertise and knowledge it can provide make it valuable to brand companies that hire it to produce their products.[20] Branded manufacturers sometimes choose to allocate some part of their available production capacity to make private-label goods, though at the risk of helping a future competitor. In the U.K. market, private labels account for more than half the goods sold in leading supermarkets.[21]

A manufacturer can produce a service too, such as the tax preparation services offered by H&R Block (franchisor) or insurance policies provided by State Farm or Allstate. These brands sell no physical products; rather, the companies create families of services to sell, which constitutes their "manufacturing" function. In turn, marketing channel functions typically focus on promotional or risk-oriented activities, such as when H&R Block promotes its services on behalf of both itself and its franchisees with a guarantee to find the maximum tax refund allowed by law. Insurance companies similarly tend to ignore physical products and focus on promotions (on behalf of independent agents in the marketplace) and risk (here, risk management is the very heart of the industry). Therefore, the lack of a physical product that needs to move through the channel does not mean that channel design or management issues disappear.

As these examples also suggest, the manufacturer is not always the channel captain. For branded, produced goods, such as Mercedes-Benz automobiles, the manufacturer clearly serves this role; its ability and desire to manage channel efforts proactively relates intimately to its investment in the brand equity of its offerings. But a private-label apparel or neutraceutical manufacturer is not evidently the owner of the brand name, at least from end-users' perspectives, who instead see another channel member (e.g., the retailer) as the apparent owner.

Nor does a manufacturer's ability to manage production mean that it excels in other marketing channel activities. An apparel manufacturer is not necessarily a retailing or logistics expert. But there are some activities that nearly every manufacturer must undertake. Physical product manufacturers must hold on to the product and maintain ownership of it, until the product leaves their manufacturing sites and travels to the next channel member. Manufacturers must engage in negotiations with buyers, to set the terms for selling and merchandising their products. The manufacturer of a branded good also participates significantly in promoting its products. Yet various intermediaries in the channel still add value through their superior performance of functions that manufacturers cannot, so manufacturers voluntarily seek them out to increase their reach and appeal.

Intermediaries: Middle-Channel Members

The term **intermediary** encompasses any channel member *other* than the manufacturer or end-user. We differentiate three general types: wholesaler, retailer, and specialized.

Wholesalers

Wholesalers include merchant wholesalers or distributors, manufacturers' representatives, agents, and brokers. A wholesaler sells to other channel intermediaries, such as retailers, or to business end-users, but not to individual consumer end-users. Chapter 7 discusses wholesaling in depth. Briefly, though, we note that merchant wholesalers take title to and physical possession of inventory, store inventory (frequently from multiple manufacturers), promote products in their line, and arrange for financing, ordering, and payment by customers. They earn profits by buying at a wholesale price and selling at a marked-up price to downstream customers, then pocketing the difference (net of any distribution costs they bear). Manufacturers' representatives, agents, and brokers rarely take title to or physical possession of the goods they sell (e.g., real estate agents do not buy the houses they have been enlisted to sell); rather, they engage in promotion and negotiation to sell the products of the manufacturers they represent and negotiate terms of trade for them. Some intermediaries (e.g., trading companies, export management companies) specialize in international selling, regardless of whether they take title or physical possession; we elaborate on these intermediaries in Chapter 9.

Retail Intermediaries

Retailers come in many forms: department stores, mass merchandisers, hypermarkets, specialty stores, category killers, convenience stores, franchises, buying clubs, warehouse clubs, direct retailers—to name just a few. Unlike purely wholesale intermediaries, they sell directly to individual consumer end-users. Their role historically entailed amassing an assortment of goods that would appeal to consumers, but today that role has greatly expanded. Retailers might contract to produce private-label goods, such that they achieve effective vertical integration upstream in the supply chain. They also may sell to buyers other than consumers; Office Depot earns significant sales by selling to businesses rather than consumers (i.e., about one-third of its total sales), even though its storefronts nominally identify the chain as a retailer. In particular, Office Depot's Business Solutions Group sells services to businesses through various routes, including direct sales, catalogs, call centers, and Internet sites, and it makes these business-to-business sales services available in the United Kingdom, the Netherlands, France, Ireland, Germany, Italy, and Belgium.[22] Chapter 6 discusses retailing in depth.

Specialized Intermediaries

Specialized intermediaries enter the channel to perform a specific function; typically, they are not heavily involved in the core business represented by the products being sold. For example, insurance, financing, and credit card companies are all involved in financing; advertising agencies participate in the channel's promotion function; logistics and shipping firms engage in physical possession; information technology firms may participate in ordering or payment functions; and marketing research firms generate marketing intelligence that can support the performance of many functions.

EXAMPLE: MTIME—BRINGING HOLLYWOOD TO ASIA (CHINA)

Established in 2005, Mtime (www.mtime.com) is China's answer to Fandango, Rotten Tomatoes, and IMDb. China is predicted to overtake the United States as the world's largest movie market, measured by box office revenues, relatively soon.[23] The Mtime online portal provides Chinese consumers with movie reviews, critics ratings, and a database of film synopses going back to 1905. It also sells movie tickets online and provides partner theaters with data about movie ticket sales, segmented by market. Mtime carries celebrity news and covers movie premieres. Most Chinese consumers do not have access to Facebook and other Western social media sites (which are blocked by the Chinese government), so portals like Mtime are a primary source of news about Hollywood and celebrities. In 2015, Mtime partnered with Dalian Wanda Group, China's largest theater chain, to sell movie-themed merchandise in theaters. Mtime also licenses products from Hasbro and Mattel, to sell through pop-up stores and its own online portal. As a result of these varied appeals, Mtime boasts an estimated 160 million unique visitors a month and has been acquired by its erstwhile partner the Dalian group for $350 million.[24]

End-Users: Downstream Channel Members

End-users (business or consumer) are channel members as well, because they can and frequently do perform channel functions, just as other channel members do. Businesses often stock up on raw materials for their operations; they are performing physical possession, ownership, and financing functions, because they buy a much larger volume of product than they will use in the near future. They also pay for the raw materials before they use them, thus injecting cash into the channel. While storing the raw materials in their factories, they reduce the need for warehouse space maintained by the supplier, thus taking on part of the physical possession function. They bear all the costs of ownership too, including pilferage, spoilage, and so forth. Naturally, these buyers expect a price cut for their bulk purchases, because they are bearing so many more channel function costs.

Combinations of Channel Members

The various channel participants can come together in various ways to create an effective marketing channel strategy. The optimal range and number of channel members depend on the needs of the end-users and manufacturers. In addition, the identity of the channel captain can vary from situation to situation. Appendix 1.1 outlines several different possible channel formats for manufacturers, retailers, service providers, and other channel structures.

Online Channels

Online channels go by many aliases: e-commerce, e-tailing, online retailing, and Internet channels, to name a few. **Online channels** offer a form of direct retailing, such that the consumer uses an Internet-enabled device to order products or services through the Internet and have them delivered, digitally or physically, to a preferred location. They provide a 24/7 shopping environment and a much wider array of goods and services available for purchase, unhindered by shelf-space constraints. In addition, they offer consumers a means to shop from anywhere and anytime, accessing vendors located in all corners of the world. Other notable strengths of online channels include their easy search functions; provision of detailed product information, both from the manufacturer or retailer and in the form of online reviews posted by other users; and helpful product and price comparison tools. Thus, by 2016, online sales accounted for 8.1 percent of all retail sales; that number is expected to grow at double-digit rates in the next several years.[25] The top 25 retailers earned combined online sales of $159 billion in 2016, and notably, 18 of these 25 companies started as traditional brick-and-mortar retailers (e.g., Walmart).[26]

Yet online channels also feature limitations, in that end-users cannot touch, feel, or try on products. Therefore, their return rates tend to be high, and the cost of those returns must be absorbed by the system. The need to wait for physical product delivery represents another drawback of online channels from end-users' perspective. In a related sense, online channels are constrained when it comes to selling items with a poor weight-to-value ratio; it even may be economically unfeasible for a channel actor to ship low-priced but heavy products like concrete or rice.

EXAMPLE: HOLLAR—TAKING THE DOLLAR STORE ONLINE (USA)

Hollar is an online dollar store, conceived of in 2015 when the founders saw that e-commerce had not really penetrated this retail space. Existing companies such as Dollar General and Dollar Tree had limited online presence, and e-commerce startups were focusing all their efforts on more affluent customer groups. For Hollar, 80 percent of its traffic comes from customers using their mobile devices to find items commonly found in drug stores, at much lower prices.[27] Many items cost $1, though the median price on Hollar is $5; nothing costs more than $10. The company boasts more than 2 million active users.[28] To deal with shipping costs, it avoids carrying heavy items (an average shipment weighs 5 pounds) and requires a minimum order of $10—though average order sizes reach about $30.

FROM A MULTI-CHANNEL TO AN OMNI-CHANNEL WORLD

Some writers use the terms "multi-channel," "omni-channel," and "cross-channel" loosely and nearly interchangeably.[29] Yet omni-channel and its variants are becoming increasingly prevalent; in Figure 1.2, we graph the frequency of searches for the term "omni-channel" in recent years.

This growth reflects market trends. The ever-growing share of online sales has prompted most manufacturers to add online channels to their existing channels mix. In certain industries (e.g., travel, books), online sales have decimated traditional intermediaries; in others, though (e.g., food retailing), the impact of online

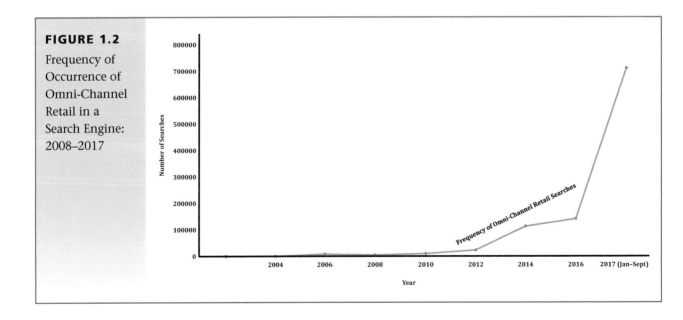

FIGURE 1.2
Frequency of Occurrence of Omni-Channel Retail in a Search Engine: 2008–2017

sales has been less dramatic. Initially, the emergence and growth of online sales led brick-and-mortar retailers to initiate multi-channel strategies, by adding online sales channels to their channel mix. More recently, some pure play online retailers, including Amazon and Warby Parker, have decided they might want to be present offline too, leading them to open a few physical stores. These choices are not limited to retailers; upstream channel members also must decide whether to add online channels.

The insurance sector offers a classic example. Most insurance companies distribute their products through independent agents, so they confronted a challenging decision about whether to offer direct online sales. The pressure to add this online channel largely came from competitive forces; online only and direct distribution insurance companies were cutting into their markets. The traditional insurers also realized that consumers' preferences were evolving when it came to ways to buy, learning valuable lessons from the fate of companies in other sectors that had been totally upended by the Internet. Yet adding an online presence created the risk that the insurance companies would alienate their primary channel partners, insurance agents. Across various sectors—insurance and otherwise—many companies sought to add online or direct channels to their traditional physical channels, while minimizing channel conflict, but for the most part, the integration across channels was minimal.[30]

The emergence of smart mobile devices, social networks, and in-store technology has blurred the line between online and physical channels, though, and this blurring is what omni-channel strategies are all about. Consumers can search for information online with their smart devices while they are still in the store, giving rise to both **showrooming** (using the store to try and touch products but buying online) and **webrooming** (searching on the web but buying in the store). The diminished boundaries between physical and online channels also precipitated the necessary shift away from a multi-channel and toward an omni-channel perspective, because firms have no choice but to find ways to integrate their operations seamlessly across channels. The lines will continue to blur with the greater penetration of smartphones, increasing investments in virtual reality, and advancing retail technologies that promise to help consumers virtually experience products and even touch, see, or smell them remotely.

DISTINCTION BETWEEN MULTI-CHANNEL AND OMNI-CHANNEL MARKETING STRATEGIES: TRENDS DRIVING THE SHIFT

A multi-channel environment sets clear demarcations and silos between channels, with the goal of optimizing the performance of each individual channel and coordinating across them. That is, a **multi-channel** strategy entails leveraging multiple channels that operate relatively independently. There may be some coordination and evaluation of the different channels, but they operate as clearly separate entities. Consumers engage in cross-channel shopping by switching among online, mobile, and physical platforms during a single purchase transaction. But in many organizations, the online and in-store experiences may be managed by separate divisions, with differing priorities, so the experience is not really seamless for the customer. Even in the face of well-entrenched cross-channel integration practices, such as when consumers can buy online and pick up products in-store, or else buy online and receive delivery, but then make returns in store, channel integration remains a challenge and a work in progress.

An omni-channel system instead harmoniously integrates functions that allow customers to shop—**research, purchase, communicate, engage with, and consume the brand**—across online, mobile, social, and offline physical channels. In an omni-channel world, channel arrangements help customers move seamlessly and however they choose, across multiple channels during a purchase transaction.[31] As another key distinction, the concept of "consumer engagement" is central to omni-channel approaches; they explicitly seek customer experience and engagement through efforts that rely on social media, email, web links, mobile platforms, store visits, promotional efforts, and so on. In this sense, an omni-channel strategy incorporates various channels of communication, in addition to channels for the physical transfer of goods.[32] Noting these differences, we also highlight several trends that are driving the shift.

Trend 1: Channel Participants Operate in a Connected World

Nearly 90 percent of Americans are online, more than three-quarters own a smartphone, nearly three-quarters have access to broadband services at home, and 70 percent of consumers use social media.[33] The ubiquity and universality of Internet access have vastly influenced people's shopping behavior. According to a Google Consumer Barometer report, 52 percent of U.S. consumers research home furnishings online prior to purchase; the incidence is even greater in Thailand, where 78 percent of shoppers do likewise.[34] This survey further revealed that across a range of 20 product categories, 35 percent of U.S. consumers sought advice through their smartphones prior to purchase, and 36 percent engaged in online comparison shopping. A high level of interconnectivity means that consumers freely move across different channels, depending on their preferences at the time.

Trend 2: Cross-Channel Shopping

Consumers use their mobile phones in stores to check and compare prices, brands, or products; they also might check out product reviews online and ask friends on social media for advice.[35] The resulting showrooming phenomenon means that many consumers visit physical stores to inspect and try products but choose to make purchases online. Such activities can lead to conflict among upstream channel members, though, because one actor is paying all the costs of informing the customer, while another one enjoys the benefits of the sale. Thus they have to devise equitable compensation systems when one channel functions as a showroom for another channel. Perhaps the most common type of cross-channel shopping behavior is webrooming, such that consumers research products online before purchasing them offline.[36] Warby Parker and Bonobos are pioneers in the online arena that now operate physical showrooms too.

Trend 3: Altered Shopping Norms

The physical storefront continues to evolve; some retail futurists predict that stores may become simply pared-down showrooms, with the mobile phone functioning as the store of the future.[37] The prediction has some reasonable support. Consider how product review sites have altered basic pricing rules. In a world devoid of product reviews, consumers tended to use price as a heuristic, often buying mid-priced items but bypassing the most and least expensive items. But today, consumers are more willing to buy the lowest-priced item in a product line, if the reviews are good.[38] The proliferation of social media sites also means that the power, reach, and frequency of word-of-mouth and shared reviews have increased manyfold. Not only do consumers share information and offer recommendations, as well as seek out information and advice from others to inform their own purchase decisions, but they also can engage with brands and become brand advocates. Marketers cannot control what consumers say, yet they can harness the power of social media as a platform for co-creating experiences and engaging with consumers. Channel managers should be mindful of privacy issues while they develop strategies to personalize their communications. A true omni-channel strategy integrates channels of communication as a key part of the channel system.

Trend 4: Move to Services

The intangible nature of services creates challenges for marketing channels, in terms of both governance and management.[39] In service channels, the focus is not on taking title and inventorying but rather on creating customer engagement and customer value. This focus provides opportunities for customization and co-creation. As we have noted, online channels also totally disrupted service industries such as travel and financial services, leading to the disappearance of many intermediaries. The ability to remove or circumvent well-entrenched intermediaries from the marketing channel and its value chain is **disintermediation**. Upstream channel members often prefer to control the customer experience, which may lead them to seek the disintermediation of downstream channel members. Tesla Motors' direct distribution model excludes traditional dealerships, because the company seeks to create a specific customer experience that goes beyond just its product offer.

The approach has prompted intense lobbying and legal action from advocacy groups and automobile associations, though,[40] which are seeking to avoid the fate of intermediaries like travel agents.

The Internet also has spawned several consumer-to-consumer service businesses with novel channel captains. For example, Airbnb enables consumers to rent out extra rooms or vacation properties to other consumers who choose to stay in these facilities rather than traditional hotel rooms. The American Hotel and Lodging Association is lobbying regulators to put curbs on Airbnb operations, arguing that the service being provided really is an unregulated hotel.[41]

Trend 5: Targeted Promotions and Customer Insights

Targeted promotions delivered via email, online couponing, price matching, and social media advertising are all tools that leverage new mass communication promotional channels. They effectively harness customer relationship marketing and social media benefits to facilitate an omni-channel strategy. For example, Walgreens and Foursquare have partnered on a location-based social networking site that provides electronic coupons to customers as soon as they enter a Walgreens store; Catalina Marketing uses in-store purchasing histories to deliver personalized mobile ads to consumers too.[42] Such technologies create a data-rich environment, as we elaborate in Chapters 10 and 11.

But many retailers have not fully developed their webpages or e-stores to ensure optimal presentations on various online and mobile platforms. In some cases, their mobile and online channels even compete directly with each other. An omni-channel strategy instead requires that upstream and downstream channel members integrate their promotion, pricing, and brand positioning across channels. For example, in their online channels, retailers are not constrained by store size or shelf space, so they can carry a wider assortment and potentially target more customers. Thus Walmart can target higher-income customers through its online and mobile platforms, competing with Costco and Amazon by selling higher-end, branded items, even while maintaining its low-price positioning for in-store shoppers. Such end-user segmentation across channels is challenging; different end-users seek varying bundles of services and thus prefer different channel arrangements. It is up to upstream and downstream channel partners to synchronize the bundle of services, and the costs involved in serving these customer segments, to find a fair, appealing, efficient pricing strategy.

CHANNEL STRATEGY FRAMEWORK

An **ecosystem**—"a complex network or interconnected system"[43] or "everything that exists in a particular environment"[44]—is an apt term to describe a firm's go-to-market strategies and associated sales channels. It involves an all-encompassing, interconnected, complex network. In a multi-channel world, firms rely on multiple routes to market, but in an omni-channel world, they must go further to develop a comprehensive framework that captures a systemic view of the flows of material, information, ownership, financing, promotion, and supporting services across channels. An omni-channel view "rises above siloed behavior, unlocks values across devices and platforms, and delivers a more curated and interactive brand experience."[45] The moving parts that form the ecosystem come together and complement one another in their capabilities.

Accordingly, an **omni-channel ecosystem** integrates domains that are often analyzed separately, namely business-to-business (B2B) and channel intermediary domains. Analyzing, designing, and developing the most effective go-to-market omni-channel structure and strategies requires a thorough understanding of both domains. This book combines them, but we also address the unique elements in separate chapters.

Specifically, in Chapters 2–5, the focus is on the **B2B domain**, starting with the assumption that developing an insightful omni-channel strategy requires being fluent in channel fundamentals. We drill down to specify various aspects of managing channel functions. In Chapter 2, we cover how channels create value and provide solutions in an omni-channel world, according to the functions and activities that exist in the channel and its participants. We also introduce the channel audits and tools that marketers can use to identify gaps in existing channels, along with a framework that can reveal if channel functions should be performed in-house or outsourced, according to a *make-or-buy channel analysis.* This chapter covers three key design questions: the degree of channel intensity, mix of channel types, and use of omni-channel distribution. Overall, the end objective must be that the channel design creates value by ensuring that the needs of both upstream and downstream members of the channel are meshed, in such a way that they can meet target end-users' demands, with minimum possible cost.

Rather than the channel design, Chapter 3 deals with *channel power.* Channel managers need to understand the source of each channel member's *power and dependence* and potential for *channel conflict* to develop before they can derive a plan for building and maintaining *relationships* with channel partners. For example, given the interdependence of channel partners who may not always have the incentive to cooperate fully, what should a channel captain do to ensure an optimal channel design? One approach is to leverage channel power. A channel member's power lies in their ability to control the strategic and tactical decisions of a channel partner. These sources could serve to further the member's individual ends, though if it uses its channel power to get channel members to perform the jobs that an optimal channel design specifies as their responsibility, the result will be a channel that delivers the demanded service outputs at a lower cost.

In Chapter 4, we go further into ways to manage channel relationships. Relationships are important for both upstream and downstream channel members, who participate in channel relationship lifecycles. We explore ways channel members might build commitment and trust, but we also cover how dysfunctional relationships, lacking in trust and commitment, can disrupt the channel. Finally, in Chapter 5 we discuss the nature and types of channel conflict and how to measure it in channel relationships, across both multi-channel and omni-channel contexts. We also identify various conflict resolution strategies.

Turning to the **channel intermediary domain**, our goal is to identify the best practices to integrate into an omni-channel system, according to the perspectives of the most common channel participants, structures, and strategies: *retailing* (Chapter 6), *wholesaling* (Chapter 7), *franchising* (Chapter 8), and *international channels* (Chapter 9). Retailing connects the channel to the end-user, and the multiplicity of retailing models available today offers testimony to the vast range of end-user segments seeking different concatenations of service outputs. We address various e-commerce topics too, such as digitization, showrooming, disintermediation, virtual and augmented reality, social commerce, and mobile commerce. Dramatic changes in the business environment—shifts from products to services, increases in e-commerce, globalization—are leading to the emergence of new channel systems, with the potential to disrupt many traditional approaches. For example, the shift to online purchases of books and music has dramatically transformed the channel system for these products. Wholesaling is distribution's "back room," moving and holding product both efficiently (i.e., to minimize cost) and effectively (i.e., to create spatial convenience and quick delivery). Franchising is an important method of selling that allows small-businesspeople to operate retail product and service outlets, with the benefits of a large-scale parent company's (franchisor's) knowledge, strategy, and tactical guidance. The channels differ somewhat in international marketing, so we also address some of these challenges, especially for firms that seek to reach the *base or bottom of the pyramid*; that is, the poorest consumers, often living in remote regions of the world.

With Chapters 10 and 11, we pull all this information together to propose omni-channel strategies. In Chapter 10, the focus is on the end-user. A fundamental principle of marketing is segmentation, which means dividing a market into groups of end-users who are (1) maximally similar to one another and (2) maximally different from other groups. For channel managers, segments can be best defined according to the service outputs the end-user needs to obtain from that marketing channel. A marketing channel is more than just a conduit for products; it is a means to add value to the products and services marketed through it. In this sense, the marketing channel represents another "production line," engaged in producing not the product (or service) that is being sold but rather the ancillary services that define how the product will be sold. Value-added services created by channel members and consumed by end-users, together with the product purchased, represent service outputs. Service outputs include (but are not limited to) bulk-breaking, spatial convenience, waiting and delivery time, assortment and variety, customer service, and product/market/usage information sharing.

In Chapter 11, we detail four pillars of an omni-channel strategy: harnessing customer knowledge, leveraging technology, managing channel relationships, and assessing channel performance. We believe that to design an optimal channel strategy for a targeted end-user market, the designer must audit the existing marketing channels serving this segment. This audit should evaluate the capabilities of each potential channel, in terms of the nine key channel functions (Figure 1.1), to determine how well it is suited to meet the segment's service output demands. Channel functions pertain to all channel activities that add value to the end-user, such that we move beyond merely moving the product along the channel to include promotion, negotiation, financing, ordering, payment, and so forth.

An omni-channel strategy is applicable both in consumer and business markets. In Figure 1.3, on the left, we present upstream sellers of raw materials or component parts. Most finished goods sellers are not fully vertically integrated, so they obtain raw materials and component parts from upstream suppliers. These suppliers may be grouped into tiers, depending on their degree of importance or the amount of business they transact with the finished goods sellers. Upstream sellers of raw materials and parts also use a variety of distribution methods to serve finished goods sellers.

Three primary drivers determine the suitability of a given channel: the size of the customer (finished goods seller) and its buying preferences, as well as the seller's willingness and ability to interact through a certain channel. To earn business from and manage relationships with larger customers, a supplier might deploy

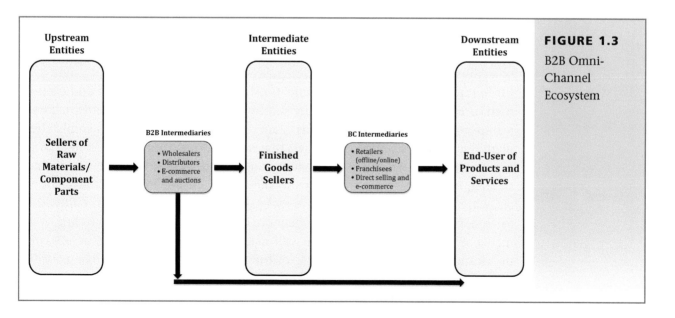

FIGURE 1.3

B2B Omni-Channel Ecosystem

an in-house direct sales force, reflecting the potential size of their order and their demand for guaranteed product availability or custom delivery options. Suppliers alternatively might hire manufacturer representatives to transact with potential customers. Some sellers (especially newer firms) may lack the resources needed to develop an in-house sales force, and agents and brokers that already have connections with customers could offer an appealing option. These agents often carry a portfolio of products from different manufacturers, which many customers prefer, rather than being limited to transacting individually with different suppliers. Finally, in globalized marketplaces, many international firms turn to agents and brokers as a key mode of entry into new overseas markets.

A firm also might go through a wholesaler or distributor. Grainger is a leading industrial distributor that stocks nearly 1.5 million items (www.grainger.com). Many finished product manufacturers source items from distributors such as Grainger, which offer one-stop shopping convenience. Furthermore, Grainger helps both suppliers and finished goods manufacturers with their supply chain functions, such as inventory management. In other industries, such as pharmaceuticals, wholesalers play a more critical role; Amerisource Bergen, Cardinal Health, and McKesson account for an estimated 90 percent of drug distribution in the United States.[46] These wholesalers often provide service for the complete inventory line produced by manufacturers and have access to a wide array of retail outlets (e.g., traditional pharmacies, supermarkets, mail order pharmacies, hospitals). In technology sectors, value-added resellers also can be critical; these distributors offer complete solutions packages that bundle components, software, or hardware from a variety of providers or add features to existing packages. If end-users need complete solutions that a single vendor is unable to provide, these resellers become critical intermediaries, because customers prefer to buy through them to obtain those value-added services.

Some firms instead turn to direct, B2B e-commerce, supported by proprietary electronic data interchange (EDI) systems or cloud computing services provided by companies like Amazon (https://aws.amazon.com/ecommerce-applications). In the automotive industry, for example, finished goods sellers can find and transact with component part suppliers using shared online platforms, some of which even feature reverse auction mechanisms, such as Covisint (www.covisint.com). These platforms allow firms to find suppliers that meet certain criteria, while also expanding the suppliers' options. Direct selling in B2B settings also can create challenges, though, because buyers readily turn to these platforms to find alternative suppliers, which might strain relationships that salespeople have spent years cultivating. Salespeople also may need to leverage more communication tools, including social media, even in a B2B context, but still deliver a consistent message across communication channels. Thus, the role of the salesperson is poised to change in the shifting omni-channel context.

Most omni-channel research tends to focus on business-to-consumer contexts, though,[47] as represented on the right side of Figure 1.3. In reality too, such considerations are prominent. Automakers are closely watching Tesla's direct distribution model to determine if it threatens to upend traditional distribution channels through franchised dealers. At the same time, dealerships themselves increasingly use the Internet to acquire customers, but they need to realize that those customers are better informed, having done plenty of research before they ever visit the dealership. Consumers also can shop among various dealerships for the same vehicle model, thus creating more intra-brand competition. For these customers, the marketer needs to find an appropriate way to synergize the offline and online experiences,[48] but also guard against the risk of revenue loss if consumers move from one channel to another. A key question is whether customers that transact with the company through a particular channel are more valuable than those that transact through other channels.[49] Most evidence indicates that customers that use multiple channels tend to be more profitable and transact more with the firm.[50,51]

Figure 1.4 summarizes the various challenges that managers face in developing an omni-channel strategy. We highlight the need to integrate across marketing and communication channels, to create unified brand experiences for customers. By necessity, an omni-channel strategy is data rich and relies heavily on data analytics. Furthermore, an omni-channel strategy demands pricing transparency and consistent pricing across channels or even globally. Certain industries are affected by the shift to an omni-channel environment more than others, though. We develop all these themes throughout this book; more briefly, in Sidebar 1.2 we highlight challenges associated with deriving a distribution strategy. We close with a brief example that highlights the opportunities and promises of an omni-channel environment.

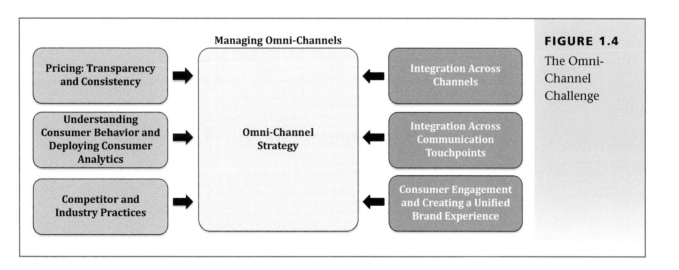

FIGURE 1.4

The Omni-Channel Challenge

SIDEBAR 1.2
E-Commerce in India: Channels Operate in an Ecosystem[52,53]

China is the world's largest e-commerce market; its 2016 sales of $681 billion made it nearly twice the size of the U.S. market. In comparison, India's e-commerce market is miniscule, currently earning sales of around $21 billion that might increase to $63.5 billion by 2021. Yet despite this relatively small size, India's e-commerce market is drawing vast attention from global e-commerce giants; Amazon has made investments of close to $5 billion, and Softbank is investing $2.5 billion. The reason for this interest actually parallels the reason that the market has remained so small thus far.

That is, e-commerce in India has not spread because the Internet has not penetrated the nation. The second most populous country in the world (more than 1.3 billion people), India also is home to an estimated 730 million mobile-phone users—but only about 450 million people use the Internet. Even as Internet penetration increases, reaching 31 percent of the country in 2017, it lags greatly behind the rates of mobile users, who were 88 percent of the population in 2016. The spread is even slower in rural areas, which are home to a population of 916 million people—all potential e-commerce customers, if only they could access the online channels.

Another challenge also represents a potential opportunity. The poor penetration of credit and debit services, along with consumer uncertainty about using them, imposes constraints on any transactions that rely on anything other than cash on delivery.[54] In such a system, channel members tasked with delivering products and services often risk theft, whether of goods or cash. These channel members cannot rely on air cargo options, though, because the available logistics in India do not reach smaller towns and cities.[55] When we include the challenges of online channels that are inherent to the medium, such as the high rate of returns, the low numbers of e-commerce customers start to make more sense.

Yet as penetration of both the Internet and credit services continues to spread, that vast untapped market offers great promise for marketers. Even the clogged and congested Indian roads may be an opportunity; people may learn to prefer to avoid the hassles of going out to shop, and rural shoppers likely will appreciate a chance to get the coolest urban styles, without having to venture into the big cities.

EXAMPLE: BEEPI/VROOM—SELLING USED CARS ONLINE (USA)

Would you buy a used car online, sight unseen? The process of buying used cars vexes many consumers, and the phrase "used car salesperson" is a widely used pejorative term to denote someone untrustworthy. But in Beepi's novel consignment model, sellers consigned the car to Beepi, which used its online portal to find buyers for the car and deliver it to them at the location of their choice. The car remained with the seller while up for sale. For sellers, Beepi promised the opportunity to get a higher return, while also eliminating the potential risk and hassle of dealing with strangers in a private-party sale. For buyers, it guaranteed a full refund if they did not like the car and returned it within seven days, certified the car with a thorough inspection, and posted several pictures of the car's interior, exterior, and engine. The target market, consumers looking for late-model used vehicles, could shop 24/7 and be freed of the challenges of haggling with a used car dealer. The company also promised that its direct model would save consumers money. Yet even after Beepi attracted funding to the tune of nearly $150 million, it could not sustain the business; it was sold and now operates under the www.vroom.com umbrella.[56]

Take-Aways

- Marketing channels are a set of interdependent organizations involved in the process of making a product or service available for use or consumption.

- Firms have to come up with a blueprint to deliver the firm's offerings to the end-user in a manner that conforms to their preferred mode and method of buying and is efficient, cost-effective, and confers competitive advantage to the firm. This is in essence the firm's go-to-market strategy.

- There are nine key channel functions that have to be performed: physical possession, ownership, promotion, negotiation, financing, risking, ordering, payment, and information sharing.

- Technological advances are changing the channel landscape and altering how end-users buy.

- The growth of online channels led firms to utilize multi-channel strategies where channels typically operate in silos as separate entities with less than optimal integration and insufficient coordination. It also led to disintermediation with well-entrenched intermediaries being removed from the channel value chain. Also some well-established formats like department stores are struggling to manage the onslaught from online channels and adapt to changes in consumer buying preferences.

- Today, the focus is moving from a multi-channel to an omni-channel strategy where firms seek integration of the customers' ability to research, purchase, communicate, engage with, and consume a brand such that the customer experience across online, physical, mobile, social, and communication channels is seamless and optimized.

- The key players in a channel system include the manufacturers who are upstream channel members, intermediaries like wholesalers, retailers who are intermediate channel members, and end-users who are the downstream channel members.

- The key distinction between omni-channel and multi-channel is one of seamless integration versus disjointed silos and that omni-channel captures the notion of customer engagement in its DNA.

- The trends driving the migration to omni-channels are that consumers live in a connected world where they engage in cross-channel shopping. Thus shopping norms have been altered and this, coupled with the move to services and the ability to generate deep consumer insights and create a custom, targeted experience for end-users, necessitates a move to an omni-channel world.

- We view channel strategy as operating in an ecosystem.

- The key to an omni-channel strategy is to integrate across channels and consumer touchpoints to create a transparent, seamless, and unified brand experience for the end-user.

APPENDIX 1.1: ALTERNATIVE CHANNEL FORMATS—DEFINITIONS AND EXAMPLES

Alternative channel formats may stem from any of the three sections of the traditional distribution channel; that is, manufacturer, distributor, or customer. But they also could have other bases. This appendix summarizes the variety of channel formats and the characteristics on which they rely to gain strategic advantages, as well as some examples of specific companies, types of companies, or product categories that use the specific channel format. By comparing each market against this information, channel managers can identify opportunities and vulnerabilities.

Manufacturer-Based Channel Formats

1. **Manufacturer Direct.** Product shipped and serviced from manufacturer's warehouse. Sold by company sales force or agents. The wide variety of products appeals to customers with few service needs and large orders. Many manufacturer-direct companies also sell through wholesaler-distributors.
   Examples: Hewlett-Packard, IBM, and General Electric sell to their largest customers using a direct sales force.

2. **Manufacturer-Owned Full-Service Wholesaler Distributor.** An acquired wholesale distribution company serving the parent's and other manufacturers' markets. Typically, diverse product lines in an industry support synergies between a company's manufacturing and distribution operations. Because of customer demand, some companies also distribute other manufacturers' products.

Examples: Revlon, Levi-Strauss, Kraft Foodservice, GESCO, clothing and apparel products.

3. **Company Store/Manufacturer Outlets.** Retail product outlets in high-density markets; often used to liquidate seconds or excess inventory of branded consumer products.
   Examples: Outlet malls, hostess bakery outlets.

4. **License.** Contracting distribution and marketing functions through licensing agreements, which usually grant exclusivity for some period of time. Often used for products in the development stage of their lifecycle.
   Examples: Mattel, Walt Disney, importers.

5. **Consignment/Locker Stock.** Manufacturer ships the product to the point of consumption, but title does not pass until consumed. Risk of obsolescence and ownership remains with manufacturer. Focus on high-price/high-margin and emergency items.
   Examples: Diamonds, fine art galleries, machine repair parts.

6. **Broker.** Specialized sales force contracted by manufacturer that also carries comparable product lines and focuses on a narrow customer segment; product is shipped through another format, such as the preceding options. Typically used by small manufacturers attempting to attain broad coverage.
   Examples: Schwan's frozen foods, paper goods, lumber, newer product lines.

Retailer-Based Channel Formats

1. **Franchise.** Product and merchandising concept is packaged and formatted. Territory rights are sold to franchisees. Various distribution and other services are provided by contract to franchisees for a fee.
   Examples: KFC, McDonald's.

2. **Dealer Direct.** Franchised retailers carry a limited number of product lines supplied by a limited number of vendors. Often these big-ticket items need substantial after-sales service support.
   Examples: Heavy equipment dealers, auto dealers.

3. **Buying Club.** Buying services requiring membership. Good opportunity for vendors to penetrate certain niche markets or experiment with product variations. They also provide buyers with a variety of consumer services; today, they are largely consumer-oriented.
   Examples: Compact disc/tape clubs, book clubs.

4. **Warehouse Clubs/Wholesale Clubs.** Appeal is to price-conscious shopper. Size is 60,000 square feet or more. Product selection is limited, and products are usually sold in bulk in a "no-frills" environment.
   Examples: Sam's Club, Costco.

5. **Mail Order/Catalog.** Nonstore selling through literature sent to potential customers. Usually has a central distribution center for receiving and shipping direct to the customer.
   Examples: Land's End, Spiegel, Fingerhut.

6. **Food Retailers.** Will buy canned and boxed goods in truckloads to take advantage of pricing and manufacturing rebates. Distribution centers act as consolidators to reduce the number of trucks received at the store. Pricing is not required, because manufacturer bar codes are available. Includes full lines of groceries, health and beauty aids, and general merchandise items. Some food retailers have expanded into other areas, such as prescription and over-the-counter drugs, delicatessens, and bakeries.
   Examples: Publix, Safeway.

7. **Department Stores.** These stores offer a wide variety of merchandise with moderate depth. The product mix usually includes soft goods (clothing, linens) and hard goods (appliances, hardware, sporting equipment). Distribution centers act as consolidators of both soft goods and hard goods. Quick response for apparel goods demands a direct link with manufacturer. A national basis motivates retailers to handle their own distribution.
   Examples: JCPenney, Federated Stores.

8. **Mass Merchandisers.** Similar to department stores, except product selection is broader and prices are usually lower.
   Examples: Walmart, Kmart, Target.

9. **Specialty Stores.** Offer merchandise in one line (e.g., women's apparel, electronics) with great depth of selection at prices comparable to those of department stores. Because of the seasonal nature of fashion goods, partnership with the manufacturer is essential. Manufacturer ships predetermined store assortments and usually prices the goods. Retailers might have joint ownership with the manufacturer.
   Examples: The Limited, The Gap, Zales.

10. **Specialty Discounters/Category Killers.** Offer merchandise in one line (e.g., sporting goods, office supplies, children's merchandise) with great depth of selection at discounted prices. Stores usually range in size from 50,000 to 75,000 square feet. Buys direct in truckloads. Manufacturer will ship direct to the store. Most products do not need to be priced. National chains have created their own distribution centers to act as consolidators.
    Examples: Office Depot, Drug Emporium, Best Buy.

11. **Convenience Store.** A small, higher-margin grocery store that offers a limited selection of staple groceries, non-foods, and other convenience items; for example, ready-to-heat and ready-to-eat foods. The traditional format includes stores that started out as strictly convenience stores, but they may also sell gasoline.
    Examples: 7-Eleven, Wawa.

12. **Hypermarket.** A very large food and general merchandise store with at least 100,000 square feet of space. Although these stores typically devote as much as 75 percent of their selling area to general merchandise, the food-to-general merchandise sales ratio typically is 60/40.
    Examples: Auchan, Carrefour, Fred Meyer.

Service Provider-Based Channel Formats

1. **Contract Warehousing.** Public warehousing services provided for a fee, typically with guaranteed serviced levels.
   Examples: Caterpillar Logistics Services, Dry Storage.

2. **Subprocessor.** Outsourcing of assembly or subprocessing. Usually performed with labor-intensive process or high fixed-asset investment when customers need small orders. These channel players are also beginning to take on traditional wholesale distribution roles.
   Examples: Steel processing, kitting of parts in electronics industry.

3. **Cross-Docking.** Trucking companies service high-volume inventory needs by warehousing and backhauling product on a routine basis for customers' narrower inventory needs. Driver picks inventory and delivers to customer after picking up the customer's shipment.
   Examples: Industrial repair parts and tools, various supply industries.

4. **Integration of Truck and Rail (Intermodal).** Joint ventures between trucking and rail companies to ship large orders door to door from supplier to customer, with one way-bill.
   Examples: Very economical for large orders, or from manufacturer to customer for a manufacturer with a broad product line.

5. **Roller Freight.** Full truckload is sent from manufacturer to high-density customer markets via a transportation company. Product is sold en route, and drivers are directed to customer delivery by satellite communication.
   Examples: Lumber products, large, moderately priced items with commodity-like characteristics that allow for routine orders.

6. **Stack Trains and Road Railers.** Techniques to speed movement and eliminate handling for product to be shipped by multiple formats. The importer might load containers directed to specific customers on a truck body in Hong Kong, ship direct, and unload onto railcars, which can eliminate two to three days' transit time. Large customer orders using multiple transportation techniques.
   Examples: Importers.

7. **Scheduled Trains.** High-speed trains leave daily at prescribed times from high-density areas to high-density destinations. Manufacturer "buys a ticket" and hooks up its railcar, then product is picked up at the other end by the customer.
   Examples: High-density recurring orders to large customers with limited after-sales service needs.

8. **Outsourcing.** Service providers sign a contract to provide total management of a company's activities in an area in which the provider has particular expertise (computer operations, janitorial services, print shop, cafeteria, repair parts, tool crib). The outsourcer then takes over the channel product function for products associated with the outsourced activity (janitorial supplies). Outsourcing has spread to virtually every area of the business (repair part stockroom, legal, accounting) and may not use merchant wholesaler-distributors. Wide variety of applications and growing.
   Examples: Infosys, R.R. Donnelly.

9. **Direct Mailer.** Direct mail advertising companies expanding services in conjunction with market research database services to directly market narrower line products. Product logistics and support performed by either the manufacturer or outsourced to a third party.
   Examples: Big-ticket consumer products, high-margin, low-service-requirement industrial and commercial equipment.

10. **Bartering.** Service provider, usually an advertising or media company, signs a barter arrangement with a manufacturer to exchange product for media advertising time or space. Bartered product is then rebartered or redistributed through other channels.
    Examples: Consumer and commercial products that have been discontinued or for which demand has slowed considerably.

11. **Value-Added Resellers (VARs).** Designers, engineers, or consultants for a variety of service industries that joint venture or have arrangements with manufacturers of products used in their designs. The VARs often get a commission or discount to service the product and carry inventory of high-turnover items.
    Examples: Computer software companies that market hardware for turnkey products; security system designers that form joint ventures with electronics manufacturers to sell turnkey products.

12. **Influencers/Specifiers.** Similar to a VAR, but these firms generally design highly complex, large projects (commercial buildings), do not take title to product, and have a group of suppliers whose products can be specified to the design. Selling effort is focused on both the ultimate customer and the specifier. Distribution of product is handled through other channel formats.
    Examples: Architects, designers, consultants.

13. **Financial Service Providers.** These formats have historically been initiated by joint ventures with financial service companies to finance margin purchases for customers or dealers (e.g., floor planning). They have been expanded to allow manufacturers to initiate distribution in new markets and assess these markets. High-capital, highly controlled distribution channel for one or two suppliers.
    Examples: Branded chemicals, construction equipment.

Other Channel Formats

1. **Door-to-Door Formats.** To some extent, these are variations on the channel formats previously listed. These formats have existed in the United States since pioneer days for products with high personal sales costs and high margins, sold in relatively small orders (encyclopedias, vacuum cleaners). A wide range of variations (e.g., home-party format) attempt to get many small buyers in one location to minimize the sales cost and provide a unique shopping experience. Variations of the format have also spread to industrial and commercial markets to capitalize on similar market needs (e.g., Snap-On Tools uses a variation of the home-party system by driving the product and salespeople to mechanics' garages and selling to them on their lunch hours). Each format is different and needs to be analyzed to understand its unique characteristics. A brief summary of the more identifiable formats follows:

   a. **Individual On-Site.** Very effective for generating new business for high-margin products requiring a high level of interaction with customers.

   Examples: Fuller Brush, Electrolux, bottled water, newspapers.

   b. **Route.** Used to service routine repetitious purchases that do not need to be resold on each call. Sometimes price is negotiated once and only changed on an exception basis. This concept was historically more prevalent in consumer lines (e.g., milk deliveries) but has recently spread to a variety of commercial and industrial segments.

   Examples: Office deliveries of copier paper and toner.

   c. **Home Party.** Similar to individual on-site sales, this format takes the product to a group of individuals.

   Examples: Tupperware, Snap-On Tools.

   d. **Multi-Level Marketing.** Salesperson not only sells products but recruits other salespeople who become a leveraged sales force that gives the original salesperson a commission on sales. Channel can be used for "high-sizzle," high-margin, fast-growth opportunities in branded differentiated products.

   Examples: Amway, Shaklee, NuSkin, plumbing products, cosmetics, other general merchandise.

   e. **Service Merchandising/"Rack Jobbing."** Similar to a route but expanded to provide a variety of services with the product. Originally, the rack jobber sold small consumer items to grocery stores, merchandised the product, and owned the inventory, merely paying the retailer a commission for the space. This concept is expanding to commercial, industrial, and home markets in a variety of niches: maintaining a stockroom of office supplies, maintaining repair parts stock, servicing replenishable items in the home such as chemicals, purified water, salt, and so on.

   Examples: Specialty items and gadgets or novelties, paperback books, magazines.

2. **Buyer-Initiated Formats.** These formats have been built on the concept of all buyers joining together to buy large quantities at better prices. It has expanded to give these buyers other securities and leverage that they might not be able to obtain on their own (e.g., private labeling, advertising design). As with the door-to-door concepts, variations of this concept are proliferating to meet individual buyers' needs.

   a. **Co-op.** Companies, usually in the same industry, create an organization in which each member becomes a shareholder. The organization uses the combined strength of the shareholders to get economies of scale in several business areas, such as purchasing, advertising, or private-label manufacturing. This format is generally designed to allow small companies to compete more effectively with large competitors. Although wholesaler-distributors can form or join co-ops, their use as an alternative channel format may direct buyers from nonwholesaler-distributors.

   Example: Topco.

   b. **Dealer-Owned Co-op.** Similar to the co-op format, except the co-op may perform many of the functions rather than contracting for them with third-party suppliers (e.g., own warehouses). Shareholders/members are generally charged a fee for usage, and all profits in the co-op at year-end are refundable to the shareholders on some prorated basis. In many instances, this format has elements of a franchise.

   Example: Distribution America.

   c. **Buying Group.** Similar to the co-op, except the relationship is usually less structured. Companies can be members of several buying groups. The loose affiliation usually does not commit the members to performance. This format has taken on a host of roles. A group can buy through the wholesale distribution channel or direct from manufacturers. Often, wholesaler-distributors are members of buying groups for low-volume items.

   Example: DPA Buying Group.

3. **Point-of-Consumption Merchandising Formats.** This concept has grown, from the practice of strategically placing vending machines where demand is predictable and often discretionary and the cost of selling through a full-time salesperson would be too high, to never-before-imagined commercial, industrial, and home markets for products and services. The increased use of technology and telecommunications has opened this channel to even more products and services.

   a. **Vending/Kiosks.** Kiosks have historically been very small retail locations that carry a very narrow product line. Through interactive video, online ordering technology, and artificial intelligence, this format has been significantly enhanced and can operate unattended. It is also being used for point-of-use dispensing of maintenance supplies and tools. "Purchases" are recorded in a log by the computer to control inventory shrinkage and balance inventory levels.

Examples: Film processing, candy, tobacco, compact discs, and tapes.

b. **Pay-Per-Serving Point of Dispensing.** Product is prepared or dispensed by vending machine at the time of purchase. Vending machines for soup and coffee, soft drinks, and candy or food are usual uses of this format, but it is expanding to include such foods as pizza and pasta.

Examples: Beverages, food.

c. **Computer Access Information.** Many of the computer access information formats have not necessarily altered the product function (products are not available online), but they have significantly altered the service and information function by uncoupling them from the product, such that the product can pass through cheaper channels.

Examples: Online information services, cable movies, news wire services, shopping services for groceries.

4. **Third-Party Influencer Formats.** These formats are designed around the concept that an organization that has a relationship with a large number of people or companies can provide a channel for products and services not traditionally associated with the organization (e.g., school selling candy to the community, using school children as a sales force). Again, the concept has broadened across both the commercial and industrial sectors and deepened in terms of the products and services offered.

a. **Charity.** This format typically involves sales of goods and services in which the sponsoring charitable organization receives a commission on the sale. All types of products can be included, shipped direct or outsourced. Sales forces may be non-paid volunteers.

Examples: Market Day, World's Finest Chocolate.

b. **Company-Sponsored Program.** Employers contract with companies for products and services for their employees or segments of employees on an as-needed basis. The provider has access to the employee base.

Examples: Healthcare and drug services, car maintenance.

c. **Premium and Gift Market.** Companies buy products customized with company logos or names for sale or distribution.

Examples: Pens, plaques, awards, T-shirts, novelties.

d. **Product Promotion Mailing with Normal Correspondence.** Promotion of products is done by mailing to customers with letters and perhaps phone call follow-up. Typically involves promotional inserts with credit card and other billings. Logistics and order fulfillment activities may be handled by others.

Examples: American Express, VISA, MasterCard.

e. **Customer List Cross-Selling.** An unusual format, in that the customer list is sold by one company to another. In effect, the marketing function is circumvented. Started in the customer industry but migrating to commercial and industrial segments.

Examples: Catalog companies, credit card companies.

5. **Catalog and Technology-Aided Formats.** The time-honored catalog marketing channel dates back to their use by department stores to extend merchandising abilities to a predominantly rural U.S. population in the late 1800s. Catalog use has expanded dramatically to follow the buying habits of consumers and institutions. Although it continues to be a threat to traditional merchant wholesaler-distributors, through mail order and links to technology, catalogs have become sales tools for some wholesaler-distributors. The format should be evaluated carefully in all sectors of the market, as follows:

a. **Specialty Catalogs.** Uses catalogs to promote a narrow range of special products or services. Mailing to potential and repeat customers. Orders come in by mail or phone.

Examples: Eddie Bauer, Bass Pro Shops, Williams Sonoma.

b. **Business-to-Business Catalogs.** Similar to specialty catalogs except that the product and customer focus is on business.

Example: Moore Business Forms.

c. **Television Home Shopping and Satellite Networks.** Heavily dependent on technology, these methods offer shopping in the comfort of people's homes. Also has business applications. Orders are placed by phone.

Example: Home Shopping Network.

d. **Interactive Merchandising.** Could embody many of the attributes of the three preceding types, but also allows for extensive, interactive, in-store capabilities, as well as online ordering. It may offer inventory checking or physical modeling capabilities and unusually extensive communication linkages.

Example: Rockar Hyundai store which dispenses with commissioned sales people and instead uses interactive hi-tech displays and gadgets along with human "brand angels" to educate consumers on car features.[57]

e. **Third-Party Catalog Services.** Catalog selling format in which one or more suppliers provide a combined catalog for a group of customers frequenting a certain place.

Examples: Airline in-flight magazines and catalogs, in-room hotel publications.

f. **Trade Shows.** A format used in some segments for direct sales order activities. Suppliers sell from booths at major trade shows or conventions. Also used for retail applications.

Examples: Boats, cars, hardware/software applications.

g. **Database Marketing.** Databases of customer buying habits and demographics are analyzed to enable the company to target customers for future mailing. Also used for retail applications.

Examples: Large grocery/consumer products companies, telephone companies.

NOTES

1 Palmatier, Robert W. and Shrihari Sridhar (2017), *Marketing Strategy: Based on First Principles and Data Analytics*, London: Palgrave Macmillan.

2 Karakiya, Fahri and Bulent Kobu (1994), "New product development process: An investigation of success and failure in high-technology and non-high-technology firms," *Journal of Business Venturing*, January, 49–66.

3 Rangan, V. Kasturi (2006), *Transforming Your Go-to-Market Strategy: The Three Disciplines of Channel Management*, Boston, MA: Harvard Business School Press.

4 Gruley, Bryan and Leslie Patton (2015), "The franchisees are not lovin' it," *Bloomberg Business Week*, September 21.

5 Taylor, Kate (2016), "Why Starbucks doesn't franchise," *Business Insider*, September 28.

6 Jargon, Julie (2013), "Starbucks tries franchising to perk up European business," *Wall Street Journal*, November 29.

7 Gensler, Lauren (2016), "The world's largest retailers 2016: Wal-Mart dominates but Amazon is catching up," *Forbes*, May 27.

8 Shi, Audrey (2016), "Amazon Prime members now outnumber non-Prime members," *Fortune*, July 11.

9 https://services.amazon.com/fulfillment-by-amazon/benefits.html, date retrieved July 28, 2017.

10 See "2011 Top 250 global retailers," *Stores*, January 2012, www.stores.org; www.naw.org, http://data.worldbank.org, and www.commerce.gov.

11 Piotrowicz, Wojciech and Richard Cuthbertson (2014), "Introduction to the Special Issue: Information technology in retail: Toward omnichannel retailing," *International Journal of Electronic Commerce*, Summer, 18 (4), 5–15.

12 Wahba, Phil (2016), "The man who's re- (re-re) inventing JC Penney," *Fortune*, March 1, 76–86.

13 McGrath, Maggie (2017), "Retail-maggedon: Macy's ugly earnings drag down entire sector," *Forbes*, May 11.

14 Brickley, Peg (2016), "Sports Authority accelerating store closings amid bankruptcy," *Wall Street Journal*, July 19.

15 Maras, Elliot (2016), "Omni-channel puts food supply chains through the wringer," *Food Logistics*, September, 16–24.

16 Gu, Zheyin (Jane) and Giri Kumar Tayi (2017), "Consumer pseudo-showrooming and omni-channel placement strategies," *MIS Quarterly*, 41 (2), 583–606.

17 Johnston, Lisa (2017), "Best Buy adds Dyson In-store experiences," *Twice*, August 7, 21.

18 Gabor, Deb (2017), "Retail is dead! Long live retail—at Best Buy, that is," *Twice*, August 7, 5.

19 See Koo, Hui-Wen and Pei-yu Lo (2004), "Sorting: The function of tea middlemen in Taiwan during the Japanese colonial era," *Journal of Institutional and Theoretical Economics*, 160 (December), 607–626.

20 Fuhrman, Elizabeth (2003), "Multibar multi-tasking," *Candy Industry*, 168 (June), 28–32.

21 Kumar, Nirmalya and Jan-Benedict E.M. Steenkamp (2007), *Private Label Strategy: How to Meet the Store Brand Challenge*, Boston, MA: Harvard School Publishing.

22 See www.officedepot.com and the company's 2016 Annual Report.

23 Ekstract, Steven (2016), "China's rising star," *www.licensemag.com*, June, 202.

24 Brzeski, Patrick (2016), "Wanda's two steps forward and one (huge) step back," *Hollywood Reporter*, 24, 18.

25 Braden, Dustin (2017), "E-tailing and the top 100," *Journal of Commerce*, May 29, 14–15.

26 Zaczkiewicz, Arthur (2016), "Amazon, Wal-Mart lead top 25 e-commerce retail list," *wwd.comi*, March 7.

27 Kokalitcheva, Kia (2016), "Hollar grabs $30 million to grow its 'online dollar store'," *Fortune*, November 18.

28 Chernova, Yuliya (2017), "Taking the dollar store concept online," *Wall Street Journal*, June 14.

29 Beck, Norbert and David Rygl (2015), "Categorization of multiple channel retailing in multi-, cross-, and omni-channel retailing for retailers and retailing," *Journal of Retailing and Consumer Services*, 27 (November), 170–178.

30 Verhoef, Peter C., P.K. Kannan, and J. Jeffrey Inman (2015), "From multi-channel retailing to omni-channel retailing: Introduction to the Special Issue on multi-channel retailing," *Journal of Retailing*, 91 (2), 174–181.

31 Piotrowicz and Cuthbertson (2014), op. cit.

32 Ailawadi, Kusum and Paul W. Ferris (2017), "Managing multi- and omni-channel distribution: Metrics and research directions," *Journal of Retailing*, 93 (1), 120–135.

33 Smith, Aaron (2017), "Record shares of Americans now own smartphone, have home broadband," www.pewresearch.org/fact-tank/2017/01/12/evolution-of-technology.

34 The Consumer Barometer Survey 2014/15, www.consumerbarometer.com/en/insights/?countryCode=GL.

35 Van Bruggen, Gerrit H., Kersi Antia, Sandy Jap, Reinartz Werner, and Pallas Florian (2010), "Managing marketing channel multiplicity," *Journal of Service Research*, 13 (3), 331–340.

36 Flavian, Carlos, Raquel Gurrea, and Carlos Orus (2016), "Choice confidence in the webrooming purchase process: The impact of online positive reviews and the motivation to touch," *Journal of Consumer Behavior*, 15 (5), 459–476.

37 Mangtani, Nitin (2017), "Why Warby Parker is the poster child for the store of the future," *Forbes*, June.

38 Simonson, I. and E. Rosen (2014), "What marketers misunderstand about online reviews," *Harvard Business Review*, 92 (1/2), 23–25.

39 Watson, George F. IV, Stefan Worm, Robert W. Palmatier, and Shankar Ganesan (2015), "The evolution of marketing channels: Trends and research direction," *Journal of Retailing*, doi.org/10.1016/j.jretai.2015.04.002.

40 Irwin, John (2016), "North Carolina denies Tesla a dealership license," *Automotive News*, May 23.

41 Shen, Lucinda (2017), "The hotel industry is striking back against Airbnb," *Fortune*, April 17.

42 Brynjolfsson, Erik, Yu Jeffrey Hu, and Mohammad S. Rahman (2012), "Competing in the age of omnichannel retailing," *Sloan Management Review*, Summer.

43 www.en.oxforddictionaries.com/definition/ecosystem.

44 www.learnersdictionary.com/definition/ecosystem.

45 Egol, Matthew, Raju Sarma, and Naseem Sayani (2013), "Reimagining shopper marketing and building brands through omnichannel experiences," *www.strategyand.pwc.com*, 4.

46 Fein, Adam J. (2016), "Top pharmaceutical distributors," www.mdm.com/2016-top-pharmaceuticals-distributors, date retrieved August 23, 2017.

47 Cummins, Shannon, James Peltier, and Andrea Dixon (2016), "Omni-channel research framework in the context of personal selling and sales management: A review and research extensions," *Journal of Research in Interactive Marketing*, 10 (1), 2–16, https://doi.org/10.1108/JRIM-12-2015-0094.

48 Herhausen, Dennis, Jochen Binder, Marcus Schögel, and Andreas Herrmann (2015), "Integrating bricks with clicks: Retailer-level and channel-level outcomes of online–offline channel integration," *Journal of Retailing*, 91 (2), 309–325.

49 Kushwaha, Tarun and Venkatesh Shankar (2013), "Are multichannel customers really more valuable? The moderating role of product category characteristics," *Journal of Marketing*, 77 (4), 67–85.

50 Venkatesan, R., V. Kumar, and Nalini Ravishanker (2007), "Multichannel shopping: Causes and consequences," *Journal of Marketing*, 71 (2), 114–132.

51 Mellis, Kristina, Katia Camp, Lamey Lien, and Els Breugelman (2016), "A bigger slice of the multi-channel grocery pie: When does consumers' online channel use expand retailers' share of wallet?" *Journal of Retailing*, 92 (3), 268–286.

52 Purnell, Newley and Mayumi Negeshi (2017), "Amazon, Softbank battle for one of last untapped Internet markets; many in India are shopping online for the first time," *Wall Street Journal*, August 11.

53 Chopra, Arushi (2017), "Number of Internet users in India could cross 450 million by June: Report," www.livemint.com/Industry/QWzIOYEsfQJknXhC3HiuVI/Number-of-Internet-users-in-India-could-cross-450-million-by.html, date retrieved August 22, 2017.

54 Verma, Sandeep (2017), "India has 28.8 million credit cards and 818 million debit cards in January 2017," www.medianama.com/2017/03/223-india-28-8m-credit-cards-818m-debit-cards-january-2017, date retrieved August 22, 2017.

55 Jindel, Vinita (2017), "Netting buyer in India," *Journal of Commerce*, February 6, 68.

56 Lunden, Ingrid (2016), "Used-car marketplace Beepi shuts down outside of CA, merges with stealth fair.com," https://techcrunch.com/2016/12/07/used-car-marketplace-beepi-shuts-down-outside-of-ca-merges-with-stealth-fair-com, date retrieved August 23, 2017.

57 www.trendhunter.com/trends/rockar-hyundai-store, date retrieved October 26, 2018.

Channel Basics

INTRODUCTION

The Importance of Marketing Channel Strategies

As outlined in Chapter 1, most products and services go through multiple marketing channels before consumers can purchase them. Thus, a central task for marketing is to design and manage a channel structure that can ensure the overall channel system operates efficiently and effectively. These challenges are compounded in omni-channel environments, where firms must integrate their operations and synchronize the customer experience across multiple channels. The channel provides a *gateway* between the manufacturer and the end-user; in few situations do end-users interact directly with the manufacturer. Therefore, their channel *experience* determines people's perceptions of the manufacturer's brand image and end-user satisfaction.

General Motors' now defunct Saturn brand transformed the car-buying experience for customers, resulting in a cult-like brand that inspired great customer loyalty. At Saturn dealerships, salespeople earned a flat fee, rather than commissions, which meant there was no high-pressure selling or haggling on price. Each car was delivered to customers with a full tank of gas, and celebratory pictures captured the moment they took possession of their new cars.[1] These channel-specific elements helped differentiate the company's market offering from those of its competitors. Such differentiation is fundamental to building and maintaining a competitive advantage, such that even as a new brand in the competitive automotive market, Saturn was able to position itself as a "different kind of car company." In short, a strong channel system is a competitive asset, not easily replicated by other firms, which means it is a source of a sustainable competitive advantage.

If it adopts a less-than-effective channel strategy, a manufacturer's products or services will suffer from limited reach and insufficient attractiveness to buyers, who may prefer to buy in a different manner. In this chapter, we take a close look at channel basics, including the functions and activities that occur in marketing channels. In doing so, we explain why marketing channels exist in the first place. We also outline how channel audits can create more efficient, responsive channel structures.

Why Do Marketing Channels Exist?

We noted in Chapter 1 that channels are essentially sets of interdependent organizations that act as teams and operate on trust. But manufacturers seemingly could just sell their products and services directly to all end-users. If they did, they could avoid depending on other parties and retain full control over their distribution. So why do marketing channels even exist? The answer involves balancing the benefits of interacting directly with end-users with its incremental costs (e.g., breaking bulk early in the distribution process, shipping many small packages to many different locations rather than large shipments to few locations). This balance shifts constantly, though, so once it is in place, a marketing channel constantly must change and develop new forms. To devise optimal channel structures and strategies, it thus is critical to understand the benefits that intermediaries in the channel provide to both upstream and downstream channel members, which we refer to as the **service outputs** provided by the channel.

Benefits for Downstream Channel Members

Search Facilitation

Marketing channels with intermediaries arise partly because they facilitate searches. The **search** process is characterized by uncertainty for both end-users and sellers. End-users need to be able to find the products or services they want; sellers need to know exactly how to reach their target end-users. If intermediaries did not exist, sellers without an already established brand name would be unable to generate many sales. For example, consumers perceive product quality as higher when they can access products through retailers with strong reputations.[2] This type of guarantee is needed, because end-users rarely have enough information to know whether to believe manufacturers' claims about the nature and quality of their products. Nor can manufacturers be certain that they are reaching the right kinds of end-user through their promotional efforts. Intermediaries such as retailers thus facilitate search on both sides of the channel.

EXAMPLE: COBWEB DESIGNS (UK)

Cobweb Designs, a high-quality needlework design firm headquartered in Scotland, is the sole licensee for needlework kits relating to the Royal Family, the National Trust for Scotland, the architect Charles Rennie Mackintosh, and the great socialist writer and designer William Morris. Cobweb's needlework kits are available at all retail outlets of the National Trust for Scotland, as well as on the company's website (www.cobweb-needlework.com), but its proprietor Sally Scott Aiton also wanted to reach the large, dispersed market of potential buyers in the United States. Aiton sought retail placements in gift shops at major art museums and botanical gardens. Gaining shelf space in a gift shop of a museum like the Smithsonian Institution in Washington, D.C. or the Art Institute of Chicago could greatly enhance the company's sales reach, because U.S. consumers who do not frequently travel to the United Kingdom still could find the company's designs (or become aware of them). Such retailers, which offer compelling brand images on their own, thus facilitate the search process on the demand side: a consumer seeking museum-reproduction needlework kits knows that she can find them at museum shops, along with other museum-reproduction products. Similarly, from Cobweb's point of view, museum shops have images that are consistent with the high quality of Cobweb Designs' kits, such that they are likely to attract visitors who tend to represent Cobweb's target market. Such access to a broad base of viable buyers again facilitates search, this time from the manufacturing end of the channel. In short, the intermediary (retail museum shop) becomes the "matchmaker" that brings the buyer and seller together.

Sorting

Independent intermediaries perform the valuable function of *sorting goods* and thus resolving the natural discrepancy between the assortment of goods and services produced by a manufacturer and the assortment demanded by the end-user. This discrepancy arises because manufacturers typically produce a large quantity of a limited variety of goods, whereas consumers demand only a limited quantity of a wide variety of goods. Intermediaries can **sort out** and break down heterogeneous supply into separate stocks that are relatively homogeneous (e.g., a citrus packing house sorts oranges by size and grade) or else perform **accumulation** and combine similar stocks from multiple sources to provide broader, more homogeneous supply (e.g., wholesalers accumulate varied goods for retailers, and retailers accumulate goods for consumers). In short, intermediaries help end-users access a unique combination of product and channel services that are attractive to them. In this sense, intermediaries *create utility* for end-users. In particular, they provide *possession, place,* and *time* utilities, such that they ensure a product is available with the assortments and in the places that are most valuable to target end-users, at the right time.

Benefits to Upstream Channel Members

Routinization of Transactions

Each purchase transaction involves ordering, determining the valuation of, and paying for goods and services. The buyer and seller must agree on the amount, mode, and timing of payment. These costs of distribution can be minimized if the transactions are routinized; otherwise, every transaction would be subject to bargaining, with an accompanying loss of efficiency.

Routinization also leads to the standardization of goods and services whose performance characteristics can be easily compared and assessed. It encourages the production of items with greater value. In short, routinization leads to efficiencies in the execution of channel activities. *Continuous replenishment programs (CRP)* remain an important element of efficient channel inventory management. First created by Procter & Gamble in 1980 to ship Pampers diapers to a retailer's warehouses automatically, without requiring retail managers to place orders, CRP came to Walmart in 1988—and the rest is retailing history. In CRP, manufacturing and retailing partners share inventory and stocking information to ensure that no products are under- or overstocked on retail shelves. These systems typically increase the frequency of shipments but lower the size per shipment, producing lower inventories held in the system and higher turnaround, both of which are sources of increased channel profitability. Moreover, CRP systems reduce inventory carrying costs, minimize the need for purchase orders, and often create closer relationships between the parties involved, resulting ultimately in greater channel loyalty.[3] However, a CRP also demands a routinized, strong relationship between channel partners. *Trust*, or confidence in the reliability and integrity of a channel partner, is required to achieve the high degree of cooperation among channel partners that is necessary to manage the CRP over time.[4]

Fewer Contacts

Without channel intermediaries, every producer would have to interact with every potential buyer to create all possible market exchanges. As the importance of exchange in a society increases, so does the difficulty of maintaining all of these interactions. Consider a simple example: in a small village of only

10 households trading among themselves, 45 transactions would be necessary to conduct decentralized exchanges at each production point (i.e., [10 × 9]/2). But if the village added a central market with one intermediary, it could reduce the complexity of this exchange system and facilitate transactions, such that only 20 transactions would be required to carry out the centralized exchange (10 + 10).

Implicit in this example is the notion that a decentralized system of exchange is less efficient than a centralized network that uses intermediaries. The same rationale applies to direct selling from manufacturers to retailers, relative to selling through wholesalers. Consider Figure 2.1. Assuming four manufacturers and 10 retailers that buy goods from each manufacturer, the number of contact lines amounts to 40. If the manufacturers sold to these retailers through one wholesaler, the number of necessary contacts would fall to 14.

The number of necessary contacts instead increases with more wholesalers. For example, if the four manufacturers in Figure 2.1 used two wholesalers instead of one, the number of contacts would rise from 14 to 28; with four wholesalers, the number of contacts grows to 56. Thus, employing more and more intermediaries creates diminishing returns, viewed solely from the point of view of the number and cost of contacts in the market. Of course, in this example we assume that each retailer contacts each of the wholesalers used by manufacturers. But if a retailer prefers a certain wholesaler, any effort by the manufacturer to restrict the number of wholesalers creates the risk of excluding the retailer's preferred wholesaler from the channel, which could leave the manufacturer unable to reach the market served by that retailer.

In this simplistic example, we also assume that the cost and effectiveness of each contact—manufacturer to wholesaler, wholesaler to retailer, manufacturer to retailer—are equivalent. Such an assumption clearly does not hold in the real world, where selling through one type of intermediary generally entails very different costs from those accrued by selling through another intermediary. Not all intermediaries are equally skilled at selling or are motivated to sell a particular manufacturer's product offering, which certainly affects the choice of which and how many intermediaries to use.

Thus we assert that it is the *judicious* use of intermediaries that reduces the number of contacts necessary to cover a market. This principle guides many manufacturers that seek to enter new markets but want to avoid high-cost direct distribution through their own employed sales forces. The trend toward rationalizing supply chains by reducing the number of suppliers also appears consistent with reducing the number of contacts in the distribution channel.

In summary, intermediaries necessarily participate in marketing channels because they both *add value* and *help reduce costs*. These roles raise another key question, then: what types of work do the channels themselves actually perform?

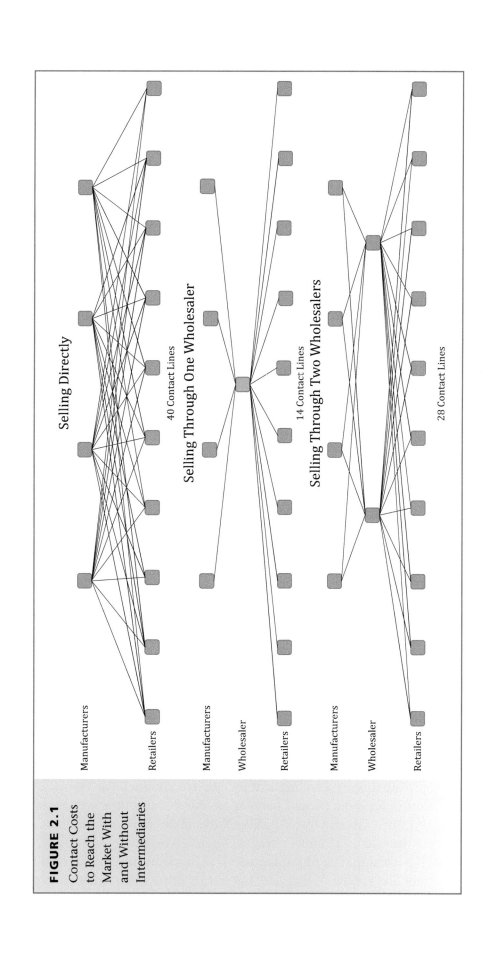

FIGURE 2.1
Contact Costs to Reach the Market With and Without Intermediaries

Selling Directly

Manufacturers

Retailers

40 Contact Lines

Selling Through One Wholesaler

Manufacturers

Wholesaler

Retailers

14 Contact Lines

Selling Through Two Wholesalers

Manufacturers

Wholesaler

Retailers

28 Contact Lines

THE KEY FUNCTIONS MARKETING CHANNELS PERFORM

Channel Functions

The marketing channel, through its members, performs a range of **channel functions** that constitute a process, flowing through the channel, performed at different points in time by different channel members. In business settings, these functions entail carrying or holding inventory, generating demand through selling activities, physically distributing products, engaging in after-sales service, and extending credit to other channel members. We introduced this list of nine universal channel functions in Chapter 1; they would be performed in a hypothetical channel that consists of producers, wholesalers, retailers, and consumers. Some functions move forward through the channel (physical possession, ownership, and promotion); others move up the channel from the end-user (ordering and payment); and still other channel functions can move in either direction or reflect activities by pairs of channel members (negotiation, financing, risk, information sharing).

Channel functions take different forms in different points of the channel. It is common for spare parts distribution to be handled by a separate third-party distributor, uninvolved in the distribution of original products, for example. Three competing manufacturers—Ingersoll-Rand International Bobcat, Clark Material Handling, and the Spicer Division of Dana Corporation—all use the same German third-party logistics (3PL) firm, Feige, to handle their non-U.S. distributions of spare parts. Feige simplifies the otherwise difficult job of managing spare parts inventories that must be shipped quickly to multiple countries with different language traditions. Feige not only receives, stores, and ships spare parts, it also provides debt, credit, and cash management services for its manufacturer clients. Dealers can order from Feige online and track their orders, after first checking that the desired parts are in stock. Feige's sophisticated information technology systems produce a remarkable 95 percent in-stock rate for its dealer customers. Customers' constant demands for quick delivery of spare parts make the use of this intermediary a superior strategy, from both cost-control and demand-satisfaction perspectives.[5] In such situations, a channel designer even might present its two physical possession activities (original equipment versus spare parts) separately, because they represent important, unique functions in the movement of products to the market.

Not every channel member needs to participate in every channel function. Specialization is a hallmark of an efficient channel. For example, physical possession of a product could move from the manufacturer to wholesalers to retailers and finally to end-users; an alternative channel might eliminate wholesalers and rely instead on manufacturers' representatives, who never take physical possession or ownership. The physical possession function still is performed by the manufacturer and retailer in this case, but not by other intermediaries. In general, channel functions get shared only by channel members that can add value or reduce costs by bearing them. However, specialization also increases interdependencies in channels, creating a need for closer cooperation and coordination in channel operations.

In addition, the performance of certain channel functions is correlated with that of other functions. Any time inventories are held and owned by one member of the channel system, financing is occurring. That is, when the wholesaler or retailer takes title and assumes physical possession of some portion of a manufacturer's output, this intermediary is financing the manufacturer, because the greatest component of carrying costs is the capital tied up by inventories held in a dormant state (i.e., not moving toward final sale). Other carrying costs include obsolescence, depreciation, pilferage, breakage, storage, insurance, and taxes. If the intermediary does not have to invest funds to pay inventory-holding costs, it can invest instead in other profitable opportunities. Capital costs thus equal the opportunity costs of holding inventory.

As this discussion suggests, given a set of functions to be undertaken in a channel, a manufacturer must assume responsibility for some, shift others to various intermediaries in its channel, or even shift everything. Accordingly, we note another important truth about channel design and management: it is possible to eliminate or substitute for the *members* of the channel but not for the *functions* they perform. When channel members leave the channel, their functions shift, either forward or backward, to be assumed by other channel members. Thus a channel should eliminate a member only if the function it performs can be done more effectively or less expensively by other channel members. Cost savings achieved by eliminating a channel member result not because that member's profit margin gets shared by the rest of the channel but rather because the functions previously performed by that channel member get completed more efficiently with another channel design.

Finally, we highlight an important channel function that permeates all value-added activities of a channel: information sharing. Manufacturers share product and sales information with their distributors, independent sales representatives, and retailers, which helps them perform the promotion function better. Consumers provide information about their preferences to the channel, which improves its overall ability to supply valued services. Producing and managing this information effectively is central to distribution channel excellence.

To design an optimal channel strategy for a targeted end-user market, the designer needs to audit the existing marketing channels serving this segment to evaluate the capabilities of each potential channel, in terms of the nine key functions and how well each version meets the segment's service output demands. Channel functions pertain to all channel activities that add value to the end-user, beyond merely handling or moving the product along the channel, and include promotion, negotiation, financing, ordering, payment, and so forth. Along with these performance considerations, channel structure decisions must reflect an effort to minimize channel function costs. Each channel member has a set of channel functions to perform;

ideally, the allocation of activities results in their most reliable performance at a minimum total cost. This task is not trivial; it involves comparing activities across different members of the channel.

Designing Channel Structures and Strategies

A channel manager conducts analyses to determine the degree of channel intensity, mix of channel types/identities, and use of dual distribution, as well as to close any service or cost gaps. By identifying demands for service outputs among different segments in the market, a channel analyst can find an optimal channel structure to satisfy them efficiently and effectively.

For each segment, the level of **intensity**, or the number of channel partners competing for customers, must be determined. A channel might include many retail outlets (intensive distribution), just a few (selective distribution), or only one (exclusive distribution) for a given market area; determining which option to choose depends on both efficiency and implementation factors. More intensive distribution makes the product more readily available to all target end-users, but it also can create conflict among the retailers that compete to sell it.

Imagine a channel manager seeking to sell a line of fine watches in retail stores. Which types and exact identities of channel partners are optimal: upscale outlets, such as Tiffany's, or family-owned local jewelers? This choice has implications for both channel efficiency and brand image. If the company also seeks to distribute its products in foreign markets, it needs to choose a distributor that can sell overseas, leveraging its good relationships with local channel partners in the target market. Therefore, this choice significantly affects the potential success of the firm's foreign market entry. Finally, the channel type decision refers to multiple levels of the channel structure. For example, an ethnic food manufacturer could sell its grocery products through small independent retailers with urban locations or with large chains that operate discount warehouse stores or by using various online-only outlets. Moving up the channel, additional decisions pertain to whether to use independent distributors, sales representative companies (called "reps" or "rep firms"), trucking companies, financing companies, export management companies, or any of a host of other possible independent distribution channel members that could be incorporated into the channel design.

Channel decisions derived from make-or-buy analyses—which indicate whether to vertically integrate or outsource—represent another critical strategic choice, because a firm's decision to own some or all of its marketing channel has an enduring influence on its ability to distribute and produce. The manufacturer becomes identified with its marketing channels, which influence its end-users and determine their perceptions of its image. The manufacturer also gains some market and competitive intelligence from these channels: what a manufacturer knows (or can learn) about its markets is heavily dependent on how it goes to market. Among downstream channel members, decisions to integrate backward would put them in conflict with other suppliers and eat up resources, which may jeopardize their ability to offer unbiased advice to their customers, yet for many, moving up the value chain seems irresistible (why let the producer take all the margins when the downstream channel member understands demand better?).

Such possibilities for unintended consequences highlight the need for a good understanding of the optimal channel structure and strategy to reach each targeted segment. This insight gives channel managers the freedom to establish the best possible channel design—as long as no other channel currently exists in the market for this segment. If a preexisting channel already is in place, though, channel managers need to undertake a gap analysis to identify the differences between an optimal and the actual current channel. For example, service output might be under- or oversupplied. Undersupply usually is obvious: the target segment expresses dissatisfaction with the insufficient level of service they receive. But the problem is more subtle in the case of oversupply, because target end-users get all the services they desire—and then some. Because that service is costly to supply, though, oversupply may lead to higher prices than target end-users ultimately will be willing to pay.

AUDITING MARKETING CHANNELS

As the previous section indicated, designing an optimal channel structure and strategy demands various analyses. A basic precept of marketing is that sellers must seek to identify and meet the needs of their end-users in the marketplace. For a marketing channel strategy, this precept means that marketers should be cognizant of how consumers prefer to buy and the type of services they want, so that the resulting marketing channel system produces the service outputs demanded by these targeted end-user segments. Thus, a key step in the process, after identifying targeted segments of end-users, is to *audit existing marketing channels*. Such audits evaluate each available channel member's capability to provide service outputs efficiently (bulk-breaking, quick delivery, spatial convenience, assortment, variety, information sharing). This evaluation must include both the level and the cost of the service outputs provided by each channel member, because end-users are sensitive to the overall utility provided by the channel (i.e., benefits at a given price). Manufacturers, wholesalers, and retailers all participate in marketing channels to create the service outputs demanded by their target end-users. Just as the machinery in a production plant produces physical products, the members of a marketing channel are engaged in **productive activity**, even if what they produce is intangible. In this sense, productivity derives from the value that end-users place on the service outputs that result from channel efforts. The activities that produce the service outputs demanded by end-users are the **channel functions**.

Auditing *what* channel functions get performed by each channel member in the existing channel system, *by whom, at what levels,* and *at what cost,* provides several important benefits:

1. Detailed knowledge of the capabilities of each channel member allows them to diagnose and remedy shortcomings in the pricing and provision of service outputs to targeted segments.

2. An audit may identify gaps in service outputs desired by targeted end-user segments, such that service providers can add necessary new channels or revise currently existing ones to address the shortcomings.

3. Knowing which channel members have incurred the costs of performing which channel functions helps members allocate channel profits equitably. In turn, channel members can better preserve a sense of fairness and cooperation and avert channel conflicts.

Our discussion in this section accordingly focuses on identifying and describing channel functions, as well as outlining how managers can audit channel systems to identify a zero-based channel, service gaps, or excessive costs.

Specific channel members can specialize in one or more channel functions, even as they remain excluded from other activities. This exclusion condition may make it appear tempting to remove another member from the channel (i.e., change the channel *structure*). But the specialized functions performed by that channel member cannot simply be eliminated. After a channel member leaves the channel, its functions must shift to some other channel member, to preserve the service output provision. An exception arises only if the eliminated channel member was performing activities that also were being addressed elsewhere in the channel, such that its contributions to the service output were redundant. For example, when an employed salesperson and an independent distributor's sales rep call on the same customer, they waste effort and resources. The channel may be better off using one or the other, not both, types of salespeople.

Every channel function contributes to the production of valued service outputs and also produces costs. Table 2.1 uses CDW as an example and offers some examples of channel cost-generating activities associated with each function.

Physical possession refers to channel activities pertaining to the storage of goods, including transportation between channel members. The costs of running warehouses and transporting products from one location to another are physical possession costs. In the case of commercial personal computer (PC) purchases, CDW's intermediary role creates significant physical possession costs and required investments, including those to maintain its 400,000-square-foot warehouse, where it houses the massive volumes of products it buys from manufacturers. For a service, such as online bill payment, physical possession costs seemingly should be lower, but they still apply to channel members who host the data (i.e., own, operate, and maintain the computer hardware and software systems to provide ready access to financial data in the system). This channel function might seem trivial at first glance, but in services markets, it is both costly and utterly crucial to the channel's success.

The costs of physical possession are distinct from the costs of **ownership**. When a channel member takes title to goods, it bears the cost of carrying the inventory; its capital is tied up in the product (whose opportunity cost is equal to the next highest value use of that capital). In many distribution systems, such as commercial PC sales, physical possession and ownership move together through the channel, but this pairing is neither necessary nor universal, as three examples show. First, *consignment selling* means that a retailer physically holds the product (e.g., painting in an art gallery), but the manufacturer (e.g., painter) retains ownership. The manufacturer gives up ownership only by selling it to an end-user. Second, ownership is separate from physical possession when a manufacturer or retailer contracts with a third-party reverse logistics specialist to handle the reverse logistic function but still retains ownership. The logistics specialist simply receives payment, as a fee for service or a percentage split of the ultimate resale revenue earned from returned merchandise. Third, a data hosting company in the online bill payment situation we mentioned previously never actually owns the data it holds.

Despite these examples, we acknowledge that physical possession and ownership move together in many channel systems. The term commonly used to designate their combined costs is **inventory-holding costs**. Inventories refer to stocks of goods or components used to make them, and they exist for several reasons:

- *Demand surges* outstrip production capacity. To smooth production, factories anticipate such surges and produce according to the forecast. Inventory results. The demand surge may be natural (e.g., ice cream in summer), or it may be due to marketers' actions, such as short-term promotions. The discipline of supply chain management emerged in the grocery industry mainly because retailers stockpiled goods to take advantage of manufacturers' promotions but then had to deal with high inventory carrying costs, including the cost of obsolescence.

- *Economies of scale* exist in production and transportation. Inventory in this case results because firms batch-process orders to make a long production run or stockpile goods to fill containers, trucks, ships, or planes.

- *Transportation takes time*, especially with greater distances between points of production and points of consumption. Downstream channel members thus maintain inventories (pipeline stock) to meet their demands until a shipment arrives and can be unpacked.

- *Supply and demand are uncertain.* Buyers can never be completely sure how long it will take to be resupplied (lead time)—or sometimes if they can get the stock at all. Thus, they acquire **safety stock** (i.e., excess of inventory, beyond the best estimate of what is needed during an order cycle) as a hedge against uncertainty. Such uncertainty often results from ignorance about what will sell (demand uncertainty).

How much inventory a channel member should hold is a very difficult question. Many models in the operations research tradition attempt to answer it, and they vary mainly in the assumptions they use to render this inventory problem mathematically tractable. The economic order quantity (EOQ) model is the oldest and likely the best known.[6]

In marketing channels, **promotion** functions take many forms: personal selling by an employee or outside sales force (e.g., brokers and registered investment advisers for mutual funds), media advertising, sales promotions (trade or retail), publicity, and other public relations activities. Promotional activities seek to increase awareness of the product being sold, educate potential buyers about products' features and benefits, and persuade potential buyers to purchase. A third-party reverse logistics specialist helps manufacturers achieve this promotional goal when it refurbishes returned products and sells them through new channels (e.g., eBay); in so doing, it targets new buyer segments and differentiates refurbished units from new products sold through standard channels. Promotional efforts also might seek to enhance overall *brand equity*, to increase sales in the future. Of course, any channel member can be involved in promotion, not just the retailer or manufacturer. Even as a distributor, CDW maintains an expensive sales force, which ultimately helps it reduce the total costs of promotion for its computer equipment manufacturers.

The **negotiation** function is present in the channel if the terms of sale or the persistence of certain relationships are open to discussion. The costs of negotiation are measured mainly on the basis of the time the negotiators need to conduct the negotiations and, if necessary, the cost of legal counsel. In a consortium with small businesses to serve the government market (Sidebar 2.1), CDW uses multiple members' capabilities to enhance the channel's joint negotiation power over the buyer: its negotiation abilities allow CDW to obtain products at low prices, so smaller businesses gain a negotiation edge in landing government contracts.

Financing costs are inherent to any sale that moves from one level of the channel to another. Typical financing terms for a business-to-business purchase require payment within 30 days and may offer a discount for early payment. With a 2 percent discount offered for payment within 10 days, for example, the terms of sale would be presented as "2–10 net 30." Regardless of the specifics, the payment terms establish the seller's willingness to finance the buyer's purchase for a period of time (here, 30 days), after the product has been delivered. In so doing, the seller accepts the financial cost of the forgone income that it could have achieved by putting that money to use in an alternative investment activity. Financing costs also may be borne by a manufacturer or intermediary, or even by an outside specialist, such as a bank or credit card company. As a distributor, CDW buys products from computer manufacturers and finances that inventory until customers buy and pay for them. It is particularly efficient in this function, according to its strong inventory turn rate and the minimal days indicated in its receivables. At the other end of the financing efficiency spectrum is a manufacturer with high product return rates that fails to manage them well. Even an average company finances its returned products for 30–70 days before reinserting them into the market.

There are many sources of **risk**. For example, long-term contracts between a distributor and end-user may specify price guarantees that lock in the distributor to a certain price. If the market price for that product rises while the contract is in force, the distributor loses revenue, because it must continue to sell at the previously determined, lower price. Southwest Airlines has been able to successfully reduce its fuel charges for years by locking in a specific price and using the savings to maintain its position as a low-cost carrier.[7] Price guarantees also may be offered to intermediaries who hold inventory, just in case the product's market price falls before the inventory is sold. This practice moves the risk from the intermediary to the manufacturer. Other risk-related costs include warranties, insurance, and after-sales service activities that attempt to mitigate concerns about unforeseeable future events (e.g., parts failures, accidents). The manufacturer or reseller usually bears these risk costs, though in some cases, a specific channel intermediary serves explicitly as a risk manager. When a CDW manager says, "We're kind of chief technical officer for many smaller firms," he is recognizing CDW's greater expertise with computer products and systems (see Sidebar 2.1). This expertise offers reduced risk to small-business customers, which know they can rely on CDW rather than try to identify the best systems on their own, with their limited knowledge.

Ordering and **payment** costs are those incurred during the actual purchase of and payment for the product. They may seem unglamorous, but innovations are radically altering the performance of these functions today. *Automatic replenishment* not only reduces ordering costs but also improves in-stock rates.

Finally, **information sharing** takes place among and between every channel member, in both routine and specialized ways. Retailers share information with their manufacturers about sales trends and patterns through electronic data interchanges; if used properly, this information can reduce the costs of many other channel functions. For example, with improved sales forecasts, the channel can lower its physical possession costs, because it holds less inventory. Such information is so important that logistics managers refer to this function as an ability to "transform inventory into information."

The costs associated with performing channel functions also demand that channels avoid performing *unnecessarily* or excessively well in any of their functions. Knowing which service outputs their target end-users demand, at what level of intensity and at what cost, helps channel managers design channel systems that provide targeted segments with the exact level of service outputs they demand, at the lowest cost.

SIDEBAR 2.1

CDW and PC Purchases by Small- and Medium-Sized Business Buyers: Channel Functions and Equity Principle Insights[8]

The success of CDW (cdw.com), a $15-billion, multi-brand technology solutions provider, lies in serving small- and medium-sized business customers with a superior provision of service outputs. Its ability to do so rests on its strategic performance of key channel functions, in a more efficient (lower-cost) and effective (better at producing service outputs) manner than other channel partners can. Key channel functions for CDW include *physical possession*, *promotion*, *negotiation*, *financing*, and *risk*. In addition, CDW offers flexibility to its buyers; not all buyers are required to pay for or solicit all of the functions that CDW offers. Instead, CDW provides differentiated function "packages" to the market, through one overall channel structure.

CDW Bears Channel Function Costs

Table 2.1 summarizes CDW's performance of key marketing channel functions, each with specific implications for channel efficiency (cost management) and channel effectiveness (minimizing total channel costs while maintaining desired service output levels).

As a channel intermediary, CDW performs *physical possession* and takes on a significant portion of the costly burden of holding inventory (in its 400,000-square-foot warehouse and large-volume purchases). The entries in Table 2.1 also suggest that CDW's participation in this function lowers the cost of inventory holding for the overall channel. In particular, CDW ships 99 percent of orders the day it receives them, reflecting its expertise in predicting demand, which minimizes its inventory-holding costs. Furthermore, CDW's "asset tagging" for government buyers constitutes a costly investment that also reduces subsequent physical possession costs, because it provides quick information to both CDW and buyers about the location of inventory. Thus it can schedule routine service and maintenance calls, as well as reduce product theft and loss. Its large-volume purchases also reduce system-wide inventory-holding costs, because it obtains reduced wholesale prices from suppliers. That is, sellers enjoy lower costs by delivering large volumes of product to CDW all at once, so they pass those savings on to CDW, while also appreciating improved channel efficiency overall.

CDW's *promotional* investments in the channel are also extensive (Table 2.1). It trains salespeople for several months when they start their jobs, so channel partners can rely on experienced promotional agents to sell their products. A salesperson is responsible for every account—even small, new accounts that initially generate low revenues. The company recognizes it cannot afford to have salespeople call on such accounts in person, so it serves them through phone or email contacts, which helps control its promotional channel function costs. But the salesperson remains available to answer customer questions, providing a well-trained sales conduit for each account. A customer with an existing, high-touch relationship with a CDW salesperson is likely to

Channel Function	CDW's Investments in the Function
Physical Possession	(a) 400,000-sq.-ft. warehouse. (b) Ships 99 percent of orders the day they are received. (c) For government buyers, CDW has instituted an "asset tagging" system that lets buyers track which product is going where; product is scanned into both buyer and CDW databases, for later ease in tracking products (e.g., service calls). (d) Buys product in *large volumes* from manufacturers, receiving approximately eight trailer-loads of product from various suppliers every day, in bulk, with few added services.
Promotion	(a) Devotes a salesperson to every account (even small, new ones), so that end-users can always talk to a real person about technology needs, system configurations, post-sale service, and so on. (b) Salespeople go through 6.5 weeks of basic training, then 6 months of on-the-job coaching, then a year of monthly training sessions. (c) New hires are assigned to small-business accounts to get more opportunities to close sales. (d) Salespeople contact clients *not* through in-person sales calls (too expensive) but by phone/email. (e) Has longer-tenured salespeople than its competitors.
Negotiation	CDW-G started a small-business consortium to help small firms compete more effectively for federal IT contracts. It gives small-business partners lower prices on computers than they could otherwise get, business leads, and access to CDW's help desk and product tools. It also handles shipping and billing, reducing the channel function burden from the small-business partner. In return, CDW gains access to contracts it could not otherwise get.
Financing	Collects receivables in just 32 days; turns inventories twice per month; and has no debt.
Risk	(a) "We're a kind of chief technical officer for many smaller firms." (b) CDW is authorized as a Cisco Systems Premier partner for serving the commercial customer market.
Information Sharing	(a) Collects information on which manufacturers' computers can best solve specific customers' needs. (b) Stores warranty information on each customer's product to facilitate servicing.

TABLE 2.1

CDW's Participation in Various Channel Functions

buy more from CDW, even if the initial purchase levels were minimal. Through these investments, CDW reaps reduced promotional costs from the long-tenured sales force it employs and keeps: a salesperson with three or more years on the job generates approximately $30,000 in sales *per day* on average, twice as much as someone with two years of experience and *10 times* as much as a salesperson with less than six months of experience!

Another example of clever management reflects the *negotiation* function in Table 2.1. The company's government arm (CDW-G) established a small-business consortium to help small computer services firms compete for U.S. government contracts. These small firms benefit from a government directive, mandating that this massive buyer award approximately 20 percent of its procurement contracts to small businesses. Although small firms thus have a *negotiation* advantage in interactions with the government as a buyer, they still must offer competitive price bids, which is difficult if they only purchase small product quantities. By providing both expertise and more competitive wholesale prices on computer equipment to small firms, CDW helps them compete on price. In this sense, CDW offers its own superior *negotiating* capability to its small partners, so that they can generate increased sales. For CDW, the benefits are obvious; it could never have qualified as a small business to win such contracts anyway. The complementary inputs of these channel partners thus jointly generate superior *negotiating* power.

In addition, CDW performs *financing* functions efficiently, as signaled by its enviable *inventory turn rate* of twice per month (this rate measures how frequently a section of shelf space, such as in the CDW warehouse, empties and is replenished with inventory). Furthermore, CDW is efficient in its *payment* collections, with just a 32-day average receivable figure (which helps it minimize the total financing cost in the channel), and the company carries no debt (which reduces the financing cost of capital).

Through extensive investments in expertise and *information sharing*, CDW reduces other channel function costs and *risk* for its buyers. As a manager quoted in Table 2.1 states, "We're kind of chief technical officer for many smaller firms." The small buyer relies on the expertise and knowledge offered by CDW to choose the right systems solutions. For commercial customers in general, CDW gained authorization as a Cisco Systems Premier partner to signal its expertise in providing full-service solutions, not just computer components. As one CDW executive explains, this authorization identifies CDW as a "trusted adviser" for the customer, such that it can "really talk technical about what a customer is trying to accomplish and really add value to the sale, as opposed to just sending out a box." CDW takes on the role of an IT strategy consultant for its customers. In this role, it also achieves channel-level efficiency in managing the cost of risk, because CDW learns relevant information and applies it to many customers, so each customer can benefit from the information-gathering economies of scale provided by CDW.

Finally, CDW offers customers a choice about which channel functions they want to transfer to it. It routinely performs substantial channel functions, but in relationships with end-users that already possess technical service capabilities or with computer manufacturers, CDW lessens its participation. For example, it serves the Kellogg School of Management at Northwestern University, which relies on CDW to provide computers for its students, faculty, and staff. After the machines have been purchased (i.e., CDW passes *physical possession* to Kellogg), the product *warranty* involves the manufacturer directly, not CDW. Kellogg has the technical capability to handle some repairs in-house, and it offers loaner machines to faculty and staff when it must ship their computers back to the manufacturer for service. Accordingly, CDW is not responsible for the post-sale services that Kellogg students and faculty enjoy when they buy a Kellogg-sanctioned laptop, because the school installs Kellogg-customized software on the machines and tests them before handing them over to the ultimate users. In this example, because the buyer can perform certain important channel functions itself, CDW responds flexibly by offering tiered service levels, such that Kellogg can select the channel functions it cannot or does not want to perform itself.

CDW Uses the Equity Principle in Function Management and Incentive Creation
In two notable ways, CDW acts in accordance with the equity principle. First, it compensates employee salespeople with a commission rate that is the same regardless of whether the sale is generated person-to-person or from online ordering (both of which CDW offers). As we discussed, every customer is assigned a CDW salesperson, in the hope that more promotional

(sales force) contacts generate greater customer lifetime value. But imagine that the customer interacts with the CDW salesperson periodically for major purchases, then buys replacement components (e.g., printer cartridges) online. Is it "fair" to award sales commissions to the salesperson for these online purchases? According to CDW, it is, because the online purchases resulted at least in part from the initial sales efforts by the salesperson to build the customer relationship. Without the salesperson, the end-user might have made these routine purchases elsewhere. Moreover, CDW recognizes that it is not just *how costly the inputs are* that matters; it is also *how the customer wants to buy*. If a customer prefers to make certain purchases online, such as when it seems easier than contacting a salesperson, CDW's internal incentive system supports the customer's freedom of choice. Its equitable commission policy also avoids a pernicious sales incentive to "force" the customer to buy in person rather than online.

Second, CDW offers a different fee schedule to the small solution providers with which it partners to serve some ultimate end-users, because it relies on them to perform on-site work, such as installation, software or hardware customization, post-sale customer service, and so forth. The equity principle suggests that these solution providers should be unwilling to undertake such costly activities unless they know they will be compensated. The fee structure offered by CDW gives them an adequate reward; by "paying them what they're worth," CDW embraces the very essence of the equity principle.

AUDITING CHANNELS USING THE EFFICIENCY TEMPLATE

To audit a channel member's capability to provide each channel function and add value, and at what cost, we can use an **efficiency template**, which describes (1) the types and amounts of work done by each channel member to perform the marketing functions, (2) the importance of each channel function to the provision of end-user service outputs, and (3) the share of total channel profits that each channel member *should* reap. Figure 2.2 contains a blank efficiency template: the rows are the channel functions, and then one set of columns indicates the *importance weights* for the functions, while the other lists the *proportional performance of each function* by each channel member.

Consider the three columns that refer to the importance weights associated with each channel function. The idea is to account for both the *cost* of performing that function and the *value added* due to that same performance in the channel. The entries in the "Cost" column should be percentages, totaling 100 percent across all the functions. If the costs of promotion account for 23 percent of all channel function costs, the analyst enters "23" in the relevant cell, then determines how the other functions account for the remaining 77 percent of the costs. To generate these quantitative cost weights, an **activity-based costing (ABC)** accounting method can measure the cost of performance for each organization.[9] For our purposes,

FIGURE 2.2
The Efficiency Template

	Importance Weights for Functions			Proportional Function Performance of Channel Member				Total
	Costs*	Benefit Potential (High, Medium, Low)	Final Weight*	1	2	3	4 (End-User)	
Physical Possession**								100
Ownership								100
Promotion								100
Negotiation								100
Financing								100
Risk								100
Ordering								100
Payment								100
Information Sharing								100
Total	100	N/A	100					100
Normative Profit Share***	N/A	N/A	N/A	N/A	N/A	N/A	N/A	100

*Entries in each column must add up to 100 points.
**Entries across each row (sum of proportional function performance of channel members 1–4) for each channel member must add up to 100 points.
*** Normative profit share of channel member *i* is calculated as (final weight, physical possession) × (channel member *i*'s proportional function performance of physical possession) +...+ (final weight, information sharing) × (channel member *i*'s proportional function performance of information sharing). Entries across rows (sum of normative profit shares for channel members 1–4) must add up to 100 points.

though, the task is more comprehensive: we need good quantitative measures of the costs of all activities performed by *all* channel members. If we know the total costs, we still need to ask: what proportion of these total channel costs is accounted for by, say, promotions?

Even without quantitative cost measures, analysts can use qualitative techniques to estimate cost weights. With a Delphi-type research technique, several expert managers in the channel might each develop their best estimates of the cost weights.[10] The output of this exercise is a set of weights, adding up to 100, that measure the proportion or percentage of total channel costs accounted for by each function.

But costs are not the entire picture. The performance of each function also creates *value*, and determining how much is a more intuitive process, linking the performance of functions to the generation of desired service outputs for a targeted segment of end-users. With this information, we can adjust the "Cost" weight to derive the final set of importance weights for each function in the channel. The adjustment process is judgmental but generally increases the weight for functions that generate "high" added value in the channel, while diminishing the value assigned to functions with "low" value added. Again in this case, the final weights must sum to 100, so if some function weights increase, others *must* decrease. A Delphi analysis can complement this approach and help channel members arrive at a final set of weights to represent both the cost borne and the value created through the performance of a channel function.

To complete the other columns in the efficiency template in Figure 2.2, the channel analyst must allocate the total cost of each function across all channel members. Again, the analyst enters figures adding up to 100, to represent the proportion of the total cost of a function that a particular channel member bears. So if a channel consists of a manufacturer, a distributor, a retailer, and an end-user, the costs of physical possession spread across these four channel members—though not all channel members bear all costs. For example, a manufacturer may use independent sales reps to help sell its product. These sales reps do not inventory any product or take any title to it; they specialize in promotional and sometimes order-taking activities. Their cost proportion entry in the physical possession row thus would be 0.

Note that the end-user is also a member of the channel. Any time end-users buy a larger lot size than they really need in the short term (i.e., forgo bulk-breaking by stocking up on paper towels at a hypermarket), they are performing some of the physical possession function, because they have to maintain the inventory of the unused product themselves. This consumer therefore bears inventory carrying costs too, which means sharing the costs of ownership in the channel. The costs of financing also might fall on an end-user who pays for the whole lot at the time of purchase. The various ways end-users can participate in channel functions thus produce costs for them; as for any channel member, these costs need to be measured.

The resulting information can be particularly useful for contrasting one segment of end-users against another, which sheds light on the fundamental question of why it costs more to serve some end-users than others. The answer is generally because they perform fewer costly channel functions themselves, thrusting this cost back onto other channel members.

After having assigned weights to each function and allocated cost proportions for the performance of each function across all channel members, the channel analyst can calculate a weighted average for each channel member, which reveals its contributions to the costs borne and value created in the channel. This weighted average is calculated as (weight × cost proportion) for each function, then summed across all functions.

These percentages have special meaning, especially when we turn to the total profit available to the channel from products sold at full-service list prices. This value equals total revenues (assuming all units sell at their list prices), minus all costs of running the channel. These percentages not only measure the proportionate value creation but also suggest the **normative profit shares** that each channel member should receive. Of course, being responsible for a larger proportion of a low-value function might not create as much value as performing even a smaller percentage of a highly valued function. Thus, being the "busy" channel member does not always signal high value creation. We return to this notion in our discussion of the equity principle in the next subsection.

In the meantime, what does it imply when an end-user generates channel profits? If end-users buy large quantities and plan to use them after the time of purchase, they pay in advance and are willing to store a product for later use. These valued channel functions are costly for the customer, just as they would be for any other channel member, so their performance merits some reward. In general, the reward for end-users who perform valued channel functions is lower prices.

In addition to determining carefully which actors to include in the efficiency template, a separate efficiency template should be devised for *each channel* that distributes the product to a targeted segment of end-users. Such separation is absolutely necessary, because a channel member involved in selling to retail buyers (e.g., retailer) does not bear any channel function costs in the direct sales channel, but it bears plenty of them in the retail channel.

Finally, the analyst might lack full financial data about the costs borne by each channel member. Without precise ratings—because we do not know precisely how much of a particular function's cost gets borne by each particular channel member—do we need to discard the efficiency template? Absolutely not, as long as *some* ranking data are available to calibrate the relative intensity of the performance of each function. Even rough rankings can provide a reasonably good approximation of the relative value created by each channel member. As with any system, the rougher the approximations, the rougher the resulting estimates, but these approximations still tend to be far more informative than an analysis that ignores the relative value added by each channel member.

In summary, the efficiency template is a useful tool for codifying the costs borne and the value added to the channel by each channel member, including end-users. Among its many uses, the efficiency template can reveal how the costs of particular functions get shared among channel members, indicate how much each channel member contributes to overall value creation in the channel, and demonstrate how important each function is to total channel performance. It also can be a powerful explanatory tool and justification for current channel performance or changes to existing operating channels. In an omni-channel design, for products sold through multiple channels, the efficiency templates can be compared to find differences in the costs of running the different channels, which may help lower costs without compromising desired service output levels.

Evaluating Channels: The Equity Principle

The normative profit shares calculated from the efficiency template for an operating channel reveal what share of the total channel profits that each channel member generates through its efforts. This normative share should relate to the *actual* share of total channel profits each channel member receives, according to our definition of the **equity principle**:

> A member's level of compensation in the channel system should reflect its degree of participation in the marketing functions and the value created by such participation. That is, compensation should mirror the normative profit shares of each channel member.

The equity principle further asserts that it is appropriate to reward each channel member in accordance with the value it creates. Not only is this equivalence fair and equitable, but it also creates strong incentives for channel members to continue generating value. Thus CDW's equal commission rates for online purchases and salesperson-handled purchases maintain employees' incentives to try to build their client accounts, regardless of how the client wants to buy. But trying to deprive any channel member of its rewards for effort and value created likely will result in subsequent underperformance. The serious channel conflicts that can result even might lead to the dissolution of the channel.

To live by the equity principle, channel members must identify the actual costs they incur and develop an acceptable estimate of the value created in the channel. Otherwise, they likely devolve into disagreements about the value each member actually has added, which represents an unwinnable argument, because it features channel members' individual perceptions of their own contributions, not facts. If the only member who recognizes the value of a contribution is the member performing it, the channel cannot effectively reinforce this high-value activity. The channel members who reward the activity also must perceive it. Although it takes substantial effort to amass the information necessary to complete an efficiency analysis, the payoffs are worthwhile.

Yet in many cases, actual profit shares do not match the normative shares suggested by the efficiency template. In this case, the solution demands further analysis of both the channel situation and the external competitive environment. In certain competitive situations, despite channel members' valiant efforts to contribute to channel performance, one of them earns less profit than the efficiency template would suggest, because the availability of competitors makes this member seem easily replaceable. Imagine, for example, a supplier of a commodity product to Walmart. When Walmart announces that its suppliers must adopt RFID (radio frequency identification) technology, our focal supplier faces significant new costs: buying the equipment to make and insert the tags; purchasing the tags themselves; training employees to handle, affix, and program the tags' contents. In addition, the cost savings promised by RFID technology must be shared between the supplier and Walmart (as well as customers). Thus the supplier might perceive that it is bearing more than its "fair share" of the cost of implementing this technology, which is a clear violation of the equity principle. Unfortunately for our supplier, though, it has little recourse: if it refuses to pay the cost of RFID tags, Walmart can simply drop it as a supplier and replace it with another that provides both the commodity and the RFID functionality. When market power and competitive pressures cause deviations from the equity principle, the channel reward system does not necessarily need to change.

In the long run, though, it might not be a bad idea for Walmart to offer some concessions to the equity principle. Channel partners who fail to receive rewards commensurate with their perceived contributions cannot remain motivated for long. They might begin looking for ways to exit the channel; at the very least, they are certain to bargain hard for favorable changes in terms. A firm that treats its channel partners poorly develops a bad reputation that will harm its long-term ability to add or manage channels in the future. Finally, violations of the equity principle constitute a primary cause of channel conflict, which in itself can be costly to manage.

Thus, astute channel managers carefully balance long-term relationship risks against the immediate gain of garnering a greater share of immediate channel profits. And we in turn reassert: If competitive conditions do not give one channel member leverage over another, profit-based rewards should spread throughout the channel roughly in proportion to the level of performance provided by each channel member. By auditing existing channels using the efficiency template, channel managers learn the suggested relative share of profit; they then can compare those shares with the actual shares of profit enjoyed by each channel member and apply the equity principle to identify any discrepancies. By determining whether the discrepancies reflect an outcome of market power or competitive pressure, the manager also can decide whether and how to address them through a channel strategy.

If no marketing channel already exists for a product, though, such as when a manufacturer seeks to sell its products in a new market or country, it needs to create a new channel. The next subsection describes how to evaluate and design new marketing channels, using a zero-based channel concept.

Evaluating Channels: Zero-Based Channel Concept

Starting from scratch and establishing a zero-based channel entails recognizing the level of channel functions that need to be performed to generate appropriate service outputs in the market. As the preceding discussion implies, though, zero-based channels may not even exist. So how can a designer possibly structure a brand new, ideal channel system? Consider the following questions as possible guidelines:

- What less or non-valued functions (e.g., excessive sales calls) can be eliminated without damaging customer or channel satisfaction?

- Are there any redundant activities? Which of them could be eliminated to lower the costs for the entire system?

- Is there a way to eliminate, redefine, or combine certain tasks to minimize the steps to a sale or reduce its cycle time?

- Is it possible to automate certain activities and thereby reduce the unit costs required to get products to market, even if fixed costs increase?

- Are there opportunities to modify information systems to reduce the costs of prospecting, order entry, quote generation, or similar activities?

For new channel designs, the planner also likely faces managerial or environmental barriers to establishing a zero-based channel. If a channel already exists, it might not be a zero-based channel.

Understanding the concept of channel functions is critical to any channel manager's ability to design and maintain an effective, efficient channel. Channel functions are both costly to offer and valuable to end-users. If managers can identify and understand the segment(s) of the market that their channel will target, they also can use sophisticated analyses of channel functions to evaluate the cost-effectiveness of various channel activities that have been designed to generate service outputs that end-users will appreciate.

AUDITING CHANNELS USING GAP ANALYSIS

By matching the service outputs demanded by targeted end-users to the offerings (service and price) provided by existing channels, managers gain a good idea of where there might be gaps in the ideal channel structure, required to meet target segments' needs. By identifying and closing these gaps, managers can build a channel that meets service output demands at a minimum cost—that is, they can design a zero-based channel.

Sources of Channel Gaps

Gaps in channel design might arise simply because management has not thought carefully about target end-users' demands for service outputs or about managing the cost of running their channel. The solution is simple: pay attention to both service gaps and cost gaps when designing the channel.

But the reality tends to be more complex. **Gaps** can arise from the limitations placed on even the best-intentioned channel managers. A manager seeking to design a zero-based channel for the company's product likely confronts constraints on his or her actions that prevent the establishment of an optimal channel design. Before diagnosing the types of gaps, it therefore is useful to discuss the limitations, or bounds, that create them. We concentrate on two: environmental and managerial.

The characteristics of the marketplace in which the channel operates can constrain the effective establishment of a zero-based channel.[11] Such **environmental bounds** create channel gaps. Two key examples of environmental bounds are local legal regulations and the sophistication of the physical and retailing infrastructure. First, legal conditions in the marketplace shape which channel partners a company may choose—that is, if they do not simply prevent the company's access to the market altogether. Recall our example of CDW, the computer reseller. Its penetration of the government market is limited by the government's stated goal of granting approximately 20 percent of its business to small- or medium-sized vendors. Therefore, CDW established a small and minority business partners program, working with independent companies whose sizes meet governmental preferences. This program creates a channel structure for CDW that is mainly the result of the imposition of a legal bound.

Second, the physical and infrastructural environment may prevent certain types of distribution channel structures.[12] Online bill payment systems demand systems that can communicate across different levels of the channel and manage information consistently over time. Not only must the bill be *payable* by the payer electronically, but it also must be *presented* electronically in a common database system. For many bill payers (consumers and businesses), the real value of electronic bill payment is the ability it provides to integrate the payment with the payer's own database of information (e.g., back-office activities, household budgets). Limitations on the integration of various electronic data sources constrain the possible spread of electronic payments in the market, though. Similarly, companies that want to manage returned products more efficiently may not be able to develop the capacity to do so themselves or to find an appropriate intermediary that can handle its specific needs. For example, in the retail book industry, processing returns represent one of the highest costs for the warehouse. The long-standing legacy of allowing free returns from retailers to publishers appears to be a hard habit to break, and this effective environmental bound persists even for those actors that would prefer to change the system.

Environmental bounds thus occur outside the boundaries of the companies directly involved in the channel and prevent channel members from establishing a zero-based channel, whether because they cannot offer an appropriate level of service outputs or because the constraints impose unduly high costs on channel members. In contrast, though managerial bounds also constrain channel design, they emanate from within the channel structure itself or from the orientation or culture of specific channel members.

That is, **managerial bounds** refer to constraints on the distribution structure that arise from the rules imposed by a company—typically, the company that manufactures the product. Sometimes a desire to control the customer, or simply a lack of trust among channel members, prevents managers from implementing a less bounded channel design.

The bounds imposed by management also may reflect a lack of knowledge about the appropriate levels of investment or activity. One computer company, whose primary route to market was online sales, found that its return rates were very high. In a (misguided) effort to minimize returns, it instituted a new policy: refunds would be offered on returned products only if the product was broken. The logic was that if the consumer received the product in good condition, it should be kept, but a nonfunctioning product that arrived at the buyer's doorstep should be taken back for a full refund or exchange. After instituting the policy, return percentages did not fall at all, but the company did notice one key change: *all* of the returned products were now broken, of course! The company had unwittingly created a managerial bound by instituting a policy that led to even worse results than the original problem. Fortunately, management realized the problem quickly and reversed course, but this example suggests that some managerial bounds are obvious enough that they should never be implemented.

Even such questionable efforts to manage the costs of returned products probably result not from some perverse desire to incur higher costs but rather from ignorance about what those costs are and what resources are available to control them. Here, we find the confluence of a managerial bound ("We don't see the value of focusing on returns and reverse logistics") and a concomitant environmental bound ("Now that we realize return costs are worth focusing on, we don't know the solution"). The goal must be to recognize all self-imposed managerial bounds and attack them whenever possible.

Whether channel gaps arise due to managerial bounds, environmental bounds, or a lack of attention to the well-being of the channel, they can profoundly affect either side of a zero-based channel, through service or cost gaps. We turn to this notion and the related taxonomy next.

Service Gaps

Think about a single service output. A **service gap** exists if the amount of a service supplied is less than the service demanded (in shorthand, SS < SD) or if the amount of service supplied is greater than the amount demanded (SS > SD). In the first case, insufficient service output is available to satisfy the target market (SS < SD). For example, customers once believed that standard music retailers offered insufficient bulk-breaking (few single-song formats), assortment, and variety; these gaps helped ensure the success of online alternatives as they came available. In this case, the service supplied by brick-and-mortar music retailers fell below the level demanded by many customers.

In contrast, a service gap may reflect a low service output offering accompanied by a low price. At Dollar Stores, everything is available at a low price, but the assortment and service provision are relatively poor. In this case, despite the very low prices, some end-users do not perceive sufficient *value* (i.e., utility for the price paid). Without sufficient value, they will not purchase the bundle consisting of the product plus its service outputs. Thus, a service gap can arise when the level of service is too low, even controlling for a lower price, such that it does not generate a sufficient amount of value for the end-user.

To describe an overly high level of service output (SS > SD), we again use the retail music example. For one target segment (e.g., younger pop music buyers who are well versed in using the Internet), the customer service provided by a standard music retailer is simply too high; they prefer do-it-yourself downloads over sales attention from possibly less well-informed in-store personnel (especially because relevant information about what music is "hot" tends to be more readily available and up-to-date on the Internet, not in stores). Most shoppers are only too familiar with the overly helpful store clerk: at first the attention may seem welcome, but eventually, it becomes irritating and distracting. These overinvestments in service outputs decrease, rather than increase, the end-user's satisfaction, even as they cost more money to provide—a dual penalty.

Businesses have to worry about not just their own service outputs but also the service outputs of other businesses. When one business offers better service, it charges a higher price for the goods it sells; when another business offers poor service, its prices tend to be lower. Some savvy consumers may take advantage of this situation by using the free services one business provides (e.g., in-store demonstrations, test drives), then purchasing the desired product at another business that does not offer these services and thus sells at a lower cost. Interestingly, such *free riding* actually can reduce the intensity of direct price competition among channel members in some cases.[13]

Of course, erring on either side is a mistake. Providing overly high service output levels can be just as bad as providing overly low levels. On the one hand, channel costs (and prices) rise too high for the value created, and on the other hand, the channel "skimps" on service outputs for which the target market would be willing to pay a premium. Profit opportunities get lost on both sides.

It also is possible to find service gaps in more than one service output. That is, the level of one service output might be too low, while the level of another is too high, as our traditional music retailing example makes clear (SS < SD for bulk-breaking and assortment/variety, but SS > SD for customer service). The channel manager might believe that such combinations balance out, such that the "extra" level of one service output should compensate for a shortfall of another. But service outputs rarely are good substitutes for each other, so no level of excess of one service output can truly compensate for too little of another. Small neighborhood variety stores offer extremely high spatial convenience, but they rarely can match the assortment and variety provided by a hypermarket, and they often charge higher prices. The decline of such stores in many urban and suburban areas in the United States suggests that consumers are not willing to trade off a poor assortment and insufficient variety for extreme spatial convenience.

Beyond finding the right combination of service outputs, it is critical to perform service gap checks, *service output by service output* and *segment by segment.* Our retail music example indicates a shortfall in the provision of some service outputs (bulk-breaking, assortment, variety), along with a surfeit of another (customer service). But the output that constitutes a service gap for one target segment (e.g., young digital natives) may represent exactly the right amount for another target segment (e.g., their grandparents, vinyl aficionados). Thus retail music stores ultimately might not disappear; instead, they may find a smaller segment of target end-users, serve them well, and continue to focus more narrowly on their needs.

Segmentation thus helps identify which service gaps exist for which clusters of potential buyers, rather than suggesting a need for global changes in the channel strategy. Identifying the segment for which a service output offering is appealing can be an enormously useful piece of information when determining how to close service gaps.

Cost Gaps

A cost gap exists when the total cost of performing all channel functions is too high, generally because one or more relevant channel functions, from physical possession to information sharing, are too expensive. Holding the level of service outputs constant, if a lower-cost way to perform the channel function in question exists, a cost gap exists too. It would be meaningless to discuss channel functions performed at too low a cost, though—as long as demanded service outputs are being produced, there is no overly low cost!

The cost of training salespeople and managing turnover in the sales force at CDW effectively illustrates a cost gap in the performance of the promotional function. The company puts all its newly hired salespeople through a very rigorous training program to enable them to provide excellent customer education and service—those service outputs most valued by small- and medium-sized business customers. But just how costly is it to generate this superior level of service outputs? Furthermore,

CDW's annual sales force turnover rate is 25 percent, which means that one-fourth of the newly hired (and expensively trained) salespeople leave the company. Their training costs are wasted investments; even worse, they may have granted one of CDW's competitors a well-trained salesperson (if that competitor engages in *poaching*, or seeking out and hiring employees trained elsewhere). If CDW could identify, before it initiated its costly training efforts, which salespeople were most likely to leave, it could lessen these promotional (sales training) costs without compromising on its delivery of service outputs.

Electronic bill presentment and payment (EBPP) services created cost gaps both before and after the onset of this new technology. Before EBPP technologies spread throughout the United States, the costs of key channel functions, including promotion, negotiation, risk, ordering, and payment, were all higher than necessary to pay bills. Adopting EBPP throughout the system undoubtedly would reduce channel costs significantly, from presentation to final bill payment and reconciliation. Yet the very introduction of this new technology created new cost gaps, because bill payers (who are channel members too) perceived greater risk associated with their new bill payment process. The shift in channel function costs from some channel members to others meant that end-users had to agree to take on the cost (i.e., risk); otherwise, the new technologies could not spread successfully. However, bill-paying end-users typically received no compensation for the time, effort, or risk associated with adopting the technology; that is, the shift in costs did not coincide with a shift in payments.

This example illustrates a general rule: if channel functions are to be shifted (even perceptually), a gap will result unless the channel member to whom the functions are shifted agrees to perform them. If the channel member is not compensated for doing so, the chances of compliance and successful implementation diminish. Over time, though, even without compensation, users and channel members often adopt the new technology if it is more efficient or becomes the widely accepted norm. Airline self-check-in is fairly well accepted, but grocery self-checkout (while growing in popularity) remains limited.

The criterion for defining a cost gap specifies that the total cost of performing all functions jointly is higher than it needs be. Therefore, a cost gap might not exist, even if one function is performed at an unusually high cost, as long as it minimizes the *total cost* of performing all functions *jointly*.[14] For example, an electrical wire and cable distributor expanded across the United States and internationally, acquiring many other independent distributors and eventually building an international network of warehouses. Some products it stocked and sold were specialty items, rarely demanded but important to include in a full-line inventory (i.e., end-users demanded a broad assortment and variety). But it was very costly to stock these specialty items in every warehouse worldwide. Therefore, the distributor chose to stock them in just one or two warehouses, which minimized the cost of physical possession of inventory. However, sometimes an end-user located far from the warehouse valued quick delivery and demanded a specialty product.

To meet that service output demand, the distributor provided air-freight services to get the required product to the end-user, incurring a seemingly inefficiently high transportation cost. Yet this high transportation cost still was lower than the cost of stocking the specialty product in all possible warehouses, awaiting a rare order. Thus, there was not any true cost gap, because the *total cost* of performing all channel functions was minimized.

In this example, it made economic sense to incur high shipping costs, in return for much lower inventory-holding costs. Furthermore, both of those costs were borne by the same channel member, namely the distributor itself. Optimal allocations of channel functions and costs are more difficult when *different* channel members perform the two functions. Say the distributor would bear the inventory-holding cost, but another intermediary (e.g., broker) was responsible for the shipping costs to get the product to the end-user. In this case, without close coordination and cooperation between the channel members, the distributor likely would benefit from lower warehousing costs at the expense of the broker, who would have to bear higher shipping costs. Even though the entire channel might benefit, this optimal solution is unlikely to arise in practice unless the distributor and broker make an explicit arrangement to share the total costs and benefits fairly.

In summary, a cost gap occurs whenever the performance of channel functions is jointly inefficient (costly). Sometimes, one or more functions may seem inefficient, but only because the channel members have purposefully traded off inefficiency in one function for super-efficiency in another, resulting in lower costs overall. More often, though, high costs are a strong signal of cost gaps. Furthermore, a cost gap might exist even without any evidence, from the end-user side, of a channel performance problem. That is, end-users may be delighted with the level of service they receive and the products they buy, and they may even consider the price for the product plus service outputs bundle reasonable. But in this scenario, chances are good that at least some channel members are not receiving a level of profit that adequately compensates them for the functions they are performing. The cost gap inflicts higher costs on channel members than are necessary. Some channel member must pay those costs, whether end-users, paying through higher prices, or upstream channel members, paying through decreased profit margins. A true zero-based channel offers the right level of service outputs at a minimum total cost to the channel.

Combining Channel Gaps

Our taxonomy of service and cost gaps implies the six possible situations in Figure 2.3, *only one of which is a zero-gap situation.* As this figure reveals, it is critical to identify the *source* of the gap. If the gap arises solely from the cost side, the channel cannot reduce or increase its service output provision in its efforts to reduce costs. Alternatively, if a service gap, involving too much of a particular service output, and a cost gap, due to inefficiently performed functions, coexist, reducing the level of service outputs offered without also increasing efficiency can never fully close the gap. If a service gap implies insufficient service outputs, combined with a high cost gap, the temptation may be to cut service provision to reduce channel costs. But this result would be doubly disastrous, in that service levels would suffer even more, and efficiency on a function-by-function basis would not improve. Without proper identification of the source of the gap, the channel could easily pursue a solution that is worse than the original problem.

To apply Figure 2.3 to a firm's channel gaps, the channel manager must specify which service gaps occur for each particular service output that is valued in the marketplace. This specification permits the manager to identify the over- and under-availability of each service output in a single framework. Figure 2.3 also is specific to unique target segments, so it needs to be applied separately for each segment in the market. A service gap for one segment may not be a gap at all in another (or the gap may differ).

Cost and service gap combinations also might arise from the links between cost decisions and the provision of service outputs. The principles of postponement and speculation offer a good example.[15] **Postponement** refers to the desires, by both firms and end-users, to put off incurring costs as long as possible. For a manufacturing firm, postponement means delaying the start of production until it

FIGURE 2.3 Types of Gaps	**Cost/Service Level**	**Service Gap (SD>SS)**	**No Service Gap (SD=SS)**	**Service Gap (SS>SD)**
	No Cost Gap (Efficient Cost)	Price/value proposition are right for a less demanding segment	*Zero-gap*	Price/value proposition are right for a more demanding segment
	Cost Gap (Inefficiently Provided Services)	Service levels are too low and cost too high	Service levels are right but costs are too high	Service levels and costs are too high

receives orders, to avoid the differentiation of raw materials into finished goods (e.g., iron ore into carbon steel). Postponement thus minimizes the manufacturer's risk of selling its production and eliminates the costs of holding relatively expensive inventory. But suppose that end-users demand quick delivery; they too want to postpone and buy at the last minute. In this situation, manufacturers engaging in postponement cannot meet the service output demands of target end-users, and though they may have avoided a cost gap, they almost certainly have created a problematic service gap.

If end-users express high demands for quick delivery, a successful channel must lessen its reliance on postponement and turn instead to greater speculation. **Speculation** involves producing goods in anticipation of orders, rather than in response to them. A lowest total cost channel that employs speculation often relies on a channel intermediary, which specializes in holding finished inventories for the manufacturer (e.g., retailer holds finished goods for consumers), in anticipation of sales to end-users. Although speculation is risky and creates inventory-holding costs, it permits economies of scale in production by allowing the manufacturer to produce in large batch-lot sizes (unlike postponement). But as demand for quick delivery increases, total channel costs ultimately must rise, which result in higher total prices for a product supplied through such a speculation-based system.

The modern retail music business faces exactly this trade-off between speculation and postponement. Previously *speculative* sales of CDs required the channel to guess in advance which CDs would sell well, so that stores could stock the right number of units. Today, more end-users engage in *postponement* sales through instant online downloads of exactly the music tracks they want to hear, at the very moment they decide they want to purchase. The tension between postponement and speculation is also evident in book sales: many book publishers still favor *speculation*, such that they supply many copies of potential bestsellers to retail bookstores, whereas *postponement* is predominant in the electronic book channel, in which a consumer can download books from the Internet on demand to read electronically. Book publishers continue to embrace speculation, out of their belief that consumers still prefer paper books and are not willing to wait to obtain the book they want, if it is not immediately available in a bookstore. That is, publishers assert that even though postponement might minimize channel costs (e.g., physical possession, ownership, financing), it compromises on the delivery of too many service outputs to be profitable overall.

Evaluating Channels: Gap Analysis Template

This chapter describes sources of channel gaps, service gaps, and cost gaps, as well as why these gaps must be considered simultaneously. Figure 2.4, the **Service Gap Analysis Template**, aims to identify service gaps explicitly according to the *targeted end-user segment*. Figure 2.5, the **Cost Gap Analysis Template**, builds on this information and identifies cost gaps, the bounds that give rise to them, and

FIGURE 2.4

Service Gap Analysis Template: CDW Example

	Service Demanded (SD: L/M/H) Versus Service Supplied by CDW (SS)						
Segment Name/Descriptor	Bulk-Breaking	Spatial Convenience	Delivery/Waiting Time	Assortment/Variety	Customer Service	Information Sharing	Major Channel for Segment
1. Small-business buyer	H (SS = SD)	Original equipment: M (SS = SD); Post-sale service: H (SS= SD)	Original equipment: M (SS > SD); Post-sale service: H (SS = SD)	M (SS > SD)	H (SS = SD)	H (Both pre-sale and post-sale) (SS = SD)	Value-added such as CDW or retailer
2. Large-business buyer	L (SS > SD)	Original equipment: H (SS = SD); Post-sale service: L (SS> SD)	Original equipment: M (SS > SD); Post-sale service: L (SS > SD)	M/H (SS = SD)	M (SS > SD)	L (SS > SD)	Manufacturer direct or large reseller such as CDW
3. Government/education	L (SS > SD)	Original equipment: H (SS = SD); Post-sale service: H (SS= SD)	Original equipment: M (SS > SD); Post-sale service: M (SS > SD)	M/H (SS = SD)	H (SS = SD)	H (both pre-sale and post-sale) (SS = SD)	Manufacturer direct or reseller; approx. 20 percent from small business

FIGURE 2.5

Cost Gap Analysis Template: CDW Example (to be used in conjunction with Service Gap Analysis Template, Figure 2.4)

Channel [Targeting Which Segments?]	Channel Members and Functions Performed	Environmental (E)/Managerial (M) Bounds	Cost Gaps [Affecting Which Functions?]	Planned Techniques for Closing Gaps	Do Actions Create Other Gaps?
1. CDW direct to buyer (→ small-business buyer)	Manufacturer, CDW, small-business buyer	[M]: no screening of recruits for expected longevity with firm	*Promotion* [sales force training/turnover]	Better screening of new recruits	No. Buying from CDW *closes* gaps for customers at risk
2. CDW direct to buyer (→ large-business buyer, government)	Manufacturer, CDW, CDW-G, large-business or government buyer	[E]: government requires 20 percent of purchases from small vendors [M]: no screening of recruits for expected longevity with firm	*Promotion* [sales force training/turnover] *Negotiation* [cannot close 20% of deals with government]	Better screening of new recruits Rely on consortium channel structure	No
3. CDW + small-business consortium of value-added resellers (VAR) (→government)	Manufacturer, CDW-G, small VAR, consortium partner, government buyer	[E]: government requires 20 percent of purchases from small vendors [M]: VAR's small-business size [M]: no screening of recruits for expected longevity with firm	*Promotion* [sales force training/turnover] *Negotiation* [small gap for a small VAR not in the CDW alliance]	Better screening of new recruits Improve negotiation through consortium with small VARs	No

Notes: All channel members perform all functions to some extent. The key channel functions of interest are *promotion, negotiation,* and *risk.*

potential actions to close them. It also can predict whether these potential actions are likely to create other, unintended gaps.

Figures 2.4 and 2.5 also provide an example analysis of CDW's situation using the Gap Analysis Templates. Service output demands differ significantly across three key segments: small businesses, large businesses, and government buyers. Spatial convenience and waiting/delivery time demands must be separated, designated to apply to original equipment or post-sale service. Small-business buyers need higher levels of post-sale service but less service for original equipment purchases (because they have no in-house servicing capabilities), whereas the opposite relationship applies to large-business buyers (which have in-house services).

After implementing changes to the channel strategy and structure to close the gaps in service and cost, the channel structure still may just approach a zero-based design, without being *fully* zero-based. That is, some environmental or managerial bounds could remain, continuing to constrain the final channel solution. Nor does the process of gap analysis ever come to a conclusion. Environmental bounds change over time, and end-users' demands for service outputs, as well as the available distribution technology, shift and transform. This propensity for change creates a never-ending opportunity for channel strategy innovations to pursue the moving target of a zero-based channel for each and every targeted segment in the market.

Make-or-Buy Channel Analysis

A fundamental question when designing a channel strategy asks, should the firm integrate vertically by performing both upstream (e.g., manufacturing) and downstream (e.g., distribution) functions? Should a single organization perform all channel functions (i.e., manufacturer, agent, distributor, retailer—all rolled into one)? Or should outsourcing apply to either distribution (upstream looking down) or production (downstream looking up), or both, such that the identities of manufacturers and downstream channel members are separate?

When a manufacturer integrates a distribution function (e.g., selling, fulfilling orders, offering credit), its employees do downstream work, and the manufacturer has integrated forward from the point of production. Vertical integration also occurs in the other direction: a distributor or retailer might produce its own branded products and thereby integrate backward. Whether the manufacturer integrates forward or the downstream channel member integrates backward, the result is that one organization does all the work in a vertically integrated channel.

Vertical integration decisions are not necessarily aggregate; rather, the decision can and should be made specifically, channel function by channel function. With sufficient power and investment, a channel member can decide to vertically integrate some subset of the channel functions, in a way that exhibits the best combination of make and buy, together in one channel structure. But managers need a structured way to analyze these issues; frame a coherent, comprehensive rationale; and reach a decision (make or buy, function by function) that can be communicated convincingly.

Make-or-buy analyses offer such a structured approach. In the base case, the manufacturer rarely should vertically integrate a downstream function, because it is typically inefficient to do so. However, a manufacturer should take responsibility for a wider set of functions in the channel if it has sufficient resources and could increase its returns on investment over time through integration. Similarly, though downstream channel members typically suffer from integrating backward, they should do so if they have the resources and would increase their long-run returns on investment.

AUDITING OMNI-CHANNELS

In an omni-channel design, the many channels grant customers numerous interfaces, giving rise to the possibility that the customer experience may vary depending on the channel used to interact with a downstream channel member (e.g., retailer). Multiple channels also create a danger of fragmentation and siloes, which can produce broken, confusing, and frustrating experiences.[16] Instead, an effective omni-channel strategy provides consumers with a cohesive, seamless, unified experience that carries across the entire spectrum of channels.[17] With an omni-channel audit, the auditor seeks to check and ensure that the myriad channels are functioning seamlessly to deliver a cohesive customer experience. Even if the firm organizes itself into distinct channels, online or offline, consumers generally perceive that they are dealing with a single entity, so they demand consistency as they move across channels. So how can an omni-channel manager make sure the customer experience is seamless? A key factor is integration across various channels, online or offline,[18] as well as across different purchase stages.

EXAMPLE: DISNEY (USA/GLOBAL)

As both an entertainment giant and a customer experience pioneer, Disney offers consumers a seamless omni-channel experience.[19] In addition to designing a user-friendly website, which functions exceptionally well on mobile platforms too, Disney encourages consumers to use mobile devices to maximize their experiences during actual visits to its theme parks. For example, with the My Disney app, they can purchase fast passes or obtain real-time dining and attraction information, including wait times for rides. Its GPS function provides customers with estimates of their distance from various rides.[20] Through their linked Magic Bands, visitors can place food orders and set appointments to take photos with Disney characters. Their phones function as hotel keys in Disney's resort hotels too. Noting its success in the parks, Disney is extending the omni-channel experience to its retail stores, by integrating its vaunted storytelling experience with technology, livestreaming the famous Disney Main Street parades in stores, and training store employees to interact with customers similar to the way staff members in the park do, to bring the Disney experience to life.[21]

Figure 2.6 outlines the steps involved in auditing omni-channels. We begin with the notions of distribution depth and distribution breadth.[22]

Distribution breadth refers to brand coverage, or the ease of finding a source for it, whether online or in a store. To achieve distribution breadth, the manufacturer needs to make its brand available in multiple venues, including the most prominent ones. **Distribution depth** instead refers to the ease of finding a brand within a particular channel or outlet. In physical stores, it entails the brand's position in prime shelf spaces and display prominence, relative to its competition. In online channels, it pertains to the position of the brand on a search result page.[23] For example, a "store within a store" presence in a retail outlet makes the brand very visible, akin to prime shelf space, which better positions this brand compared with its competition.

In Table 2.2, we outline various metrics to assess distribution breadth and depth. The breadth metrics mainly relate to the number, importance, and ease of shopping in various outlets. The depth metrics focus on the prominence of the manufacturer's brand in the various channels and in relation to competition, as well as the support it receives from various outlets that help end-users purchase its product easily. Therefore, the first step in an omni-channel audit is gathering a full sense of the brand's presence in the marketplace.

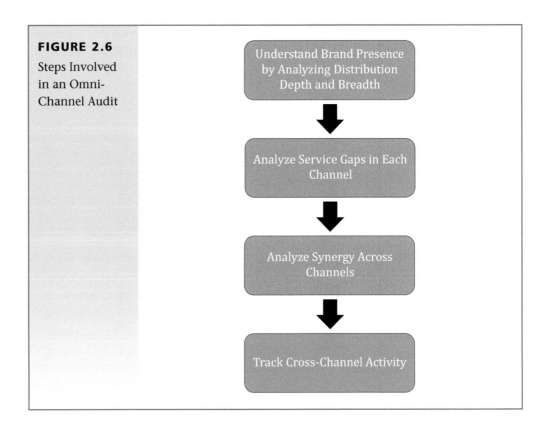

FIGURE 2.6

Steps Involved in an Omni-Channel Audit

Understand Brand Presence by Analyzing Distribution Depth and Breadth

Analyze Service Gaps in Each Channel

Analyze Synergy Across Channels

Track Cross-Channel Activity

Breadth Metrics		**TABLE 2.2**
	• Number of offline and online outlets in which the brand is available • Percentage of outlets in which brand is available for purchase • Brand is present in the largest, most prominent outlets • Presence of a brand app and number of app downloads • Ease of finding brand in online searches	Metrics for Measuring Omni-Channel Distribution Breadth and Depth
Depth Metrics		
	• Number of outlets where brand maintains a "store within a store" • Average number of units carried per outlet compared with total brand units • Share of shelf space relative to competition • Position of brand in retailer search results page • Option to buy online and pick up in-store • Sales support available in stores	

With this complete understanding of the brand's presence in various channels, the next step is to analyze the service and cost gaps in each channel, using the process outlined previously. Such an analysis can reveal how each channel in the omni-channel ecosystem is performing, as well as its role in serving end-user needs. A myth that persists in many omni-channel contexts is that online shoppers are least expensive to serve, yet the reality is that the most profitable consumers usually patronize multiple channels. Still, consumer behavior varies widely across segments. According to a study of apparel shopping in the United Kingdom, only 7 percent of consumers shopped both online and offline for apparel, while a majority (three-fourths) only purchased offline, and 19 percent only bought online.[24] Yet among older consumers, the incidence of online shopping was much lower, and online shoppers gave greater weight to different factors than did the offline shoppers. Many retailers have effectively synchronized their product assortments across channels, but synchronizing service delivery represents a much greater challenge,[25] especially when we note that online shoppers tend to prioritize the ease of use of the website, delivery options, and speed, while offline shoppers emphasize price, staff knowledge, and stock availability. Such distinctions clearly can create both cost and service gaps and leave an omni-channel company wondering if it should pay more attention to its older, offline shoppers or devote more resources to the smaller, younger, faster-growing base of online shoppers. Moreover, if it explicitly aims to provide high levels of service to offline customers, does it also need to configure its website to offer high service levels (e.g., chat feature)?

The ultimate answer to these questions is: it depends. An omni-channel design needs to serve each customer in the manner he or she desires, without wasting resources on less valued aspects.[26] It is pointless for companies to promise same-day delivery to consumers who are in no rush. It also needs to rebalance channel functions to ensure efficient operations. For example, existing distribution centers rarely are equipped to ship to individual customers. As manufacturers increasingly take on retailing functions (e.g., ordering and shipping capabilities on manufacturer websites) and retailers increasingly engage in private-label manufacturing, the potential for channel conflict rises in omni-channel settings.

A possible resolution to such conflict might come from synergies across channels, suggesting the need to assess the strength of the cross-channel capabilities of each partner.[27] Unfortunately, though, few omni-channel systems are set up to synchronize supply chains across channels.[28] In many cases, channel partners fail to encourage customers who visit a store to order out-of-stock items online, with free shipping, nor do they accept product coupons seamlessly across channels.[29] As a notable exception, Walmart's scan-and-go app allows consumers to scan items while in the store and pay through the app. As they exit the store, a customer service associate verifies the payment, but they do not need to stand in a checkout queue.[30]

An omni-channel audit also might track cross-channel activities. Consumers have incentives to visit stores to make purchases, such as when they want to inspect a product physically, avoid shipping charges, or obtain the item immediately. A true omni-channel setup thus accepts and encourages consumers who search on a retailer's website but then purchase products in stores. Doing so means making sure the item is in stock, rather than offering certain items only online. As stores undergo digital conversions, they also must be integrated carefully with the online channel,[31] such that the detailed product information available online should be available to consumers shopping inside the store.

In Figure 2.7, we present a checklist for determining the seamlessness of omni-channel operations and tracking cross-channel synergies. Ideally, a firm operates according to how consumers actually shop, rather than on the basis of legacy approaches. Pricing, promotions, ordering, and returns should be synchronized across channels. Accordingly, we close this chapter with an example from the Swedish retailer H&M, which performs well when it comes to certain aspects of cross-channel shopping but not on others, limiting consumers' true omni-channel experience.

EXAMPLE: H&M (SWEDEN/GLOBAL)

A smartphone app allows consumers to shop online while they are in H&M stores,[32] using a "scan and buy" feature. Consumers can scan a product tag and learn whether the item might be available in different colors or sizes online. They also can chat with customer service reps. However, H&M does not offer a store pickup option or free or expedited shipping, nor does it permit online purchases to be returned to stores, and it imposes a shipping charge on all returned items. Thus the synergies across channels are limited. In the crowded apparel market, H&M has curtailed its ambitious plans to increase the number of stores and instead is focusing on growing through same-store sales and 35 online marketplaces.[33] It also plans to support in-store pickup and return of online orders, and it has signaled that it is working to facilitate mobile payments.[34]

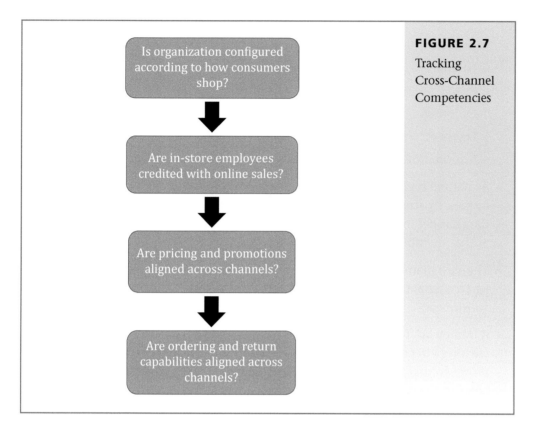

FIGURE 2.7

Tracking Cross-Channel Competencies

Take-Aways

- Both upstream and downstream factors affect the development of channels and provide reasons to adjust channels over time. Upstream factors include:

  ○ Routinization of transactions.
  ○ Reduction in the number of contacts.

 Downstream factors include:

  ○ Search facilitation.
  ○ Sorting.

- Marketing functions are elements of work, performed by members of the marketing channel. There are nine universal channel functions:

  ○ Physical possession.
  ○ Ownership.
  ○ Promotion.

- o Negotiation.
- o Financing.
- o Risk.
- o Ordering.
- o Payment.
- o Information sharing.

- A channel member can be eliminated from a channel, but the functions performed by that member cannot be. Before eliminating a channel member, the channel manager should consider the cost of replacing the performance of that member's channel functions.

- The key members of marketing channels are manufacturers, intermediaries (wholesale, retail, and specialized), and end-users (business customers or consumers).

- A framework for analyzing channel design and implementation is crucial for creating effective (i.e., demand-satisfying) and efficient (i.e., cost-effective) routes to market, in which members continue to be willing to perform the channel functions assigned to them.

- Just as production plants produce physical products, the members of a marketing channel engage in *productive activity*. We call the activities of the channel its *functions*.

- Detailed knowledge of function performance in the channel improves service output provision, facilitates channel design or redesign, helps determine rewards for channel members, and can mitigate channel conflicts.

- Every channel function not only contributes to the production of valued service outputs but is also associated with a cost.

- The drive to minimize channel management costs implies that it is important to avoid performing unnecessarily high levels of any of the functions; knowing which service outputs are demanded by target end-users is the key to knowing which levels to adopt to create the right level (neither too low nor too high) of service outputs that will be most valued by target end-users.

- The efficiency template describes (a) the types and amounts of work done by each channel member to perform marketing functions, (b) the importance of each channel function to the provision of consumer service outputs, and (c) the resulting share of total channel profits that each channel member *should* reap.

- A separate efficiency template should be created for *each channel* used to distribute the product and, ideally, for *each market segment* that buys through each channel.

- A zero-based channel design meets the target market segment's demands for service outputs, at the minimum cost of performing the necessary channel functions that produce those service outputs.

- Comparing a zero-based efficiency analysis with the channel's efficiency analysis can inform the channel analyst of situations in which a channel member may be busy (with high channel function costs) yet not adding commensurate value to the channel's overall operations.

- The equity principle states that compensation in the channel system should reflect the degree of participation in the marketing functions and the value created by this participation. That is, compensation should mirror the normative profit shares for each channel member.

- Channel gaps arise as a result of *bounds* that prevent the channel manager from optimizing the channel structure.

  - *Environmental* channel bounds are constraints imposed from outside the channel, such as legal restrictions or a lack of adequate infrastructural capabilities in the market that can support an optimal channel structure.

  - *Managerial* channel bounds are constraints imposed from inside the channel, usually due to channel managers' lack of knowledge about the full implications of channel actions or reflecting optimization at a higher level than the channel.

  - The channel structure can be optimized *subject to these bounds*, but this solution will not be quite as efficient, nor will it do quite as good a job of satisfying target end-users' service output demands, as would an unconstrained channel.

- *Service gaps* can arise because a particular service output, provided to a particular target segment of end-users, is too *low* and the service outputs demanded exceed the service outputs supplied (SD > SS); or because a particular service output, provided to a particular target segment of end-users, is too *high* and the service outputs supplied exceed the service outputs demanded (SD < SS).

  - When SD < SS, the channel is operating inefficiently, because consumers are not willing to pay for the high level of service offered, due to their low valuation of that service.

○ In general, service gaps may remain if competitors are no better at providing these service outputs than the channel is. However, persistent service gaps provide an ideal opportunity for the channel to build overall market demand and steal market share, by investing in improved service output levels.

- *Cost gaps* arise when one or more channel function(s) are performed at high costs. A superior technology might exist to decrease the cost of performing that function, without compromising service output provision.

- The Gap Analysis Templates provide tools for codifying knowledge of both the service and cost gaps facing the channel in its channel management tasks.

- Omni-channels require extended audits, to determine whether the various channels in the system are seamless and synchronized and whether the incentives of each channel are aligned with that of the whole system.

NOTES

1 Hughes, Charles and William Jeanes (2008), *Branding Iron: Branding Lessons from the Meltdown of the US Auto Industry*, Marshalltown, IA: Racom Communications.

2 Purohit, Devavrat and Joydeep Srivastava (2001), "Effect of manufacturer reputation, retailer reputation, product warranty on consumer judgments of product quality," *Journal of Consumer Psychology*, 10 (3), 123–134.

3 Partida, Becky (2014), "Continuous replenishment can boost logistics efficiency," *Supply Chain Management Review*, May/June, 70–72.

4 Fang, Eric, Robert W. Palmatier, Lisa Scheer, and Ning Li (2008), "Trust at different organizational levels," *Journal of Marketing*, 72 (March), 80–98.

5 See "Outsourcing: A global success story," *Logistics Management*, 42 (2, February 2003), 60–63.

6 For a discussion of these models, see Chopra, Sunil (2012), *Supply Chain Management*, 5th ed., Englewood Cliffs, NJ: Prentice Hall.

7 Woodyard, Chris (2016), "Airlines' fuel prices bets not always paying off," *USA Today*, January 25, www.usatoday.com/story/money/cars/2016/01/25/airlines-fuel-price-bets-not-always-paying-off/79288102, date retrieved September 10, 2018.

8 Information for Sidebar 2.1 is drawn from Campbell, Scott (2003), "CDW-G calls on VARs," *Computer Reseller News*, November 17 (No. 1071), 162; Campbell, Scott (2004), "CDW snags companywide Cisco Premier status—relationship advances reseller's bid to build services business," *Computer Reseller News*, 12, April 12; Gallagher, Kathleen (2002), "CDW computer remains afloat despite market's choppy waters," *Milwaukee Journal Sentinel*, September 29, 4D; Jones, Sandra (2004), "Challenges ahead for CDW; Dell deals make inroads in already difficult market," *Crain's Chicago Business*, June 28, 4; Kaiser, Rob (2000), "Vernon Hills, Ill., computer products reseller has an approach to win business," *Chicago Tribune*, August 16; McCafferty, Dennis (2002), "Growing like gangbusters—sales at Chicago-area CDW-Government shot up 63 percent from 2000 to 2001," *VAR Business*, July 8; Moltzen, Edward (2003), "Looking for SMB traction, gateway inks reseller pact with CDW," *CRN*, May 26, 55; O'Heir, Jeff (2003), "CDW teams with small VARs to

access government biz," *Computer Reseller News*, August 25 (No. 1059), 6; O'Heir, Jeff (2003), "Time to move on," *Computer Reseller News*, October 20 (No. 1067), 98; Rose, Barbara and Mike Highlett (2005), "Balancing success with high stress," *Chicago Tribune*, June 5; Schmeltzer, John (2003), "CDW pulls out the stops to reach small business," *Chicago Tribune*, September 8; Zarley, Craig and Jeff O'Heir (2003), "Seeking solutions—CDW, Gateway and Dell come calling on solution providers for services expertise," *Computer Reseller News*, 16, September 1; CDW Brandvoice (2016), "Small business growth requires strategic IT planning," *Forbes*, July 6, www.forbes.com/sites/cdw/2016/07/05/small-business-growth-requires-strategic-it-planning/#62ce1f275969, date retrieved September 10, 2018.

9 We do not develop an in-depth discussion of activity-based costing in this text. Interested readers should visit the following sources: Horngren, Charles T. (2011), *Cost Accounting*, 14th ed., Englewood Cliffs, NJ: Prentice Hall; Cooper, Robin and Robert S. Kaplan (1991), "Profit priorities from activity-based accounting," *Harvard Business Review*, 69 (3, May–June), 130–135.

10 See, for example, Forsyth, Donelson R. (1983), *An Introduction to Group Dynamics*, Monterey, CA: Brooks/Cole. The RAND Corporation is credited with developing the Delphi technique in the 1950s to forecast where the Soviet Union would attack the United States, if it were to launch an attack. It originally put U.S. generals and Kremlinologists into a room to discuss the issue, but they made very little progress. Thus, the RAND Corporation developed the Delphi technique to arrive at an orderly consensus.

11 See, for example, Achrol, Ravi S., Torger Reve, and Louis W. Stern (1983), "The environment of marketing channel dyads: A framework for comparative analysis," *Journal of Marketing*, 47 (Fall), 55–67; Achrol, Ravi S. and Louis W. Stern (1988), "Environmental determinants of decision-making uncertainty in marketing channels," *Journal of Marketing Research*, 25 (February), 36–50; Etgar, Michael (1977), "Channel environment and channel leadership," *Journal of Marketing Research*, 15 (February), 69–76; Dwyer, F. Robert and Sejo Oh (1987), "Output sector munificence effects on the internal political economy of marketing channels," *Journal of Marketing Research*, 24 (November), 347–358; Dwyer, F. Robert and M. Ann Welsh (1985), "Environmental relationships of the internal political economy of marketing channels," *Journal of Marketing Research*, 22 (November), 397–414.

12 Achrol and Stern (1988), op. cit., refer to the present and projected state of technology, the geographic dispersion of end-users, and the extent of turbulence and diversity in the marketplace as factors that can inhibit optimal channel design. These are all examples of infrastructural dimensions. Achrol and Stern also consider a set of competitive factors, such as industry concentration and competitors' behavior, which constitute different dimensions of the infrastructure facing a firm seeking to manage its channel structure appropriately.

13 Shin, Jiwoong (2007), "How does free riding on customer service affect competition?" *Marketing Science*, 26 (July–August), 488–503.

14 Louis P. Bucklin calls this phenomenon "functional substitutability." See Bucklin, Louis P. (1966), *A Theory of Distribution Channel Structure*, Berkeley, CA: University of California, IBER Special Publications.

15 Bucklin, Louis P. (1967), "Postponement, speculation and the structure of distribution channels," in Bruce E. Mallen (ed.), *The Marketing Channel: A Conceptual Viewpoint*, New York: John Wiley & Sons, Inc., pp. 67–74.

16 Saghiri, Soroosh, Paul Wilding, Carlos Mena, and Michael Bourlakis (2017), "Towards a three-dimensional framework for omni-channel," *Journal of Business Research*, 77, 53–67.

17 Verhoef, Peter C., P.K. Kannan, and Jeffrey Inman (2015), "From multi-channel retailing to omni-channel retailing: Introduction to the Special Issue on multi-channel retailing," *Journal of Retailing*, 91 (2), 174–181.

18 Herhausen, Dennis, Jochen Binder, Marcus Schoegel, and Andreas Hermann (2015), "Integrating bricks with clicks: Retailer-level and channel-level outcomes of online-offline channel integration," *Journal of Retailing*, 91 (2), 309–325.

19 Agius, Aaron (2018), "Seven outstanding examples of omni-channel experience," https://blog. hubspot.com/customer-success/omni-channel-experience, date retrieved March 9, 2018.

20 Larsen, Gil (2017), "What Disney and IBM can teach omnichannel marketers," *Chief Marketer*, www. chiefmarketer.com/what-disney-ibm-can-teach-omnichannel-marketers, date retrieved March 9, 2018.

21 Wilson, Marrianne (2017), "Disney testing new store design as part of omnichannel update," *Chain Store Age*, September 26, www.chainstoreage.com/article/disney-testing-new-store-design-part-omnichannel-update, date retrieved March 9, 2018.

22 Farris, Paul W., James Olver, and Cornelius DeKluyver (1989), "The relationship between distribution and market share," *Marketing Science*, 8 (2), 107–128.

23 Ailawadi, Kusum L. and Paul W. Farris (2017), "Managing multi- and omni-channel distribution: Metrics and research directions," *Journal of Retailing*, 93 (1), 120–135.

24 Berg, Achim, Leonie Brantberg, Louise Herring, and Patrik Silen (2015), "Mind the gap: What really matters for apparel retailers in omnichannel," *McKinsey & Company*, www.mckinsey.com/~/media/mckinsey/dotcom/client_service/retail/pdfs/mind%20the%20gap%20what%20really%20matters%20for%20apparel%20retailers%20in%20omnichannel_final.ashx, date retrieved March 11, 2018.

25 Davey, Neil (2016), "Omnichannel: Are companies closing the gap on customer expectations?" *MYCustomer*, July 7, www.mycustomer.com/service/channels/omnichannel-are-companies-closing-the-gap-on-customer-expectations, date retrieved March 10, 2018.

26 Kumar, Raj, Tim Lange, and Patrik Silen (2017), "Building omnichannel excellence" (April), www.mckinsey.com/industries/consumer-packaged-goods/our-insights/building-omnichannel-excellence, date retrieved March 11, 2018.

27 Okamura, Jim (2006), "Gaps across the channel," *Multichannel Merchant* (May), 68–70.

28 Bhatnagar, Amit and Siddhartha S. Syam (2014), "Allocating a hybrid retailer's assortment across retail stores: Bricks and mortar vs. online," *Journal of Business Research*, 67 (6), 1293–1302.

29 Hamory, Mark, Scott Rankin, Colleen Drummond, and Duncan Avis (2016), "Customers don't have time for half-baked omnichannel," *kpmg.com*, https://advisory.kpmg.us/content/dam/advisory/en/pdfs/customers-dont-have-time-for-half-baked-omnichannel.pdf, date retrieved March 11, 2018.

30 BI Intelligence (2017), www.businessinsider.com/walmart-refocuses-on-omnichannel-2017-2, date retrieved March 12, 2018.

31 Kumar, Raj and Michael Hu (2015), "Is your supply chain ready for the omni-channel revolution?" *Supply Chain Management Review* (September/October), 76–78.

32 Ewoldt, Michelle (2015), "Omni-channel audit: H&M," www.linkedin.com/pulse/omnichannel-audit-hm-michelle-ewoldt, June 30.

33 Howland, Daphne (2017), "H&M reverses store expansion plans to focus on omnichannel," www. retaildive.com/news/hm-reverses-store-expansion-plans-to-focus-on-omnichannel/435251.

34 Mau, Dhani (2017), "H&M announces bigger focus on ecommerce expansion, will still open 430 new physical stores this year," *Fashionista*, https://fashionista.com/2017/01/hm-earnings-2016-new-brand.

CHAPTER 3

Channel Power

LEARNING OBJECTIVES

After reading this chapter, you will be able to:

- Appreciate the role of power in managing channel relationships.
- Describe the relation between power and dependence and define when dependence exists.
- Distinguish five sources of power, as well as the importance and uses of each.
- Appreciate the advantages of a mutually dependent relationship.
- Distinguish six communication strategies for converting power into influence and their effects in channel relationships.
- Appreciate how the omni-channel landscape affects the nature of power in marketing channels.

INTRODUCTION: THE NATURE OF MARKETING CHANNELS

Managing channels is a fundamental and substantial task, requiring efforts to motivate and incentivize a range of independent but also interdependent entities to work toward the common good. In an effective channel relationship, two or more organizations must function as if they are pursuing a **single shared interest**. Channel management becomes even harder in an omni-channel environment, which involves more varied actors, activities, and channels, often with conflicting interests. In Figure 3.1, we outline three approaches to managing channels; this chapter covers one of them, namely managing by exerting power. The other two approaches, building relationships and managing conflict, are the focus of subsequent chapters.

Virtually every element of marketing channels is permeated by considerations of **power**, because marketing channels themselves are systems of players that depend on one another but have competing objectives and may not march to

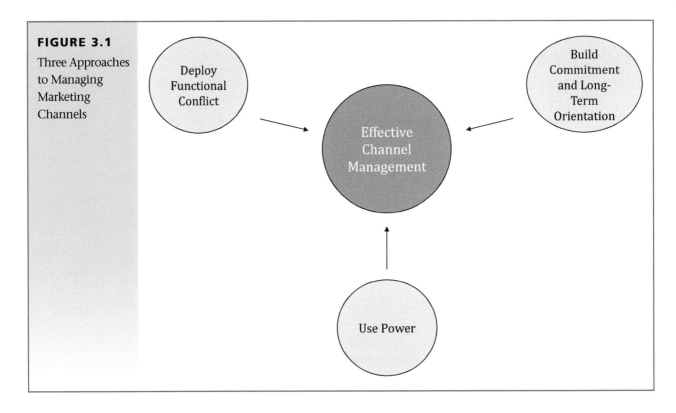

FIGURE 3.1

Three Approaches to Managing Marketing Channels

the beat of the same drummer, without some force that requires them to do so. In highlighting the importance and role of power in managing channels, we start with the premise that marketing channel members must work together to serve end-users. But such interdependence does not mean that what is good for one is equally good for all. Each channel member seeks its own profit. Maximizing the system's profits is not the same as maximizing each member's profits. All else being equal, each member of the system is better off to the extent that it can avoid costs (or push them onto someone else) while garnering revenues (perhaps by taking them from someone else). And one party's costs may generate disproportionate benefits for another party.

For example, imagine a manufacturer that would like to set a high wholesale price, to gain more revenue from its exclusive retailer. The retailer, to preserve its margins, sets a higher retail price (and exclusivity enables it to impose this price). As a result, retail demand diminishes, compared with the level that would maximize the total channel's profits. This problem is called **double marginalization**, because the inefficiency results from two margins, rather than one, in the channel. If the manufacturer were vertically integrated forward (or the retailer were vertically integrated backward), the single organization, generating one income statement, would set a lower retail price, following a strategy of lower overall margins but higher volumes.[1] Both the channel (higher profits) and the final customer (lower prices) would benefit. But because the retailer has one income statement and the manufacturer has another, retail prices will stay higher, and unit sales will remain low. But Apple was able to leverage its power when it initially selected an exclusive channel partner for the iPhone, ensuring that the powerful manufacturer would earn significant revenue sharing rate on all sales.[2]

There is usually a "better way" to operate a marketing channel that increases overall system profits. But the organizations in the channel may be unwilling to adopt this approach, because what is best for the system is not necessarily best for each member of it. *Left alone, most channel members will not cooperate to achieve system-level goals.*

Enter power. It provides a way for one player to convince another to change what it is about to do. This change can be for the good of the system or for the good of a single member.

POWER

Power is the ability of one channel member (A) to get another channel member (B) to do something it otherwise would not have done. Simply put, power is the potential for influence.

EXAMPLE: TENCENT (CHINA)

The Chinese Internet company Tencent was founded in 1998. Its WeChat app has nearly a billion users, and nearly one-third of them spend more than 4 hours daily on the app.[3] In addition, its WeChatPay app is used by nearly 600 million users—a significant factor, considering that more than half of all Internet commerce in China takes place through mobile phones.[4] Chinese consumers use the company's products for messaging, chatting, shopping, social networking, gaming, ordering food, and hailing taxis. As a result of its huge user base and dominance in the Chinese market, Tencent exerts substantial market power relative to its partners and other entities that seek access to its enormous customer portfolio. Such power derives from the partner companies' worry that Tencent could partner with or even invest in a competitor if they do not let the company have its way. Even the Chinese government has grown wary of Tencent's massive market power, reportedly asking for a stake in the company.[5]

Power as a Tool

Power is a term laden with negative connotations, often implying abuse, oppression, or exploitation. And properly so: power can cause great damage. In channels especially, power can be used to force another channel member to generate some value, without granting it equitable compensation for that effort. The party in the stronger power position can grab a disproportionate share of the benefits of the relationship,[6] and when used in this way, power is (and should be) condemned.

But this critical view is one-sided. Because power represents the potential for influence, great benefits can be achieved through its judicious use, to drive a channel toward more efficient, more coordinated operations. For example, at one point in its history, Hewlett-Packard (HP) made complete printers in a factory, then shipped them into the channel, hoping that end-users would buy them. But because different customers demanded many versions of each printer, this policy resulted in high inventories, often of the wrong products. In response, HP pioneered a strategy to achieve mass customization at low prices. Its printer designs featured standardized, independent modules that could be combined and assembled easily to make many variations of the core product. Channel partners could stock the generic modules and assemble them, according to customers' distinct needs.

With its considerable power in the printer channel, HP thus pushed light manufacturing and assembly out of the factory and down the channel. The move generated conflict, but it also resulted in lower inventories throughout the channel *and* fewer stockouts, an ideal (and often seemingly impossible) combination. End-users enjoyed the benefits of greater choice, at lower prices. Other downstream channel members could appreciate the benefits of increased customer satisfaction, along with lower inventory-holding costs. And HP expanded the market for printers while also taking a greater share of the bigger pie. Careful to preserve its sterling reputation for fair play, though, HP never sought to appropriate downstream channel members' share of the new wealth that the channel generated.

A tempting alternative might imagine that HP could achieve this win–win result without wielding power or pressuring its reluctant channel members. It had strategic alliances in place with its distributors; why not just work with them, instead of exercising power over them? Had the channel recognized how well the modular approach worked, it theoretically would have assumed some of the factory's functions, because channel members would have adopted the approach of their own free will. But such clarity and certainty exist only with the benefit of hindsight. Mass customization, achieved through the postponement of assembly, was a radical idea at the time, and even today, it is not widely used. Embracing the idea would have required an act of faith; absent faith, it required HP's exercise of power.

The Five Sources of Channel Power

How can we take an inventory of an organization's ability to change the behavior of another organization? There actually are many ways; the debate is about which way is best.[7] One way of thinking about indexing power, called the French and Raven approach, has proven particularly fruitful in marketing channels, even though it came from psychology.[8] It holds that the best way to **measure power** is to count its genesis from five sources: reward, coercion, expertise, reference, and legitimacy. Each source is reasonably observable, so even though power is hidden, it can be approximated by compiling the estimates of its sources.

Power can be accrued and exerted only by a producer with a viable value proposition that appeals to the end-user. If the producer suffers a serious deficiency in this basic element, no amount of power in the channel can compensate for it. Specifically, the producer must offer:[9]

- a product or service whose quality level meets the needs of a substantial segment of end-users,

- at a price these end-users consider paying,

- such that it is saleable enough that the terms of trade offered to other channel members enable them to earn minimum acceptable financial returns at the price end-users are willing to pay,

- backed by a minimally acceptable producer reputation, and

- delivered reliably, such that the producer honors any delays it has negotiated with channel members or their customers.

These five thresholds are fundamental; without them, the downstream channel member has limited ability to create demand and no reason to bother to try to do so, regardless of the power exerted by the upstream member. Figure 3.2 gives a bird's-eye view of the five sources of power.

Reward Power

A **reward** is a benefit, given in return for a channel member's agreement to alter its behavior. In distribution channels, the emphasis is mainly on financial rewards. Financial returns need not be immediate, or precisely estimable, but expectations of

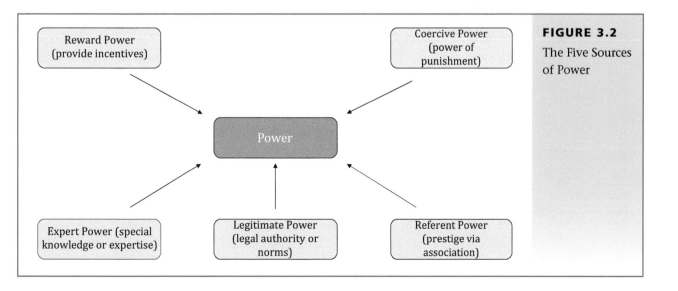

FIGURE 3.2

The Five Sources of Power

eventual payoffs, even indirect ones, pervade channel negotiations. Reward power is based on a belief by actor B that actor A has the ability to grant it something valuable. The effective use of reward power rests on A's possession of some resource that B values and believes it can obtain by conforming with A's request. But the *ability* to grant rewards is not sufficient; B must also perceive that A is *willing* to grant rewards. Therefore, B must be convinced that what A desires really will create benefits, and then that B will receive a fair share of those benefits.

Many channel initiatives create reward power in various forms. For example, efforts to boost a reseller's capabilities enable it to increase its profits. Excellent logistics also can increase downstream channel members' rewards indirectly, because their interactions with the producer are more efficient and profitable—which has the added advantage of being difficult to imitate.[10] Not only do producers gain the ability to alter downstream behavior by increasing rewards, but downstream channel members also can reward producers by more effectively establishing markets for the producers' product or service offers.

Coercive Power

Coercive power stems from B's expectation of punishment by A if it fails to conform with A's influence attempt. In the United States, large supermarket chains extract substantial slotting allowances (fees) from branded producers before they will agree to stock new products. Regardless of the potential economic rationale for this practice,[11] empirical evidence suggests that these fees really exist because the retailer has the ability to block market access by a manufacturer that refuses to pay.[12] Other examples of coercive power include margin reductions, a withdrawal of previously granted rewards (e.g., exclusive territorial rights), and slower shipments.

In this sense, **coercion** is synonymous with the potential to threaten another organization, whether implicitly or explicitly. The threat of being dropped from Walmart's approved vendor list has led most of its suppliers to adopt expensive electronic data interchange (EDI) systems and agree to perform bulk-breaking to support its various stores. Sock manufacturers might be required to mix different kinds of socks on a pallet to fit a specific Walmart store's requirements, rather than shipping complete pallets and thrusting the costs of recomposing the pallets onto Walmart. This shift is not trivial; the processes required to mix sock types on a pallet costs the manufacturer .15 cents per pair—and each pair sells to Walmart for $2.00.[13]

While some might suggest that coercive power represents the flip side of reward power, many channel members do not see it this way. They view **negative sanctions** not as the absence of rewards but as an attack on themselves and their business. Coercion in this sense is synonymous with aggression, such that it provokes self-defense responses. Channel members that perceive low rewards likely react with indifference or withdrawal, but when they perceive a pathological form of coercion, they consider a counterattack. This defensive reaction means that coercive power is less functional over time than other sources of power that produce more positive side effects.[14] Therefore, coercion should be the last tactic used to evoke change, because it is likely to provoke retaliation.

We might make this recommendation, but coercive power often persists, and its users often appear surprised by the intensity of the target's reaction—especially if the reaction is delayed so that the target can marshal its forces and compose its counterattack. Department store chains, such as Saks Fifth Avenue and Bloomingdale's, likely perceive the opening of factory outlet stores as an effort by a manufacturer to coerce them into greater cooperation. Rather than cooperating, they generally **retaliate** in the short run by canceling orders and in the long run by opening their own factory outlet stores, in which they underprice their own suppliers' stores.[15] Other forms of retaliation may be less dramatic or could even pass unremarked. In general, though, when a target perceives the use of threats, it downgrades its estimation of the value of the business of the coercive actor.[16]

In the short term, the relationship suffers three types of damage. First, the target of coercive power is less satisfied with the financial returns it derives (a reaction that tends to be part perception and part reality). Second, the target is less satisfied with the nonfinancial side of the relationship, because a coercive partner seems less concerned, respectful, willing to exchange ideas, fulfilling, gratifying, or easy to work with. Third, the target assumes the relationship has become more conflict-laden.

But so what? A powerful actor seemingly might care little about disillusionment by the target of its coercive power. But in the short run, the target grows less cooperative; in the medium term, the target expresses less trust; and in the long run, the target grows less committed to the relationship.[17] What the powerful member gains from its coercion thus may be lost later; there are always opportunity costs associated with alienating other channel members. Coercion erodes the relationship—even if it does so slowly enough that the influencer fails to realize what it is losing.

And yet, there are times when the benefit of coercion may be worth its cost. Here, we return to our Walmart example, in which it demanded suppliers adopt EDI to automate their purchasing processes. The vast potential of EDI to reduce costs has led many firms to adopt it proactively, but those benefits are far clearer in hindsight. Thus, approximately half of the early EDI adopters actually were forced to buy the related tools by other members of their supply chains—in many cases, by Walmart, which imposed adoption deadlines by threatening to stop its orders.[18] When it became clear that EDI benefitted the entire channel, the coerced targets were willing to forgive their partner. Surviving this particular crisis even seems to have strengthened their channel relationships. But if the coerced channel member does not benefit, or does not perceive a benefit, the relationship can be seriously and irreparably damaged.[19]

Expert Power

Expert (or expertise) power is based on the target's perception that the influencer has special knowledge or expertise that is useful and that the target does not possess. Of course, such expertise power is at the heart of the division of labor, specialization, and comparative advantages in channel functions.

EXAMPLE: FARMACIAS SIMILARES (MEXICO)

The poor often pay more than wealthy people for the same items because poor neighborhoods are underserved, in terms of distribution.[20] Victor Gonzalez was determined to do something about it.[21] The laboratory Gonzalez owns produced generic, less expensive, legal copies of branded pharmaceuticals. But despite the lack of legal barriers to selling generics, pharmacies chose to stock only expensive, patented foreign drugs, on which they enjoyed a large margin. So he founded Farmacias Similares, a drugstore chain that sells generic medications (mostly older drugs whose patents have expired). The highly successful chain has opened more than 2,000 stores, most of them located next to clinics that Gonzalez has founded and underwritten through a nonprofit group. The clinics handle 800,000 visits a month, at far lower costs than private clinics charge. The independent doctors who staff them are free to prescribe as they see fit, and the visitation fees are low. In effect, Gonzalez has built an alternative health system. Farmacias Similares prompted a boom in generics, raising their profile and bringing new suppliers into the market. Gonzalez's generic laboratory now provides only one-fifth of the pharmacy chain's stock, with the rest made by local companies. However, the pharmacy chain retains expertise power, due to its vast knowledge of Mexico's drug market and regulations. The firm also is the acknowledged expert at spotting gaps and convincing laboratories to create supply to fill them.

Although it takes substantial time and effort to build expert power, this power can dissipate or even disappear in an instant.[22] Expert advice, once given, grants the recipient the ability to operate without further assistance, so the original expert's relationship power drops immediately. A firm that wishes to retain its expert power over the long run thus has three options.

1. It can dole out expertise in small portions, always retaining enough vital data to ensure other channel members' continued dependence. This option implies purposefully keeping other channel members uninformed about some critical aspect of channel performance, though. Such a strategy can be self-defeating, because all channel members need to work up to their capacities if the channel as a whole is to succeed.

2. The firm can continually invest in learning, to ensure it always has new, important information to offer channel partners. Its learning might focus on market

trends, threats, and opportunities that other channel members would find difficult to generate. Thus the cost of this option is substantial, but so are the benefits, in terms of achieving channel goals.

3. It might transmit only customized information and encourage channel partners to invest in transaction-specific expertise, which is so specialized that they cannot transfer it easily to other products or services. The specific nature of the expertise, along with the costs involved in acquiring it, thus impedes exit from the channel.

Some writers subdivide expert power into expertise and information sources. The former implies the provision of good judgments (forecasts, analyses); the latter involves the provision of data (e.g., news that a competitor has just dropped prices).[23] Information is not identical to expertise. Supermarkets, for example, receive huge amounts of consumer purchase data from their checkout scanners. To turn this information into insight, they send the data for each product category to selected suppliers ("category captains"), who use their knowledge of the type of product to discern patterns from millions of transactions. Supermarkets have information power over suppliers, which convert the data they receive into expertise power over supermarkets. This exercise is so important that both sides view it as an investment in building a strategic alliance.

Using expert power is not as easy as it may sound, even for an organization that holds considerable amounts of it. First, to exercise expert power, a channel member must be trusted. Otherwise, expert advice looks like an attempt at manipulation. Second, experts are usually accorded very high status, which makes them difficult to identify with and perhaps impedes necessary trust building. Third, independent-minded, entrepreneurial businesspeople don't like to be told what to do. They believe that *they* are the experts (and they are often right!). If an influencer is to employ expert power, the target has to be willing to accept this expert's information and judgments. Such acceptance is far more likely if a good working relationship exists, such that the target believes in the basic competence and trustworthiness of the influencer.[24] It is also easier if the target needs (i.e., is dependent on) the influencer.

Legitimate Power

To be **legitimate** is to be perceived as right and proper, in accordance with normative or established standards. **Legitimate power** thus stems from the target company's sense that it is in some way obligated to comply with the requests of the influencer, because such compliance seems right and proper by normal or established standards. That is, the influencer has legitimate power if the target feels a sense of duty and bound to carry out the influencer's request. This sense of responsibility comes from two main sources: the law (legal legitimate power) and norms or values (traditional legitimate power).

Legal legitimate power is conferred by governments, stemming from each nation's laws of contracts and commerce. For example, patent and trademark laws give owners some freedom and justification to supervise the distribution of their products. Commercial laws allow firms to maintain agreements, such as franchises and other contracts, that confer on them the legitimate power to demand behavior that is not required in conventional channel arrangements.

EXAMPLE: *POONIWALA V. WYNDHAM WORLDWIDE CORPORATION (USA)*

In a franchise agreement, Wyndham Worldwide assigned Pooniwala to operate various motels under the Travelodge, Super 8, and Days Inn brand names. But Wyndham Worldwide decided to terminate the agreements, with the claim that the motels operated by this franchisee failed a series of quality assurance tests.[25] In addition to questioning the quality assurance process overall, Pooniwala alleged that Wyndham actually was withdrawing the agreement in retaliation for a separate litigation between the parties, over a different contract. Then it asserted that Wyndham issued perverse incentives to employees to sign up new franchisees, even for existing properties, to gain additional incentives. A federal court acknowledged that terminating the franchise agreement would harm Pooniwala, but it also weighted the potential damage to the Wyndham brand if the franchise agreement were to remain in place. Ultimately, the court sided with Wyndham, noting the detailed documentation it offered of quality assurance violations by Pooniwala.[26]

Even when channel members invest in crafting thorough contracts—which still is common, particularly in franchise arrangements—a well-considered contract rarely covers all the power that any channel member might need. Franchisees sign contracts with franchisors, obliging them to maintain their facilities with a certain appearance, honor the standards and procedures set by the franchisor, pay advertising fees or royalties, and buy from approved sources. But franchisees regularly violate these terms and assume the franchisor will tolerate their breaches of contract. And the franchisors often express just such tolerance, because enforcing a contract is expensive and might prompt backlash against the franchisor. Even with the legitimate right to punish violators, franchisors thus engage in cost–benefit analyses about whether it is worthwhile to punish a contract violation. It often isn't.[27]

Of course, legitimate power exists in dealings between organizations; it just does not stem from hierarchical authority. Rather, it comes from **norms, values,** and **beliefs**. One firm may believe that a channel member deserves to be accorded certain deference, because of its successful track record or exemplary management. The largest firm could be considered the leader (channel captain) by other channel members. In all these cases, that firm enjoys legitimate power.

Behavioral norms, or expectations of "normal" behavior, arise in a channel to define roles and effectively confer legitimate power on certain channel members. For example, distributors in the information technology (IT) industry work according to norms different than those that mark many other industries: they are far more likely to honor a supplier's request to name their customers and detail their shipments. Norms exist not only within industries but in certain channels, some of which manage to build expectations,[28] such as:

- *Solidarity*. Each side expects the other to focus on the relationship in the whole, rather than thinking transaction by transaction.

- *Role integrity*. Each side expects the other to perform complex roles that cover not just individual transactions but also a multitude of issues not related to any single transaction.

- *Mutuality*. Each side expects the other to divide up its joint returns in a way that assures adequate returns to each side.

These norms, once created, give one channel member the ability to exert legitimate power over the other, by appealing to the norms as a reason to comply with a request.

Referent Power

Referent power exists when B views A as a standard of reference and therefore wishes to identify publicly with A. In a marketing channel, one organization might seek to be publicly identified with another in search of prestige. Downstream channel members seek to carry high-status brands to enhance their own image; upstream channel members "rent the reputation" of prestigious downstream firms.[29]

The existence of referent power is undeniable. It is especially visible when wholesalers or retailers pride themselves on carrying certain brands (e.g., Harley-Davidson motorcycles, Ralph Lauren clothing, Intel semiconductors), and manufacturers pride themselves on having their brands carried by certain outlets (e.g., Neiman Marcus in the United States, Mitsukoshi in Japan, value-added resellers known for exceptional service in business-to-business realms). Creating and preserving **referent power**, defined as the ability to confer prestige, is a key reason manufacturers restrict their distribution coverage to selected outlets, as well as an explanation of why downstream organizations restrict representation to selected brands.

A firm with proprietary know-how might begin with legitimate power, in the form of patent protections, then use this basis to expand its referent power, as Sidebar 3.1 suggests in the example of Gore-Tex®.

SIDEBAR 3.1
Gore-Tex® Changes Its Power Base

Gore-Tex® is a family-owned firm, built on the basis of a revolutionary invention by William Gore, a former DuPont researcher. An additive for textiles uses a series of tiny pores to block wind and water, together with a series of large pores to permit perspiration to exit. Although its benefits are easy to present, the technical product is difficult to communicate about convincingly, because most users find it hard to believe that the same product can keep them warm and dry without trapping sweat.

Gore-Tex's® customers are manufacturers, usually of high-end outdoor clothing, that use Gore-Tex® in their production processes and then sell to retail outlets. These customers in turn are channels of distribution to end-users (clothing wearers). The producer has always sought to control these complex distribution channels. Initially, it did so by relying on the legitimate power of the Gore-Tex® patent and the lack of comparable alternatives. Although it thus induced dependence based on legitimate power, the company wisely used its patent-protected period as a window of opportunity to build referent power too, by practicing the art of making itself indispensable.[30]

This referent power now exists by virtue of more than 30 years of heavy investments in marketing the Gore-Tex® trade name to outdoor enthusiasts, leading to high brand awareness among end-users across the world (with a peak of 70 percent in Sweden). The resulting pull effects in the channel make sales easier for retailers and producers. Moreover, to reinforce the perception that the Gore-Tex® name provides reward power, the firm spends heavily on advertising, then reinforces its mass media efforts with its own sales force, which works with vendor salespeople to share expertise. Gore-Tex® salespeople train customer salespeople (i.e., clothing makers), as well as *their* customers (i.e., retailers), including providing kits to enable salespeople to demonstrate Gore-Tex® properties (e.g., spray bottle for product demonstrations). Patagonia, as a well-known name in outdoor clothing, resisted labeling its products as made with Gore-Tex® for years and conceded only after its own and retail salespeople argued that it would be easier to invoke the Gore-Tex® name than to keep explaining what Gore-Tex® does to end-users. Today, the company's legitimate power has largely disappeared, because the Gore-Tex® patent has expired. But its referent power, built over years of effort, effectively has replaced it.

Of course, this power is relationship specific. Gore-Tex® uses its power to oblige manufacturers to submit to rigid testing, involve the firm in their design processes, and bar certain choices (e.g., no Gore-Tex® can be incorporated in private-label merchandise). Producers accept this influence because, as a salesperson for a leading retailer puts it, "Hikers want first of all a Gore-Tex® vest, and the brand comes before everything else." As it seeks to expand, though, Gore-Tex® has moved into designer clothing markets, where its advantages are less well known and valued. In these arenas, the firm cannot induce the same level of cooperation from producers that it enjoys in the outdoor market. When it pursues partnerships with brands such as Boss, Prada, or Armani, the firm has been forced to concede, "Our logo is not as decisive in the act of purchase. It is just a complement."

DEPENDENCE AS THE MIRROR IMAGE OF POWER

Considering the various elements of power, what we really need is a practical, concrete way to observe and measure the potential for influence. According to sociology, it actually is pretty simple: *A's power over B increases with B's dependence on A.*[31] If it depends on party A, party B also is likely to change its behavior to align with A's desires. Thus, B's dependence gives A greater potential for influence.

Defining Dependence

For our purposes, we recognize that B depends more heavily on A when it

1. Obtains greater *utility* (value, benefits, satisfaction) from A; and

2. Has access to *fewer alternative* sources of that utility.

Dependence equals utility multiplied by alternative scarcity (in mathematical terms, $D = U \times S$). However, if B derives little value from what A provides (U is null), it is irrelevant whether alternative providers exist: B's dependence is low. If A provides great value but B can readily find other sources to provide just as much value (S is null), it is irrelevant whether A offers benefits: B's dependence again is low. Again, we can apply a mathematical metaphor. Low utility (U) or low alternative scarcity (S) is like multiplying by 0, so the product (D) is 0.

Thinking of one actor's power as the other actor's dependence is useful, because it focuses the analysis on **scarcity**, or how readily B can replace A. This point is easy to overlook. Channel members often consider themselves powerful because they deliver value to their counterparts, but counterparts just don't need them if they are easy to replace, which reduces their power.

EXAMPLE: CNH GROUP (USA)

A manufacturer of construction and farm equipment, CNH Group owns two well-regarded brands, Case and New Holland. It was producing high-quality products and devoting considerable resources to marketing and engineering. However, sales had dropped by 30 percent. The Group soon realized that it had neglected relationships with its 1,200 dealers, which instead were being heavily courted by competitors like Kubota. In response to those efforts, the dealers moved CNH-branded products to the back of their showrooms. To address the issue, CNH began investing to make itself harder to replace by offering dealers an inimitable benefit: sophisticated market research, conducted by CNH, *for dealers*, that specified how those dealers compared with competitors in their markets and how they could beat their competition. This investment in expert power offered a route to reinventing CNH as a more responsive, helpful, irreplaceable business partner.[32]

Measuring Dependence

Utility and Scarcity

A more reasonable estimate of another channel member's dependence on the focal actor comes from assessing both elements (utility and scarcity) separately, combining them only later. To assess **utility**, let's assume you represent the focal actor, and you need to tally up the benefits your firm offers. To do so, you must recognize your channel partner's goals and how your offering helps it meet those pursuits. You might estimate your utility by inventorying your five bases of power, or you could obtain a rough estimate of the profits you generate for your partner, both directly and indirectly. However you choose to assess your worth, you must remember to focus on what is important to the partner (e.g., volume rather than profits).

To assess alternative **scarcity**, or how easily you could be replaced, you need to consider two additional factors. First, who are your (potential) competitors? That is, what other organizations exist (or might enter the market) that can supply what you provide or an acceptable equivalent? When no other options exist, alternative scarcity is very high, so your partner's dependence on you also is high. Second, if alternatives exist (i.e., alternative scarcity is low), you need to determine how easily the channel member can switch from your organization to a competitor. If switching is easy, your partner does not depend on you, and you have essentially no real power. If switching away from your organization is impractical or prohibitively expensive, you enjoy a high alternative scarcity value in the market (even if alternatives exist in principle).

Now return to the benefits you provide, and combine your estimates with your assessment of the difficulty your channel partner would have replacing you. The **combined analysis** reveals the dependence of your channel member on you and thus your level of power. Try not to be too upset when you realize that you *are* replaceable, despite the value of your offerings. This realization is common and sobering—but also informative and likely accurate.

Let's consider a hypothetical example of a manufacturer P of specialty steel, which supplies distributors X and Y. For both X and Y, manufacturer P's brand attracts end-users, which also helps the distributors' salespeople sell other products in their portfolios. Its utility, both direct and indirect, is thus substantial. But three competitors also offer equivalent products, so P looks easily replaceable. Distributor Y, which is a large, well-known firm, works with whatever manufacturer gives it the best deals at any time, switching readily across the four manufacturers in the market. Thus, P has little power over Y. In contrast, X is a small distributor that continues to struggle to establish itself in its marketplace. Unimpressed by its sales volume, the other three manufacturers in the market refuse to supply X on the same friendly terms that P offers. Because X has no realistic alternative to P (it cannot afford the terms the other manufacturers demand), X depends on P, and P has greater power in this relationship.

Manufacturer P could increase its power over both distributors if it could induce them to make investments that would be difficult to transfer to another manufacturer, such as adopting P's proprietary ordering software, getting training about the unique features of P's products, participating in joint advertising campaigns, or forging close relationships with P's personnel. Any distributor that has invested time and energy in such pursuits likely is reluctant to sacrifice its investments by switching suppliers. The high **switching costs** make P a *de facto* monopolist; even in the face of apparent competition, the distributor's dependence confers power on manufacturer P.

Other methods to approximate dependence seek a rougher proxy indicator, in lieu of a thorough and detailed (also known as slow and costly) assessment of utility and scarcity. Each proxy indicator suffers drawbacks, but these methods are easier to implement and frequently offer a reasonable approximation.

Percentage of Sales or Profits

A quick method estimates the **percentage of sales or profits** earned by the partner that the focal channel member provides. The higher this percentage, the higher the partner's dependence and thus the more powerful the focal member is. That is, an important (powerful) channel member provides high benefits, and switching threatens the loss of those benefits to partners, which implies higher switching costs. If the benefits also account for a significant proportion of the partner's sales or profits, those switching costs may grow astronomical. This argument has considerable merit. But the percentage of sales/profit method also represents an approximation. It cannot capture all benefits, nor does it assess scarcity directly. Thus in some situations, the method works poorly. For example, franchisees likely derive 100 percent of their sales and profits from the franchisor, yet some franchisees still are more or less dependent than others.[33]

Role Performance

Dependence approximations can come from assessments of how well the focal actor performs its role compared with competitors. Greater superiority implies higher **role performance**, such that few alternatives can offer a similar level of performance, even if their product offerings appear similar.[34] This direct method comes closer to assessing scarcity, but it cannot address role importance. That is, you may perform a role better than competitors, but your partners depend on you only if they derive utility from the performance of this specific role. Furthermore, your partner likely can access meaningful alternatives if it is willing to accept some diminishment in role performance.

In other circumstances, role performance simply does not capture dependence well. For example, many emerging economies feature sellers' markets, in which demand far outstrips supply, barriers to entry restrict supply, and there are many reseller candidates. In these sectors, every channel member depends on every supplier, regardless of its role performance.[35] Yet role performance remains a reasonable proxy for dependence in many other circumstances. Service excellence confers uniqueness (scarcity), even for commodity products. In this case, superb role performance creates dependence (and power), because excellence is nearly always scarce *and* valuable.

Balancing Power: A Net Dependence Perspective

Dependence is never one way. Dependence assessments must take both channel partners' perspectives. Just as X depends on P to provide utility, P needs X for a different type of utility. They are interdependent, which blunts P's ability to pressure X to alter its behavior. High mutual dependence, or **interdependence**, is synonymous with high mutual power. High mutual power also gives channel members greater ability to achieve very high levels of value.[36] Each party has leverage over the other, which should drive their coordination and cooperation.[37]

Consider the example of beer brewers. In the United States, SABMiller Brewing covers the large market with relative ease, because 470 wholesalers span the country, though most of them also carry competing brands. Each side needs the other (high utility); both sides have alternatives (low scarcity). East African Breweries Ltd. (EABL) also covers the large market of Kenya, but its ease of access is much lower, because there are only 30 wholesalers in the area. Despite this challenge, EABL achieves 98 percent market coverage, even in rural areas, which enabled it to drive SABMiller right out of Kenya. The key is high mutual dependence: EABL holds a few house accounts and grants exclusive territories. Its wholesalers carry only beer—often only EABL brands. Thus the great benefits and great utility that each side earn through the channel would be at risk were either side to choose to stop being exclusive and consider alternatives.

High, balanced dependence blocks exploitation, because each side has countervailing power, which it can use for self-protection. Without a notably weaker party in the relationship, each side forces the other to share gains, which fosters norms of fairness and solidarity. This level of symmetric dependence promotes bilateral functioning by increasing each side's willingness to adapt in dealing with the other.[38]

Of course, symmetry also might imply low mutual dependence, such that neither side has much need of the other. This low–low combination is so common in marketing channels that it represents a baseline condition for many channel management recommendations. When each side is dispensable, the channel tends to operate in accordance with classic economic relationship predictions.[39]

Finally, to assess countervailing power, as part of the calculation of net dependence, a decision maker might consider the relationship level and calculate net dependence with one other channel member. But in some cases, single-channel members (upstream or downstream) can radically and quickly shift the calculation by coming together in a **coalition**. Suddenly, one party faces a bloc—which usually raises both the benefits and alternative scarcity of the other side.

Imbalanced Dependence

After such sudden shifts, one channel member may become much more dependent than the other. The balance of power favors the less dependent member, whereas the more dependent member suffers exposure to **exploitation**.[40] All too often, that exposure leads to problems. The more dependent party loses out, in both economic terms and noneconomic benefits,[41] even if the more powerful (less dependent) channel member does not actively attempt to appropriate rewards. That is, the weaker member might suffer simply because the fortunes of the stronger member decline. In addition, facing the specter of exploitation, the weaker (more dependent) party senses its own vulnerability and is quick to suspect the stronger party of acting in bad faith. Asymmetric relationships thus tend to be more conflict-laden, less trusting, and less committed than interdependent relations.[42] What are channel members to do then?

Strategies for Balancing Dependence

There are three countermeasures available to the weaker party to reduce its dependence. That is, if B depends more on A than A depends on B, then B can

1. Develop alternatives to A.

2. Organize a coalition to attack A.

3. Exit the situation and no longer seek the benefits that A provides.

In channels, the first reaction is the most common. Fear of exploitation drives channel members to develop countervailing power, especially as their dependence increases. For example, some sales agents (e.g., manufacturers' representatives, or reps) tailor their operations to key principals, which creates potentially dangerous dependence imbalances for them. These reps go to great lengths to cultivate their relationships with end-users as well, to build customer loyalty to the reps' agency. With this power relation, the rep can induce customers to change to another brand if necessary. Because the rep can take end-users elsewhere, it achieves countervailing power against the principal. These reps generally earn better profits than those that neglect to balance their dependence after they have tailored their operations to a principal.[43]

This measure also involves the potential ability to add a supplier, if necessary. Many channel members deliberately maintain a diversified portfolio of counterparts, to allow them to react immediately if any one organization exploits a power imbalance. For example, in line with industry norms, U.S. automobile dealers once represented only one brand of car each, making them highly dependent on the manufacturer. After the oil crisis of the early 1970s encouraged dealers to add more fuel-efficient cars, often produced by other brands, it was a short step to broad diversification. Now many auto dealers rely on multiple locations, each of which represents a different brand, or even a single location selling multiple brands. This diversified portfolio reduces the dealer's dependence on any single manufacturer and enables it to resist any given automaker's pressure attempts.

The second countermeasure, organizing a coalition, involves a strategy of bringing in third parties. There are several ways to do so. A common method in Europe is to write contracts that require mandatory arbitration of any disputes. The arbitrators are usually private entities, but the third party also could be a government body. Other coalitions emerge when channel members band together into trade associations. Just as much as they used the first countermeasure, automobile dealers in the United States rely on this tactic. By organizing and lobbying state legislatures, dealers have pushed through "Dealers' Day in Court" laws in many states that limit automakers' ability to coerce or pressure them through lawsuits or penalties. For example, when General Motors vertically integrated forward in selected markets, an organized coalition of dealers demanded it reverse its strategy, leading the CEO to admit: "I learned a lot. Having your key constituents mad at you is not the way to be successful."[44]

The third countermeasure is to withdraw from the business and therefore from the relationship.[45] Exiting the business and moving resources elsewhere (e.g., selling off an auto dealership) may seem unthinkable, but it also constitutes the most conclusive way to escape dependence. In retail channels, powerful retailers like Walmart use their substantial power to demand reduced prices from dependent manufacturers. Even if those manufacturers might prefer to sell through Walmart's extensive distribution system, they have the option of offsetting the lower prices they offer the retail giant with higher prices charged to weaker retailers and shifting more of their sales focus to these higher-margin channels through advertising and promotion efforts.[46]

Perhaps none of these dependence-reduction strategies is appealing. In that case, to address imbalanced dependence, the weaker member might seek to increase the other party's dependence by offering greater utility and making itself less replaceable. The best method often is to improve its service levels. If a weaker party begins to offer quicker delivery, for example, its partner may find the service offer nearly irresistible. A manufacturer that guarantees on-time deliveries eliminates the threat of stockouts for the retailer, which should lead the retailer to come to rely more on its products. Of course, such a tactic also implies that the manufacturer is devoting substantial resources to its relationship with the retailer, so this strategy might be risky. But ultimately, it could ensure greater mutual dependence between them.

Strategies for Tolerating Imbalanced Dependence

The most common reaction by weaker parties is no reaction. That is, more often than not, a dependent party simply accepts the situation and tries to make the best of it. It might even deliberately devote a high proportion of its effort or sales to the other party, in the hope that it becomes so important that the stronger party values its contribution and actively avoids taking advantage of its vulnerability. Weaker parties also might rely on internal norms of joint decision making and trust the other party to take its interests into account. Firms are (perhaps surprisingly) willing to be vulnerable in this manner. Clothing suppliers often make investments in a single powerful retailer and reassure themselves that the retailer will not abuse its position, because they are an important supplier or have a long tradition of joint decision making.[47]

But especially in globally consolidating markets and industries,[48] we need to ask: are stronger parties always exploitative? Do weaker parties always suffer? Should imbalanced relationships be avoided?

Some imbalanced dependence relationships actually work well. When department store buyers, who select merchandise for each department, rely on manufacturers to supply appealing merchandise with a strong brand name, they willingly grant far greater power to the suppliers, which might not depend on the store as a major outlet. Despite this imbalance, department stores generally benefit from this dominant supplier relationship, especially if the market environment remains stable and *predictable*. That is, if the dominant supplier's product enjoys predictable demand, the department stores minimize their own need to take price reductions. In addition, in this setting, suppliers normatively refrain from exploiting buyers' vulnerability.

In unpredictable settings, though, supplier dominance may quickly become a liability. As demand fluctuates, the store cannot oblige the dominant supplier to be more flexible, such as by taking back more unsold merchandise. Thus, in highly *uncertain* market environments, high mutual dependence is preferable, to ensure that both suppliers and buyers are motivated to find common solutions to complex stocking problems. Low mutual dependence is another option, because in that case, the buyer has the option of switching suppliers.

In short, imbalanced dependence is not necessarily detrimental in stable environments and when the less dependent party voluntarily refrains from abusing its power. A channel can function effectively if the stronger party takes care to treat the more vulnerable party equitably.[49] Equitable treatment also improves relationship quality, which enhances the functioning of the channel. Finally, because every channel member's reputation is at stake, unfair treatment creates reputation risks that may make it more difficult for a powerful, exploitative actor to attract, retain, and motivate other channel members in the future.

On the whole, we suggest examining both dependence and interdependence to get a complete picture. They are not two sides of the same coin. Dependence motivates relationship quality and cooperation; interdependence encourages relationship-specific investments and performance improvements by increasing the stakes for both parties.[50] Parties even may choose to enter into imbalanced relationships that are exploitative and coercive—as long as they obtain "acceptable" benefits from those interactions.[51]

POWER-BASED INFLUENCE STRATEGIES

In Figure 3.3, we outline six power-based influence strategies.

Converting the potential for influence into demands for real changes in another party's behavior requires communication, and the nature of that communication influences the channel relationships.[52] Most channel communications can be grouped into six categories, or *influence strategies*:

1. **Promise.** If you do what we wish, we will reward you.

2. **Threat.** If you don't do what we wish, we will punish you.

3. **Legalistic.** You should do what we wish, because you have agreed to do so (whether in a contract or through an informal working understanding of how we do business).

4. **Request.** Please do what we wish.

5. **Information exchange.** Let's pursue a general discussion about the most profitable way for you to run your business, without mentioning exactly what we want. This oblique strategy seeks to change your perceptions of what is effective, in a way that favors us. We hope this subtle form of persuasion prompts you to draw conclusions about what you should do—and that those conclusions match what we want you to do.

6. **Recommendation.** Similar to an information exchange, let's discuss profitable methods, but we will provide you with the conclusion, namely you would be more profitable if you would do what we wish. This more overt strategy tends to generate skepticism and counterarguments.

Channel members that have not invested in building corresponding power bases likely find that their influence attempts fail. Again, we caution that power, and thus

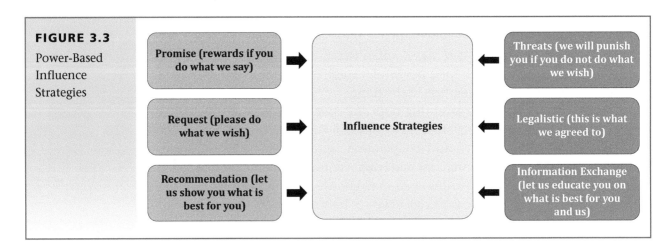

FIGURE 3.3
Power-Based
Influence
Strategies

Promise (rewards if you do what we say)

Request (please do what we wish)

Recommendation (let us show you what is best for you)

Influence Strategies

Threats (we will punish you if you do not do what we wish)

Legalistic (this is what we agreed to)

Information Exchange (let us educate you on what is best for you and us)

power bases, are specific to each relationship: Nestlé has far more reward power (and thus can use a promise strategy effectively) with a small retailer than with an international hypermarket chain.

As a general rule, boundary personnel eventually use all six strategies in each relationship they develop. But each relationship also exhibits a particular style that reflects which strategies are most common. The predominant style, or influence strategy used most often, determines how well the firm converts its power into actual behavioral changes by its partner. Yet evidence indicates that the two lightest-handed strategies, recommendation and request, are the ones used most often (whereas the heaviest-handed, threats and legalisms, are used least often).[53]

Most available, systematic evidence from Western cultures suggests that more subtle influence strategies improve interpersonal relationship quality, whereas overt influence strategies risk resentment. Non-Western cultures often are more tolerant of coercive strategies; coercive strategies also appear more acceptable for dealing with upstream channel members, outside of franchising arrangements.[54]

OMNI-CHANNELS AND POWER

Multiple channels have always existed, but at one time, companies tended to prefer a single, primary route to market and turn to other routes only as secondary, downplayed, or disguised methods, in their effort to avert channel conflict and avoid confusing customers. For example, suppliers might quietly open their own sales and distribution organizations, competing directly but not obtrusively with their own channel customers for end-users (dual distribution). But today, the use of multiple channels is the visible norm rather than the hidden exception.[55] Heightened competition has driven many suppliers to change and expand their channels; fragmented markets make it harder to serve customers efficiently through only one channel type. In addition, whereas channels once had to remain simple, to facilitate their administration, technological advances have made it feasible to manage far more complex channel structures.

Moreover, suppliers and customers like multiple channels. For suppliers, they increase market penetration, giving them a better view of multiple markets, while also raising entry barriers to potential competitors. As their various channels compete, suppliers enjoy the benefits of this "healthy" competition. For customers, multiple channels increase the chances of finding one that meets their service output demands. Multiple channel types also make it easier for customers to pit one channel against another when they seek more services at lower prices. Thus, multiple channels even create markets: suppliers and customers can more easily find one another and fulfill their needs by using the most appropriate channel types.[56] In an omni-channel world, manufacturer and retailer power accordingly gets diffused.

Manufacturers now routinely sell their products directly to the consumer and have effectively become direct competitors of retailers, both offline and online.[57]

At the same time, retailers increasingly have expanded their private-label offerings. As these developments reveal, the exercise of power is not a static phenomenon. Power equations change over time, and parties must adapt to changing situations.[58] At one time, manufacturers ruled the roost. But power shifted to retailers with the emergence of mega-stores, for which the retailers controlled significant shelf space. The power balance may be swinging again, with the advent of multi-channel retailing, because manufacturers gain new avenues and options for reaching consumers, and retailers face ever-intensifying competition.

These trends do not suggest that concentration in retail markets has completely disappeared, though. Two giant retailers, Woolworth and Coles, account for 80 percent of the Australian grocery market, but the power of these giants varies greatly depending on the product category.[59] They do not have much power over manufacturers with strong brands (e.g., Huggies diapers). In other categories, though, their private-label brands are virtually destroying the manufacturer brands. So the extent to which omni-channel shopping affects power dynamics is determined, in large part, by the characteristics of the specific industries. Smaller suppliers in asymmetrically dependent relationships can use their expert power to exert influence over larger partners in an omni-channel context if they can provide value to end-users by enabling them to shop when, where, and how they want.

Take-Aways

- The three ways to manage a relationship are to (a) foster commitment, (b) exercise power, or (c) capitalize and learn from functional conflict.

- Channel power is the ability to alter another organization's behavior. It is a tool, neither good nor bad.

- Power permeates all aspects of marketing channels. The interdependence of channel members makes power a critical feature of their functioning.

- Channel members must invest over time to build power, then assess their power accurately and use it wisely, whether to achieve their own initiatives or to protect themselves from others' influence attempts.

- The power of A is equal to the dependence of B. The dependence of B increases when

  o B derives great utility from dealing with A.

  o B cannot find that utility easily among A's competitors, because there are few competitors, or B faces very high switching costs.

- Power comes from five sources:
  - Reward.
  - Coercive.
  - Expert.
  - Legitimate.
  - Referent.

- Power is a two-sided affair, specific to each relationship at any given time. Any assessment of power must consider the countervailing power of the other side. The best indicator of power is the net dependence of the two sides.

- Mutually dependent relationships often generate exceptional value added, because each side has sufficient leverage to ensure win–win solutions.

- Imbalanced dependence is very common. In these relationships,
  - The stronger party can exploit or ignore the weaker one.
  - The weaker party can take countermeasures, including diversifying, forming a coalition, or exiting the business.
  - Channel success requires the stronger party to exhibit restraint, act equitably, and appear fair.

- Translating power, a latent ability, into influence involves communication (influence strategies). The most common (and effective) methods are:
  - making promises;
  - issuing requests;
  - exchanging information; and
  - making recommendations.

NOTES

1 Jeuland, Abel P. and Steven M. Shugan (1983), "Managing channel profits," *Marketing Science*, 2 (3), 239–272.
2 Kai, Gangshu, Yue Dai, and Sean Zhou (2012), "Exclusive channels and revenue sharing in a complementary goods market," *Marketing Science*, 31 (January–February), 172–187.
3 Stone, Brad and Lulu Yulin Chen (2017), "Tencent dominates in China: Next challenge is rest of the world," *Bloomberg Business Week*, June 28, www.bloomberg.com/news/features/2017-06-28/tencent-rules-china-the-problem-is-the-rest-of-the-world.
4 Xiao, Evan (2017), "How WeChat became Alipay's largest rival," April 20, www.techinasia.com/wechat-pay-vs-alipay.

5 Yuan, Li (2017), "Beijing pushes for a direct hand in China's big tech firms," *The Wall Street Journal*, October 11.

6 Rehme, Jakob, Daniel Nordigarden, Daniel Ellstrom, and Daniel Chicksand (2016), "Power in distribution channels: Supplier assortment strategy for balancing power," *Industrial Marketing Management*, 54, 176–187.

7 Brown, James R., Jean L. Johnson, and Harold F. Koenig (1995), "Measuring the sources of marketing channel power: A comparison of alternative approaches," *International Journal of Research in Marketing*, 12 (2), 333–354.

8 French, John R., Jr. and Bertram Raven (1959), "The bases of social power," in Dorwin Cartwright (ed.), *Studies in Social Power*, Ann Arbor, MI: University of Michigan, pp. 150–167.

9 Narus, James A. and James C. Anderson (1988), "Strengthen distributor performance through channel positioning," *Sloan Management Review*, 29 (4), 31–40.

10 Mentzer, John T., Daniel J. Flint, and G. Tomas M. Hult (2001), "Logistics service quality as a segment-customized process," *Journal of Marketing*, 65 (4), 82–104.

11 Chu, Wujin (1992), "Demand signalling and screening in channels of distribution," *Marketing Science*, 11 (3), 327–347; Bloom, Paul N., Gregory T. Gundlach, and Joseph P. Cannon (2000), "Slotting allowances and fees: School of thought and the views of practicing managers," *Journal of Marketing*, 64 (2), 92–108.

12 Rao, Akshay R. and Humaira Mahi (2003), "The price of launching a new product: Empirical evidence on factors affecting the relative magnitude of slotting allowances," *Marketing Science*, 22 (2), 246–268.

13 Zimmerman, Ann (2003), "To sell goods to Wal-Mart, get on the net," *The Wall Street Journal* (November 21), 1–2.

14 Gaski, John F. and John R. Nevin (1985), "The differential effects of exercised and unexercised power sources in a marketing channel," *Journal of Marketing Research*, 22 (May), 130–142.

15 Munson, Charles L., Meir J. Rosenblatt, and Zehava Rosenblatt (1999), "The use and abuse of power in supply chains," *Business Horizons*, 30 (January–February), 55–65. This article gives many examples of channel power in operation.

16 Geyskens, Inge, Jan-Benedict E.M. Steenkamp, and Nirmalya Kumar (1999), "A meta-analysis of satisfaction in marketing channel relationships," *Journal of Marketing Research*, 36 (May), 223–238.

17 Geyskens, Inge, Jan-Benedict E.M. Steenkamp, and Nirmalya Kumar (1998), "Generalizations about trust in marketing channel relationships using meta analysis," *International Journal of Research in Marketing*, 15 (1), 223–248.

18 Munson, Rosenblatt, and Rosenblatt (1999), op. cit.

19 Hart, Paul and Carol Saunders (1997), "Power and trust: Critical factors in the adoption and use of electronic data interchange," *Organization Science*, 8 (January–February), 23–42.

20 Agnihotri, Aripita (2013), "Doing good and doing business at the bottom of the pyramid," *Business Horizons*, 56 (5), 591–599.

21 Luhnow, David (2005), "In Mexico, maker of generics adds spice to drug business," *The Wall Street Journal* (February 22), A1, A6.

22 Rosencher, Anne (2004), "Le Client Mystère, Ou l'Art d'Espionner Ses Point de Vente," *Capital* (November), 124–126.

23 Raven, Bertram H. and Arie W. Kruglanski (1970), "Conflict and power," in P. Swingle (ed.), *The Structure of Conflict*, New York: Academic Press, pp. 69–99.

24 Anderson, Erin and Barton Weitz (1989), "Determinants of continuity in conventional channel dyads," *Marketing Science*, 8 (Fall), 310–323.

25 See https://law.justia.com/cases/federal/district-courts/minnesota/mndce/0:2014cv00778/137395/36.

26 See http://franbuslaw.com/blog/?p=713.

27 Antia, Kersi D. and Gary L. Frazier (2001), "The severity of contract enforcement in interfirm channel relationships," *Journal of Marketing*, 65 (4), 67–81.

28 Heide, Jan B. and George John (1992), "Do norms matter in marketing relationships?" *Journal of Marketing*, 56 (April), 32–44.

29 Chu, Wujin and Woosik Chu (1994), "Signaling quality by selling through a reputable retailer: An example of renting the reputation of another agent," *Marketing Science*, 13 (Spring), 177–189.

30 Bouillin, Arnaud (2001), "Gore-Tex ou l'Art de se Rendre Indispensable," *Management* (October), 30–32.

31 Emerson, Richard M. (1962), "Power–dependence relations," *American Sociological Review*, 27 (February), 31–41.

32 Donath, Bob (2002), "Value studies reveal insufficient attention to dealers plenty costly," *Marketing News* (October 28), 8–9.

33 Kale, Sudhir H. (1986), "Dealer perceptions of manufacturer power and influence strategies in a developing country," *Journal of Marketing Research*, 23 (November), 387–393.

34 Frazier, Gary L. (1983), "On the measurement of interfirm power in channels of distribution," *Journal of Marketing Research*, 20 (May), 158–166.

35 Frazier, Gary L., James D. Gill, and Sudhir H. Kale (1989), "Dealer dependence levels and reciprocal actions in a channel of distribution in a developing country," *Journal of Marketing*, 53 (January), 50–69.

36 Lusch, Robert F. and James R. Brown (1996), "Interdependency, contracting, and relational behavior in marketing channels," *Journal of Marketing*, 60 (October), 19–38.

37 Hallén, Lars, Jan Johanson, and Nazeem Seyed-Mohamed (1991), "Interfirm adaptation in business relationships," *Journal of Marketing*, 55 (April), 29–37.

38 Heide, Jan B. (1994), "Interorganizational governance in marketing channels," *Journal of Marketing*, 58 (January), 71–85.

39 Palmatier, Robert W., Rajiv P. Dant, and Dhruv Grewal (2007), "A comparative longitudinal analysis of theoretical perspectives of interorganizational relationship performance," *Journal of Marketing*, 71 (October), 172–194.

40 Provan, Keith G. and Steven J. Skinner (1989), "Interorganizational dependence and control as predictors of opportunism in dealer–supplier relations," *Academy of Management Journal*, 32 (March), 202–212.

41 Ross, William T., Erin Anderson, and Barton Weitz (1997), "Performance in principal–agent dyads: The causes and consequences of perceived asymmetry of commitment to the relationship," *Management Science*, 43 (May), 680–704.

42 Kumar, Nirmalya, Lisa K. Scheer, and Jan-Benedict E.M. Steenkamp (1994), "The effects of perceived interdependence on dealer attitudes," *Journal of Marketing Research*, 32 (August), 348–356.

43 Heide, Jan B. and George John (1988), "The role of dependence balancing in safeguarding transaction-specific assets in conventional channels," *Journal of Marketing*, 52 (January), 20–35.

44 Taylor, Alex (2002), "Finally GM is looking good," *Fortune* (April 1), 42–46.

45 Yang, Donghoon, Eugene Sivadas, Bohyeon Kang, and Sejo Oh (2012), "Dissolution intention in channel relationships: An examination of contributing factors," *Industrial Marketing Management*, 41 (7), 1106–1113.

46 Geylani, Tansev, Anthony J. Dukes, and Kannan Srinivasan (2007), "Strategic manufacturer response to a dominant retailer," *Marketing Science*, 26 (March–April), 164–178.

47 Subramani, Mani R. and N. Venkatraman (2003), "Safeguarding investments in asymmetric inter-organizational relationships: Theory and evidence," *Academy of Management Journal*, 46 (1), 46–62.

48 An excellent discussion of this trend and its implications appears in Fein, Adam J. and Sandy D. Jap (1999), "Manage consolidation in the distribution channel," *Sloan Management Review*, 41 (Fall), 61–72.

49 Kumar, Nirmalya, Lisa K. Scheer, and Jan-Benedict E.M. Steenkamp (1995), "The effects of supplier fairness on vulnerable resellers," *Journal of Marketing Research*, 32 (February), 54–65.

50 Scheer, Lisa K., C. Fred Miao, and Robert W. Palmatier (2015), "Dependence and interdependence in marketing relationships: Meta-analytic insights," *Journal of the Academy of Marketing Science*, 43, 649–712.

51 Cowan, Kirsten, Audhesh Paswan, and Eric Van Steenburg (2015), "When inter-firm relationship benefits mitigate power asymmetry," *Industrial Marketing Management*, 48, 140–148.

52 This discussion is based on Frazier, Gary L. and John O. Summers (1986), "Perceptions of interfirm power and its use within a franchise channel of distribution," *Journal of Marketing Research*, 23 (May), 169–176.

53 Frazier, Gary L. and John O. Summers (1984), "Interfirm influence strategies and their application within distribution channels," *Journal of Marketing*, 48 (Summer), 43–55.

54 Johnston, Wesley James, Angelina Nhat Hanh Le, and Julian Ming-Sung Cheng (2017), "A meta-analytic review of influence strategies in marketing channel relationships," *Journal of the Academy of Marketing Science*, DOI 10.1007/s11747-017-0564-3.

55 Frazier, Gary L. and Tasadduq A. Shervani (1992), "Multiple channels of distribution and their impact on retailing," in Robert A. Peterson (ed.), *The Future of U.S. Retailing: An Agenda for the 21st Century*, Westport, CT: Quorum Books.

56 Cespedes, Frank V. and Raymond Corey (1990), "Managing multiple channels," *Business Horizons*, 10 (1), 67–77; Moriarty, Rowland T. and Ursula Moran (1990), "Managing hybrid marketing systems," *Harvard Business Review* (November–December), 146–150.

57 Karray, Salma and Simone Pierre Sigue (2018), "Offline retailers expanding online to compete with manufacturers: strategies and channel power," *Industrial Marketing Management*, https://doi.org/10.1016/j.indmarman.2018.01.004.

58 Low, Wen-Shinn and Han-Tzong Lee (2016), "The exercise and acceptance of power in an industrial channel dyad," *Journal of Business-to-Business Marketing*, 23, 135–151.

59 Sutton-Brady, Catherine, Patty Kamvounias, and Tom Taylor (2015), "A model of supplier–retailer power asymmetry in the Australian retail industry," *Industrial Marketing Management*, 51, 122–130.

CHAPTER 4

Channel Relationships

LEARNING OBJECTIVES

After reading this chapter, you will be able to:

- Describe the motivations for and importance of building channel relationships.
- Distinguish upstream and downstream motivations for forming a relationship.
- Recognize why multiple channels represent the norm and describe ways to build relationships therein.
- Explain how to extend the time horizon of a relationship and why doing so is critical.
- Explain the role of relationship velocity.
- Differentiate the five phases of a close marketing channel relationship.

INTRODUCTION

Why Do Relationships Matter in Marketing Channels?

Channel relationships go by many labels, including partnerships, relational governance, hybrid governance, vertical quasi-integration, and strategic alliance. Channel management is about motivating and incentivizing interdependent yet independent entities to maximize the common good. As noted in Chapter 3, in an effective channel relationship, two or more interdependent organizations need to function as if they are pursuing a **single shared interest**. Channel management also becomes more challenging in an omni-channel environment, in which firms must deal with and synergize their channel activities and conflicting interests across different channels.

The hallmark of strong channel relationships is a genuine commitment and willingness to engage in give-and-take interactions to achieve and reflect the objectives of the partnership. **Commitment** exists when one organization wants the relationship to continue indefinitely; however, it is not sufficient by itself to ensure an effective channel relationship. The organization also must be willing to **sacrifice** to maintain and grow the relationship. Sacrifices may take the form of giving up short-term profits or not pursuing other opportunities, preferring instead to devote organizational resources to the relationship. In general, a committed party works hard to maintain and advance the relationship. As the Sears example indicates, commitment is not a given, even in long-standing relationships.

EXAMPLE: SEARS (USA)[1]

Sears Roebuck was established in 1893 as a mail order company that catered mostly to rural America, offering consumers access to products that previously had been available only to city dwellers. It later started operating large department stores in cities and small towns to expand its reach. A pioneer in multi-channel retailing, Sears was one of the first brick-and-mortar companies to move online. It had nearly the breadth of Amazon, before Amazon existed, selling everything from insurance products (it owned All-State Insurance) to appliances to clothing. But in more recent years, it has fallen on hard times, losing more than $10 billion since the start of the 2010s. Sales fell to $22.14 billion, substantially down from $41.57 billion in 2011, following the corporation's decisions to spin off some of its divisions and close stores throughout the United States. Sears also remains straddled with long-term debt. Such factors have had detrimental implications for its relationship with suppliers, even those with which it has had lengthy relationships. For example, Sears came to Whirlpool's rescue in the 1920s, and in 2002, it accounted for 20 percent of Whirlpool's revenues. But that percentage has fallen to just 3 percent today, as Whirlpool, concerned about Sears' financial health, ships fewer products at higher prices, with more stringent payment terms, in an effort to reduce its own risk. Insurers and banks similarly are concerned about guaranteeing Sears' ability to pay vendors.[2] Thus LG demands cash upfront, before it will supply Sears; United National Consumer Suppliers allows it one month to make a payment, but that is far less than the two-month grace period it provides Sears' competitors.[3]

In Chapter 3, we presented the use of power as one approach to managing channels. In this chapter, our goal is to highlight an alternative approach while also stressing the importance of deploying relational tools to manage channel relationships. This chapter begins by considering fundamental questions: *what are the key motives for building channel relationships, and why are they so important in marketing channels?*

Upstream Motives for Building a Strong Channel Relationship

Why should an upstream channel member, such as a manufacturer, want to build a committed relationship with a downstream channel member, such as a distributor?

Channel relationships begin with the manufacturer's recognition that it potentially can profit from the many advantages a downstream channel member can offer. Chief among these, manufacturers tend to appreciate the ability to achieve better coverage, and at lower cost (including lower overhead).

It is surprising how often manufacturers fail to appreciate the value that channel members provide them, or else overestimate their own ability to duplicate, effectively and efficiently, another party's performance of key channel functions. For some manufacturers, their "'do it in-house technical' culture . . . prevents them from understanding, respecting, and trusting intermediaries to any degree."[4] For example, their internal selling arm might view independent channel members as competition. Or companies may be staffed by people who have never worked in channels and distrust partners in general, with the assumption "they will screw things up and . . . will be very expensive."[5] In contrast, a channel-centric supplier understands and respects how each independent channel member undertakes activities and converts them into meaningful service outputs, to generate effective results.

Once appreciation for the downstream organization exists, manufacturers seek relationships to **motivate** channel members to represent them better, in their current markets, in new markets, or with new products. Building commitment is an effective, durable way to motivate downstream channel members, particularly when the organization must assume the significant risks of performing channel functions for new products or in new markets. Sidebar 4.1 shows how John Deere motivated dealers to adapt to changing buyer behavior in the highly competitive market for lawn maintenance equipment, even as it broadened its distribution and deepened its dealer relationships.

SIDEBAR 4.1
John Deere Helps Dealers Reach Out to Women

John Deere is a venerable manufacturer of premium equipment for farmers and homeowners. Its trademark green tractors are fixtures on farms, in parks, and across private yards and gardens. Cheryll Pletcher, the director of channel marketing, and David Jeffers, the manager of the retail brand experience, play important roles in Deere's Commercial and Consumer Division. Their jobs focus on helping the firm's 3,200 U.S. dealers adjust to radical changes in their markets.[6]

John Deere invests heavily in consumer research, from which it learned that the firm enjoyed a high reputation but prompted low intentions to buy among consumers. Sales were concentrated in "pro-sumer" segments (i.e., consumers who like to buy products that offer professional specifications). People who simply wanted a lawn tractor were not persuaded. In particular, women—who influence some 80 percent of household purchases—did not show high awareness or purchase intentions toward John Deere products.

A review of the dealer network helped explain why. Of the 3,200 dealers, 1,500 also sold agricultural products to farmers. Many of the close channel relationships also were very old (lasting more than a century in some cases). As U.S. cities sprawled into the country, these dealers increasingly discovered that their farmer customers were being replaced by homeowners, a completely different market. Many dealers had difficulty adapting to these non-technical, time-pressed customers, who demanded solutions to their own unique problems, like cup holders for their coffee mugs, not necessarily greater engine horsepower. Many of these prospective customers also had no idea where to find the dealers, who tended to be located beyond retail shopping districts. Says Jeffers, "We always joke that we have a great dealer network—cleverly hidden all over America!"

Many manufacturers might have reacted to this information by severing or downgrading their relationships with the downstream channel members. But John Deere has always been a channel-centric supplier that values continuity and trust, so it chose to do the opposite. It worked to help dealers through the transition to serving homeowner customers, including training for dealer salespeople. John Deere also helped the stores redesign their store layout, working from a flexible format that could be adapted to the dealer's business mix—and to the other brands that John Deere freely acknowledged the dealer needed to carry to generate sufficient sales volume. Says Pletcher,

> Consumers are used to malls. They have told us that with some dealers, they just don't feel they have been invited in. You know the four Ps of marketing—price, place, product, and promotion? We know that even if you have the right products, at the right price, and with the right promotions, everything will come to naught unless the place is right. For consumers it really matters what the store looks like.

As a policy, John Deere pilots all new programs with small groups of dealers, to garner their feedback and testimonials to use when it ultimately rolls out the program. Thus, it encourages dealers to try the new format by showing them how it has worked for other dealers. Notes Pletcher, "We have to convince them—they are not franchises."

But if John Deere refused to abandon its dealer network, how could it still grow sales? One solution was to offer a limited line of the firm's entry-level lawn tractors through Home Depot— the big box building supply store that many of its dealers saw as a prime competitor. Home Depot wanted an exclusive line; it also noted its disappointment with the high rates of returns it was encountering with the brands it was carrying. Rather than going ahead unilaterally, though, John Deere consulted its dealer advisory council. The dealers reluctantly accepted the idea, and even asked to carry the same model line themselves, on the condition that John Deere sell no other models to Home Depot.

The outcomes thus benefitted John Deere, its dealers, and Home Depot. Every machine sold through Home Depot would be inspected first by a dealer mechanic, resulting in very low return levels. The dealers service the machines and affix their identifying plates, even though Home Depot makes the sale. The dealership still can contact the customer directly for ongoing support and service. Simply seeing the green machines in Home Depot prompted many customers to visit John Deere dealers, especially those pro-sumers who decided to find the dealer to see the full assortment, beyond the entry-level model they found in a place they visit regularly.

John Deere also uses other resources to generate business for its dealers. For example, though the products are available on a corporate website, all sales generated by the site go to the local dealers, to "keep them in the loop." Similarly, John Deere advertises expressly to women and runs clinics for women in its dealers' showrooms; sales to women have soared as a result. By driving prospective customers to find the dealers, it also enables dealers to convert the leads into a pattern of repeat sales.

As a side effect, some dealers have consolidated into multi-unit dealerships, with three to five locations and stronger, closer relationships with John Deere. Some suppliers worry when consolidation forces them to deal with fewer, larger, more powerful channel members. But not John Deere. According to Pletcher, "Frankly, we like it. You get a change of philosophy—they manage their dealership like a business and less like people who run a dealership because it is where they want to go to work everyday."

This story illustrates a crucial point: Because John Deere already had created strong, committed relationships through decades of working with its dealer network, it was able to convince dealers to accept its distribution of lower-end products through Home Depot and build a win–win solution that actually *rewards* dealers for Home Depot sales. Augmenting specialty dealers with generalist mass-market competitors usually prompts a bitter conflict. It is not at all clear that John Deere could have pushed through such an expansion of its distribution channels without its existing (and very valuable) asset of dealer relationships.

A manufacturer also may seek a relationship to coordinate its marketing efforts with distributors more tightly, which would enable it to reach end-users better. It may seek greater cooperation related to the exchange of information in particular. Through their relationships, manufacturers hope to gain information about the marketplace, even though downstream channel members have economic motives to withhold that information. Distributors may withhold market information to prevent the manufacturer from using the information against them in negotiations. Or they may withhold information for a simpler reason: because it takes time to brief a principal, and that time has other, more productive uses. Downstream channel members are like a wall between the manufacturer and the final buyer, blocking the manufacturer's view and reducing its understanding of the end-user. By gaining distributor commitment, the manufacturer hopes to peek over the wall; that is, to increase information sharing. Most large U.S. grocery retailers share weekly, or even daily, sales data with suppliers.[7] Distributors tend to be more willing to share strategic information with their suppliers if those suppliers depend more on them than the other way around and when both parties have committed significant transaction-specific investments to the relationship.[8]

Another emerging motive to forge a relationship with downstream channel members stems from the growing wave of **consolidation** in wholesaling. Mergers and acquisitions in many industries are transforming the wholesale level, from many smaller players (fragmentation) to a handful of giant players (consolidation). Manufacturers seek relationships because they see the pool of potential partners drying up. They fear losing distribution access, not only due to the few players left standing but also because the survivors themselves are powerful organizations that enter into more or less privileged relations with selected manufacturers. A strong relationship helps rebalance the power arrangement, while also ensuring consistent access to markets.[9]

In the longer term, the manufacturer seeks to erect **barriers to entry** against future competitors. One of the best possible barriers is a good distribution network. Unlike a price cut or a product feature, a channel is hard to duplicate. A committed channel partner in particular may refuse to carry or actively promote a new entrant's brands, as the widely celebrated channel relationship between Procter & Gamble (P&G) and Walmart reveals.[10] Both of these one-time adversaries are noted for using their considerable power to sway the trade. In particular, P&G's brand appeal and market expertise with hundreds of fast-moving consumer goods is so dominant that it has been described as a "self-aggrandizing bully."[11] Walmart, the massive retailer, uses its volume and size to oblige suppliers to do business as it dictates: no intermediaries, extraordinarily low prices, extra service, preferred credit terms, investments in electronic data interchange (EDI) and radio frequency identification (RFID) technology, and so forth.

But these upstream and downstream giants also built a strong channel relationship, using the techniques described in this chapter. Most notably, they made investments tailored to each other. For P&G, the payoffs have come in several forms: it receives continuous data by satellite from individual Walmart stores (not pooled over the entire store network), covering sales, inventory levels, and prices for each stock-keeping unit (SKU) of each brand P&G sells. Then P&G takes responsibility for reordering and shipping, often directly to the stores (a practice called **vendor-managed inventory**). The cycle is completed by electronic invoicing and electronic funds transfer. With this paperless system, P&G can manufacture to demand, cut inventories, *and* still reduce stockouts. Overall logistics costs accordingly have declined. Furthermore, P&G does enormous business with Walmart, protected from competition by the investments it has made and its intimate knowledge of Walmart's needs. Finally, P&G gains an excellent source of market research, in the store-level data it garners from its partner.

In recent years, the partnership has hit some rough patches, though, demonstrating that even strong relationships require constant maintenance. Recent figures indicate that P&G still accrues nearly $10 billion in sales through Walmart, yet both companies have suffered sales slowdowns, driven by the tight budgets of their target markets of modest-income consumers.[12] In their individual attempts to deal with these challenges, the partners have adopted some behaviors that threaten their partner. For example, Walmart, in the face of intense competition from Amazon and discounters like Aldi, has demanded that P&G cut the costs of its goods and has introduced store brand alternatives to P&G offerings. At the same time, P&G made the decision to sell fragrances through Aldi.

Downstream Motives for Building a Strong Channel Relationship

The motives for downstream channel members to build strong relationships revolve around having an assured and stable supply of desirable products. Consolidation is a motive here again: As mergers and acquisitions concentrate market share among a few manufacturers in many industries, downstream channel members commit to the survivors to maintain product supply. Channel members also build relationships to ensure the success of their own marketing efforts. By coordinating their efforts with a supplier, channel members seek to work better together, though this is not an objective in itself. Rather, it matters because it helps each channel member serve its customers better, which in turn translates into higher volumes and higher margins.

Channel members further seek to cut costs through their strong channel relationships. For example, by coordinating logistics, a channel member can increase inventory turnover, keep lower levels of stocks, and take fewer write-downs of obsolete stock. The best of all worlds arises when stock costs get cut *and* the channel member suffers fewer out-of-stock situations.

Downstream channel members, such as distributors, build strong relationships with suppliers to **differentiate** themselves from other distributors too. By positioning themselves as the manufacturer's preferred outlets for desirable brands or selected SKUs, distributors differentiate their assortments and related service provision. By differentiating themselves, downstream channel members also discourage new competitive entries into their markets.

Distributor differentiation is often based on a strategy of offering value-added services, such as preventive or corrective maintenance, application assistance, on-site product training, engineering and design, technical expertise on call, special packaging and handling, or expedited and free telephone assistance. Distributors pursuing this strategy are more likely to work closely with their suppliers, which helps the distributor set itself apart from fierce competition, while simultaneously helping the manufacturer build a market for its products.[13]

Returning to the relationship between P&G and Walmart, what benefits does the downstream retailer gain? Its inventories are lower, but without risking stockouts, and the chain can offer customers lower prices and greater availability of well-known brands. Walmart also is no longer responsible for managing its inventory (which is only a benefit if the function is done well, as it is in this case). The paperless transaction system permits Walmart to enjoy float, in that the retailer does not pay its supplier until after the consumer pays for the merchandise. This system, though difficult to build and duplicate, has given Walmart a formidable competitive advantage in the saturated retail arena.

The upstream and downstream motives to forge strong relationships thus are more similar than they appear at first glance. Figure 4.1 summarizes the preceding discussion and notes the parallels in the interests of both sides. As this figure shows,

FIGURE 4.1
Motives to
Create and
Maintain
Strong Channel
Relationships

Motives to Ally Strategically	The Upstream Channel Member	The Downstream Channel Member
Fundamentals	Motivates downstream channel members to represent it better • In current markets • With current products • In new markets • With new products	Avoids stockouts while keeping costs under control • Lowers costs of all flows performed, such as lower inventory-holding costs
Generate customer preference	Coordinates marketing efforts more tightly with downstream channel members • Get closer to customers and prospects • Enhance understanding of the market	Coordinates marketing efforts more tightly with upstream channel members • Serve the customer better • Convert prospects into customers • Net effect: higher volume and margins
Preserve choice and flexibility of channel partners	Guarantees market access in the face of consolidation in wholesaling • Keep routes to market open • Rebalance power between the manufacturer and surviving channels	Ensures a stable supply of desirable products, even as manufacturers consolidate • In current markets • Selling current products • Opening to new markets • With new products
Strategic preemption	Erects barriers to entry to other brands • Induce channels to refuse access • Induce channels to offer low levels of support to entrants	Differentiates itself from other downstream channel members • Supplier's preferred outlet • Value-added services, difficult to copy and of high value to customers
Superordinate goal	Seeks an enduring competitive advantage leading to profit • Reduces accounting and opportunity costs	Seeks an enduring competitive advantage leading to profit • Reduces accounting and opportunity costs

upstream and downstream channel members fundamentally pursue relationships for the same reasons: to attain an **enduring competitive advantage that leads to profit**. Both parties seek to improve their coordination within the channel, to serve customers better, and to reduce their accounting and opportunity costs. Both parties also seek to build stable relationships that are difficult to duplicate, which will discourage entry into their respective businesses.

BUILDING CHANNEL COMMITMENT

Need for Expectations of Continuity

A channel member that wants to build commitment in a relationship must begin by building the expectation that prospective partners will be doing business for a long time. The expectation of continuity is essential before any organization can cooperate and invest to build a future.[14] Yet continuity can never be taken for granted. Channel members know that they will be replaced if their performance fails to satisfy.

In environments in which legal barriers to termination are low (such as the United States), channel members also fear they will be replaced even if their performance *does* satisfy! For example, principals often engage agents or resellers to represent secondary products or to penetrate markets that they consider peripheral. If the downstream channel member makes a success of the business, it logically should fear that the manufacturer will take business away or renegotiate the terms of the arrangement, to appropriate some of the unexpected gains.[15]

What inspires confidence that a business relationship will last?[16] Continuity expectations increase in the presence of:

- Trust.

- Two-way communication.

- A reputation for fair dealing.

- A long-standing, stable relationship.

- Balanced power.

- Combined stakes.

Specifically, when downstream channel members expect to do business on behalf of a principal, they likely *trust* the manufacturer (as we discuss in a subsequent section) and enjoy *two-way communication*, including the active give-and-take of ideas, with that manufacturer. Trust and communication operate in a reinforcing cycle: more trust leads to more communication leads to more trust leads to more communication, and so forth. Thus, frequent, candid, detailed mutual communication is a must for a healthy channel partnership.[17] However, more than a few members of would-be channel partnerships assume they enjoy better communication and higher trust levels than they really do.

Downstream channel members also expect continuity when their manufacturer partners have a *reputation* for treating other channel members fairly, as well as when they have been doing business with their manufacturer partner for some time already. But long-standing, seemingly *stable* channel relationships can hide problems. In particular, communication is often rather low in older relationships; rather like an old married couple who sits in silence over the dinner table, the two parties might assume they know each other so well that communication is superfluous. Older channel relationships frequently look stronger than they really are, because both sides take them for granted and permit communication to decline. Eventually, their lack of communication will damage the trust that has built up in these old, stable relationships.

Continuity expectations are higher when power is *balanced* in a relationship. Imbalanced power causes the weaker party to fear being exploited, such that it is more likely to defect. Knowing this, the stronger party discounts the potential for a future relationship, because it expects the weaker party to withdraw or go out of business. Thus, even when one party has the upper hand, it has less confidence that its relationship will last, compared with a balanced power scenario. But balanced power does not ensure a strong relationship, despite its continuity, as we noted previously.

Finally, the *combined stakes* of the two parties also play a role: the more both sides get from the relationship, the more they expect it to continue. At least one party has too much to lose to let the relationship end without fighting to preserve it. Ideally, both parties have stakes (e.g., both derive substantial revenues from the arrangement), so both parties have an interest in avoiding a capricious end to the relationship.

The belief among channel partners that their relationship has a future is a minimal condition for commitment. But to erect a true, strong, relational-based partnership, the next step demands that each side also *believe* that its partner is committed. In Figure 4.2, we present a summary view of what a committed relationship entails.

Need for Reciprocation: Mutual Commitment

With some expectation of continuity, a strong relationship requires each party's commitment.[18] **Asymmetric commitment** is rare. Any partner to a relationship is going to do its own calculations. Why should it accept the obligations of being committed, unless it believes its counterpart is also committed and ready to assume its own obligations? Channel members that doubt the commitment of another organization may proclaim themselves partners, in the interest of preserving appearances, but they do not believe in, nor do they practice, commitment.

		FIGURE 4.2
A committed party to a relationship (manufacturer, distributor, or other channel member) views its arrangement as a long-term relationship. Some manifestations of this outlook show up in statements such as these, made by the committed party about its channel partner.		Symptoms of Commitment in Marketing Channels
We expect to be doing business with them for a long time.	We are willing to grow the relationship.	
We defend them when others criticize them.	We are patient with their mistakes, even those that cause us trouble.	
We spend enough time with their people to work out problems and misunderstandings.	We are willing to make long-term investments in them, and then to wait for the payoff to come.	
We have a strong sense of loyalty to them.	If another organization offered us something better we would not drop this organization, and we would hesitate to take on the new organization.	

Clearly, these statements do not reflect normal operating procedures for two organizations. Commitment involves more than an ongoing cordial relationship. It demands confidence in the future and a willingness to invest in the partner, at the expense of other opportunities, to maintain and grow the business relationship.

Deception certainly seems possible in this case, such as when one party seeks to convince its channel partner that its commitment is genuine, even when it is not. Yet most evidence suggests that this strategy rarely works. Upstream and downstream channel members are usually well informed about each other's true level of commitment. And they carefully and dynamically condition their own attitudes, depending on what they (reasonably accurately) believe about the other party's commitment. These accurate assessments are possible because organizations, unlike some people, are not very good actors. Even if every boundary spanner and point of contact were instructed to put up a façade, the counterpart ultimately can see through it. This works both ways: truly committed firms may claim externally that they are questioning their commitment, in an attempt to conceal their dependence or vulnerability. But this projection fails too, and partners are rarely misled for long.

Strategies for Building Commitment

Imagine you are a distributor, dealing with a supplier. You gauge the supplier's commitment to you on the basis of its past behavior, focusing on two critical questions: (1) Have you had an acrimonious, conflict-laden past with this supplier? and (2) What actions do you anticipate the supplier taking, to tie itself to your business?

These anticipated actions take two forms: selectivity and specialized investments. First, a higher degree of **selectivity** by the supplier gives you some degree of protection from competitors that might sell the same brand. With such high selectivity exercised by the supplier in its coverage of your market, you likely come to believe that the supplier is truly committed to a business partnership with you. At the limit, if you obtain territory exclusivity, you will regard the supplier as highly committed. Conversely, if nearly every other competitor in your market sells this brand too, you perceive little commitment from your supplier.

This question becomes somewhat more complicated when your supplier practices direct selling and maintains **house accounts** to serve some of its customers directly, in direct competition with you. Although such competition seemingly should destroy your confidence in its commitment, manufacturers often practice direct selling, even to a rather substantial degree, while still inspiring confidence in their commitment. Regardless of what you might say, you likely tolerate some direct selling, because you know some customers will only deal directly with the supplier. In that case, the supplier's direct selling does not take away any of your business. It might even relieve you of some channel duties that you do not want to perform, for specific customers with substantial demands. Other manufacturers may try to camouflage the full extent of their direct selling, but this fib is not really a major factor. Rather, the key point is your *perception* that the manufacturer is handling its direct business fairly, as opposed to being greedy and stealing business you could have earned.

Second, suppliers might seek to build assets that are dedicated to your relationship and that cannot be redeployed in connection with another distributor. These **idiosyncratic investments** are customized to your relationship; if the supplier were to replace you, it would need to write off (or at least greatly write down) this investment. To duplicate the value it has created through this investment and in its relationship with you, the supplier would need to make a new investment in a competitor that replaces you. Some notable, difficult-to-redeploy investments include:

- Supplier personnel and facilities dedicated to a single distributor.

- A supplier's stock of learning about you—such as your methods, your people, your strengths, and your weaknesses.

- Compatible reporting systems, geared to the peculiarities of your system (especially if your system is proprietary).

- Investments designed to identify your business and its business, in the minds of customers.

- Investments in general training programs and other resources that help you run your business better.

- A location near you but at a remove from your competitors.

These assets vary in how easy they are to deploy, but all of them are costly to move. A switch in distributors means employees must be disrupted. Dedicated personnel may be reassigned, if there is other work for them, but their relationships with you become worthless. Facilities may be retrofitted, if they are still needed, but only with additional effort. Learning about you must be discarded. The supplier could offer training programs to your replacement, but doing so does not recoup the training expenses and efforts already invested in you. The supplier also could serve your competitors from a distant location, but that would incur extra costs. Worst of all for the supplier, it will be forced to explain to customers why its downstream representation has changed.

Such idiosyncratic investments are known as **credible commitments**, **pledges**, or **relationship-specific investments**. When manufacturers invest in you, your confidence in their commitment should soar, because they are erecting barriers to their *own* exit from their relationship with you.

Now take the perspective of the other side of the relationship: you are the supplier, gauging how committed the distributor is to its relationship with you. You likely discount pledges of commitment from partners who previously have had acrimonious relationships with you. You instead believe in the commitment of a distributor that gives you some degree of selectivity in your product category. At the limit, you will be inspired by the apparent commitment of a distributor that gives you category exclusivity (i.e., in your category, the distributor carries only your brand). And you will believe in the commitment of a distributor that invests in you in an idiosyncratic manner, such as one that:

- Dedicates people and facilities to your line.

- Invests in upgrading and training the personnel serving your line.

- Seeks to learn about you and build relations with your people.

- Trains its customers in the use of your line.

- Attempts to ally its name and yours in customers' minds.

- Invests in a reporting system that is particularly compatible with yours (especially if yours is proprietary).

- Locates its facilities near you and far from your competitors.

As these parallel signals of commitment reveal, suppliers and distributors, upstream and downstream, look for similar things from their partners. A partner that makes idiosyncratic investments, offers greater selectivity, and is not stained by the lingering sense of conflict is one that is committed, which likely causes you to believe in the future of your relationship and commit yourself as well.

How Downstream Channel Members Commit

An exhibition of commitment inspires commitment. But other options are available for encouraging downstream channel members to commit to a supplier. At a fundamental level, a distributor enters relationships if it believes the payoffs will justify the costs. Therefore, it expects results that it cannot get through a more conventional, less committed relationship.

To achieve these results, the distributor dedicates resources to the supplier, including dedicated personnel, joint marketing, and so forth. These investments represent the distributor's efforts to expand the pie; that is, to generate exceptional results for the entire marketing channel.[19] If these investments are well considered, if the supplier works with the distributor, and if the distributor collects an equitable share of the pie, the distributor is motivated to invest more in the future. Over time, the accumulated investments a distributor has made become a motive to commit. The distributor works to keep its relationship going to protect its accrued investments.

In addition, two-way communication, involving the free exchange of information (even, or perhaps especially, sensitive details), close participation in the supplier's marketing efforts, allowing suppliers to see its weaknesses and strengths, and giving advice to the supplier can enhance commitment. Of course, no distributor will undertake these actions if the supplier expresses unwillingness. Two-way communication is a two-way street.

How Upstream Channel Members Commit

So what actions do suppliers take that commit them to their downstream channel member? Before making investments, many rigorously verify the downstream channel member's ability and motivation.[20] Once they have identified viable distributors, they can make idiosyncratic investments to expand the channel pie, such as training, mingling their brand image with the distributor's image, and so forth. Such investments both grow the pie and strengthen the relationship.

Two-way communication again plays a substantial role,[21] because it enables the manufacturer to look over the wall and see the market that the distributor serves. This transparency is somewhat dangerous for the distributor, because the supplier can use that information to exploit or compete against the downstream channel member.

Finally, it is worth highlighting that firms can create a close, committed relationship without creating a successful channel. The simple fact that two firms work together in a closely coordinated way does not ensure their success or the success of the channel. Some close, committed firms merely reinforce each other's dedication to a poor strategy.

BUILDING CHANNEL TRUST

Another element is essential to strong relationships: trust. To some extent, trust can be created by making relationship-specific investments and communicating. But trust also is far more complex. It is a function of daily interactions, many of which are beyond top management's control. We therefore move next to the question of how to use the **concept of trust** to build stronger channel relationships.

Trust, though easy to recognize, is difficult to define.[22] Trust in a channel member is usefully conceptualized as confidence that the other party is **honest** (stands by its word, fulfills obligations, is sincere), together with assessments of the other party as **benevolent**, implying confidence that the other party is genuinely interested in one's welfare and interests, such that it will seek mutual gains rather than manipulate all the gains for itself. Overwhelming field evidence shows that in channel relationships, honesty and benevolence go together; where one is missing, so is the other. To trust a channel member is to believe in its integrity and concern for mutual well-being. To distrust is to fear deception and exploitation.

A strong relationship requires mutual commitment, and commitment cannot occur without trust. Such behavior is rational. It obviously would be a mistake to invest resources, sacrifice opportunities, and build a future with a party bent on exploitation and deception. A reasonable level of trust is necessary for *any* channel relationship to function and for the maintenance and management of business relationships.[23] Trust assumes an even stronger role in building and sustaining channel relationships in settings marked by weak or underdeveloped legal systems, such as in China.[24] Distrust cannot characterize channel relationships for long, though; it either gets resolved, or the channel dissolves. But committed relationships exhibit higher-than-usual trust levels.

Need for Economic Satisfaction

Channel members commit with a rational expectation of financial rewards. They will not commit without the prospect of financial returns, nor will they wait indefinitely for those rewards to materialize. Economic satisfaction plays a fundamental role in building and maintaining trust, which is necessary for committed relationships.[25]

Economic satisfaction is a positive, affective (emotional) response to the economic rewards generated by a channel relationship. Economic rewards are ultimately financial. So why cast them as an emotional state, rather than as utility? Why not speak in terms of money rather than affect?

The reason is that channel members simply don't compare money directly. It is difficult to put a precise accounting valuation on many outcomes (e.g., higher market share, greater store traffic). Even were a valuation to be made, it cannot be compared directly across organizations: 100,000 euros in economic returns might thrill one channel member but disappoint another member of the same channel.

Furthermore, channel members do not react to straightforward results. They react to how the results *compare* against several baselines they consider important, such as what they had expected, what they consider possible, what they consider equitable, or what they expect to gain from their next best alternative use of resources. The more the returns exceed a channel member's "reference value," the higher its likely level of satisfaction. Once an excess in returns exists, the channel member has every reason to believe that the channel can continue to generate similarly high returns.[26] Therefore, economic *satisfaction*, rather than economic *outcomes*, increases trust.

Economic satisfaction is so important that many firms agree to make risky, **generic investments** in channel members. These investments create vulnerability, because they empower the recipient to use the invested asset in the service of competitors. Yet firms that take this risk often are rewarded with higher commitment, especially if they are industry leaders and think to combine generic and idiosyncratic assets together in a package.[27] Sidebar 4.2 offers an example from the tobacco industry.

SIDEBAR 4.2
Philip Morris Substitutes Channels for Advertising

Consider an example of generic investment.[28] Philip Morris operates in France, a country with a complex set of tobacco limitations. On the one hand, cigarette advertising is totally forbidden and has been replaced by vigorous antismoking campaigns by the Ministry of Health. On the other hand, high tobacco taxes are a major source of revenue for the country, so government regulations oblige tobacco stores to accommodate smokers with long opening hours and a complete assortment of the 350 brands available in France. The government also seeks to ensure that rural smokers have easy access, so small tobacconists have sprung up all over the country, struggling to maintain the broad assortment. Jeanne Polles, the sales and marketing director for Philip Morris in France, explains, "Tobacconist shops are cluttered, not always very clean, and yet, under the new laws, it is the only place we have left to talk to our consumers."

For this supplier, the solution was training: a free half-day seminar on the importance of merchandising to any tobacco shops that wanted to join. The training, conducted by Philip Morris sales reps, offers different information than their once-a-month sales visit. The generic training actually benefits any products sold in the shops, including Philip Morris's competitors. The focus is solely to convince tobacconists of a seemingly obvious argument: better merchandising and shelf placement boosts sales.

Philip Morris also makes no special effort to protect its generic investment from free riding, though in the process, it tries to create two idiosyncratic assets. First, the Philip Morris sales reps build good relationships with tobacconists. Second, they offer a key merchandising lesson by explaining to the tobacconists that "more people will come in if they put Marlboro in the window." This credible statement does not detract from the generic appeal of the training; it simply reflects the advantages of being a leading firm and a global brand.

Unfortunately, we've established some circular logic here. Organizations build strong channel relationships to produce outcomes and increase economic satisfaction. Economic satisfaction increases trust and therefore builds relationships. So is economic performance a cause or an effect of committed relationships?

Well, it's both. The better the channel partnership performs financially, the more satisfied the parties are (at least roughly), and the more they trust the relationship. This trust builds commitment, which helps the parties expand their pie, which increases satisfaction (unless the baseline comparison jumps higher than the results), which enhances trust, and so forth.

This description suggests a virtuous cycle. But the situation also can be difficult, in that we need good results to build a relationship, but we need a relationship to generate good results. This process has to start somewhere. The question is where. How do we build relationships without economic performance to establish trust?

Strategies for Building Channel Partners' Trust

A substantial body of evidence indicates that trust is associated with several other properties, many of which involve psychological notions of noneconomic satisfaction. Because of their positive, affective (i.e., emotional) response to psychosocial aspects of the relationship,[29] satisfied channel members find interactions with their channel partners fulfilling, gratifying, and easy. They appreciate contacts and like working with their partner, who appears concerned, respectful, and willing to exchange ideas (a foundation for two-way communication).

Role of Noneconomic Factors

Many noneconomic drivers of trust appear purely interpersonal, but they also apply to the interorganizational level, such that they get reproduced over and over, through daily interactions among people working for channel organizations. In some short-sighted channels, these positive sentiments get dismissed as "nice but not necessary," or perhaps even irrelevant or insufficiently "business-like." Yet study after study demonstrates that noneconomic satisfaction is tightly bound to trust, which is critical for building financially desirable relationships.

What produces noneconomic satisfaction? Two drivers stand out due to their absence, namely the **absence of dysfunctional conflict**, or lingering, unresolved, intense disputes over major issues, and the **absence of coercion** by the other side. A party that perceives pressure, punishment, threats, and retribution from its partner experiences a rapid decline of positive sentiment, even if the relationship moves in a direction the channel member prefers. In contrast, the liberal use of noncoercive influence strategies, such as exchanging information, offering assistance, and making requests, effectively increases noneconomic satisfaction. These methods help resolve conflict without blunt intrusiveness. By trying to influence partners in a noncoercive way, organizations create the impression of being accommodating, responsive problem solvers.

Noneconomic satisfaction also is bound up with perceptions of fairness, on two fronts:[30] **procedural fairness**, or the sense of being treated equitably on a day-to-day basis, regardless of the rewards derived from the relationship, and **distributive fairness**, or gaining equitable rewards from the relationship, regardless of daily interaction patterns. Distributive and procedural equity reinforce noneconomic satisfaction.

Many organizations accordingly seek to build on what they already have. If parties have prior social and economic ties, they possess the invaluable asset of **social capital**, which they seek to leverage by developing their ties further. In foreign markets, for example, firms with an existing marketing arrangement with a distributor might add new products to the channel, even if that channel is not ideal for the product otherwise. As the old saying goes, familiarity breeds trust. For most firms, doing business with firms they know is the safest bet, and if they need to extend their networks, they do business with firms known to the firms they know (i.e., referrals).[31] Personal relationships and reputations in channel organizations help intensify existing relationships, increasing the social capital already embedded in them.[32]

Of course, organizations cannot always work with organizations they already know, and social capital is not necessarily related to firm size or profitability. Sometimes the best partner is a smaller account that is critical to the firm's future (e.g., because it is an innovator that influences other firms). Thus, firms often adopt elaborate **qualifying** strategies to learn about potential partner firms before doing business with them. For example, to build new forms of trust, it can be useful to identify and select new partners with similar goals. **Goal congruence** effectively dampens conflict and can lead to rapid relationship building.

In addition to goal congruence, the qualifying process for retailers seeking garment manufacturers, for example, might include assessments of their actual garment quality, manufacturing capacity, price competitiveness, general business philosophy, reputation with other apparel companies and retailers, and reputation for garment quality and on-time delivery. To conduct this sort of investigation, the retailer needs the cooperation of resellers, which is not easy to achieve. As a signal, though, resellers that cooperate in the qualification phase likely are already inclined to work with the prospective supplier. Therefore, qualification tactics screen which channel members are most willing and able to partner in a trustworthy manner, leading to relationships that tend to be unusually flexible, especially in the face of uncertainty.[33]

Yet we still find firms that engage in virtually no screening, content to trust their impressions or assurances. In one notable example, a channel manager of a motorcycle manufacturer was confident in his judgment, based on his excellent track record in picking good distributors. He used his instincts to award exclusive distribution rights for Costa Rica to a seemingly impressive firm that promised a large initial order. But the partner never delivered the promised order. After some months, the manufacturer investigated, only to learn that the owner of his exclusive distributor had a brother who was also a distributor—representing a directly competing line of motorcycles![34]

Some people simply are trusting—it is part of their personality (whereas others are prone to cynicism and unlikely to trust in any circumstances). This personality trait also appears among organizations, as part of their corporate **culture**. These companies actively seek to cultivate a reputation for being trustworthy (while others seek to disguise their culture of exploitation and dishonesty). To some extent, then, an organization's trustworthiness is a part of its culture.[35]

Finally, some environments are conducive to building trust. Trust increases in generous, or munificent, environments that offer resources, growth, and ample opportunity. These environments provide every incentive to work together, with rewards for everyone. Trust instead declines in volatile, complex, unpredictable environments. These risky, treacherous, and difficult environments require constant monitoring and fast adaptation. Such conditions strain any relationship and create opportunities for both misunderstanding and disputes.

Decision-Making Processes

The decision making that takes place within a marketing channel is closely structured. Perhaps the most important element of that structure is how much decision making gets centralized within the upper reaches of an organization's hierarchy, whether upstream or downstream. Whatever its source, **centralization** hurts trust.[36] Concentrating decision power in the upper echelons of one organization (rather than delegating decision making to the field, across organizations) undermines participation, cooperation, and daily interactions that promote trust. Yet centralization also offers a way for an organization to marshal its own resources to get things done. That is, we cannot blindly condemn centralized decision making, but we do recognize the need to acknowledge its costs in terms of building trust.

The channel decision-making structure also consists of **formalization**, or the degree to which decision making relies on rules and explicit procedures. Formalization tends to hinder trust, because a mechanistic approach to interactions robs the players of their autonomy. Formalization also might signal that one party mistrusts the other, inviting reciprocal mistrust. However, some evidence suggests that it is the *nature* of the formalization that really matters. That is, formalization can enhance positive attitudes and trust if it helps clarify how to perform tasks and who is responsible for them.[37] Formalization that clarifies roles thus could be helpful, rather than constraining, such that when more channel members agree about who is responsible for what (i.e., domain consensus), their level of trust rises.

In this context, we also note that the more channel members communicate, the more they cooperate on a daily basis. The more they cooperate, the more they come to trust one another. working together on issues with mutual relevance, such as market decision making and planning, builds a basis for trust. But here again, we achieve a circular logic: working together is both a cause (immediately) and an effect (later) of trust. This circularity, by which actions that enhance trust and commitment create further trust and commitment, helps explain why strong channel partnerships take time to build—especially when the channels are marked by distrust from the start.

Overcoming Channel Distrust

Imagine you manage a downstream channel member and want to build a strong relationship with one of your suppliers, but the level of overall trust in the channel is low. What should you do first? Increase communication? Seek greater cooperation? Reduce conflict? Make conflict more functional? Align your organizations' goals? Reduce your efforts to influence the other party through coercion and substitute reasoned arguments and greater accommodation instead? Pay more attention to issues of fairness?

Well, yes. But here is the paradox: even as you, the top manager, dedicate yourself to building trust, neither your employees nor the employees of your counterpart are inclined to implement your plans. Why? *Because they don't trust one another.* Even if you can induce your own employees to make the effort, your channel counterpart may block implementation or ignore your best efforts.

All top management can do is attempt to create a structure that is conducive to building trust and hope that employees will adjust their everyday behavior accordingly. For example, organizations might balance each other's dependence by granting selectivity and making idiosyncratic investments. In addition, they can eschew centralized decision making and use their influence over their own personnel to elicit the desired behaviors, hoping for reciprocity.

Ultimately, though, the structures and policies that are instituted to implement trust only create a foundation for it. From that foundation, daily interactions among people and accumulated experience can transform the structural opportunity into an operational reality. The bad news is that it is a slow, expensive, uncertain process. The good news is that trust encourages behaviors that reinforce trust. And if you can achieve it, a marketing channel with high levels of trust is nearly impossible to imitate.

Preventing Perceptions of Unfairness

Relationships can be easily damaged by unresolved perceptions of unfairness.[38] Unfairness not only directly undermines channel partners' trust and commitment but also aggravates the negative effects of any unresolved conflict or perceived opportunism. Contracts are not the answer; they can enhance the negative effects of unfairness on cooperative behaviors and performance. Instead, channel members need to recognize what causes their partners to perceive unfair treatment. For example, many automobile dealers depend on manufacturers with strong brand names and invest heavily in these brands. Those investments would be difficult to salvage or reassign, so the dealership has high switching costs. The manufacturer instead has multiple candidates that want to become dealerships and thus is less dependent on any one of them. Accordingly, the automotive industry is filled with examples of dealers that accuse their manufacturer partners of exploitation.

To avoid such accusations and the relationship deterioration that comes with them, the manufacturer needs to ensure that it exhibits **distributive fairness**, such that it determines the profits it shares with dealers by considering more than absolute rewards. Both parties need to compare the benefits they derive from the relationship against four baselines:

- Their own inputs, or what they put into the relationship.

- The benefits derived by comparable dealers.

- The benefits available from the next best alternative (e.g., for dealers, selling another make of car or investing capital elsewhere).

- The other party's inputs, or what it puts into the relationship.

Low absolute rewards shared with the dealer may seem fair if:

- The dealer invests little.

- Other dealers gain little.

- The dealer has no better use for its resources.

- The manufacturer invests heavily in the relationship.

Conversely, even very high absolute rewards may seem unfair or inequitable to dealers if:

- The dealer invests heavily.

- Other dealers are very profitable.

- Other opportunities are appealing.

- The manufacturer invests little.

As we have noted, another facet of fairness is **procedural justice**, which depends on how the stronger party treats the weaker party on a day-to-day basis (i.e., normal operating procedures). This issue is separate from the fairness of rewards. For example, auto dealers consider their supplier fairer if the manufacturer communicates both ways (listens as well as talks), appears impartial, and remains open to argument and debate. In this case, the manufacturer's personnel are critical, because procedural justice perceptions stem from how they interact with the dealer, such as whether they explain themselves clearly, act courteously, and exhibit knowledge about their channel partner's situation.

Some field evidence suggests that procedural justice actually has more impact than distributive justice on the more vulnerable party's sense that the relationship is equitable—regardless of whether the relationship achieves objective equity. A key reason is that distributive justice is not readily observable (who really knows all the factors that influence it?), whereas procedural justice is readily and regularly observable.

THE CHANNEL RELATIONSHIP LIFECYCLE

The Five Stages of a Channel Relationship

A close marketing channel relationship is like a living creature, moving through its biological lifecycle by proceeding through stages of development. Let's take a hypothetical supplier, Omega Industries, and a hypothetical distributor, Annecy Ltd. These two organizations may form a marketing channel through a series of ongoing transactions, each evaluated on its own merits, such that each side is ready to terminate or reduce its business dealings. This series of discrete transactions is a marketing channel, but it is not a close relationship. To develop into an ongoing, committed relationship, the channel would need to pass through five development stages,[39] as listed in Figure 4.3.

Stage 1: Awareness. Omega is aware that Annecy is a feasible exchange partner, but neither party has made any specific contact to explore doing business or upgrading their transactional business dealings into a stronger, more continuous relationship. (Our hypothetical example could easily go the other way, making Annecy the focal party that recognizes that Omega is a feasible supplier to upgrade to a preferred partnership level.) This stage can last a very long time, with no real progress, and it may simply dissipate if either firm decides its counterpart is not a good partnership candidate, for whatever reason. Or the arrangement could progress.

Stage 2: Exploration. Omega and Annecy investigate forging a stable relationship. They likely test each other during a trial-and-evaluation period (which can be lengthy, especially for important, risky, complex channel functions). Each side forecasts and weighs the costs and benefits of creating a close marketing channel together. When the managers of each firm describe this stage, they might comment:

> *You can't start out with a full-blown relationship. It's got to be incremental. You get closer as each side takes small steps.*
>
> *If it's going to be long-lasting, it doesn't happen overnight.*[40]

FIGURE 4.3

Relationship Phases in Marketing Channels

Relationship Phase 1: Awareness	Relationship Phase 2: Exploration	Relationship Phase 3: Expansion	Relationship Phase 4: Commitment	Relationship Phase 5: Decline and Dissolution
• One organization sees the other as a feasible exchange partner • Little interaction • Networks are critical: one player recommends another • Physical proximity matters to make parties aware of each other • Experience with transactions in other domains (other products, markets, functions) can be used to identify potential partners	• Testing, probing by both sides • Investigation of each other's nature and motives • Interdependence grows • Bargaining is intensive • Selective revealing of information is initiated and must be reciprocated • Great sensitivity to issues of power and justice • Norms begin to emerge • Role definitions become more elaborated • Key feature: each side draws inferences and tests them • This phase is easily terminated by either side	• Benefits expand for both sides • Interdependence expands • Risk taking increases • Satisfaction with results leads to greater motivation and deepening commitment • Goal congruence increases • Cooperation increases • Communication increases • Alternative partners look less attractive • Key feature: momentum must be maintained. To progress, each party must seek new areas of activity and maintain consistent efforts to create mutual payoffs	• Each party invests to build and maintain the relationship • Long time horizon • Parties may be aware of alternatives but do not court them • High expectations on both sides • High mutual dependence • High trust • Partners resolve conflict and adapt to each other and to their changing environment • Shared values and/or contractual mechanisms (e.g., shared risk) Reinforce mutual dependence • Key features: loyalty, adaptability, continuity, and high mutual dependence set these relationships apart	• Tends to be sparked by one side • Mounting dissatisfaction leads one side to hold back investment • Lack of investment provokes the other side to reciprocate • Dissolution may be abrupt but is usually gradual • Key feature: it takes two to build but only one to undermine. Decline often sets in without the two parties' realization

But if the players both achieve promising calculations, they engage in communication and negotiation. Norms (i.e., expected patterns of behavior) begin to form, as do mutual trust and joint satisfaction. In this delicate stage, the relationship is just emerging from its cocoon. The behaviors that each party adopts in this early stage have substantial impacts on the future survival of the relationship. In particular, each side makes inferences about the other, though without much of a basis of prior knowledge. Intangible perceptions (e.g., goal congruence) play a major role, informed by early interactions and outcomes. Such relationships can accelerate sharply if the two sides make idiosyncratic investments.[41] In addition, each partner's use of its power determines whether both sides want to continue to evolve, and the expectations developed during this exploration phase determine whether a partnership ultimately is achievable.

Stage 3: Expansion. In its adolescence, the relationship starts to grow rapidly. Each side derives greater benefits, develops greater motivation, and elaborates on the relationship. If management can ensure that each side perceives the benefits are being shared equitably, trust spirals upward, and interdependence increases. In this exciting stage, morale is high, leading Annecy and Omega to cooperate and perceive that they are pursuing common goals. Interaction becomes even greater than is strictly necessary, in part because each side's personnel likes the communication, such that they might acknowledge:

> *Over time, you build a history of situations, compromises, and solutions. You learn the unwritten rules and how they want to play the game, which makes it increasingly easier to do business.*[42]

Managers on both sides should use this moment to deepen their interdependence, setting the stage for commitment to stabilize.

Stage 4: Commitment. The relationship is easily recognizable and stable—fully grown, in a sense. It has developed a substantial history, marked by investments, interdependence, and strong norms. The intangible factors (e.g., perceived goal congruence) are less important, simply because the partnership can rely instead on its rich infrastructure. Thus both Annecy and Omega count on the relationship and invest heavily to maintain the strong partnership they have achieved. Neither side is very open to overtures by other firms; they prefer doing business with each other and may say:

> *We are constantly changing things to try to improve the way we do business together. We will experiment with new ideas, test new processes, try something different. Costs are incurred on both sides but we are willing to pay them. We have learned a lot from them. They have made us a better . . . company because they are demanding, innovative, and willing to try things.*[43]

Yet management also must be attentive to maintaining the relationship, lest it slip into decline and dissolution. Even in the strongest relationship, strains occur.

Stage 5: Decline to dissolution. When the relationship starts to die, Omega and Annecy cease to have a close partnership. They may resume their old transactional links, though they are more likely to cease doing business at all. Dissolutions are usually accompanied by acrimony, after having been initiated by one side that has grown dissatisfied with the arrangement. This side begins to withdraw and behave in a manner inconsistent with commitment. The annoyed other side reciprocates with neglectful, damaging, or destructive behavior. Decline rapidly takes a momentum of its own.

Decline and dissolution also can happen when one party takes the relationship for granted and fails to work to keep it going. Alternatively, one party might sabotage the relationship, to free itself to move on to other opportunities. But decline can be like a cancer, a lingering process that is unapparent to the parties until it is too far advanced to be cured.

Managing the Stages

One implication of the notion of these five stages of development is that relationships are difficult to build quickly and from the ground up. Development takes time, particularly if the targeted partners do not currently do business together. Every existing channel member is a potential asset in this respect, because extant business links, even minor ones, help the awareness and exploration phases proceed much faster and can upgrade the relationship more swiftly and surely.

But a caveat also is in order. Despite the appeal of the stages-of-development idea as a way to think about creating a relationship and keeping it going, relationship development rarely is as linear, orderly, and sequential as the five stages imply.[44] On a daily basis, relationships constitute a series of episodes or critical incidents that help the players define their common purpose, set boundaries on their relationship, create value (and claim their share of it), and evaluate their returns from the relationship. Through their repeated interactions, firms may develop sufficient critical incidents to move their relationship from a series of transactions to a real partnership, and in retrospect, managers might even remember their experiences as corresponding to stages, though they recognize those stages only after considerable development has occurred.

At the time of their development, though, relationships often do not progress in an orderly way. Thus, it is difficult to say with confidence what stage a relationship is in for much of its history. However, the good news is that if a relationship seems to be regressing (e.g., moving from expansion to exploration), there is no real cause for alarm. In retrospect, the regression could be just a blip, and it does not mean the relationship is doomed to deteriorate.[45]

We thus might consider an alternative perception on categorizing relationships into phases, one that describes the state of a relationship at a specific point in time, by capturing **relationship velocity**, or the rate and direction of change in commitment. Relationship velocity offers a stronger predictor of performance than relationship level, due to people's propensity to use trend extrapolation as a decision heuristic.[46] For example, as shown in Figure 4.4, relationships may display the same level of commitment at two points in a relationship lifecycle (dotted line), one with positive and one with negative velocity. Accounting only for their level, a channel member might predict that its customers will make similar choices at both points. Instead, and more accurately, by accounting for relationship velocity, it can include additional, behavior-relevant information. Its customers likely will make their decisions on the basis of their perceptions of the direction and rate of change in the relationship. Managers who know the velocity or trend of their relationships can better predict channel members' decisions.

FIGURE 4.4

Role of Relationship Velocity Versus Level of Commitment

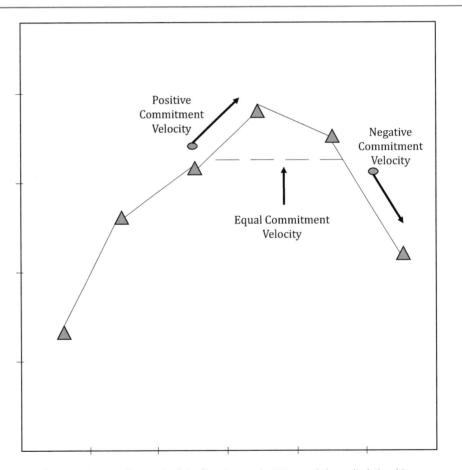

Note: Means for commitment reflect each of the first six years in 433 tested channel relationships.

Adapted from Palmatier, Robert W., Rajiv P. Dant, Dhruv Grewal, and Mark B. Houston (2013), "Relationship velocity: Toward a theory of relationship dynamics," *Journal of Marketing*, 77 (January), 136–153.

Managing Troubled Relationships

Relationships require maintenance, though they also can wear out, even if maintained properly. In a common scenario, one partner might begin to suspect that the other partner is taking advantage of the spirit of their understanding and failing to live up to its promises, actual or implied. This suspicion can poison even effectively functioning relationships, creating a self-fulfilling prophecy in which the suspicious party angrily withholds its effort and prompts the suspected party to reciprocate. The relationship then spirals downward, as performance declines.

Some kinds of relationships can better withstand the pressures of suspicion, though. Research indicates that relationships bound by mutual idiosyncratic investments continue to perform even as suspicion increases.[47] Relationships with a foundation of congruent goals also continue to perform. In this case, the parties take their congruent goals for granted and forget about them when all is well, then rediscover this relationship property and use it to enhance their joint results when they face the pressure of mounting suspicion. In contrast, dyads that rely on interpersonal trust between a key person on each side likely suffer performance decrements with greater suspicion, because the two "custodians" come under scrutiny. Other players (accountants, sales managers, finance managers) question their relationship and intervene, offsetting the beneficial effects of the trust between these key individuals.

As in this case, some of the best, most trusting relationships hold within them the seeds of their own decline.[48] Trust induces hidden costs, because at very high levels, people may not ask enough probing or difficult questions. If relationships lack enough constructive conflict, settle on agreements too easily, or become too homogeneous, they dampen creativity. Worst of all, trusted parties may exploit their partners, using their accumulated confidence to ensure that the trustor never sees what is going on.[49]

Relationship Portfolios

So even trusting relationships can fail, and relational-based partnerships may not be worth their accounting and opportunity costs. Faced with both positive and negative assessments of close relationships, it should come as no surprise that most firms maintain a broad portfolio of channel partners, representing a wide spectrum of relationship strength levels. Ultimately, manufacturers need a portfolio of downstream relationships to cover the market and meet multiple service output demands. Downstream channel members need a portfolio of suppliers and brands to cover the assorted needs of their customers and prospects. All firms need some strong relationships with channel partners to gather information and calibrate strategy and tactics, but they can function efficiently and effectively in more conventional business interactions too.[50] Firms even might gain some unique benefits from weak ties. For example, when buying complex, information-intensive, high-risk products (e.g., IT systems), customers might prefer resellers with strong ties to IT manufacturers. Yet they also appreciate a reseller that has weak ties with multiple IT makers, because they can scan varied sources of supply to get innovative ideas and create new possibilities, without committing to any one supplier.[51]

Relationship Quality

Researchers have found it useful to refer to the notion of *relationship quality* to encompass a range of variables that reflect the overall status of a relationship. In most cases, relationship quality entails a combination of commitment, trust, and satisfaction, such that higher levels of these three variables indicate better relationship quality.[52] An argument also can be made to include a broader set of variables, such as communication or the level of cooperation in the relationship, to provide a clearer sense of overall relationship quality.[53] The increased presence and level of certain variables—such as commitment, satisfaction, and trust—indicates that a relationship is on a strong footing. Other factors instead structurally bind the relationship,[54] including dependence, termination costs, and relationship-specific investments. Finally, there are the factors that threaten relationships and even can lead to their dissolution, such as unfairness, conflict, and goal incongruence.[55]

MULTI-CHANNEL VERSUS OMNI-CHANNEL RELATIONSHIPS

As we outlined in Chapter 1, an omni-channel approach requires deep, seamless integration across multiple channels. In a multi-channel setup, the channels instead tend to act as separate entities, each seeking to maximize its own utility, with minimal regard and awareness for others. Demands for seamless integration instead require the parties to commit at a deeper level, which may include relationship-specific investments. Accordingly, interdependence often is greater in an omni-channel context, due to this need for greater coordination to achieve a truly synergistic experience and operations across channels. As such, we expect that in an omni-channel context, interdependence and commitment are greater than they would be in a multi-channel context. In Figure 4.5, we compare some aspects of relationships in these two contexts.

Companies can design their multi-channel organizations in several ways. For example, they might serve different customer segments through different channels, or they could serve all segments through multiple channels but compartmentalize the functions performed by each channel. These design considerations in turn determine the relationships that arise within each channel. Segment differentiation tends to reduce horizontal conflict within the channel but also reduces cooperation among the parties; differentially allocated tasks instead reduce vertical conflict and improve cooperation.[56] Segment differentiation has a canceling-out effect, such that

Relationship Facet	Omni-Channel	Multi-Channel
Integration	Seamless	Siloed
Commitment	Deep	More Perfunctory
Relationship-Specific Investments	Higher	Variable
Interdependence	Maximum	Variable

FIGURE 4.5

Relationships in Omni-Channels Versus Multi-Channels

the positive effects of reduced horizontal conflict get canceled out by the creation of siloes, whereas task differentiation generally boosts sales. In an omni-channel setup, which demands seamless approaches, an improper design can lead to not just a breakdown of the consumer experience but also heightened conflict among the channel partners. Thus it is essential that the parties, which must synchronize their operations to provide a seamless omni-channel experience, have trust in and commitment to the process and each other. They also need to perceive the design as clearly transparent and fair to all parties. The example below illustrates the challenges of moving from a multi-channel to an omni-channel setup.

EXAMPLE: DELIVERY HERO (GERMANY/GLOBAL)

Delivery Hero is a German-based company that refers to itself as the leading global online food ordering and delivery firm. It operates in more than 40 countries and partners with more than 150,000 restaurants worldwide.[57] The main way customers order food from restaurants is by calling them directly. Smaller restaurants thus have to take individual orders and process payments, as well as maintain a delivery force that, rather inefficiently, delivers small orders to individual households. They thus can only access restricted delivery zones; it would be inefficient to deliver a small order to someone living many miles away and then drive back. As an appealing alternative, customers can order through Delivery Hero's online portal, which contains a wealth of information, such as restaurant reviews and details about specialty restaurants' (e.g., vegan, ethnic) unique offerings. Restaurants that partner with Delivery Hero thus gain operational efficiency, as well as access to a much wider base of customers, which generally improves their profitability. In these partnerships, Delivery Hero promises to share detailed data with its restaurant partners, which restaurants can use to develop new menu items, according to what is selling well in other locations, or identify sources of customer disaffection and which promotions have been most effective.[58] The company's success has not gone unnoticed. Amazon and Uber are seeking to enter this lucrative sector of the market.[59]

Let's dissect this example from the perspective of an individual restaurant. To partner with Delivery Hero, the restaurant needs to trust that Delivery Hero agents will arrive, collect the food on time, and deliver it accurately to the customer. Delivery Hero collects payments from customers who order through Delivery Hero's own portal, so the restaurant also needs to trust that the service provider will offer timely, accurate payment reimbursement. But does this collaborative service represent a short-term multi-channel experiment, or do the partners expect a long-term partnership where there will be a seamless experience for the customer? If they enter into a partnership, should it represent a multi-channel or an omni-channel operation? To answer these questions, the restaurant has to consider various elements. For example, it could retain its own delivery service or outsource all deliveries to Delivery Hero (i.e., make-or-buy decision). In terms of costs, the service charges that it must pay Delivery Hero need to be added to the prices it charges customers. If it pursues a classic multi-channel design, the restaurant might charge different prices to customers who dine in, order directly from the restaurant, or order through Delivery Hero. It also might impose distinct delivery policies across channels if it worries that it cannot guarantee the same experience from Delivery Hero that it mandates when operating with its own delivery agents. If it decides to add even more channels, the restaurant might partner with Amazon or Uber to provide additional delivery options for customers.

All of these decisions must stem from the restaurant's prior experiences with and perceptions of the success it has achieved with similar cooperative arrangements. It also can consider the reputation of Delivery Hero and the level of commitment it wants to make to any individual channel partner. These factors in turn establish its trust in the system[60] and thus the form that the channel relationship takes.

The siloes in this example (e.g., different offerings in the restaurant, delivery, and external delivery channels) would need to be eliminated if the restaurant were to pursue seamless omni-channel operations. But how would that work in practice? To illustrate such an approach, we switch to another example that outlines how the retailer Van Heusen is leveraging digital technology to provide seamless customer experiences and adopting digital tools to enhance in-store operations.

EXAMPLE: VAN HEUSEN (GLOBAL)

In Van Heusen's stores in India, the "best-selling shirt brand in the world"[61] greets customers with large digital displays of information about new fashion trends and new arrivals.[62] A measurement scanner, called the style pro, allows customers to specify their precise measurements to ensure a good fit of various clothing items.[63] In addition, its style bar helps consumers solidify and voice their own style preferences, which prompt in-store personnel to offer innovative styling tips. Shoppers even can use a virtual trial mirror, to preview how various clothing items would look on them, without ever having to try them on.

Take-Aways

- A relational channel partnership exists when two or more organizations have enduring, substantial connections that cause them to function according to their perceived single, shared interest. Committed parties:
  - Desire the relationship to continue indefinitely.
  - Are willing to sacrifice to maintain and grow the relationship.
- Relationships serve both upstream and downstream needs to create enduring competitive advantages, leading to profits.
- Relationships require an expectation of continuity, which grows with:
  - Mutual communication.
  - Balanced power.
  - Higher combined stakes of both parties.
- The foundation of a strong relationship is trust, which combines confidence in the other party's honesty with a sense of its genuine interest in welfare.
- Trust flourishes in response to satisfaction with noneconomic outcomes, including the absence of coercion and dysfunctional conflict. (Functional conflict and trust coexist easily.)
- Perceptions of procedural and distributive fairness support trust, both directly and by enhancing noneconomic satisfaction.
- Economic satisfaction drives and results from relationships. As a party derives more financial rewards from the relationship, its trust increases, which strengthens the relationship, which works together more effectively, which generates more rewards and reinitiates the upward spiral of commitment.
- The move to omni-channel necessitates deeper relationships with greater trust and commitment amongst the parties.

NOTES

1 Kapner, Suzanne (2017), "To the worsening troubles at Sears, add skittish suppliers," *The Wall Street Journal*, October 31, A1, A8.
2 DiNapoli, Jessica and Richa Naidu (2017), "Without insurance, some vendors balking at stocking Sears' shelf," *Reuters*, August 24, www.reuters.com/article/us-sears-vendors-insight/without-insurance-some-vendors-balk-at-stocking-sears-shelves-idUSKCN1B50E9, date retrieved November 3, 2017.
3 Unglesbee, Ben, "Sears reportedly losing suppliers as vendor insurance rises," *Retail Dive*, www.retaildive.com/news/sears-reportedly-losing-suppliers-as-vendor-insurance-rises/503770, date retrieved November 3, 2017.

4   Frazier, Gary L. (1999), "Organizing and managing channels of distribution," *Journal of the Academy of Marketing Science*, 2 (2) (Spring), 226–240.

5   Hotopf, Max (2004), "The beefs of channel managers," *Routes to Market* (Spring), 3–4.

6   Hotopf, Max (2004), "Making a multi-channel strategy work," *Routes to Market* (Autumn), 7–8.

7   Mittendorf, Brian, Jiwong Shin, and Dae-Hee Yoon (2013), "Manufacturing marketing initiatives and retailer information sharing," *Quantitative Marketing & Economics*, 11, 263–287.

8   Frazier, Gary L., Elliot Maltz, Kersi Antia, and Aric Rindfleisch (2009), "Distributor sharing of strategic information with their suppliers," *Journal of Marketing*, 73 (July), 31–43.

9   Fein, Adam J. and Sandy D. Jap (1999), "Manage consolidation in the distribution channel," *Sloan Management Review*, 41 (Fall), 61–72.

10 Kumar, Nirmalya (1996), "The power of trust in manufacturer–retailer relationships," *Harvard Business Review*, 60 (November–December), 92–106.

11 Kumar, Nirmalya (2000), "The power of trust in manufacturer–retailer relationships," in *Harvard Business Review on Managing the Value Chain*, Boston, MA: Harvard Business School Press, 91–126.

12 Nassaeur, Sarah and Sharon Terlep (2016), "The $10 billion tug-of-war between Wal-Mart and P&G," *The Wall Street Journal*, June 15, A1.

13 Kim, Keysuk (1999), "On determinants of joint action in industrial distributor–supplier relationships: Beyond economic efficiency," *International Journal of Research in Marketing*, 16 (September), 217–236.

14 Heide, Jan B. and Anne S. Miner (1992), "The shadow of the future: Effects of anticipated interaction and frequency of contact on buyer–seller cooperation," *Academy of Management Journal*, 35 (June), 265–291.

15 Weiss, Allen M., Erin Anderson, and Deborah J. MacInnis (1999), "Reputation management as a motive for sales structure decisions," *Journal of Marketing*, 63 (October), 74–89.

16 Anderson, Erin and Barton Weitz (1989), "Determinants of continuity in conventional channel dyads," *Marketing Science*, 8 (Fall), 310–323.

17 Mohr, Jakki and John R. Nevin (1990), "Communication strategies in marketing channels: A theoretical perspective," *Journal of Marketing*, 54 (October), 36–51.

18 Much of this section draws on Anderson, Erin and Barton Weitz (1992), "The use of pledges to build and sustain commitment in distribution channels," *Journal of Marketing Research*, 24 (February), 18–34.

19 Jap, Sandy D. (1999), "'Pie-expansion' efforts: Collaboration processes in buyer–supplier relationships," *Journal of Marketing Research*, 36 (November), 461–475.

20 Stump, Rodney L. and Jan B. Heide (1996), "Controlling supplier opportunism in industrial relations," *Journal of Marketing Research*, 33 (November), 431–441.

21 Palmatier, Robert W., Rajiv P. Dant, Dhruv Grewal, and Kenneth R. Evans (2006), "Factors influencing the effectiveness of relationship marketing: A meta-analysis," *Journal of Marketing*, 70 (October), 136–153.

22 Geyskens, Inge, Jan-Benedict E.M. Steenkamp, and Nirmalya Kumar (1998), "Generalizations about trust in marketing channel relationships using meta analysis," *International Journal of Research in Marketing*, 15 (1), 223–248.

23 Shahzad, Khuram, Tahir Ali, Josu Takala, Petri Helo, and Ghasem Zaefarian (2017), "The varying roles of governance mechanisms on ex-post transaction costs and relationship commitment in buyer–supplier relationships," *Industrial Marketing Management*, https://doi.org/10/1016/j.ind marman.2017.12.012.

24 Wang, Cheng Lu, Yizheng Shi, and Bradley R. Barnes (2015), "The role of satisfaction, trust and contractual obligation on long-term orientation," *Journal of Business Research*, 68, 473–479.

25 Ganesan, Shankar (1994), "Determinants of long-term orientation in buyer–seller relationships," *Journal of Marketing*, 58 (April), 1–19.

26 The concept of a "reference value" for a monetary cost or profit also appears in pricing literature, where a consumer's reference price is the price she or he expects to pay for an item; a price lower than that value has a positive impact on purchase intentions. See Kalyanaram, G. and Russell S. Winer (1995), "Empirical generalizations from reference price research," *Management Science*, 14 (3), G161–169; Winer, Russell S. (1986), "A reference price model of brand choice for frequently purchased products," *Journal of Consumer Research*, 13 (September), 250–256.

27 Galunic, Charles D. and Erin Anderson (2000), "From security to mobility: An examination of employee commitment and an emerging psychological contract," *Organization Science*, 11 (January–February), 1–20.

28 Hotopf, Max (2002), "Skilling your channel," *Routes to Market* (Autumn), 4–7.

29 Geyskens, Inge, Jan-Benedict E.M. Steenkamp, and Nirmalya Kumar (1999), "A meta-analysis of satisfaction in marketing channel relationships," *Journal of Marketing Research*, 36 (May), 223–238.

30 Kumar, Nirmalya, Lisa K. Scheer, and Jan-Benedict E.M. Steenkamp (1995), "The effects of supplier fairness on vulnerable resellers," *Journal of Marketing Research*, 32 (February), 54–65.

31 Gulati, Ranjay (1998), "Alliances and networks," *Strategic Management Journal*, 19 (1), 293–317.

32 Weitz, Barton A. and Sandy D. Jap (1995), "Relationship marketing and distribution channels," *Journal of the Academy of Marketing Science*, 23 (4), 305–320.

33 Wathne, Kenneth H. and Jan B. Heide (2004), "Relationship governance in a supply chain network," *Journal of Marketing*, 68 (1), 73–89.

34 Thomas, Andrew R. and Timothy J. Wilkonson (2005), "It's the distribution, stupid!" *Business Horizons*, 48 (1), 125–134.

35 Dyer, Jeffery H. and Harbir Singh (1998), "The relational view: Cooperative strategy and sources of interorganizational competitive advantage," *Academy of Management Review*, 23 (4), 660–679.

36 Frazier (1999), op. cit.

37 Dahlstrom, Robert and Arne Nygaard (1999), "An empirical investigation of ex post transaction costs in franchised distribution channels," *Journal of Marketing Research*, 36 (May), 160–170.

38 Samaha, Stephen A., Robert W. Palmatier, and Rajiv P. Dant (2011), "Poisoning relationships: Perceived unfairness in channels of distribution," *Journal of Marketing*, 75 (3), 99–117.

39 Dwyer, F. Robert, Paul H. Schurr, and Sejo Oh (1987), "Developing buyer–seller relationships," *Journal of Marketing*, 51 (April), 11–27.

40 Larson, Andrea (1992), "Network dyads in entrepreneurial settings: A study of the governance of exchange relationships," *Administrative Science Quarterly*, 37 (1) (March), 76–104.

41 Jap, Sandy and Shankar Ganesan (2000), "Control mechanisms and the relationship lifecycle: Implications for safeguarding specific investments and developing commitment," *Journal of Marketing Research*, 37 (May), 227–245.

42 Larson (1992), op. cit.

43 Larson (1992), op. cit.

44 Anderson, James C. (1995), "Relationships in business markets: Exchange episodes, value creation, and their empirical assessment," *Journal of the Academy of Marketing Science*, 23 (4), 346–350.

45 Narayandas, Das and V. Kasturi Rangan (2004), "Building and sustaining buyer–seller relationships in mature industrial markets," *Journal of Marketing*, 68 (July), 63–77.

46 Palmatier, Robert W., Rajiv P. Dant, Dhruv Grewal, and Mark B. Houston (2013), "Relationship velocity: Toward a theory of relationship dynamics," *Journal of Marketing*, 77 (January), 13–30.

47 Jap, Sandy and Erin Anderson (2004), "Safeguarding interorganizational performance and continuity under *ex post* opportunism," *Management Science*, 49 (12), 1684–1701.

48 Anderson, Erin and Sandy D. Jap (2005), "The dark side of close relationships," *Sloan Management Review*, 46 (3), 75–82.

49 Selnes, Fred and James Sallis (2003), "Promoting relationship learning," *Journal of Marketing*, 67 (July), 80.

50 Cannon, Joseph P. and William D. Perreault (1999), "Buyer–seller relationships in business markets," *Journal of Marketing Research*, 36 (November), 439–460.

51 Wuyts, Stefan, Stefan Stremersch, Christophe Van Den Bulte, and Philip Hans Franses (2004), "Vertical marketing systems for complex products: A triadic perspective," *Journal of Marketing Research*, 41 (4), 479–487.

52 Athanasopoulou, Penelope (2009), "Relationship quality: A critical literature review and research agenda," *European Journal of Marketing*, 43 (5–6), 583–610.

53 Woo, Ka-Shing and Christine T. Ennew (2004), "Business-to-business relationship quality: An IMP interaction-based conceptualization and measurement," *European Journal of Marketing*, 38 (9–10), 1252–1271.

54 Kang, Bohyeon, Sejo Oh, and Eugene Sivadas (2013), "Beyond relationship quality: Examining relationship management effectiveness," *Journal of Marketing Theory & Practice*, 21 (3), 273–287.

55 Samaha, Palmatier, and Dant (2011), op. cit.

56 Furst, Andreas, Martin Leimbach, and Jana-Kristin Prigge (2017), "Organizational multichannel differentiation: An analysis of its impact on channel relationships and company sales success," *Journal of Marketing*, 81 (1), 59–82.

57 Delivery Hero, www.deliveryhero.com, date retrieved March 13, 2018.

58 Schumacher, Thomas and Dennis Swinford (2016), "How a tech unicorn creates value," *McKinsey Quarterly* (June), www.mckinsey.com/business-functions/strategy-and-corporate-finance/our-insights/how-a-tech-unicorn-creates-value, date retrieved March 13, 2018.

59 Thomasson, Emma and Nadine Schimroszik (2018), "Delivery Hero sees Amazon, Uber squeezing online food market," *Reuters*, February 14, www.reuters.com/article/us-delivery-hero-ceo/delivery-hero-sees-amazon-uber-squeezing-online-food-market-idUSKCN1FY204, date retrieved March 13, 2018.

60 Del Campo, J.D.S., I.P. Garcia Pardo, and F. Hernandez Perlines (2014), "Influence factors of trust building in cooperation agreements," *Journal of Business Research*, 67 (5), 710–714.

61 Van Heusen, https://vanheusen.com, date retrieved March 13, 2018.

62 Girish, Devika (2016), "Omnichannel retail in India: 5 brands that are doing it right," *Beaconstac*, March 22, https://blog.beaconstac.com/2016/03/omnichannel-retail-in-india-5-brands-that-are-doing-it-right, date retrieved March 13, 2018.

63 Srivastava, Aditi (2015), "Van Heusen: Transforming Indian apparel retailing," *Afaqs!*, December 25, www.afaqs.com/news/story/46692_van-Heusen-Transforming-Indian-Apparel-retailing, date retrieved March 13, 2018.

CHAPTER 5

Channel Conflict

LEARNING OBJECTIVES

After reading this chapter, you will be able to:

- Outline inherent sources of conflict in channel relationships and define its three main causes: goals, perceptions, and domains.
- Recognize the different types of conflict.
- Develop an understanding of how conflict can be measured.
- Understand the ways in which partner conflict can be resolved.
- Describe the negative effects of high conflict on channel performance but also identify circumstances in which conflict is neutral or even positive.
- Recognize why multiple channels represent the norm and describe ways to address the conflict they create.
- Explain why many suppliers like gray markets (while protesting to the contrary).

INTRODUCTION

In Chapters 3 and 4, we outlined two approaches to manage channels, namely the exercise of power and the deployment of relational mechanisms. Given the interdependence that is omnipresent in channels, though, conflict is inherent to channel relationships. **Channel conflict** arises when behavior by one channel member is in opposition to the wishes or behaviors of its channel counterparts. The channel actor seeks a goal or object that its counterpart currently controls. Accordingly, channel conflict implies that one member of a channel views its upstream or downstream partner as an **adversary** or opponent. These interdependent parties, at different levels of the same channel (upstream and downstream), contest with each other for control. Manufacturers might decide to remove their products from certain retail establishments; retailers can choose not to carry certain manufacturers' products in their stores. But these responses to conflict hurt both parties.[1]

In an omni-channel context, conflict also can be exacerbated if the firms treat each channel separately, rather than ensuring synergy. Such approaches even create new forms of conflict across channels,[2] such as when online channels cannibalize the sales of traditional in-store channels.

THE NATURE OF CHANNEL CONFLICT

Conflict per se need not be a problem in distribution channels. Rather than disuniting or antagonizing channel members, some conflict, in some forms, actually strengthens and improves the channel—as long as the channel manager deals with it effectively and appropriately.

Types of Conflict

Conflict implies incompatibility at some level. It frequently exists at such a low level, due mainly to the surrounding conditions, that channel members do not even really sense it. Such **latent conflict** is a norm in most marketing channels, in which the interests of channel members inevitably collide as the parties pursue their separate goals, strive to retain their autonomy, and compete for limited resources. If each player could ignore the others, latent conflict would disappear. But companies linked in a channel are fundamentally interdependent.[3] Every member needs all other members to meet end-users' service output demands economically.

This fundamental interdependence is taken for granted in marketing channels. Because the organizations in these channels face constant conflicts, they lack the time or capacity to deal with each one explicitly. Instead, they focus on a few latent conflicts at any one time,[4] while strategically overlooking others. Although this strategic choice enables the firms to function more efficiently on a day-to-day basis, the failure to account for latent conflict may become a problem if the partners develop new channel initiatives that transform the latent conflict and spark active opposition from channel partners.

In contrast with the latent form, **perceived conflict** arises as soon as a channel member senses opposition of any kind: of viewpoints, of perceptions, of sentiments, of interests, or of intentions. Perceived conflict is cognitive, emotionless, and mental, resulting simply from the recognition of a contentious situation. Thus even if two organizations perceive their disagreement, their individual members likely experience little emotion or frustration. They describe themselves as "businesslike" or "professional" and consider their differences "all in a day's work." This scenario also describes a normal (and often preferable) state in marketing channels, with little cause for alarm. These members might not even describe their dealings as conflict-laden, despite their opposition to each other on important issues.

When emotions enter the picture, though, the channel experiences **felt (or affective) conflict**. The reasons that this type of conflict arises can vary, but the outcomes are similar: individual players start mentioning conflict in the channel, as a result of the negative emotions they experience, including tension, anxiety, anger, frustration, and hostility. Organizational members personalize their differences, such that their descriptions of their business interactions begin to sound like interpersonal disputes (i.e., "That company is so rude! They don't even care how I feel about things"). Economic considerations fade into the background, and the antagonists impute human features and personal motives to their channel partners. If feelings of outrage and unfairness reach a breaking point, boundary spanners and their managers even might refuse economically sensible choices, harming their own organizations in their efforts to "punish" their channel counterparts.[5]

If left unmanaged, felt conflict thus can escalate quickly into **manifest conflict**. This opposition is expressed visibly through behaviors, such as blocking each other's initiatives or goal achievement and withdrawing support. In the worst cases, one side tries to sabotage the other or take revenge.

Measuring Conflict

In Figure 5.1 we provide an overview of a four-step approach to measuring conflict in channels and elaborate on the steps below.

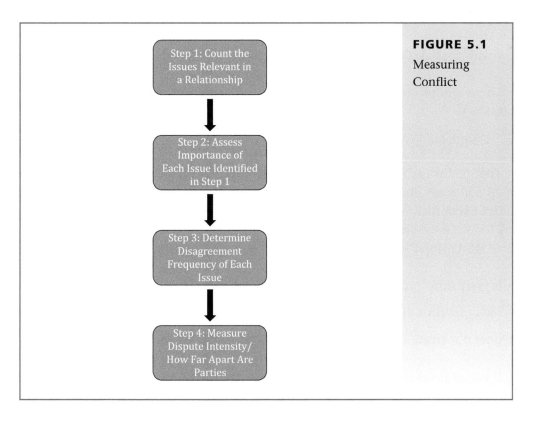

FIGURE 5.1

Measuring Conflict

The true level of conflict in a channel relationship depends on four elements. Here, we present those elements as a hypothetical assessment of how much conflict automobile dealers experience in their relationships with car manufacturers.[6]

> Step 1. **Count the issues.** Which issues are of relevance to the two parties in the channel relationship? For car dealers, there are dozens of relevant issues in their relationships with manufacturers, such as inventories (vehicles and parts), allocation and delivery of cars, dealer staff size, advertising, allowances, reimbursement for warranty work, and so forth. It does not matter whether the issues are in dispute at any particular moment; the count must include all major aspects of the channel relationship.

> Step 2. **Assess importance.** For each issue, some measure must exist to ascertain how important it is to the dealer. For example, dealers might indicate, on a 0–10 scale (very unimportant to very important), how important they consider each issue to their profitability.

> Step 3. **Determine disagreement frequency.** How often do the two parties disagree about each issue? Dealers could be asked to recall their discussions with the manufacturer about each issue during the past year and indicate, on a 0–10 scale (never to always), how frequently those discussions involved disagreement.

> Step 4. **Measure dispute intensity.** For each issue, how far apart are the two parties' positions? Using another 0–10 scale (not very intense to very intense), dealers can indicate how strongly they disagree during a typical discussion with their dealer about each issue.

These four pieces of information then combine to form an **index of manifest conflict**:

$$\text{Conflict} = \sum_{i=1}^{N} \text{Important}_i \times \text{Frequency}_i \times \text{Intensity}_i$$

That is, for each issue i, we multiply its importance, frequency, and intensity, then add the values for all N issues (for car dealers, perhaps $N = 15$), to form an index of conflict. A manufacturer then might compare these estimates across dealers to locate the site of the most serious conflict. This simple formula also offers a profound insight into channels: no real argument exists over any issue if it:

- is petty (low importance),
- rarely sparks a difference of opinion (low frequency), or
- does not create substantial distance between the two parties (low intensity).

If *any* of these elements is low, the issue is *not* a genuine source of conflict (i.e., multiplying by 0 creates a product of 0). Parties to a conflict often can become so emotional that they forget this simple rule. But if allowances are a minor issue, the dealer's and manufacturer's positions about car allowances are not far apart, or allowances seldom come up as topics of discussion, there is little need for concern—even if it might seem so during the height of a heated discussion about allowances.

This conflict formula effectively captures the overall sense of frustration in a channel relationship. Thus, relationship diagnosticians can use it to pinpoint where and why parties have come into opposition, especially when the combatants themselves are unable to identify the sources of their friction. Particularly in conflict-laden channels, the parties involved often become polarized and sense that they disagree more than they really do, because their high-running emotions cause them to double count issues, overlook points on which they agree, or exaggerate the importance, intensity, and frequency of their differences. A third party can help them locate the true sources of their disagreement, which is a first step to finding a solution.

CONSEQUENCES OF CONFLICT

Functional Conflict: Improving Channel Performance

Despite a widespread (and sometimes accurate) view of conflict as dysfunctional, such that it harms relationship coordination and performance, on some occasions, opposition actually makes a relationship better. **Functional conflict** implies that members recognize each other's contributions and understand that their success depends on others, so they can oppose each other without damaging their arrangement. As a result of their opposition, they:

1. Communicate more frequently and effectively.

2. Establish outlets for expressing their grievances.

3. Critically review their past actions.

4. Devise and implement a more equitable split of system resources.

5. Develop a more balanced distribution of power in their relationship.

6. Develop standardized ways to deal with future conflict and keep it within reasonable bounds.[7]

Overall, conflict is functional when it drives channel members to improve their performance. For example, functional conflict might increase motivation and knowledge sharing among the parties to a relationship.[8] By raising and working through their differences, they push each other to do better and break out of old habits and assumptions, as Sidebar 5.1 describes.

SIDEBAR 5.1
Functional Conflict in Plumbing and Heating Supplies

The use of cooperative (co-op) advertising money has been marked by a long history of conflict. In co-op advertising programs, suppliers share the cost of local advertising by downstream channel members when it features the supplier's products. In principle, co-op advertising is in the interests of both parties and effectively builds partnerships. In practice, it is a source of considerable conflict. Resellers accuse suppliers of exercising too many bureaucratic controls over their ads, delaying payments of co-op funds, and finding pretexts to refuse to pay at all. Suppliers accuse downstream channel members of diverting co-op money to other purposes, running poor ad campaigns, and featuring their products together with those of competitors.

In the plumbing and heating supplies industry, some channel partners thus have sought creative new approaches to joint advertising. Wholesalers create their own internal advertising staff to increase their promotion competence. Suppliers revisit their procedures to devise streamlined approval and reimbursement policies, remove hurdles to reimbursement, eliminate bureaucratic rules, and signal their willingness to trust and collaborate with channel partners to run joint campaigns.

Other suppliers copy techniques from other industries, such as building a predefined co-op allowance into their wholesale prices. This sum (e.g., $2 on a $122 faucet) gets tracked and set aside as co-op money. If the distributor runs a sufficiently large campaign by a fixed date, it collects the fund; otherwise, it reverts to the supplier. Procter & Gamble uses a similar method to sell fast-moving consumer goods. The very existence of the fund pressures distributors to advertise (to avoid "losing" their "advance") and puts pressure on the supplier to be flexible (to avoid appearing as though it has appropriated money for which it is the custodian).[9]

In principle, all channel conflict should be functional. In practice, it is not. So we must ask: *what makes conflict functional?*[10] From a downstream channel member's viewpoint, functional conflict is a natural outcome of close cooperation with the supplier. Cooperative relationships are noisy and contentious, because working together to coordinate inevitably generates disputes. But as long as channel members are committed, the resulting conflict should be tolerated, and even welcomed as normal, because it can improve performance in the short term and is unlikely to damage the level of trust in the relationship in the long term, especially if the downstream channel member has considerable influence over the supplier. An influential channel member is a **disputatious** one—willing to give and take to push channel performance.

In contrast, suppliers that prefer to find weaker channel members they can dominate might enter into relationships that appear harmonious but that never quite realize their full potential. Harmonious, peaceful channels also might arise when channel members express little opposition, mostly because of their general **indifference**. The two parties simply do not bother to disagree about anything.

There is no issue about which they have a strong opinion, that is really important to them, that they care to invest the effort to argue about. These two sides are not in agreement; they simply don't disagree—because they don't care. Consider, for example, a downstream channel member that partners with so many principals that it simply cannot pay attention to all of them. In this case, a harmonious channel signals neglect, and such neglect frequently is mutual. The relationships exist on paper (and may entail some transactions), but the parties never really engage, whether in conflict or in cooperation. Regardless of the reason for their existence, these harmonious channels need to increase their activity and communication levels to improve their performance, and such steps will, happily, increase their conflict.

Put another way, channel performance depends on communication and cooperation among channel members, which means that inevitably they will discover some points of opposition and perceive conflict. Managed properly, these emerging disagreements can be channeled into constructive conflict. Even if perceived conflict becomes felt (i.e., emotions get aroused), channel members may prod their partners to achieve better results, through functional conflict. Only when conflict escalates into substantial manifest conflict does it create tension and frustration, in which case managers must step in to keep it from damaging or ultimately destroying the channel.

Manifest Conflict: Reducing Channel Performance

If some channel friction is mundane, then we should just accept it as inevitable and dismiss it as normal, right? Not quite. High channel friction still creates costs. Substantial field research documents the outcomes of literally thousands of channel relationships in developed, mostly Western economies.[11] The distillation of that research indicates that constantly high levels of manifest conflict reduce an organization's satisfaction and damage the channel's long-term ability to function as a close partnership. These findings imply that channel partners cannot focus just on their share of the overall pie; they also need to enhance cooperation while simultaneously seeking to reduce the conflict their cooperation might induce, to increase the size of the overall pie that the parties share.[12]

Consider a focal firm in a channel that encounters higher levels of tension, frustration, or disagreement in a channel relationship. Perceived conflict will increase, as will felt (affective) conflict and manifest conflict (blocking behaviors). Because of this increased conflict, the focal firm derives less value from the channel, as well as less satisfaction from the business rewards (financial and strategic) that result from this relationship. Some decrease in satisfaction is objective: Profit indicators decline when conflict increases. But there is another element too, because in judging its satisfaction, the focal firm also includes its assessment of what it might expect to gain from alternative uses of its resources. Conflict may increase its anticipated disappointment by inflating the focal firm's belief that there are better alternatives available. Beyond these financial aspects, the focal firm's satisfaction with the psychological and social elements of its relationship declines as well.

It is tempting to disregard these "fuzzier" outcomes of conflict, because they do not translate easily into profit terms. But to the focal firm, interpersonal dissatisfaction is serious. It makes each workday less gratifying to the people involved, and it damages the solidarity of the relationship.

Unsatisfactory social relationships also diminish trust in the channel counterpart. **Trust** is a critical foundation for durable, well-coordinated relationships. A belief that the other party will act with fairness, honesty, and concern for well-being is essential to building committed relationships, in which the parties make sacrifices to build and maintain their channel. Conflict undermines this channel commitment by damaging a focal party's trust in its counterpart, in that not only does conflict directly shake the focal firm's confidence in its counterpart's benevolence and honesty, but it also reduces interpersonal satisfaction, which then delivers another blow to trust.

Finally, conflict is costly, and some costs take years to emerge fully. Therefore, channel managers need to make careful calculations to determine if the costs of conflict are worth the benefits that the conflict might induce. For example, initiatives to change the way things are done in the channel will spark conflict and costs. But the benefits of this initiative might outweigh the costs of the conflict. Conflict does not always need to be minimized; rather, it inherently needs to be managed, such that each member of the channel rationally and realistically chooses to enter into a conflict, rather than being surprised to discover that its initiatives were not worth the costs of the opposition they created.

MAJOR SOURCES OF CONFLICT IN CHANNELS

Most conflict is rooted in differences in (1) channel members' goals, (2) perceptions of reality, and (3) perceived domains, or areas in which they should be able to operate with autonomy. The last is the most complex of these three sources, because domain conflict comprises many subdimensions. For example, in the product market subdimension, we find that manufacturers today go to market through so many different routes that their channel partners are bound to compete for some of the same business. If the channels are redundant, competition over customers can quickly turn into conflict with the supplier. Other subdimensions include clashes over each party's role and sphere of influence. We therefore build up to this complex discussion and begin instead with one of the most intractable problems: clashing goals.

Sidebar 5.2 illustrates how the sunglasses manufacturer Oakley effectively used coercion when its largest retailer created a conflict of interest by vertically integrating backward into production.

SIDEBAR 5.2
Oakley Battles Its Biggest Customer

Oakley is a California-based manufacturer of high-technology, high-design, premium-priced sunglasses. Its biggest distribution channel customer is Sunglass Hut, a prominent retail chain whose specialty stores offer excellent coverage in malls, airports, and business districts. Sunglass Hut's trained salespeople counsel browsers as they shop a deep assortment (many brands and models) in a narrow category (sunglasses). The chain excels at converting lookers into buyers and finding prospects willing to pay a high price for technology, design, and innovation in a highly competitive product category.

In April 2001, Sunglass Hut was purchased by Luxottica Group, the world's largest maker of eyewear. Luxottica manufactures many of Oakley's competitors, including Ray-Ban, Armani, Bulgari, and Chanel. In a matter of months, Luxottica drastically reduced its Oakley orders. By August of the same year, Oakley was forced to issue an earnings warning that lowered its stock price. Oakley charged that Sunglass Hut engineered the sales decline by paying its floor salespeople higher commissions on Luxottica's products. Indeed, a Luxottica spokesperson admitted, "Our idea is to increase the percentage of sales that will be Luxottica brands." Oakley thus went to battle with its biggest customer, retaliating on multiple fronts:

- It contacted Oakley customers by mail and web with communications suggesting that Sunglass Hut salespeople were more interested in their commissions than in customers' best interests, so they might want to shop elsewhere.

- It launched a reward-based program to cultivate other retailers, using product exclusives, merchandise display fixtures, special point-of-sales materials, and marketing materials designed to drive traffic to these stores.

- It convinced sporting goods stores (e.g., Champs, Foot Locker), department stores (e.g., Nordstrom), and optical stores to open or enlarge their sunglasses counters, even adding "Oakley corners" within the stores. Effectively, Oakley created new retail competition for Sunglass Hut.

- It accelerated its program to open its own stores that would sell the brand's apparel, footwear, prescription glasses, and watches, along with its sunglasses.

- In a direct attack on the parent company, Oakley sued Luxottica and its multiple manufacturing and retailing subsidiaries (e.g., Ray-Ban, Lenscrafters, Sunglass Hut) for patent infringement, for making and selling selected lens colors. Oakley successfully secured a restraining order. This move was particularly interesting, because it had been common practice for distribution channels to reverse engineer their suppliers' products, then incorporate the features into their own house brands. Suppliers often tolerate such behavior as a cost of doing business, and Oakley may have done so—until Sunglass Hut reduced the benefits that made its tolerance worthwhile.

Sunglass Hut capitulated quickly. By November 2001, it had signed a new three-year agreement, restoring its status as Oakley's biggest customer, and Oakley's stock price rebounded.

But the damage to the relationship was done. Oakley settled its lawsuit, but it also stated it would continue its channel diversification, determined never again to depend so much on one channel member.

This pledge turned out to be easier said than done. In the three years following the battle, many of Oakley's new channels (e.g., Foot Locker) were badly hurt by the return of Sunglass Hut and withdrew their Oakley presence. Oakley management professed to be surprised; like many suppliers, they may have overestimated their brand's appeal and believed that coverage, once gained, would remain stable. Oakley's other businesses also have fluctuated, even as Luxottica continues to pursue its own interests. In 2003, it acquired OPSM, a prominent Australian sunglasses retailer, and promptly reduced OPSM's business with Oakley. And though Sunglass Hut's business with Oakley is strong, it also has fluctuated.

Oakley's communications to potential investors thus contain "safe harbor" disclaimers, warning of its "dependence on eyewear sales to Luxottica Group S.p.A., which, as a major competitor, could materially alter or terminate its relationship" with Oakley. Thus its "major competitor" is, at the same time, Oakley's largest distribution channel! Luxottica's position as a manufacturer that has vertically integrated forward into distribution creates a divergence of goals that suggests Oakley will always be in conflict with its largest channel member.

Competing Goals

Each channel member has a set of **goals and objectives** that differ from the goals and objectives of other channel members. This built-in difference is fundamental to all businesses, not just channels. A notable theory, called agency theory, highlights the clash between the desires of the principal (who creates work) and the agent (to whom the principal delegates the work). The inherent difference in what they want to achieve and what they value causes principals to seek ways to monitor and motivate agents. **Agency theory** underscores how competing goals create conflict in any principal–agent relationship, regardless of the personalities of the players involved or the history of their relationship. Channel members who personalize conflicts and believe that a change of partner will solve their problems are thus likely to be sorely disappointed, because their fundamental goal conflict remains.[13]

The relationship between the athletic wear manufacturer Nike and the retailer Foot Locker offers a good example of a generic and perennial form of goal conflict, in this case between suppliers and resellers. Foot Locker carries Nike products because it wants to maximize its own profits, whether by increasing unit sales, achieving higher gross margins per unit (i.e., paying Nike less while charging the customer more), decreasing inventory, reducing expenses, or receiving higher allowances from Nike. In contrast, Nike wants to maximize its own profits, so its preferences are nearly the reverse of the retailer's: it wants Foot Locker to increase unit sales, accept lower gross margins (i.e., pay it more while charging customers less), hold more inventory (to avoid stockouts and maximize selection), spend more to support the product line, and get by without allowances. The two parties' overall profit goals lead them to collide nearly every time they meet, on every objective except one, namely to raise unit sales.

Surprisingly, though, much of the tension, anxiety, and frustration in a channel results not from actual goal clashes but from the channel members' *perceptions* of goal divergence. The misperception that their goal incongruity is higher than it actually is continues to fuel conflict and leads to a remarkable practice by supposed channel partners: Salespeople and sales managers express more willingness to deceive distributors than to mislead customers or their own employers.[14]

Differing Perceptions of Reality

Distinct **perceptions of reality** induce conflict, because they imply the likelihood of divergent responses to the same situation. As a general rule, channel members are confident that they know what's going on, but when they compare their perceptions with others', the results are so different that it is difficult to believe they are members of the same channel. Perceptions differ markedly,[15] even in relation to seemingly basic questions such as:

• What are the attributes of the product/service?

• What applications does the product/service support, and for which segments?

• Who is the competition?

With divergence in such basic ideas, it is not surprising that channel members also disagree about more subjective, judgment-laden subjects, such as how readily a product or service can be sold, what added value each channel member offers, or how each side behaves. With inaccurate expectations about what other channel members are likely to do, our focal firm also will choose suboptimal strategies, which can heighten conflict further. Inaccurate expectations spark surprise and opposition when other parties "fail" to react as expected.[16]

Why are such misperceptions so common—and so serious? A major reason is **focus**. The supplier focuses on its product and its processes. The downstream channel member instead focuses on its functions and customers. These differences expose channel members to very different information and influences, such that they each start to build different segments of the overall puzzle.

Seldom do channel members cooperate enough to assemble the entire puzzle to develop a complete picture. But a lack of communication exacerbates the conflict that results from different perceptions of reality, whereas frequent, timely, and relevant communication at least can align—if not totally match up—with perceptions and expectations.[17] When a top manager for Toyota invested the time and effort to visit U.S. dealers regularly and engage in conversations about problems district managers had failed to resolve, for example, "I found out that out of ten complaints from each dealer, you could attribute about five or six to simple mis-understandings, another two or three could be solved on the spot, and only one or two needed further work."[18]

In domestic markets, channel members disagree in their views of the situation; the problem is exacerbated in international settings due to cultural differences. In the clash of cultures, differences in perception and interpretations of the channel environment are prominent and frequent.[19] Regardless of the product or service sold, channel members experience substantial friction generated by members' culturally divergent ideas of what behavior is appropriate. One solution is to generate greater sensitivity to the business culture of the channel partner. Greater cultural sensitivity demands a foundation of respect for and understanding of the other culture's language, customs, values, attitudes, and beliefs. Channel members who slight another national culture or economize on communication pay a steep price: excessive conflict, with negative impacts on channel performance.

Intrachannel Competition

From an upstream perspective, suppliers may sense conflict if their downstream partners represent their competitors—as they often do, so that they can provide a large assortment and exploit economies of scale by pooling demand for a class of products. Even though agents and resellers rely on this tactic to provide high coverage and lower prices, such **intrachannel competition** still can spark disputes, especially if the downstream agent appears insufficiently dedicated to meeting its responsibilities to the supplier.

More acrimonious disputes arise if the upstream party believes it has established an understanding to limit competition, on which its downstream partner is reneging. A California medical supply firm won almost $5 million in damages from one of its distributors when an arbitration panel found that the downstream member violated its contract by promoting a competitor's products.[20] However, a more common situation involves an "unspoken understanding" that cannot be proven but still can provoke conflict. From a downstream perspective, intrachannel competition implies that the supplier relies on various direct competitors to sell its products to the market.

EXAMPLE: CISCO (USA/GLOBAL)

Approximately 85 percent of Internet traffic flows through Cisco's systems.[21] The company maintains a complex distribution system; in addition to a direct sales model, it relies on value-added resellers and other third-party distributors. Specifically, Cisco's direct sales model focuses on its 30 largest, enterprise customers; then it partners with 60,000 distributors to sell to smaller buyers, which accounts for approximately 85 percent of its revenues.[22] Through its sophisticated, tiered partner program, Cisco provides extensive training and certifications to partners, which in turn invest their considerable resources in gaining familiarity with Cisco products across different sectors, including security, data centers, and enterprise networks. However, noting the shift from hardware-based networking to software-oriented options, Cisco also is on an acquisition spree. For example, it acquired Broadsoft to gain a foothold in the voice marketplace. Yet some partners have expressed concern that Cisco may start to compete directly with its many partners that already have invested heavily in their own voice offerings.[23]

OMNI-CHANNELS

As outlined in Chapter 1, an omni-channel strategy can be a breeding ground for conflict. Multiple channels have always been common, but at one time, companies tended to use a single, primary route to market and turn to their other routes only as secondary, downplayed, or even disguised methods, to avert channel conflict and avoid confusing customers. For example, suppliers might quietly open their own sales and distribution organizations, competing directly but not obtrusively with their own channel customers for end-users (dual distribution). But today, an explosion in the use of multiple channels has made them the norm rather than the exception.[24] Why? Heightened competition has driven many suppliers to change and expand their channels; fragmented markets make it harder to serve customers efficiently through only one channel type. In addition, whereas channels once had to remain simple, to facilitate their administration, technological advances have made it feasible to manage far more complex channel structures.

Moreover, suppliers and customers like multiple channels. For suppliers, they increase market penetration, giving the suppliers a better view of multiple markets, while also raising entry barriers to potential competitors. As their various channels compete, suppliers enjoy the benefits of this "healthy" competition. For customers, multiple channels increase the chances of finding one that meets their service output demands. Multiple channel types also make it easier for customers to pit one channel against another when they seek more services at lower prices. Thus, multiple channels even make markets: suppliers and customers can more easily find one another and fulfill their needs by using the most appropriate channel types.[25]

However, the dangers of multiple channels are similar to the dangers of intensive distribution: downstream channel members may lose motivation and withhold support (a passive response), retaliate, or exit the supplier's channel structure (active responses). Such threats are particularly intense when customers can free ride, gaining services from one channel but buying from another. By adding channel types, the supplier ironically may reduce, rather than increase, the breadth and vigor of its market representation.

Suppliers fail to anticipate this outcome because they think of their markets as distinct, well-behaved segments, in which a particular type of customer always wants to buy in one manner (e.g., convenient and cheap, with few services), while another type always prefers another manner (e.g., full support, after spending time negotiating and paying a higher price). Each segment calls for different service outputs and thus different channel types (in our examples, a discount catalog and a value-added reseller, respectively). By offering these multiple channels, suppliers seemingly can better serve multiple segments, without the various channels ever really competing head to head.

That image may hold on a spreadsheet, where buyers can be neatly categorized and served by a single type of channel. But the strategy often collapses when it moves off the page, where customers can move about rather than sticking to their assigned categories. Customers love to free ride (e.g., get advice from the value-added reseller, then order from the discount catalog), especially business-to-business customers that hire purchasing agents explicitly to find the maximum value at the lowest delivered price. Furthermore, the same customers often behave differently, depending on the *occasions* for their purchase of the same item.

However, four general types of environments usually can support multiple channels without increasing conflict to ruinous levels:[26]

- Growing markets, which offer opportunities to many players.
- Markets in which customers perceive the product category as differentiated (so channel members can distinguish their offerings).
- Markets in which buyers' consistent purchasing style involves one type of channel member (so customers are less likely to seek competing channels).
- Markets that are not dominated by buying groups.

Still, specifying the environment may not be sufficient to establish the clear presence of multi-channel conflict. That question demands more in-depth analysis.

Identifying Multi-Channel Conflict

Multiple channels do not automatically compete. Companies can design their channels in such a way that each one serves a distinct customer segment or so that different channels perform different tasks.[27] Channel members might believe they are serving the same customer, even if they are not. Coca-Cola faced strong opposition from retailers in Japan when it started installing vending machines, but through its market research, it ultimately was able to prove that consumers used vending machines for totally different occasions and obtained different value from them than they sought when purchasing from the retailers.[28]

Multiple channels can even help one another by building **primary demand** for the product category. A classic example is the combination of a store and a direct marketing operation (e.g., catalog, website). Potential customers encounter the brand in both channels and thus can purchase as they wish. Some retailers use this synergy to explore markets: when catalog sales in an area reach a certain level, they take it as a sign that it is time to open a store there. The accounting methods for these combinations are necessarily approximate, though, in that the supplier cannot know for certain how many customers might try on clothing in the store, go home to think about it, and then order from a website or catalog. In response, many combination sellers represent the same owner (e.g., Victoria's Secret for lingerie, Land's End for clothing), which hires a corporate accountant to allocate costs or revenues and a human resources manager to administer compensation—that is, to reduce channel conflict. When channels are independent, it is not as easy to settle disputes, and suppliers have not paid enough attention to mechanisms for compensating the victims of excessive channel conflict.

It is fair to say that online and offline stores can be substitutes or complementary for consumers. Offline stores might cut into the sales of online stores if retailers have a strong local presence, but they can help boost online sales if the retailer's presence in the region is limited.[29]

Identifying multi-channel conflict also requires a clear recognition of the various benefits of the multiple channels to the supplier. Better coverage is an obvious benefit; other motives, usually unspoken, also arise because one channel might help the supplier manage another. For example, many suppliers serve industrial customers by sending manufacturers' representatives to them, but in the same market, they might reserve some customers (house accounts) to be served only by company employees. This dual distribution (vertically integrated *and* outsourced) practice is so common that it rarely creates enough conflict to harm a channel relationship, especially when the selling task is (1) ambiguous, such that it would be difficult for the supplier to determine how well an external rep is really performing (performance ambiguity problem) or (2) complex, putting the salesperson in a position to learn so much about a particular sales task that she or he becomes too valuable to replace (lock-in problem). These circumstances increase the supplier's dependence on a rep but make it more difficult to identify poor performers. Thus, the integrated channel provides a partial solution: from its small, in-house sales force, the supplier learns more about the task, including appropriate performance benchmarks, and develops a credible threat to terminate the rep and bring the account in-house. In short, a second channel can be useful for learning and keeping options open.[30]

EXAMPLE: SAMSUNG/LENOVO/CANON (INDIA)

In India, consumer electronics are mostly distributed through brick-and-mortar stores; they account for 80 percent of retail sales volume. Many giant electronics goods manufacturers maintain their own company-owned retail stores. But India's e-commerce giants are challenging this

(continued)

(continued)

dominance, because the offline stores cannot compete on price with e-tailers such as Flipkart (for which the largest shareholder is Walmart[31]), Snapdeal (in which eBay and Alibaba are investors), and Amazon. In their pursuit of sales growth, many small retailers also are turning to the marketplace features supported by Amazon and Flipkart to sell their electronics at prices much lower than what they charge in their own offline stores.[32] In response, some manufacturers such as Canon and Lenovo have sought to undercut the e-tailers by offering longer warranty deals for consumers who purchase through traditional, "authorized" channels. However, consumers continue to be attracted by the low prices and effective customer service available through e-commerce channels. Manufacturers have little choice but to acknowledge the market power of these online competitors. Ultimately, realizing the slowing sales in its home market of China, Lenovo decided to embrace e-commerce channels, rather than face the daunting challenge of building offline channels quickly in a country as large as India.[33]

Managing Multiple Channels

When they have identified the presence of conflict and determined whether it is threatening or not, suppliers also must consider what responsibility they have to protect their multiple channels from one another. Some suppliers assume no such responsibility and thus take no action; others question what action they possibly *could* take, even if they wanted to protect their channels. Actively trying to prevent one channel from competing with another (e.g., terminating discounters) can provoke legal action and is often futile anyway. Suppliers that try to manage the problem by devising different pricing schemes for different channels also enter legally dubious territory, creating an opportunity for arbitrage (as we discuss in relation to gray markets in a subsequent section).

More proactive options include offering more support, more service, more products, or even different products to different channel types to help them differentiate themselves. In general, suppliers gain more cooperation from their multiple channels, in terms of pricing, stocking, and display, if they can supply differentiated product lines (from the end-user's perspective) to different groups of retailers.[34] To do so, they likely need to *reserve* higher-end models for one channel and the rest of the line for another.

A variation on this theme would be to offer essentially the same product under different brand names to different channels—a common strategy in automobile and appliance markets.[35] It is effective when buyers do not know the products are virtually identical, though the channels know, and they often share that information with customers. Third-party buying guides also point out that model X of brand Y is the same as model A of brand B. The strategy thus can be futile, unless both brands possess considerable brand equity.

At the extreme, differentiation through different brands or products in different channels no longer entails a multi-channel strategy, such as when the supplier sells a "flagship" segment of its product line through one channel and provides secondary or peripheral products only in a separate channel. For example, in high-tech settings, some firms sell their major IT through distributors and everything else over the Internet. Customers thus can access anything the supplier makes, but most of the business goes to independent resellers. The supplier contents itself with product sales that do not interest this channel anyway.

Still, some channels demand **active intervention**. For example, durable products are distinctive in that they can be rented or sold, and then later resold by various members of the channel. In the 1990s, U.S. automakers needed a reason to keep their factories running, so they sold huge volumes of cars at ridiculously low prices to rental agencies—many of which were partially owned by the automakers. Nearly as soon as they had purchased the cars, these rental agencies began reselling the fleet, filling their parking lots with barely used cars for sale at very attractive prices. Of course, this newly introduced channel hurt auto dealers, and the resulting conflict was important, intense, and frequent enough to bring the issue into the court system. To lessen the conflict, several carmakers intervened by buying the gently used cars back from rental agencies and reselling them to dealers. This interventionist shift in inventory allowed carmakers to eat their cake and have it too, for a time. They maintained production volume and avoided a war between two important channels, but to the detriment of the channels, and ultimately themselves.[36]

UNWANTED CHANNELS: GRAY MARKETS

One of the most pressing issues for channel managers, especially in global markets, is the existence and persistence of gray markets.[37] **Gray marketing** is the sale of authorized, branded products through unauthorized distribution channels—usually bargain/discount outlets that provide less customer service than authorized channels do. A great variety of products get sold through gray markets, including luxury watches and designer clothing. Gray marketing is not the same as black marketing or **counterfeiting**. Counterfeiting refers to the selling of fake goods and knock-offs and trying to pass them off as the real thing. Counterfeiting remains illegal in most markets around the world. Unlike counterfeiting, gray marketing is completely legal in most situations.[38] Who supplies these unauthorized outlets? The usual suppliers include:[39] (1) authorized distributors and dealers, often from other markets; (2) professional arbitragers, including import/export houses; and (3) professional traders, many of whom live near market borders, who buy huge amounts in one market that offers low prices, then transport them to another market where prices are higher. The ultimate source and victim of such gray marketing is the supplier itself, whether its home office or its foreign divisions.

EXAMPLE: COSTCO (USA/GLOBAL)

Costco offers consumers a great place to obtain great deals on designer clothing and watches. But it obtains many of these products through gray markets, prompting some manufacturers to bring suits against it. A well-known, long-running legal battle involved Omega Watches.[40] Costco obtained Omega Seamaster watches from an authorized Omega distributor in Europe and sold them in the United States, at a much lower price than that charged by authorized U.S. Omega retailers. After some initial setbacks in lower courts, Costco eventually prevailed in the case, based on the doctrine that a firm can resell anything acquired legally. Yakima similarly has expressed frustration with Costco for selling gray market Yakima products in its stores,[41] but the justification by the retailer remains the same.

Several factors create a ripe environment for gray markets. One is **differential pricing** to different channel members: one channel over-orders to get a discount, then sells off the excess to unauthorized channels, at a non-discounted price. Similarly, different prices charged in different geographic markets, whether because of taxation, exchange rate differences, or varying price sensitivities across regions, encourage gray markets to arise. For example, foreign companies producing and selling in the People's Republic of China (PRC) sometimes must compete for sales with smugglers who sell branded products that were exported out of China and then reimported, to avoid local taxes. The product is an authorized branded product, but it also has been illegally smuggled, because it avoids import taxes on its re-entry into the PRC. Juul does not sell vaping devices to those under the age of 21 through their own website, but teenagers often purchase these vaping products through eBay and Alibaba which are an unauthorized gray market channel for these devices.[42]

When domestic products are sold through high-service, high-price channels, an opportunity also arises to introduce gray-marketed goods through discount retailers. For example, gray marketers regularly attempt to buy designer fashions in Louis Vuitton and Chanel outlets in Europe, bring the goods back to Japan (legally), and then put them on sale in Japanese stores at a price lower than the prevailing retail prices in authorized outlets in Japan. An unaware shopper may be surprised to encounter the elaborate security measures and limitations on purchase volume used by Louis Vuitton's flagship store in Paris, which exist mainly to block gray marketers.

The development of emerging markets and the worldwide liberalization of trade also favor the growth of gray markets. These **economic fundamentals** create incentives for firms to capitalize on brand equity and volume potential by offering similar products across countries. However, optimal prices naturally vary across countries, due to differences in exchange rates, purchasing power, and supply-side factors (e.g., distribution, servicing, taxes). The moment price differences arise between territories, substantial gains become available through arbitrage. Gray markets need not even involve cross-border trade, though; they are also common in domestic markets in which suppliers want to keep their products out of certain channels (e.g., discount chains).

Purchasers gain value from the wider availability of gray goods (due to their lower prices), but other members of the channel may suffer from them. Manufacturers complain that gray goods impair their ability to charge different prices in different markets. If the service levels provided by gray market retailers are lower than those of authorized dealers, brand equity may suffer, which also is a serious concern for manufacturers. But perhaps the strongest complaints about the escalation of gray marketing come from authorized dealers. Gray markets unequivocally erode potential volume for authorized dealers and can place severe pressure on after-sales service functions. All in all, then, when it is feasible to intercept and monitor gray goods, it seems to be in a producer's interest to do so.

Yet gray markets persist—and even are growing in many settings. They seem particularly active in developed economies, such as the United States, Canada, and the European Union, where manufacturers have both the means and the legal framework to stop them. That is, despite manufacturers' legal recourse to limit the proliferation of gray goods, they rarely do so,[43] especially when:

- Violations are difficult to detect or document (e.g., in distant markets, when customers are geographically dispersed).

- The potential for one channel to free ride on another is low anyway (e.g., resellers provide little service or charge separately for services rendered).

- The product is more mature.

- The distributor supplying the gray market does not carry competing brands in the focal product category.

This last item may be the most surprising, because these distributors seemingly should be far more vulnerable to pressure applied by the supplier. But suppliers appear to indulge these distributors, because they perform well and exhibit a form of loyalty that is stronger than that displayed by a diversified distributor. By granting gray market distributors some market protection, the supplier can invoke a pledge of exclusive dealing in the category. In this mutual dependence scenario, the supplier may hesitate to alienate an important distributor, even a gray market one.

It thus appears that manufacturers weigh the (often high) costs and (sometimes low) benefits of enforcement action and simply *decide to look the other way*. They are particularly forgiving of channel members that have made a powerful pledge (exclusive dealing), and they seem philosophical about gray markets for maturing products, which already are subject to greater price competition.

Some indications even imply that some manufacturers could be *positively disposed* toward gray markets, which seemingly would require other incentives to be at work. Perhaps these markets help manufacturers increase their market coverage. For suppliers of mature products, gray markets also put implicit pressure on authorized channels to compete harder, and they make the product more widely available to a price-sensitive segment. Such suppliers could profit from privately tolerating gray markets—while publicly objecting to them—as long as their authorized channels do not cut back their own purchases or support in protest.

In this sense, gray markets might allow a supplier to serve two segments, even as it proclaims it is serving only one. The segment that visits traditional market resellers cares about the shopping experience (e.g., displays, atmosphere, sales help, seller's reputation) but is less concerned about price. The segment that shops in gray markets, in contrast, will buy anywhere and from anyone, as long as the price is low. The former, price-insensitive segment is the supplier's formal target; the latter, price-sensitive segment represents a surreptitious target that the supplier serves through gray markets, even as it maintains a more highbrow image to continue appealing to its primary target.

As a result, gray markets are a major cause of channel conflict, because both upstream and downstream channel members are of two minds about them. Suppliers bemoan them in public and encourage them in private. Downstream channel members protest their "unfair" competition even as they supply these markets with goods. Even if all channel members agreed that they really wanted to stop gray marketing, the many economic incentives achieved from selling through unauthorized outlets leave sought-after products almost invariably subject to some gray market activity, because enforcement is not easy. It thus is little wonder that gray markets remain so common and cause so much channel conflict.

Industrial marketing channels in developed economies are usually good examples of **balanced power**.[44] Each side tends to be differentiated and has many alternatives to the current channel partner. Thus, upstream and downstream channel members are both powerful, so they tend to be **intolerant** of coercive tactics.

MITIGATING THE EFFECTS OF CONFLICT IN BALANCED RELATIONSHIPS

Dealers carry a limited number of product lines, supplied by a limited number of vendors. Often they sell expensive items that demand high after-sales service support, such as automobiles, garden equipment, or tires. Because they depend on a narrow range of products and suppliers, dealers are vulnerable to coercion or threats by the manufacturers whose lines they carry. Such relationship-damaging actions might include adding a mass merchandiser, adding a new dealer to the existing dealer's territory, withdrawing a product line, or imposing an outside credit agency to approve the dealer's credit applications for new customers. In an extensive study of how dealers react to such **destructive actions**,[45] five different reactions emerge:

- Passive acceptance; that is, saying or doing very little in response.
- Venting by complaining vigorously without taking action.
- Neglecting the supplier by relegating the line to a lower priority and cutting back on resources.
- Threatening to stop selling the line (even if it means closing the business).
- Engaging the supplier in constructive discussion to try to work things out and improve the situation.

An increasingly popular solution relies on **dealer councils**. These groups of carefully selected dealers work with the supplier to reduce the destructive impact of its actions and facilitate communication between dealers and suppliers.

PERCEIVED UNFAIRNESS: AGGRAVATING THE EFFECTS OF CONFLICTS

Research investigating the negative effects of conflict, opportunism, and unfairness indicates that **perceived unfairness** exerts the greatest negative impact on channel member cooperation and flexibility.[46] It also aggravates the negative effects of conflict and opportunism on channel performance. This "relationship poison" not only hurts the relationship directly but also amplifies the negative impacts of any background conflict.

When channel members perceive greater unfairness, they often attribute negative motives to the seller. Rather than giving their channel partner the benefit of the doubt, they assume some deliberate intention to take advantage of the situation to gain an unfair share. These channel members respond severely to conflict, often with strong negative emotions, including anger, that in turn increase the severity of their further responses. Then of course they seek retribution, and the negative spiraling of action and reaction begins.

CONFLICT RESOLUTION STRATEGIES

How do channel members cope with conflict? We distinguish two approaches. First, they can try to keep conflict from escalating into a dysfunctional zone, by developing institutionalized mechanisms, such as arbitration boards or norms of behavior, that help defuse disputes before they harden into hostile attitudes. Second, they might adopt patterns of behavior for resolving conflicts after they become manifest.

Forestalling Conflict through Institutionalization

Channel members sometimes institute policies to address conflict in early stages, or even before it arises. Such policies become **institutionalized** (i.e., part of the environment, unquestioned and taken for granted), in forms such as joint memberships in trade associations, distributor councils, and exchange-of-personnel programs. Other channels, from their very start, rely on built-in appeals to third parties, such as referrals to boards of arbitration or mediation (as is particularly popular in Europe). These policies serve subtle conflict-management functions. In Figure 5.2 we outline the four approaches to resolving channeling conflicts and discuss them in detail below.

Information-Intensive Mechanisms

Some mechanisms head off conflict by creating a better means to share information. But information-intensive mechanisms also are risky and expensive, because each side risks divulging sensitive information and must devote resources to communicating. Thus trust and cooperation are helpful, in the sense that they keep the conflict manageable.

When channel partners agree to **joint membership in trade associations** (e.g., a committee founded by the Grocery Manufacturers of America and the Food Marketing Institute developed the universal product code), they have devised a new mechanism to contain conflict through an institutionalized approach. **Personnel exchanges** as an institutional vehicle seek to turn channel members' focus toward devising solutions rather than engaging in conflict. The exchanges may be unilateral or bilateral, usually for a short, specified period. For example, the close connections between Walmart and Procter & Gamble have been greatly facilitated

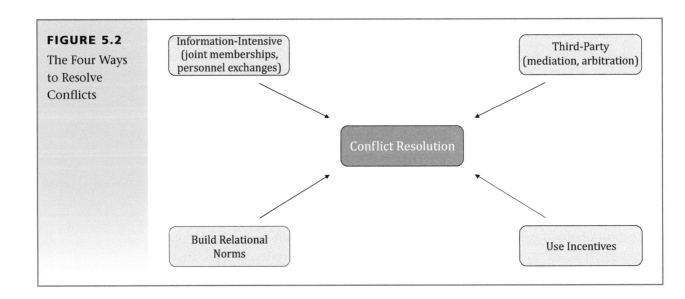

FIGURE 5.2
The Four Ways to Resolve Conflicts

Information-Intensive (joint memberships, personnel exchanges)

Third-Party (mediation, arbitration)

Conflict Resolution

Build Relational Norms

Use Incentives

by their personnel exchanges. Although such exchanges require clear guidelines, because of the likely disclosure of proprietary information, the participants return to their employers with a new, interorganizational view of their jobs, greater personal and professional involvement in the channel, and additional training. Participants also have an opportunity to meet with channel counterparts who have similar task responsibilities, professions, and interests.

Third-Party Mechanisms

Mediation and arbitration, the most widely used third-party mechanisms, introduce external parties that are not involved in the channel. **Mediation** is a process whereby a third party attempts to settle a dispute by persuading the parties to continue their negotiations or consider the mediator's procedural or substantive recommendations. The mediator typically offers a fresh view of the situation, which may enable it to perceive opportunities that "insiders" cannot. Mediators also help disputing parties find underlying points of agreement and promote integrative (win–win) solutions. Solutions might become acceptable simply because they have been suggested by the mediator. Mediation in business settings thus enjoys a high settlement rate (60–80 percent), though neither party is obliged to accept the recommendations. Such success may arise because the mediator allows both parties to save face, by making concessions without appearing weak. And disputants often perceive the overall process as fair.

An alternative to mediation is **arbitration**, in which the third party actually makes the decision, and both parties state in advance that they will honor whatever decision the arbitrator makes. Arbitrators often begin with a formal fact-finding hearing that operates much like a judicial procedure, with presentations, witnesses, and cross-examinations. Arbitration may be compulsory or voluntary. In **compulsory arbitration**, the parties are required by law to submit their dispute to a third party, whose decision is final and binding. In a **voluntary arbitration** process, the parties voluntarily submit their dispute to a third party, whose decision still is final and binding, such that reneging on the decision represents a major breach of confidence. Arbitration offers all the advantages of mediation, plus the advantage that the disputants can blame the arbitrator if their constituents object to the settlement.

Some firms practice sequences of mediation and arbitration. That is, they agree upfront that if the mediator cannot settle the issue, it will pass to an arbitrator—usually the same person who served as the mediator. In an arbitration–mediation sequence, the arbitrator instead places his or her secret decision in a sealed envelope, and then the issue passes to mediation. If the parties cannot agree, they open the envelope and abide by that decision. Such sequential approaches threaten to reduce each party's decision control, which not only lowers each party's expectations (i.e., making them more reasonable) but also motivates them to negotiate cooperatively. If all else fails, the process ultimately seems more fair than simple arbitration, and the parties are more likely to comply with the ruling than they might be with simple mediation.

Institutionalizing the practice of taking disputes to third parties can also forestall conflict. Because they know they face the prospect of outside intervention, disputants work to settle their differences internally. If they cannot, the third parties provide a sort of safety net for dealing with conflict *after* it climbs too high. The input of third parties to an ongoing conflict also can contribute to the success of channel relationships, because third-party interventions prompt greater satisfaction among channel members with the financial rewards they derive from their relationship.[47]

Building Relational Norms

The preceding mechanisms are policies that can be proactively devised, consciously put into place, and continually maintained by management to forestall conflict or address it once it occurs. But another important class of factors can forestall or direct conflict, even though management cannot directly create or control them. That is, norms govern how channel members manage their relationship over time, according to the functioning of that relationship. Take the case of contracts. Moderately detailed contracts reduce "destructive" conflict, by leaving sufficient room for give-and-take negotiations but still providing a framework that regulates behaviors. Overly detailed contracts instead lead to behavioral rigidity and create potential problems in the relationship.[48] In a channel, norms entail expectations about behavior, shared (at least partially) by all channel members. In alliance channels, common norms include:

- **Flexibility**: channel members expect each other to adapt readily to changing circumstances, with a minimum of obstruction and negotiation.

- **Information exchange**: channel members share all pertinent information—no matter how sensitive—freely, frequently, quickly, and thoroughly.

- **Solidarity**: everyone works for mutual, not just one-sided, benefits.

These **relational norms** tend to come in a package: a relationship attains high levels of all these norms if it reaches a high level of any of them.[49] A channel with strong relational norms is particularly effective at forestalling conflict, because it discourages parties from pursuing their own interests at the expense of the channel. These norms also encourage various players to refrain from coercion and make an effort to work through their differences, which keeps conflict within functional zones.[50]

Unfortunately, management cannot decide one day to create relational norms and then "just do it." Norms emerge from the daily interactions of the people who constitute the marketing channel. They also can be positive or negative.

A channel might embrace a destructive norm of cutthroat competition or pure self-interest seeking. Unlike policies, norms are not easy to observe, announce, publicize, or control.

Using Incentives to Resolve Conflict

Depending on the conflict resolution style a negotiator chooses, the best arguments for persuading its counterpart differ. However, economic incentives work well almost universally, regardless of the personalities, players, or history of the relationship. Just as reward power is a highly effective way to influence a channel member, appealing to economic self-interest is a highly effective way to settle a dispute. Thus, good negotiators find ingenious ways to base their arguments on economics, then combine them with a strong program of communications in a good interpersonal working relationship.

Consider, for example, manufacturer-sponsored promotion programs aimed at retailers. In fast-moving consumer goods industries, suppliers spend enormous sums to create point-of-purchase advertising and displays for in-store use. These programs are major sources of contention. Manufacturers accuse retailers of taking the promotion money and then not mounting the promised promotion. Retailers complain that manufacturers never pony up their fair share of promotion allowances, even while they promise more than they can deliver. The resulting acrimony has consumed reams of pages of discussion in the grocery trade press.

But most of this acrimony could be resolved if the manufacturer would simply combine appealing economic incentives that encourage participation in a pay-for-performance system with a presentation by a salesperson who has developed a good working relationship with the retailer. The economic incentives have obvious appeal; the good relationship helps the salesperson direct the retailer's attention to the incentives. A pay-for-performance system in particular (i.e., the retailer pays for items sold on promotion rather than all items ordered) screens out retailers that are fundamentally uninterested in cooperating with the supplier.[51]

To function effectively, though, economic incentives must do more than offer a better price or higher allowance, options that are visible and easy for competitors to match. Rather, persuasive economic arguments feature a portfolio of elements that collectively create positive financial returns for a channel partner.[52] For example, independent sales agencies strongly appreciate a product that can generate profits by:

- Compensating for lower-volume sales with a higher commission rate, or vice versa.

- Overcoming lower commission rates by being easier to sell, such that it demands less sales time (i.e., cuts costs).

- Establishing the sales agent in a growing product category, to contribute to future profits.

- Increasing overall sales synergy and spurring sales of other products in the agent's portfolio.

In addition, independent agencies respond to indirect, risk-oriented arguments. A principal should try to convince its agents that sales of its products are not unpredictable but rather can be accurately forecasted. Such arguments can be conveyed far more effectively by principals that invest in vigorous, two-way communication programs within the channel.[53] Unfortunately, though, economic incentives can rapidly multiply and become difficult to administer. Channel networks often have so many points of contact, across so many organizations, that the sheer task of keeping track of the channels and their incentives grows daunting.

Because the distinct entities in an omni-channel setting try to coordinate their activities, to deliver a seamless experience to the end-user, conflict is inevitable. But much of this conflict is likely to be functional, in that it goads the parties to work together to iron out their various issues and debates. In contrast, conflict in multi-channel settings may be more dysfunctional; these parties are concerned about cannibalization and confront frustrated end-users, confused by the separate offerings in the various channels (e.g., promotions in one channel are not honored in another). In Figure 5.3, we compare this relational landscape in omni-channel versus multi-channel contexts. It shows that partners in an omni-channel context, to provide the seamless experience, must exhibit

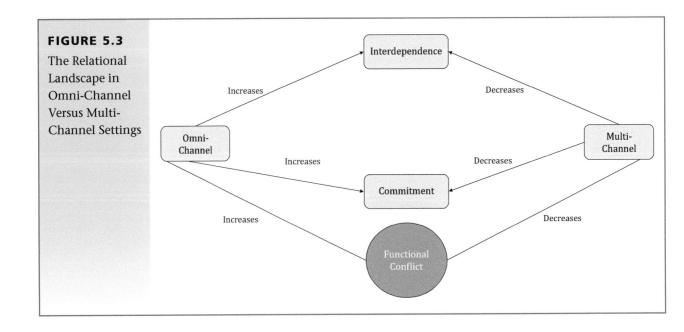

FIGURE 5.3

The Relational Landscape in Omni-Channel Versus Multi-Channel Settings increased coordination and teamwork. In this sense, both interdependence and commitment should be greater in omni-channel contexts. In contrast, in multi-channel siloes, interdependence and commitment likely diminish, because the parties have little motive to synchronize their offerings. In turn, we expect greater functional and productive conflict in omni-channel contexts as the parties work together to devise a seamless experience for customers. In multi-channel contexts, we expect less functional conflict and knowledge sharing; instead, more destructive conflict is likely.

Take-Aways

- A good way to assess the true degree of conflict is to index, for each relevant issue, the:
  - Frequency of disagreement.
  - Intensity of disagreement.
  - Importance of the issue.
- If any element is low, the issue is not a real source of conflict.
- Conflict is inevitable in marketing channels because of their:
  - Built-in viewpoints and goal differences.
  - Perceptual variations, which arise because channel members see different pieces of the channel environment.
  - Clashes over domains (roles, responsibilities, territories).
- Domain conflict is especially prominent in multi-channel situations, which demand creative solutions, such as communication, concession, compensation, win–win approaches, product differentiation, or acceptance.
- Gray markets are growing rapidly, because both upstream and downstream channel members have reasons to permit them, regardless of their complaints.
- Institutionalized mechanisms to contain conflict early include information-intensive strategies and the use of third parties.
- Conflict also can be resolved through economic incentives, which should be less visible, combine with good communication, and encourage channel members to make some investment.
- Conflict can be more functional in omni-channel situations.

NOTES

1 Der Maelen, Sara Van, Els Breugelmans, and Kathleen Cleeren (2017), "The clash of the titans: On retailer and manufacturer vulnerability in conflict delistings," *Journal of Marketing*, 81 (1), 118–135.

2 Bianchi, Raffaella, Michal Cermak, and Ondrej Dusek (2016), "More than digital plus traditional: A truly omnichannel customer experience," *McKinsey Quarterly* (July).

3 Stern, Louis W. and James L. Heskett (1969), "Conflict management in interorganizational relations: A conceptual framework," in Louis W. Stern (ed.), *Distribution Channels: Behavioral Dimensions*, Boston, MA: Houghton-Mifflin, pp. 156–175.

4 Pondy, Louis R. (1967), "Organizational conflict: Concepts and models," *Administrative Science Quarterly*, 14 (1), 296–320.

5 Zwick, Rami and Xiao-Ping Chen (1999), "What price fairness? A bargaining study," *Management Science*, 45 (June), 804–823.

6 Brown, James R. and Ralph L. Day (1981), "Measures of manifest conflict in distribution channels," *Journal of Marketing Research*, 18 (August), 263–274. This article is the basis for the following discussion and examples of measuring channel conflict.

7 Dwyer, F. Robert, Paul H. Schurr, and Sejo Oh (1987), "Developing buyer–seller relationships," *Journal of Marketing*, 51 (April), 11–27.

8 Tang, Thuong Pat, Xiaorong Fu, and Qinhong Xe (2017), "Influence of functional conflicts on marketing capability in channel relationships," *Journal of Business Research*, 78, 252–260.

9 Webster, Bruce (1998), "Uses and abuses of co-op advertising," *Supply House Times*, 15 (March), 57–64.

10 Anderson, James C. and James A. Narus (1984), "A model of the distributor's perspective of distributor–manufacturer working relationships," *Journal of Marketing*, 48 (Fall), 62–74.

11 Geyskens, Inge, Jan-Benedict E.M. Steenkamp, and Nirmalya Kumar (1999), "A meta-analysis of satisfaction in marketing channel relationships," *Journal of Marketing Research*, 36 (May), 223–238.

12 Draganska, Michaela, Daniel Klapper, and Sofia B. Villas-Boas (2010), "A larger slice or a larger pie? An empirical investigation of bargaining power in the distribution channel," *Marketing Science*, 29 (January–February), 57–74.

13 Bergen, Mark, Shantanu Dutta, and Orville C. Walker Jr. (1992), "Agency relationships in marketing: A review of the implications and applications of agency and related theories," *Journal of Marketing*, 56 (3), 1–24.

14 Ross, William T. and Diana C. Robertson (2000), "Lying: The impact of decision context," *Business Ethics Quarterly*, 10 (2), 409–440.

15 John, George and Torger Reve (1982), "The reliability and validity of key informant data from dyadic relationships in marketing channels," *Journal of Marketing Research*, 19 (November), 517–524.

16 Brown, James R., Robert F. Lusch, and Laurie P. Smith (1991), "Conflict and satisfaction in an industrial channel of distribution," *International Journal of Physical Distribution & Logistics Management*, 21 (6), 15–26.

17 Palmatier, Robert W., Rajiv P. Dant, and Dhruv Grewal (2007), "A comparative longitudinal analysis of theoretical perspectives of interorganizational relationship performance," *Journal of Marketing*, 71 (October), 172–194.

18 Johansson, Johnny K. and Ikujiro Nonaka (1987), "Market research the Japanese way," *Harvard Business Review*, 65 (3), 1–5.

19 LaBahn, Douglas W. and Katrin R. Harich (1997), "Sensitivity to national business culture: Effects on U.S.–Mexican channel relationship performance," *Journal of International Marketing*, 5 (December), 29–51.

20 "Newsmakers: Acacia Inc.," *Sales and Marketing Management*, 148 (April), 20.

21 "Who is Cisco," www.cisco.com/c/en_au/about/who-is-head.html, date retrieved March 14, 2018.

22 Haranas, Mark (2016), "5 surprising statistics about Cisco's channel strategy," www.crn.com/slide-shows/networking/300081194/5-surprising-statistics-about-ciscos-channel-strategy.htm/pgno/0/5, date retrieved March 14, 2018.

23 Haranas, Mark (2017), "Unified communications blockbuster: Cisco to acquire Broadsoft for $1.9B, partners fear channel conflict," www.crn.com/news/networking/300094321/unified-communications-blockbuster-cisco-to-acquire-broadsoft-for-1-9b-partners-fear-channel-conflict.htm, date retrieved March 14, 2018.

24 Frazier, Gary L. and Tasadduq A. Shervani (1992), "Multiple channels of distribution and their impact on retailing," in Robert A. Peterson (ed.), *The Future of U.S. Retailing: An Agenda for the 21st Century*, Westport, CT: Quorum Books.

25 Cespedes, Frank V. and Raymond Corey (1990), "Managing multiple channels," *Business Horizons*, 10 (1), 67–77; Moriarty, Rowland T. and Ursula Moran (1990), "Managing hybrid marketing systems," *Harvard Business Review* (November–December), 146–150.

26 Sa Vinhas, Alberto and Erin Anderson (2005), "How potential conflict drives channel structure: Concurrent (direct and indirect) channels," *Journal of Marketing Research*, 42 (November).

27 Furst, Andreas, Martin Leimbach, and Jana-Kristin Prigge (2017), "Organizational multichannel differentiation: An analysis of its impact on channel relationships and company sales success," *Journal of Marketing*, 81 (January), 59–82.

28 Bucklin, Christine B., Pamela A. Thomas-Graham, and Elizabeth A. Webster (1997), "Channel conflict: When is it dangerous?" *McKinsey Quarterly*, 7 (3), 36–43.

29 Wang, Kitty and Avi Goldfarb (2017), "Can offline stores drive online sales?" *Journal of Marketing Research*, 54 (October), 706–719.

30 Dutta, Shantanu, Mark Bergen, Jan B. Heide, et al. (1995), "Understanding dual distribution: The case of reps and house accounts," *Journal of Law, Economics, and Organization*, 11 (1), 189–204.

31 Chanchani, Madhav and Chaitali Chakravarty (2018), "Walmart set to be largest shareholder in Flipkart," *Economic Times*, March 14, https://economictimes.indiatimes.com/small-biz/start ups/newsbuzz/walmart-set-to-be-largest-shareholder-in-flipkart/articleshow/63292655.cms, date retrieved March 14, 2018.

32 Mehta, Jaideep (2014), "Retail boom: Why traditional and online retailers need to solve their disputes on pricing," *Economic Times*, May 4, https://economictimes.indiatimes.com/industry/services/retail/retail-boom-why-traditional-online-retailers-need-to-solve-their-disputes-on-pricing/articleshow/34601080.cms, date retrieved March 14, 2018.

33 Datta, Aveek (2016), "Enter the dragon: Lenovo counts on India to offset troubles at home," *Forbes India*, November 7, www.forbesindia.com/article/boardroom/enter-the-dragon-lenovo-counts-on-india-to-offset-troubles-at-home/44695/1, date retrieved March 14, 2018.

34 Villas-Boas, Miguel (1997), "Product line design for a distribution channel," *Marketing Science*, 17 (2), 156–169.

35 Sullivan, Mary W. (1998), "How brand names affect the demand for twin automobiles," *Journal of Marketing Research*, 35 (May), 154–165.

36 Purohit, Devarat (1997), "Dual distribution channels: The competition between rental agencies and dealers," *Marketing Science*, 16 (3), 228–245; Purohit, Devarat and Richard Staelin (1994), "Rentals, sales, and buybacks: Managing secondary distribution channels," *Journal of Marketing Research*, 31 (August), 325–338.

37 This section is adapted from Coughlan, Anne T. and David A. Soberman (2005), "Strategic segmentation using outlet malls," *International Journal of Research in Marketing*, 22 (March), 61–86; Soberman, David A. and Anne T. Coughlan (1998), "When is the best ship a leaky one? Segmentation, competition, and gray markets," INSEAD working paper 98/60/MKT; Champion, David (1998), "Marketing: The bright side of gray markets," *Harvard Business Review*, 76 (September/October), 19–22.

38 Weigand, Robert E. (1991), "Parallel import channels: Options for preserving territorial integrity," *Columbia Journal of World Business*, 26 (Spring), 53–60; Assmus, Gert and Carsten Wiese (1995), "How to address the gray market threat using price coordination," *Sloan Management Review*, 36 (Spring), 31–41.

39 Henricks, Mark (1997), "Harmful diversions," *Apparel Industry Magazine*, 58 (September), 72–78.

40 Post, David (2015), "Costco can keep selling gray market Omega watches at a discount without copyright liability," *Washington Post*, January 21.

41 Brain Staff (2014), "Yakima says Costco bought its product on gray market," *Bicycle Retailer*, March 20.

42 Tolentino, Jia (2018), "The promise of vaping and the rise of Juul," *The New Yorker*, May 14, www.newyorker.com/magazine/2018/05/14/the-promise-of-vaping-and-the-rise-of-juul, date retrieved September 26, 2018.

43 Cespedes, Frank V., E. Raymond Corey, and V. Kasturi Rangan (1988), "Gray markets: Causes and cures," *Harvard Business Review*, 88 (July–August), 75–82; Myers, Matthew B. and David A. Griffith (1999), "Strategies for combating gray market activity," *Business Horizons*, 42 (November–December), 2–8; Bergen, Mark, Jan B. Heide, and Shantanu Dutta (1998), "Managing gray markets through tolerance of violations: A transaction cost perspective," *Managerial and Decision Economics*, 19 (1), 157–165.

44 This discussion is based on Frazier, Gary L. and Raymond C. Rody (1991), "The use of influence strategies in interfirm relationships in industrial product channels," *Journal of Marketing*, 55 (January), 52–69.

45 Hibbard, Jonathan D., Nirmalya Kumar, and Louis W. Stern (2001), "Examining the impact of destructive acts in marketing channel relationships," *Journal of Marketing Research*, 38 (1), 45–61.

46 Samaha, Stephen, Robert W. Palmatier, and Rajiv P. Dant (2011), "Poisoning relationships: Perceived unfairness in channels of distribution," *Journal of Marketing*, 75 (May), 99–117.

47 Mohr, Jakki and Robert Spekman (1994), "Characteristics of partnership success: Partnership attributes, communication behavior, and conflict resolution techniques," *Strategic Management Journal*, 15 (1), 135–152; Mohr, Jakki, and Robert Spekman (1996), "Perfecting partnerships," *Marketing Management*, 4 (Winter/Spring), 34–43.

48 Yang, Wei, Yu Gao, Yao Li, Hao Shen, and Songyue Zheng (2017), "Different roles of control mechanisms in buyer–supplier conflict: An empirical study from China," *Industrial Marketing Management*, 65, 144–156.

49 Heide, Jan B. and George John (1992), "Do norms matter in marketing relationships?" *Journal of Marketing*, 56 (April), 32–44.

50 Heide, Jan B. (1994), "Interorganizational governance in marketing channels," *Journal of Marketing*, 58 (April), 71–85.

51 Murray, John P., Jr. and Jan B. Heide (1998), "Managing promotion program participation within manufacturer–retailer relationships," *Journal of Marketing*, 62 (January), 58–68.

52 Anderson, Erin, Leonard M. Lodish, and Barton Weitz (1987), "Resource allocation behavior in conventional channels," *Journal of Marketing Research*, 24 (February), 85–97.

53 Mohr, Jakki and John R. Nevin (1990), "Communication strategies in marketing channels: A theoretical perspective," *Journal of Marketing*, 54 (October), 36–51.

CHAPTER 6

Retailing Structures and Strategies

LEARNING OBJECTIVES

After reading this chapter, you will be able to:

- Describe the types of retail structures that exist worldwide.
- Explain how a retail positioning strategy flows from both cost-side and demand-side factors.
- Define the retailer's positioning strategy as a set of service outputs delivered to the market, which helps differentiate a retailer from its competitors, even if the products sold are identical.
- Recognize important trends and developments on the consumer and channel sides that affect retail management.
- Develop an understanding of the retail strategic profit model.
- Outline the power and coordination issues facing retailers and their suppliers, as well as how suppliers respond to retailers' use of power to influence channel behavior.

THE NATURE OF RETAILING

Merriam-Webster's dictionary defines **retailing** as "the activities involved in the selling of goods to ultimate consumers for personal or household consumption."[1] Thus in a **retail sale**, the buyer, rather than a business or institutional purchaser, is the ultimate consumer. The **buying motive** for a retail sale is personal or family satisfaction, stemming from the consumption of the item being purchased by an end-user. We expand on Merriam-Webster's definition and suggest that retailing also includes sales of services, not just goods. For example, child daycare centers, auto rental companies, restaurants, banks, and hair salons are engaged in service retailing.

Retailing accounts for a substantial portion of the U.S. and world economy. The United States is the world's largest retail marketplace, and U.S. retail sales were to the tune of nearly $5 trillion in 2016, while worldwide retail sales exceeded $20 trillion.[2] As we briefly discussed in Chapter 1, the retailing landscape is undergoing significant changes in the omni-channel era. We thus begin by outlining various retailing formats, then highlight various trends in retailing, especially those shaped by this modern omni-channel environment.

CLASSIFICATION OF RETAILERS

Retailers come in many shapes and forms, as outlined in Table 6.1, and there are many ways to classify retailers. Retail establishments vary in size, ownership arrangements, breadth and depth of assortments provided, and service levels. Many retail establishments are embracing multi-channel delivery and making an effort to incorporate omni-channel experiences, in keeping with evolving customer buying trends and expectations. We next take a look at the major retail formats in brief.

Supermarkets

Supermarkets are self-service stores that traditionally specialized in food retailing. However, over the years U.S. supermarkets have made significant in-roads into non-food retailing and provide many other services under their roofs, such as florist and pharmaceutical services. The supermarket industry operates on low margins but has exhibited a wide-ranging push into higher-margin lines, such as pharmacy services. Prepared foods are another notable initiative by many U.S. supermarkets, to the extent that many of them represent bona fide competitors of fast food and quick-service restaurants. Other supermarkets offer private-label or store-branded merchandise.

In keeping with practices first originating in Europe, some supermarkets have adopted or face competition from the **hypermarket** or **supercenter** format, which combines groceries with a range of other offerings, from clothing to household items to jewelry. Evidence of this strong competition from hypermarkets comes in the form of some recent statistics: Walmart owned 25 percent of the total U.S. grocery market in 2017, compared with 10 percent accounted for by Kroger, the largest U.S. grocer.[3] Supermarkets thus are working to expand their specialized offerings, such as ethnic, organic, or private-label merchandise explicitly to attract shoppers and compete more effectively against hypermarkets, warehouse clubs, and limited assortment supermarkets.

Traditional supermarkets also find themselves in competition with **limited assortment supermarkets** like Aldi and Save-A-Lot. Whereas supermarkets usually carry about 50,000 stock-keeping units (SKUs), limited assortment stores carry far fewer (typically 2,000–5,000) SKUs and mainly or almost exclusively feature store brands, such that their assortments represent about 80 percent of the selection that would be available in a traditional supermarket.[4]

EXAMPLE: THE LIMITED ASSORTMENT AT ALDI (GERMANY/USA/GLOBAL)

Founded in Germany in 1914, Aldi maintains more than 10,000 stores globally; it expects to operate nearly 1,400 stores in the United States soon and has plans to expand to 2,500 stores by 2022. Typical stores carry about 2,000 SKUs, mainly private-label products that it subjects to blind taste tests to prove its offerings are as tasty as national brand options.[5] The limited selection has enabled Aldi to keep its operating costs low, and it passes on those savings to consumers, such that it charges prices that are about 17 percent lower than Walmart's.[6] The efficient operations and low operating costs result from its frequent turnover, smaller storefronts, store designs that eliminate decorations and other amenities, and production of its own private-label products.

Warehouse Clubs

Warehouse clubs such as Sam's Club and Costco were initially targeted at small businesses. They sold wholesale quantities at a discounted "wholesale" price, in a retail format. Warehouse clubs typically charge a membership fee, which becomes an important and significant revenue stream for these retailers, and they restrict their offerings to members. Members must buy in bulk, and by doing so, they in effect take over some of the warehousing function from upstream channel members. The typical warehouse club tends to have a relatively small assortment of options or varieties within each product category at any given time, but its pricing is low, and shoppers often run across premium brands, alongside the clubs' own private-label brands.

Department Stores

As the name suggests, department stores are organized into departments, offering a wide assortment of products and services. They first arrived on the scene in the 19th century, providing clothing, shoes, electronics, jewelry, furniture, and home improvement items in a single location. Because of their appeal to customers who appreciate one-stop shopping, department stores have long represented shopping destinations, such that they anchor malls and thereby benefit other **specialty stores**. However, this format appears to be entering a decline stage, such that many of the retailers that once anchored shopping malls, such as JCPenney, Macy's, and Sears, are shuttering their stores. The cascading effects of these trends have strongly influenced U.S. retailing, including transformations and closures of enclosed shopping malls throughout the nation. When anchor stores close, smaller specialty retailers often follow suit and leave the mall too, because without a destination store to attract them, customers stop visiting malls in general.[7]

Still, many of them remain, so considering their unique features can be instructive. A traditional department store does not use centralized checkout systems; shoppers can check out and continue shopping as they move from department to department. Department stores vary in the level of service they provide: "Tier 1" department stores like Neiman Marcus offer more personalized service than "tier 2" stores like Macy's. "Tier 3" department stores such as JCPenney and Sears provide little service; they also face intense competition from discounters (e.g., Target). The higher service levels can be offered only at higher price levels, due to the costs involved in producing such service outputs. In this sense, department stores are inevitably constrained by their target consumers' willingness to pay, which must inform what services they choose to offer, or not. Finally, many department stores carry exclusive merchandise to draw shoppers. Some retailers are experimenting with **store-within-a-store** formats, such that the department store carves out a space for a well-known brand to establish a mini "specialty" store inside its locations.

Specialty Stores

Specialty stores offer a much narrower product assortment, equivalent to a single department in a department store. But within this narrow assortment, they carry a much **deeper** set of offerings (e.g., more sizes, colors, designs). They also provide knowledgeable salespeople. Until recently, such stores have often located in malls anchored by department stores and operated at price points similar to those of the department stores with which they compete, while still providing a higher level of service. The Gap and Victoria's Secret are key examples; manufacturers such as Apple and Godiva also maintain their own specialty stores.

Discount Stores

Discount stores such as Walmart and Target require a primarily self-service approach and rely on their lower prices to attract shoppers. Similar to department stores, they carry a broad assortment of products; in many sectors, such as toys, small appliances, and packaged goods, they dominate the marketplace. With their low margins, these retailers cater to a lower-income target segment, relative to department or grocery stores. They also require frequent turnover and high volumes to make up for the low margins. For certain product lines, such as clothing, they thus are unlikely to carry many prestigious or expensive brands. Moreover, many discount stores offer grocery items, with the recognition that consumers shop frequently for groceries. When a discount store adds a grocery section, consumers may be more likely to visit it, perhaps with greater frequency, and buy more of the expanded range of products once they are in the store.

Specialty discount stores are similar to discount stores but offer a narrower assortment of merchandise. Some specialty discount stores, due to their size and market dominance, are referred to as **category killers**, such as Home Depot and Best Buy.

Convenience and Drugstores

Convenience stores mostly locate in residential areas or in association with gas stations. Their depth and breadth of assortments identify them as mini-versions of grocery stores, though they usually charge a convenience premium. Customers visit convenience stores such as 7-Eleven for four main reasons:[8] (1) to replenish their stocks of everyday products they are running low on, between their more extensive trips to grocery stores; (2) to purchase tobacco or newspapers; (3) to grab snacks and drinks; and (4) to find quick, cost-efficient meal solutions. Many convenience stores earn substantial portions of their revenues from selling prepared foods.

Drugstores function as pharmacies, but the advent and expansion of new medical markets, established through managed care and mail-order pharmacies, has created a new and challenging business environment for these retailers. In response, many drugstores have started operating walk-in medical clinics and offering expanded assortments of cosmetics, food, and convenience products.

Table 6.1 provides a snapshot of this summary of retail types, along with a classification of the different classes of retailers according to their positioning strategies. Their differences allow for the presence of multiple types of retail outlets, selling the same physical merchandise, even in the same geographic market. Comparisons across the rows in Table 6.1 further suggest that by making strategic choices that reflect these dimensions, a store can establish a position in the marketplace to survive and thrive, even when competitors offer seemingly similar products and pursue the same target markets of customers.

THE RETAIL LANDSCAPE

The Big Players

Stores magazine publishes an annual list of the 100 largest retailers (https://stores.org/2017/06/26/top-100-retailers) in the United States and another list cataloging the 250 largest retailers in the world. A quick perusal of the 100 largest U.S. retailers reveals that only two (Amazon and QVC) generate the majority of their sales through nonstore retailing. In addition, food retailing is a component for many of the biggest of the big retailers: 8 of the top 10 sell at least some food (all retailers except Home Depot and Lowe's; even Walgreens has some food sales). Discount stores, warehouse clubs, drugstores, and supermarkets all are well represented in this top 10 list.[9] However, we cannot ignore or underestimate the dominance of Walmart in retailing worldwide. Walmart achieves more than three times the sales of the second largest U.S. retailer (Kroger). Finally, the largest service retailer, McDonald's, ranks at number 12; Aldi, the largest limited assortment supermarket, reaches position 19.

The global top 250 list (https://nrf.com/2017-global-250-chart) reaffirms Walmart's dominance in particular, as well as the strong positions of U.S. retailers

TABLE 6.1 A Taxonomy of Retailer Types	Retailer Type	Main Focus on Margin or Turnover?	Bulk-Breaking
	Department store (e.g., Macy's)	Margin	Yes
	Specialty store (e.g., The Gap)	Margin	Yes
	Mail order/catalog (e.g., Land's End)	Both	Yes
	Convenience store (e.g., 7-Eleven)	Turnover	Yes
	Category killer (e.g., Best Buy)	Turnover	Yes
	Discount store (e.g., Wal-Mart)	Turnover	Yes
	Hypermarket (e.g., Carrefour)	Turnover	Yes
	Warehouse club (e.g., Sam's Club)	Turnover	No

Spatial Convenience	Waiting and Delivery Time	Variety (Breadth)	Assortment (Depth)
Moderate	Low wait time	Broad	Moderate/Shallow
Moderate	Low wait time	Narrow	Deep
Extremely High	Moderate/High wait time	Narrow	Moderate
Very High	Low wait time	Broad	Shallow
Moderate	Low wait time	Narrow	Deep
Low	Moderate wait time (may be out of stock)	Broad	Shallow
Low	Moderate wait time	Broad	Moderate
Low	Moderate wait time (may be out of stock)	Broad	Shallow

in general. This dominance by U.S. retailers is not surprising; the United States remains the world's largest retail marketplace. Yet several European (German, French, U.K., Swedish, Dutch) and Japanese retailers also rank high,[10] and Chinese retailers have started to make their presence felt in the top 250 list.

Modern Shifts and Challenges

Some of the most prominent trends that modern retailers confront include the move to an omni-channel age and the explosion and continuing enhancements of big data and their related technology.

Omni-channel trends. The distinction between online and physical retailing continues to be blurred in the age of omni-channel retailing,[11] which constitutes a challenge because of the different essential characteristics of physical and online retailing. Retailers cannot ignore either form; even if most growth is coming from online retailing, a bulk of retailing still takes place in physical stores. Thus, consumer preferences necessitate the shift to multi- and omni-channel retailing.[12]

As we have noted, online and physical stores once operated in separate siloes, but their integration increases customers' willingness to pay, purchase and search intentions, and the perceived service quality of the online store.[13] Thus, retailers increasingly pursue such integration to ensure they establish stellar customer experiences in both formats. While many consumers may first go to well-known online retailers like Amazon, many consumers perusing online channels prioritize familiar names, such that they search first through the online stores of the offline, physical stores that they already patronize. However, with increased experience with online shopping, they likely engage in greater comparison shopping.[14]

With a multi-channel setup, a key choice is whether to stock the same items online and offline. A major constraint in online retailing is the weight-to-value ratio. Low-value items that weigh a lot (e.g., concrete, rice) are not optimal online offerings, because it is not economical to ship them to individual consumers. However, online retailers are not constrained by shelf space, so they can carry a wider array of SKUs and add assortments that they might not list in their stores.

Such distinct constraints also raise some exciting possibilities for targeting different audiences across their physical and online stores. In the United Kingdom, Aldi does not offer much food in its online stores and instead focuses on selling small appliances, household items, and wines.[15] Such considerations also are closely related to pricing transparency. A standardized pricing scheme across in-store and electronic channels can be a challenge, because the economics of selling vary between physical and online formats. For example, to account for the costs of real estate and salespeople, physical stores might need to charge more. But a lower price online also might lead to cannibalization of in-store sales. A higher, standardized price online instead could make the retailer potentially less appealing than its online-only competitors.[16]

Physical stores instead might focus on service. They can leverage convenient locations and allow customers to pick up items ordered online. Many previously online-only retailers have opened physical stores; Amazon even acquired Whole Foods, confirming its embrace of physical retailing. This development mirrors earlier trends when catalog retailers like J. Crew opened physical stores. When catalog and online-only retailers add physical stores, their sales to existing customers tend to increase, due to more frequent shopping trips rather than larger orders. Yet catalog sales generally are negatively affected, while Internet sales tend to remain the same.[17]

Explanations for why sales by such omni-channel retailers often exceed those of online-only retailers might refer to consumers' sense of trust. Many shoppers reject retailers that lack any physical presence; the absence of this physical presence creates a sense of psychological distance that reduces their level of trust.[18] Yet adding a physical store also creates some risk for online retailers. For example, showrooming represents a pertinent challenge: customers visit stores to learn about available options, establish a sense of trust, and obtain expert advice from salespeople. But after receiving these expensive service offerings, they switch channels and purchase online, often at a lower price. Such threats reflect a salient shift in consumer mindsets, in that they view the store mainly as a place to inspect the product, not the place to buy it.[19]

Technology and data trends. For most consumers, retailing offers two perceptual categories. On the one hand, both product and service retailing can be associated with chores and mundane tasks, such as visiting the grocery store or dry cleaner. On the other hand, retailing may be perceived as a fulfilling, fun, and entertaining experience. When retail shopping is a chore, retailers can rely on predictive analytics to simplify the task, such as with automatic replenishment programs that deliver replacements of routinely consumed products. Many dry cleaners offer pickup and delivery services, coordinated through mobile apps, to make it easier for consumers to purchase their service offerings. In addition to minimizing consumers' annoyance and saving them time, such technologies create switching barriers, because they encourage customers to build an ongoing, habitual relationship with the retailer. In particular, replenishment services that integrate mobile technologies can be very effective. They increase purchase frequency and order sizes, leading to more habitual purchases from the retailer.[20]

When shopping is fun, big data offer a different set of tools for retailers to appeal to consumers looking for enjoyable experiences. In particular, big data are better data (i.e., more complete, more interlinked, more current). With them, retailers can target individual consumers according to their prior purchases, demographics, social activities, shopping habits, and geographic locations.[21] For example, location-based social networking sites (e.g., Foursquare) deliver electronic coupons to customers' mobile phones, at the very moment they encounter the related retail offer. Despite the promise of such big data, their effective use continues to be limited among retailers, especially smaller ones. Empirical evidence shows that retailers that leverage their data-rich environments have much to gain—even more than actors in other industries—including clear returns on investments in customer analytics programs. Failures to take advantage of big data thus are short-sighted and problematic.[22]

Other technological advances rely less on big data but still offer compelling opportunities to retailers, especially for engaging in co-creation with customers. Co-creation can range from the simple (e.g., Build-a-Bear customers create stuffed animals, using standard components that they can combine as they choose) to the extreme (e.g., innovation contests involving customers).[23] Procter & Gamble and Starbucks both sell products successfully co-created with customers, who have offered innovative ideas or suggestions for improving store designs. The Korean cosmetics retailer Missha instead saw that the cosmetics market was dominated by high-priced competition and worked closely with their suppliers to cut costs and co-create affordable high-quality cosmetics.[24]

In new channel applications that can enhance perceptions of both the chore and fun types of shopping, retailers increasingly use chatbots to communicate with online customers or robots to interact with them in stores or else to complete orders in distribution and fulfillment centers. Chatbots support anytime, anywhere customer service, but they also deepen customer engagement, such that Domino's relies on chatbots to keep customers informed of the precise location of their pizza delivery. Macy's storehelp bot helps customers locate items within stores.[25]

Another recent development pertains to the emergence of **social shopping**, which uses social media networks and technologies to help users research and purchase products. For example, on Instagram, users can tap on logos within posts, which takes them directly to purchase sites. To some extent, though, social commerce has been stymied by a lack of consumer familiarity.[26]

EXAMPLE: POSHMARK (USA)

Poshmark, a fashion social network site, attracts more than 2.5 million users,[27] seeking access to the 5,000 brands and more than 25 million items available on the site.[28] But Poshmark does not carry or hold any inventory. Instead, during virtual shopping parties, sellers and buyers interact, and buyers can search the site at any time. Then following a sale, each seller ships the items to buyers, using postage-paid Poshmark envelopes. The site reports $500 million in gross merchandise transactions in a recent year; it takes a 20 percent cut on all merchandise sold, such that its revenue in that year was approximately $100 million. Although it began as a forum for women to sell fashionable items to friends, it has expanded to include men's and children's items. The social shopping site enables sellers to recommend products that might suit their customers' style; in essence, sellers act like virtual stylists. The hosted parties and social nature of the site also gives all the participants a sense of community. Poshmark thus has begun to attract small boutiques to its site and has added the Amazon Alexa app, so users can call on Alexa to help them find various themed or dedicated looks and items.[29]

Finally, augmented reality technology integrates virtual objects into a real-world setting, to enhance the virtual experience, and it appears poised to exert a substantial influence on retailing.[30] The Swedish furniture maker IKEA relies on augmented reality to help customers have a virtual experience of new designs, such that they can understand how they would interact with the kitchen layout or feel in a bedroom decorated according to the virtual design.[31] Such technologies offer great promise for personalizing each shopper's experience too.

EXAMPLE: BOON + GABLE (SA)

Boon + Gable combines advanced technology with the appeal of personal, in-home shopping consultants. Time-pressed professionals who need help with their wardrobe choices can download the company's app, which asks about their brand preferences, styles, body measurements,

(continued)

(continued)

and budgets. A stylist then schedules an in-home consultation, bringing along items that may interest the shopper. Customers can purchase the items immediately, receiving advice from the expert consultant about how to mix and match the items with clothing they already own. Boon + Gable works both with small boutiques and large department stores; an average order is $700, or about six times the sales earned through a traditional e-commerce order.[32] By gathering information from various consumers and their preferences, it also has built a recommendation engine. Thus Boon + Gable combines the best of online (never having to leave the house, relying on technology to predict user preferences) with a personalized human touch that helps shoppers feel confident in their purchases.[33]

RETAIL POSITIONING STRATEGIES

The retail sector is very competitive, so retailers must carve out a clear positioning strategy to attract customers. When a retailer chooses its positioning strategy, it must do so with a recognition of the significant potential effects on its competitiveness and performance. Having determined these effects, it can select specific cost-side and demand-side characteristics. For example, on the cost side, a retailer might focus on its margin and inventory turnover goals. On the demand side, the retailer needs to determine which service outputs to provide its shoppers. We discuss each of these issues in turn, then summarize our discussion by detailing how these choices help shape the retailer's overall strategy.

COST-SIDE POSITIONING STRATEGIES

In a high-service retailing system, **margins** are higher, but **turnover** (i.e., the number of times inventory on the shelf turns over in a specified period, usually a year) is lower. In low-price retailing systems, the opposite holds: low margins, high inventory turnover, and minimal service levels. Although the retail marketplace is filled with both types, excitement and attention often focus on the revolutionary volume efficiencies achieved by the advanced practitioners of low-price retailing systems (e.g., Walmart, Home Depot), which attain not only low margins and high turnover but also add in pretty good service. They are able to pay for such expensive service provision largely because of the high rates of return on their investments they earn, by always improving their asset management, using sophisticated information systems.

Historically, the low-margin/high-turnover model sought high operational efficiency so that it could pass any savings on to the customer. But as our channel perspective has taught us, passing savings on to the customer actually entails a *transfer* of costs (i.e., opportunity and effort costs), rather than their elimination. A consumer who shops at Costco, Sam's Club, or Carrefour may gain the benefit of a lower price but pays for it by taking on channel functions, such as bulk-breaking, transportation from a less convenient location, and higher self-service levels. This operational philosophy, such that the retailer trades off its margin and its turnover, reflects the recognition that certain segments of consumers are willing to absorb certain costs for some of their purchasing behaviors. But if consumers remain unwilling to trade off lower service levels (i.e., take on more channel functions themselves) for lower prices, retailers need to avoid such low-price, low-margin retail operations.

At the same time, lowering operational costs does not always require lowering the levels of *all* service outputs. Fashion-forward clothing retailers such as Zara and H&M offer end-users up-to-date assortments (i.e., excellent assortment and variety) and quick delivery of the hottest new styles but still hold costs down and thus can also provide competitive prices. Sidebars 6.1 and 6.2 highlight the different ways these two retailers have built their channel systems to meet these seemingly contradictory goals: Zara uses a highly vertically integrated path, whereas H&M relies on much more outsourcing. As long as the retailers hold their costs down, either method seems feasible.

SIDEBAR 6.1
Zara: A European Retailer Using the Low-Margin, High-Turnover Model of Retailing

Zara was founded in Spain in 1975, and in the few decades of its existence, it has built and fine-tuned a particular model of fashion retailing that appears to balance the need to control costs with the need to meet the demands of its fashion-forward, trendy target market.

Zara's target consumer in Europe is a fashion-conscious, young female who values novelty and exclusivity but is also quite price-sensitive. The most important service output demands of this consumer are therefore *assortment and variety* (which should be extensive and novel) and *quick delivery* (i.e., extremely fashion-forward and available to buy). Providing a quickly changing, market-responsive assortment of reasonably priced, fashion-forward clothing has long been one of the thorniest challenges for retailers. Zara has met this challenge through a combination of strategies:

- It makes 40 percent of its own fabric and owns its own dyeing company, which permits it to buy undyed fabric from outsiders and postpone coloring fabric until it knows what colors are really popular in a given season.

- It owns its own production for more than 50 percent of its clothes, thus retaining control over production from start to finish.

- It concentrates all of its owned production and warehousing in one area, in Galicia in northern Spain.

- It purposely makes small amounts of product at a time, rather than large-batch volumes.

- It owns its own logistics and trucking operations, which in some cases may mean sending a half-empty truck through Europe.

- It has invested in significant communications capabilities, from the store manager-level back to the designers, from designers to production, from production to warehousing, and from the warehouse back to retail stores.

- It sticks to a rigid reordering, production, and shipping schedule that makes restocking stores extremely predictable to everyone in the system, including consumers.

- It favors introducing new styles over restocking styles it has already shipped once and has invested in an extremely flexible manufacturing operation to permit this approach.

These policies actually contradict many practices throughout retailing today—from the highly vertically integrated set of operations Zara pursues, to the rigid controls it exerts throughout its logistics and ordering systems, to its small-batch production practices, to the constant revamping of product lines in the stores. So how can Zara possibly make money with such a topsy-turvy retailing system?

The answer lies in its apparently high-cost methods of operation, which actually *maximize turnover and save costs* in other parts of its business. Because Zara has invested in significant amounts of communication at all levels of its business (which is also possible because of its investments in vertical integration), designers at headquarters learn about new "hot" styles mid-season, before any of Zara's competitors are able to see the trends and respond to them. With its flexible manufacturing operations, its well-integrated clothing designers can work closely with manufacturing operations to create cutting-edge designs and feed them to manufacturing with no delay. It also is more feasible to respond to this information, because Zara has chosen *not* to make large-batch volumes of any styles it innovates; thus, it has the space in the stores to accommodate new styles. Furthermore, it does not suffer from large overstocks and thus does not need to mark down merchandise as heavily as its competitors do. That is, it never produces large volumes of any style, and it only produces styles for which it has market-level indications of demand.

Because Zara actually cultivates slack (i.e., unused) capacity in its factories and warehouse, it can accommodate rush jobs that would cause bottlenecks in standard retail systems. And because Zara's consumers *know* that Zara is constantly coming out with new styles (as well as *exactly when* the stores are restocked), they shop more often (particularly right after a new shipment comes in), to keep up with the new styles. For example, a shopper in London visits a standard clothing store (where she shops routinely) about four times per year; the same shopper visits a Zara store 17 times per year! The Zara shopper feels a certain urgency to buy a garment when she sees it at the store, because she may not be able to find it again if she waits to get it. This increases sales rates and merchandise turnover.

So what are the results of Zara's retailing strategy?

1. Zara has almost no inventories in its system:

   o An item sits in its warehouse only a few *hours* on average (not days or weeks!).

   o Store deliveries occur (on schedule) twice per week to each store in the system, worldwide.

   o Most items turn over in less than one week (significantly less than its competitors' inventory turn rates).

2. Zara can create a new design, manufacture it, and have it on its stores' shelves in just *two weeks*, versus 9 to 12 *months* for other retailers (e.g., The Gap, VF Corporation).

3. Zara's shipments are 98.9 percent accurate, and it enjoys a very low shrinkage rate of 0.5 percent (i.e., loss of inventory due to theft or damage).

4. Its designers bring over 10,000 new designs to market (versus 2,000–4,000 items introduced by The Gap or H&M) each year.

5. Zara maintains net profit margins of about 10 percent annually, as good as the best retailers in the business, even though its prices are fairly low.

6. It does little advertising, spending only 0.3 percent of sales on ads, versus the more typical 3 to 4 percent of sales for its competitors. It does not need to spend on advertising, because its shoppers are in the stores so many times a year that there is no need for advertising to remind them to come.

7. On average, Zara collects 85 percent of list price on its clothing items, versus an industry average of only 60 to 70 percent (including markdowns). This rate leads to higher net margins; in one year, Zara's net margin was 10.5 percent, H&M's was 9.5 percent, Benetton's was 7 percent, and The Gap's was 0 percent.

In short, Zara's formula for success rests on its highly centralized control, all the way from its input sourcing (dyes, fabrics), to design, to logistics and shipping, and finally to retailing. Given the high cost of owning all of these resources, Zara has to maximize the value created from them—which it does very well, by excelling at meeting the core service output demands of its target market, namely novel and extensive variety and assortment, quickly.[34]

SIDEBAR 6.2
H&M: Another Low-Margin, High-Turnover European Retailer, with a Different Channel Strategy

In contrast to Zara, described in Sidebar 6.1, consider the strategy of H&M, an international retailer founded in 1947 in Sweden. Like Zara, it sells "cheap chic" clothing, and its core consumer is similar to Zara's (though its stores also offer men's, teens', and children's clothing). The average price of an item in H&M in 2002 was just $18, and shoppers look there for current-season fashions at bargain prices.

H&M's formula for offering this assortment to its consumers at aggressively low prices is somewhat different than Zara's, however. H&M does not own any manufacturing capacity, relying on outsourcing relationships with a network of 900 suppliers located in low-wage countries like Bangladesh, China, and Turkey. It frequently shifts production from one supplier to another, depending on demand in the market for various fabrics, styles, and fashions. All of H&M's merchandise is designed in-house by a cadre of 95 designers in Stockholm

(Zara has about 300 designers, all at its headquarters in Spain). The management style is extremely frugal; not only does the company control manufacturing costs, but its managers do not fly business class and try not to take cabs when traveling.

H&M focuses on minimizing inventory everywhere in its system. It has the ability to create a new design and get it into stores in as little as three weeks (a bit longer than Zara, but still extremely impressive, given industry norms). It restocks stores on a daily basis, which is not always frequent enough; when it opened its flagship store in New York City, it had to restock on an *hourly* basis. Because its merchandise turns over very quickly, it can charge very low prices for it yet maintain good profitability.

H&M has chosen a more aggressive store growth strategy than Zara, which has caused it some problems in recent years. Its entry into the United States was plagued by poor location choices, as well as leases for stores that were too big. It worked on these problems and reached a breakeven point in the United States in 2004.

Whether the H&M-style model—farming out production to third parties and ruthlessly cutting costs everywhere in the system—or the Zara model—purposely cultivating slack capacity and investing in highly flexible but vertically integrated facilities—will dominate is not at all clear. It is entirely possible that both will flourish in the future, as both have well-integrated systems in place that meet the needs of the market, albeit in different ways.[35]

Like all organizations, retailers have to achieve financial targets. Of critical importance in determining the retail strategy is whether they should emphasize low margins and high turnover or else seek high margins at low turnover. Managers must arrive at their best estimates of the organization's chances for achieving its financial targets, often using a **strategic profit model (SPM)**,[36] which proposes that retailers need to manage either their margins or their assets, or both. It starts with the concept of **net sales**, defined as gross sales less customer returns and allowances. Then the SPM highlights three components:

1. **Margins**, or the ratio of profit to sales. Every retailer should seek to manage its margins (net profit/net sales).

2. **Asset turnover** (net sales/total assets), which captures the retailer's efficiency in creating revenue from the assets it has deployed. Put another way, it captures the amount of assets that need to be deployed to generate a certain amount of revenue.

3. **Financial leverage**, measured by an equity multiplier (total assets/net worth), which demonstrates how leveraged a retailer is. The conventional goal is to secure a **target return** on its net worth (net profit/net worth).

Accordingly, we can present the SPM with the following equations:

$$\frac{net\ profit}{net\ sales} \times \frac{net\ sales}{total\ assets} = \frac{net\ profit}{total\ assets},\ and$$

$$\frac{net\ profit}{total\ assets} \times \frac{total\ assets}{net\ worth} = \frac{net\ profit}{net\ worth}.\ Thus:$$

$$\frac{net\ profit}{net\ sales} \times \frac{net\ sales}{total\ assets} \times \frac{total\ assets}{net\ worth} = \frac{net\ profit}{net\ worth}.$$

If competition or economic conditions exert strong downward pressure on margins, management can pursue asset turnover more actively, using more appropriate designs that improve sales per square foot (which reflects space and location productivity), sales per employee (labor productivity), or sales per transaction (merchandising program productivity).

In retail setting, three interrelated performance measures also suggest ways for retailers to improve their profitability (see also Appendix 6.1). First, **gross margin return on inventory investment (GMROI)** is equal to the gross margin percentage, multiplied by the ratio of sales to inventory (at cost). This combination of margin management and inventory management can be calculated for companies, markets, stores, departments, classes of products, or SKUs. With the GMROI, the retailer can evaluate its performance according to the returns it earns on its investments in inventory. Several tactics offer means for retailers to use this information to improve their inventory returns. For example, efficient consumer response (ECR) initiatives in the grocery industry seek to reduce average inventory levels while maintaining sales by relying on just-in-time shipments, electronic data interchange (EDI) linkages between manufacturers and retailers, and the like. Such actions reduce the GMROI denominator without changing the numerator.

However, GMROI suffers a few notable limitations. Items with widely varying gross margin percentages appear equally profitable, as in the following example.

	Gross Margin	×	Sales-to-Inventory Ratio	= GMROI
A	50%	×	3	= 150%
B	30%	×	5	= 150%
C	25%	×	6	= 150%

The gross margin only accounts for the cost of goods sold, not for differences in the variable costs associated with selling different kinds of merchandise. Other measures that include more comprehensive measures tend to be more difficult to derive, though.

Second, when it comes to the **gross margin per full-time equivalent employee (GMROL)**, retailers' goals are to *optimize*, not maximize. As sales per square foot rise, some fixed costs (e.g., rent, utilities, advertising) might not increase but even could decline as a percentage of sales. Imagine, for example, that a retailer stocks up on inventory before the busy holiday shopping season. By also hiring some additional salespeople to help out in December, it suffers lower average sales per employee, but profitability still jumps, because these additional employees are better able to facilitate sales, by getting the new inventory onto the sales floor faster and leveraging other fixed assets (e.g., opening all the checkout lines, making sure displays are clean and uncluttered) in the store. Of course, during conventional sales periods, comparisons across companies still can reveal that one achieves better GMROL than others.

Third, the **gross margin per square foot (GMROS)** supports an assessment of how well retailers use a unique and powerful asset: the shelf or floor space that they agree to allocate to manufacturers' products.

Retailers' uses of such gross margin measures exert pressure on suppliers, which need to find a way to secure sufficient margins for retailers, earned through their brands. Those margins depend on the sales volume their brands generate, the amount of shelf or floor space consumed by their brands, and the costs incurred to store, handle, and sell their brands.

In response, upstream channel members increasingly seek to speed up inventory replenishment steps, because replenishing stocks more quickly means the retailer can devote less costly shelf space to the frequently replenished items, as well as suffer fewer inventory-holding costs. Although related *fixed-cost* investments, such as inventory management systems, eventually reduce marginal costs, they can be difficult to introduce into the channel, because the various channel partners have to bear their substantial costs upfront.

For example, Michaels Craft Stores, the leading craft retailer worldwide, tried to start small by educating suppliers about the benefits of incorporating bar coding, common SKU numbers, computerized labels, and electronic invoicing into the channel. Yet suppliers—often small, local, artisanal organizations—resisted the initial costs of incorporating such technologies into their relatively non-computerized businesses.[37] Such resistance might reflect two key problems. First, the channel partner might not *understand* the marginal cost savings it (and the channel overall) ultimately will accrue by making immediate fixed-cost investments in improved technologies. Second, if various members of the channel do not *trust* the channel manager, they may suspect opportunism, such that their high upfront costs might generate benefits only for one member of the channel. The former problem requires expertise power to educate channel partners about the cost reduction benefits; the latter demands more investments in conflict reduction and trust building.

Finally, we need to consider the effects of one other major retailing cost and its implications for retail strategy choices, namely the rent that bricks-and-mortar stores pay their landlords. In shopping malls, for example, the largest "anchor" stores traditionally have generated disproportionate benefits for the developer, because they attract shoppers who also patronize other stores in the mall. In return, according to one study, they paid significantly lower rental rates (up to 72 percent lower per square foot!) than non-anchor stores.[38] Such subsidies even persist despite the generally lower sales per square foot that anchor stores generate, compared with specialty and other smaller stores. In some malls, the anchor tenants are being replaced by multiple (two to five) mid-sized stores such as Dick's Sporting Goods, T.J. Maxx, and the Container Store and landlords are able to charge more rent per square foot from these tenants.[39] Thus, the economics of a retail store, which inform its strategic position choices, depend on internal cost factors but also on the cost factors determined by the retail environment in which the store functions.

Demand-Side Positioning Strategies

Every retailer would love to earn higher margins and higher merchandise turnover and lower retailing costs. But this ideal combination is likely impossible; instead, retailers combine these variables strategically in their various efforts to attain approximately equitable financial outcomes. Beyond these decisions, then, the retailer must consider what service outputs it will supply to make the best use of its combination of characteristics and appeal effectively to its chosen target market.

Bulk-Breaking

This function is classically the provenance of a retail intermediary. Manufacturers make huge batches of products; consumers want to consume just one unit. Therefore, traditional, service-oriented retailers buy in large quantities and offer consumers exactly the quantity they want. Some grocery retailers even go beyond conventional bulk-breaking. They first separate the pallets of eggs they receive into individual, one-dozen cartons for customers. But they also might allow customers to break the dozen-egg bundle into smaller portions, based on their needs.

Other retailers, such as warehouse stores (e.g., Sam's Club, Costco), offer consumers a lower price but require them to buy larger lot sizes (i.e., break bulk less). Consumers whose transportation, storage, and financing costs already are relatively low may choose to buy a case of paper towels or 10-pound bags of frozen vegetables at lower per unit prices (though they must expend more monetary costs upfront). More traditional grocery retailers also often encourage, but do not force, larger lot-size purchases through special pricing, such as "buy one, get one free" deals or bundle pricing (e.g., "three for $1").

On the other end of this trend spectrum are so-called dollar stores, which offer very small quantities of products at very low prices. Thus a consumer can purchase a small bottle of dishwashing detergent or a package of two or three cookies. The unit price on these items is higher than in other retailers, but consumers enjoy the benefits of massive bulk-breaking, which is particularly valuable if they are unable or unwilling to perform financing or inventory-holding channel functions.

Spatial Convenience

Products can be classified as convenience, shopping, or specialty goods, and this categorization depends on the extent of search or shopping activity the consumer is willing to undertake. To determine its positioning strategy, a retailer must recall that convenience goods should require little effort to obtain, whereas considerable effort may be required to secure highly regarded, relatively scarce specialty goods. *The retail location decision, and the resulting service output of spatial convenience, thus is inextricable from the type of goods the retailer chooses to offer.* As a general rule, retail locations should be convenient to their target market, a lesson that H&M might have forgotten for its introduction to the United States (see Sidebar 6.2), when it chose locations in suburban New Jersey and Syracuse, New York.

Furthermore, the balance of search/shopping behavior, and thus demand for spatial convenience, varies across consumer segments and with changing demographic and lifestyle trends. Households in which all the adults work face higher opportunity costs for time, such that the effective costs of searches and shopping increase. Thus one shopper might be impressed with the service offerings of a SuperTarget store (i.e., a format that includes both food and non-food items) in her area—though not quite impressed enough to overcome the lack of spatial convenience it offers. Because it is farther away than her local grocery store, "It won't replace my weekly grocery store trip."[40] In contrast, Walgreens' drug and convenience store chain purposefully seeks out locations that are conveniently on consumers' usual shopping paths, often finding sites near major grocery stores. By adding service offerings that decrease the average transaction time in the store to 14 minutes, Walgreens also increases the chances that a shopper will get a parking space close to the store, another form of spatial convenience.[41]

Waiting and Delivery Time

Consumers differ in their willingness to tolerate out-of-stock situations when they shop; even the same consumer exhibits differential willingness across different purchase occasions. Intense demand for this channel function translates into a demand that a product be in stock at all times, which in turn means retailers must take on more of the expensive inventory-holding function, by holding extra safety stocks in their stores. To fine-tune its strategy, each retailer must gauge how damaging an out-of-stock occurrence would be. Most grocery retailers make it a high priority to avoid out-of-stock situations for basic products, such as milk or bread, but may feel more confident about running out of an exotic, perishable, specialty fruit.

For a furniture retailer, in-store stocks tend to be so low that consumers seeking to purchase likely would not expect to take their desired sofa home with them and instead anticipate waiting (up to 8 to 12 weeks) to receive delivery (which implies that they trade off long wait times for better delivery service outputs).

Not every combination of waiting and delivery service outputs represents such a clear trade-off, though. One furniture manufacturer, England Inc., refigured its manufacturing operations to be able to build 11,000 upholstered sofas and chairs per week, each made to order, for delivery to consumers within three weeks of their order. This speed greatly diminished the wait time required by its traditional competitors, but it did so without requiring consumers to give up delivery capacity (or assortment and variety), as they would have to do if they purchased a ready-made sofa from Walmart or another alternative source. By improving both service outputs, England has enjoyed strong sales performance.[42] This provision suggests changing competitive norms in the marketplace as well. When competitors improve their provision of a key service output, the old performance norms may be insufficient to keep consumers loyal, such that constant updates to the retail strategy become necessary. When Lowe's and Home Depot promised quicker delivery of the large appliances on their showroom floors for example, Sears had little choice but to try to keep pace with next- or same-day delivery offers.[43]

Other retailers continue to deviate purposefully from standard competitive norms, expressly to establish unique retail positions in the market. Zara's planned stockout policies (see Sidebar 6.1) have served to both minimize inventory-holding costs and create consumer excitement and urgency to purchase. Discount club retailers offer no guarantee of in-stock status, so if consumers find their preferred brand of fabric softener on the shelves, they know they had better purchase immediately. Otherwise, they may be forced to wait a long (and perhaps more critically, *unpredictable*) amount of time before finding the product in the store again. A very brand-loyal consumer finds this scenario intolerable, but "treasure hunters" love the prospect of finding a one-of-a-kind item on sale at Costco, never to be seen again on its shelves.

Product Variety

Variety describes different classes of goods that constitute the product offering; that is, the *breadth* of the product lines. **Assortment** instead refers to the *depth* of product brands or models offered within each generic product category. Discounters such as Target and Walmart offer limited assortments of fast-moving, low-priced items across a wide variety of goods; a specialty store dealing in only, or primarily, home audiovisual electronic goods, such as Listenup, instead stocks a very large and complete line of a smaller variety of items, offering the deepest assortment of models, styles, sizes, prices, and so on.

Sometimes a retailer's variety and assortment choice is purposefully narrow, to appeal to a particular niche (e.g., pregnant women shopping at maternity clothing stores). If such a retail concept saturates the market, though, further attempts at growth are challenging, as Gymboree learned. The upscale children's clothes stores, located mainly in malls, had to expand into different **store concepts**, rather than trying to extend its own specific assortment or variety. To start, it began opening Janie and Jack stores that could sell a specific assortment of upscale baby gifts. In addition, it has sought to advance into an array of related but distinct retail concepts, allowing the corporate channel to increase both its assortment and its variety, while leaving these factors consistent in each store line.[44] In so doing, it also needs to beware of several pitfalls: avoid cannibalization of the core retail concept while exploiting its knowledge of the retailing concepts that made it successful to begin with.

The variety and assortment dimension clearly demands the careful and strategic attention of top management, because these decisions determine the entire character of the enterprise. After the basic strategy has been established, though, the task of choosing *specific* products or brands usually falls to the buyers. **Buyers** play a central role in retailing; some retailers even generate more profits through the trade deals and allowances that their buyers negotiate than they earn through their merchandising efforts. Because buying is such a critical aspect of retailing, it is important to understand the evaluative processes and procedures involved in merchandise and supplier selection. The appendices to this chapter seek to improve such understanding: Appendix 6.1 is a glossary of pricing and buying terms commonly used by retailers, and Appendix 6.2 briefly describes some of their merchandise planning and control procedures.

Customer Service

Virtually all major retail innovations in the past century have relied on manipulating the customer service variable, to greater or lesser degrees. Consider in-store sales help, for example. In warehouse clubs that have eliminated expert sales clerks who can help customers locate and compare the various personal computers on offer, the locate–compare–select process becomes the consumer's responsibility. But in Apple stores, the resident Geniuses provide not only detailed, extensive advice about the products for sale but also post-sales service, to the extent they will transfer data from the customer's old computer to his or her new Mac while the customer waits.

Retailing is one of the few industries that remains highly labor-intensive. **Sales, general, and administrative (SG&A)** expenses for retailers thus must include the cost of keeping salespeople on the floor to help shoppers. As a percentage of net sales, SG&A tends to be higher for specialty stores (e.g., Ann Taylor, The Gap) and department stores (e.g., Nordstrom) than for office supply or drug stores (e.g., Walgreens). The retailers with the lowest SG&A percentages are general merchandise retailers and hypermarkets (e.g., Costco, Walmart).

Table 6.2 summarizes the net sales, SG&A expenses, and SG&A-to-net sales percentages for several stores in each category. As these data show, providing better

	Net Sales ($million)	SG&A Expenses ($million)	SG&A as % of Net Sales	**TABLE 6.2**
General Merchandise, Hypermarkets, Category Killers				Net Sales and SG&A Expenses of Retailers
Walmart	481,317	101,853	21.16	
Costco	126,127	12,950	10.26	
Home Depot	94,595	17,132	18.11	
Target	69,495	13,356	19.22	
Lowe's	65,017	15,129	23.27	
Drugs, Home Electronics				
Walgreens	118,214	23,740	20.08	
Best Buy	39,403	7,547	19.15	
Department Stores				
Kohl's	18,686	4,435	23.73	
JCPenney	12,547	3,557	28.35	
Nordstrom	14,757	4,315	29.24	
Dillards	6,418	1,681	26.19	
Specialty Stores				
The Gap	15,516	4,140	26.68	
Ann Taylor	6,649	2,068	31.1	
Chico's	2,480	772	31.13	

Source: Annual reports for 2017 for each company.

service is a costly function for retailers. Lower service retailers such as Costco appear to compensate the consumer for the lack of service provision, with lower costs. On the flip side, a higher SG&A percentage for Ann Taylor or Chico's may be entirely consistent with the very high level of in-store service that its salespeople offer, such that the retailer is able to charge commensurately higher prices. However, it appears somewhat disconcerting when a retailer that adopts a low service strategy also features a high SG&A percentage, as is the case for JCPenney.

These variations reflect the costs of customer service but also its remarkable benefits. Retailers continue to invest in customer service because it can bring about these substantial benefits. Consider a seemingly humble example: the provision of shopping carts in retail stores. Carts are common in grocery stores, as well as in mass merchandisers or hypermarkets. But apparel retailers generally resist them as inconsistent with their images, especially for high-end offerings such as Nordstrom offers. At the same time, shoppers in mass-market retail outlets buy an average of 7.2 items when using a cart, compared with only 6.1 items without a cart. A department store shopper with a child in the cart's seat, another child hanging onto the cart's handle, and multiple, bulky boxes of children's shoes in the basket seems highly likely to appreciate this service offering! Furthermore, this relatively small investment (each cart costs about $100) generates substantial consumer service benefits for broad segments of shoppers,[45] because it removes the costs of performing a channel function from consumers' shoulders.

In all these demand-based dimensions of retailing strategy, the goal thus is to identify the functions that consumers are (or are not) willing to assume. With that information, the retailer can select its positioning and calculate the cost—in time, money, effort, and convenience—of taking on additional service output functions, if doing so might make it more attractive to consumers.

RETAIL CHANNELS

Consumers are increasingly comfortable with buying through multiple channels and types of outlets, such that their purchase behavior varies not just by segment but also by purchase occasion.[46] Some consumers like to browse through bricks-and-mortar bookstores, because they hope to stumble on a surprise and enjoy a cup of coffee while they review book jackets. Another segment of consumers prefers to order books through Amazon, because their tastes are so unique that they are unlikely to find their favorite texts in a regular store. Other consumers have eliminated traditional books from their reading habits altogether, downloading everything they read through Kindle. And yet other consumers practice "hybrid shopping," using online, bricks-and-mortar, and electronic versions of products to complete their shopping process, perhaps by browsing the bookstore on their way home to find a new novel, checking prices on Amazon, and then selecting the Kindle or paperback version, whichever is less expensive, for their final purchase.

This broad array of shopping behaviors means that designing a retail strategy involves careful consideration of the entire process the consumer undergoes, which eventually may culminate in a sale. But the firm needs to be present in many more channel locations before it gets to that point. In this section, we consider some new locations in the retail channel, including current uses of the Internet as a retail outlet and retail facilitator, direct selling as an alternative mode to reach consumers, and hybrid shopping behavior.

Internet Retail Channels

Worldwide retail e-commerce sales have reached about $2.290 trillion.[47] The dominant consideration that propels e-commerce transactions by most consumers is convenience, defined in terms of ease and speed of access. The increased use of home shopping technologies (e.g., catalogs, online, televised, digital assistants) also is testimony to the importance of spatial convenience, in this expanded sense.

That is, the critical consideration may still be "location, location, location," but the placement of physical outlets is less of an issue for many firms.

In the first quarter of 2012, U.S. retail e-commerce sales were $53.1 billion. By the third quarter of 2017, they had more than doubled, to $115.3 billion, accounting for 10.2 percent of global retail sales in 2017.[48] Figure 6.1 summarizes e-commerce and total retail sales from 1998 to 2015, revealing that though offline sales still dominate, e-commerce sales continue to increase each year. Not only have e-commerce sales steadily increased, but they have increased at a rate greater than the rate of total U.S. retail sales growth, so that the proportion of all retail sales consummated through e-commerce channels keeps increasing. For example, when comparing third-quarter retail sales from 2016 to 2017, e-commerce showed a 15.1 percent increase, relative to the much lower 4.3 percent increase for total retail sales.[49]

In the United States, nearly two-thirds of the population makes an online purchase in a given year; China exhibits a higher share of online sales, but only about one-third of customers make online purchases.[50] Rather, the bulk of online sales come through mobile channels, which account for 58.9 percent of online sales. Such growth in mobile commerce is largely driven by the Chinese market, which accounts for two-thirds of worldwide e-commerce.

Online retailers also have emerged as "information storehouses" that incorporate video and detailed text descriptions of products, product reviews, and

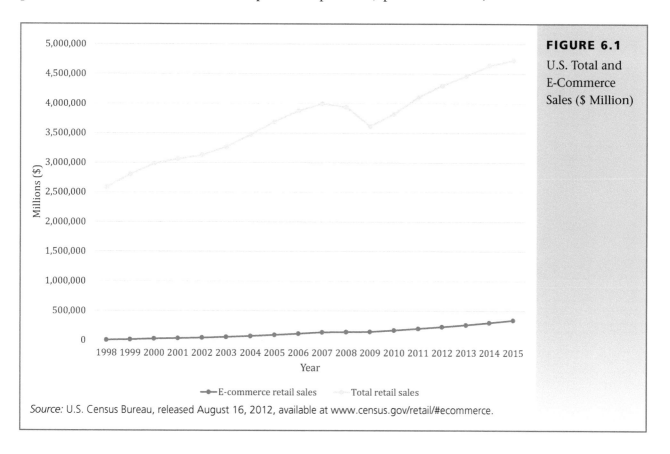

FIGURE 6.1

U.S. Total and E-Commerce Sales ($ Million)

Source: U.S. Census Bureau, released August 16, 2012, available at www.census.gov/retail/#ecommerce.

recommendation algorithms.[51] In this sense, the high quality of information available online represents another driver of consumers' preferences for online channels, where they also can find a wider selection of products. Among the information they can gather, online channels enable consumers to compare prices easily across retailers.

Direct Selling Channels

Direct selling involves "the sale of a consumer product or service in a face-to-face manner away from a fixed retail location."[52] Direct selling organizations (DSOs) use such techniques to reach final consumers, relying on personal selling as a key to their channel structure and retail positioning. Well-known DSOs include Amway (household cleaning products, personal care products, appliances), Mary Kay (cosmetics), Herbalife (nutritional supplements and vitamins), Avon (cosmetics), Pampered Chef (cookware and bakeware), and Tupperware (household storage containers)—though various brands sell almost every type of good and service that consumers can buy. The most popular items are consumable products that can be purchased repeatedly, often by the personal network that an independent distributor develops. Direct selling is a very old method of distribution that remains viable because of consumers' interest in personal interactions, combined with the low cost of forming and running these channels.

Nearly 20.5 million people engaged in direct selling in the United States in 2016, 74 percent of whom were women.[53] Their direct selling generated more than $35 billion in retail sales across wellness, home and family care, and personal care industries, in addition to various services. Yet typical members of this sector do not make a living or support their families solely through direct selling; they tend to be married women who work for the DSO part-time. Some people certainly earn substantial amounts, but a more common scenario involves supplemental earnings, to complement the family's main source of income.

Some of these pay discrepancies stem from the unique channel structures of DSOs. Whether the DSO brand manufactures the goods it sells or contracts for their manufacture with other companies, it relies on downstream intermediaries, variously called "distributors," "consultants," or "salespeople" (we use the term "distributors" here). These **distributors** are independent contractors, rather than employees of the companies, who purchase inventory at a lower price, then resell it at a markup to downstream end-users. They thus bear physical possession and ownership, risking, ordering, and payment flow costs—though perhaps their most important function is promotion, in that standard advertising is very rare among DSOs.

In a multi-level DSO (or MLDSO), distributors earn compensation in three ways. First, they earn the distributor-to-retail markup on the goods they buy wholesale from the DSO. Second, the DSO pays them a commission on every sale. Third, a distributor who recruits other distributors also makes commissions on the sales those recruits make. Compensation plans differ widely in MLDSOs, but for illustration, consider the example in Figure 6.2:[54] Catherine has been recruited directly by Janet. Janet is Catherine's "upline," and Catherine, Susan, Kent, and all their recruits collectively constitute Janet's "downline." Janet sells $200 worth of products in a month; Catherine, Susan, and Kent each sell $100; and Catherine's three recruits each sell $50 of product. Thus, Janet's personal volume is $200, but her group volume is $650 (the sum of her volume and the volumes of every distributor in her downline). Because Janet's group volume commission rate is 7 percent, she earns $45.50 on her group volume, less the net commissions earned by her downlines. Susan, Kent, and Catherine receive a lower commission rate of 5 percent, so on the $450 they collectively sell, they receive $22.50 (or 5 percent of $450). Janet's net *commission* earnings are therefore $23.00 ($45.50 – $22.50); she also earns money on the wholesale-to-retail markup (usually 40 to 50 percent) she garners on her own personal sales.

The structure of the compensation system in a MLDSO creates different incentives for direct selling versus building a direct selling network, which requires a delicate balance by the DSO. The more time current distributors spend recruiting new distributors, the bigger the DSO's network gets. But recruiting new distributors without spending sufficient time selling products does not generate revenues or profits for the DSO.[55] This balance illustrates the clear distinction between legitimate DSOs and illegitimate pyramid schemes. A **pyramid scheme** is a fraudulent mechanism

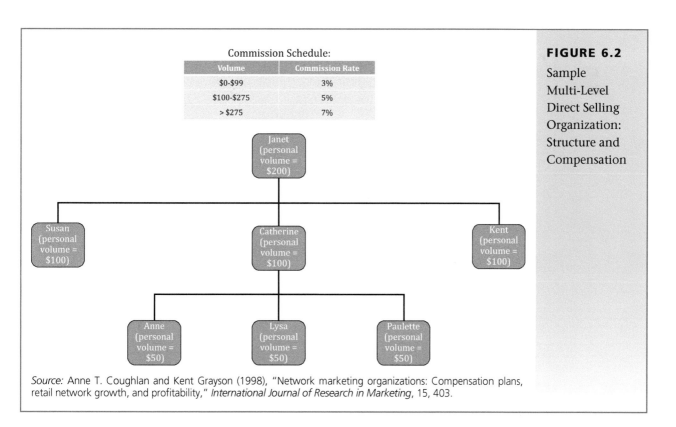

FIGURE 6.2

Sample Multi-Level Direct Selling Organization: Structure and Compensation

Commission Schedule:

Volume	Commission Rate
$0-$99	3%
$100-$275	5%
> $275	7%

Janet (personal volume = $200)

Susan (personal volume = $100)

Catherine (personal volume = $100)

Kent (personal volume = $100)

Anne (personal volume = $50)

Lysa (personal volume = $50)

Paulette (personal volume = $50)

Source: Anne T. Coughlan and Kent Grayson (1998), "Network marketing organizations: Compensation plans, retail network growth, and profitability," *International Journal of Research in Marketing*, 15, 403.

that demands new recruits pay a non-refundable fee to become a distributor, and existing distributors earn rewards simply for getting new recruits to sign on and pay this fee. Both the company and the distributor earn money without selling a product or service, which means they do not provide any value or benefits in exchange for customer payments. Many pyramid scheme victims do not appreciate the risk of this inherent instability; people who do often try to take opportunistic advantage of the system before it collapses. Although they were not retailers, financiers also have famously exploited pyramid schemes, such as when Bernard Madoff convinced investors to keep adding money to his investment schemes, without ever providing any actual service.[56]

To guard against illegal pyramid schemes, legitimate DSOs have created a code of ethics for their industry. Thus, some positioning choices are made in advance for legitimate DSOs: they offer low entry barriers, or costs, of joining (e.g., a reasonable fee for a "starter kit"); accept unsold merchandise for a nearly complete refund (e.g., 90 percent); and provide rewards based primarily on product sales, not the recruitment of downline members of the network. However, this distinction between a legitimate DSO and an illegal pyramid scheme is not always obvious to casual observers, which means that a legitimate DSO has other positioning choices to make. In particular, because it is relatively easy to sign on as a distributor, many people do so without serious consideration of what it takes to run a part-time sales business. Recruits without the right business acumen may make costly mistakes before they quit, and though no DSO can protect its distributors from making some bad decisions, each of them has a vested interest in trying to select and manage new recruits to minimize such problems. Doing so avoids the image problems that continue to plague fraudulent direct selling activities, ensuring a better reputation, and thus stronger sales, for that DSO.

Hybrid Retail Channels

No single retail form is likely sufficient to reach a market or satisfy a particular target segment's set of service output demands. Some firms are pure online sellers, but most combine bricks-and-mortar stores with online selling strategies. As we noted in Chapter 1, many of the biggest brick-and-mortar retailers also dominate the online space. Even with Amazon's remarkable successes, it is moving beyond an exclusive focus on online selling, as we noted previously in describing its acquisition of Whole Foods. The persistence of mixtures of retail solutions in various product categories suggests that on the demand side, consumers value having more than one way to access desired products. This value may be a segmentation indication (i.e., some consumers always shop online, others always shop in brick-and-mortar stores, so to attract both segments, a retailer must use both retail outlets) or else an indication that any single consumer routinely can and does use multiple retail outlets to complete a purchase.

The implications of these parallel indications are multiple. First, even if sales appear to be shifting from one type of outlet to another, it may be a bad idea to shut down the former, because its role may have shifted as well, namely from a place to complete the sale to a place to gather other valued service outputs, such as information provision or customer service. Determining the true economic value added of this type of retail outlet may not be easy, but clearly it offers some economic value by preserving multiple retail routes to market. If these hybrid channels are not vertically integrated, the channel manager's task becomes even more difficult: an information provider likely is not sufficiently compensated for its costly service outputs if another member of the channel earns all the sales. In this case, *free riding* becomes a natural byproduct of hybrid retail channel usage, and the channel manager must decide how to maintain equity.

Second, the question of whether hybrid shopping involves multiple consumers or one consumer using multiple channels is far more critical than it may seem at first. Imagine you are the retail manager for a manufacturer that contracts with both independent brick-and-mortar retailers and Internet retail outlets (which might be owned by the brick-and-mortar retailers as part of their own hybrid retailing strategy). Both outlets are retail outlets, because both can (and do) sell to end-users. However, the brick-and-mortar store also serves as an infomediary for consumers who like to look in person, then buy online—the showrooming phenomenon we mentioned previously. In this increasingly common situation, there really are *three* routes to market: (1) brick-and-mortar channel (consumers ignore the online channel), (2) online channel (consumers ignore the brick-and-mortar channel), and (3) **hybrid channel** (consumers obtain some service outputs online and others offline). Only by recognizing the three-part channel structure can channel managers measure the incremental effectiveness of any individual outlet accurately. The measurement grows even more complex if we add in other channels. Such a view of the channel structure can be especially useful in negotiations among channel members who worry that their markets are being stolen or that they are not being fairly compensated for the services they render. Also, consumers do not just migrate between online and offline channels. They follow different paths to purchase and often switch among devices online. In Figure 6.3, we highlight how consumers simultaneously use multiple channels to search for and purchase products and services.

Third, manufacturers and retailers that use multiple retail routes to market to create broader brand awareness and market reach still need to find a way to control channel conflict. For brick-and-mortar retailers, catalog channels are an excellent way to increase their reach; Neiman Marcus, the upscale retailer based in Dallas, Texas, has published a Christmas catalog since 1926 and sends out approximately 90 different catalogs annually to more than 100 million potential consumers who would be hard pressed to find a store in their nearby vicinity.[57] In this case, the additional route to market did not create much conflict, because the retailer owns both the brick-and-mortar stores and the catalog effort (as well as its online channels).

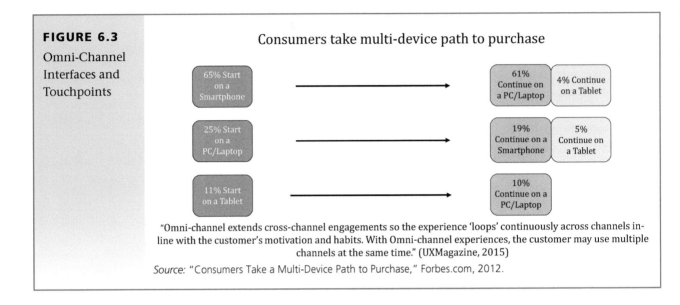

FIGURE 6.3

Omni-Channel Interfaces and Touchpoints

Consumers take multi-device path to purchase

65% Start on a Smartphone → 61% Continue on a PC/Laptop | 4% Continue on a Tablet

25% Start on a PC/Laptop → 19% Continue on a Smartphone | 5% Continue on a Tablet

11% Start on a Tablet → 10% Continue on a PC/Laptop

"Omni-channel extends cross-channel engagements so the experience 'loops' continuously across channels in-line with the customer's motivation and habits. With Omni-channel experiences, the customer may use multiple channels at the same time." (UXMagazine, 2015)

Source: "Consumers Take a Multi-Device Path to Purchase," Forbes.com, 2012.

For direct sellers, it appears that the hybrid channel challenge has been a bit more stressful, especially as a result of modern demographics. With women just as likely to work out of the home as within, the "stay-at-home mom" model that supported so many companies' direct selling operations suffered a blow. Thus, Avon yielded to the strong temptation to add online selling to its cosmetics channel mix—only to hear from angry "Avon ladies" (its independent distributors) that their newest competitor was also their DSO. Avon's initial hybrid strategy was to sell online directly to end-users, bypassing Avon ladies entirely and not granting them any sales credit for online sales. But after a period of some disarray and the loss of many distributors, Avon modified its model, allowing each distributor to set up her own website, on which she received sales credit for her online sales. In this case, the issue was not *whether* to go online but rather *how* to do so to gain the benefits without incurring the costs of increased channel conflict and cannibalization.[58]

Managing multiple retail routes to market remains a challenge for manufacturers and their retail partners, yet hybrid shopping behavior has penetrated all the combinations of multiple channels. The successful response to its challenges is rarely to shut down an "offending" channel—one with fewer sales, or one that appears to be free riding on the others—because it likely is providing some valued service outputs. Rather, the solution involves offering the right performance rewards for all valued channel functions, to ensure that all the channel members have strong incentives to perform in accordance with the channel design. There is some evidence that the online and offline physical channels are both substitutes for and complements of each other. When a retailer has a strong presence in a geographic area, opening more physical stores could diminish online sales; if a retailer has a relatively weak presence, though, the arrival of a new store might increase online store sales.[59] Offline stores also serve a marketing communications function: they increase the retailer's visibility. Consumers encounter vast amounts of information in the offline world, so in this sense, marketers also can leverage online resources to help consumers process and make sense of these inputs.[60] For example, stores might grant consumers access to detailed product descriptions, product reviews, and product comparison tools online, so they can make informed choices rather than giving up and walking away from the store.

As we have noted before, an ongoing challenge for hybrid retailers is providing customers with a seamless experience across channels. What makes the experience less than seamless? For retailers operating through multiple channels, it could be that store coupons they honor in physical stores are not applicable online, or vice versa. Shoppers who identify a desirable item in the online store and make the effort to come to the store to check it out should not be hindered by the discovery that the store does not carry it or the item is out of stock. Different prices in online versus offline channels also can be a source of frustration and confusion for consumers. Even if retailers do not explicitly adopt a hybrid strategy, they still must recognize the demands of the modern omni-channel context. Pure brick-and-mortar retailers still need means to offer information online and increase their service levels to justify visits to their store. Pure online retailers have to invest in convenient pickup options, give consumers opportunities to inspect products in person, and help make experience goods searchable in some way.[61]

RETAILER POWER AND ITS EFFECTS

At one time, companies such as Procter & Gamble, Colgate, Kraft, and Clorox dominated retailers; now the retailers tend to dominate them. What channel developments have led to such a shift?

First, sales of items normally sold by grocery, drug, and mass merchandise retailers often are approaching saturation, such that they cannot increase at rapid rates. For the retailers to grow, they must steal sales from their competitors, rather than waiting for overall demand to expand. Competition for market share exerts enormous pressure on retailers to perform; most chains tend to carry similar products, so their competition is largely based on price. Because better prices (coupled with excellent locations, appealing stores, and reasonable service) have become a primary route to survival and success, the chain retailers have had little choice but to pressure suppliers for price concessions of their own. In food retailing in particular, warehouse clubs, general merchandise supercenters, deep-discount drugstores, and mass merchandisers have been growing more rapidly than traditional food stores, allowing them to expand, at the expense of supermarkets, especially among particular niche markets of consumers that value price and a selected set of services.[62]

Because supermarket profit ratios (net profits-to-sales) already were low, at about 1 percent, any loss of sales to alternative formats, especially from heavy buyers (e.g., large households), could be disastrous. Even as the power of these traditional retailers has been hemmed in by new entrants, they remain the primary channel for many consumer goods suppliers, which means they can move price pressures immediately back up the channel to manufacturers.

Second, retailers continuously seek to improve their productivity and thereby lower costs, while keeping their prices the same or slightly lower than competitors'. If they can achieve economies of scale, they simultaneously might be better able to provide consumers with the convenience of one-stop shopping in larger store formats. This approach elevates their fixed costs, though, forcing supermarket and mass merchandisers to increase their emphasis on generating enormous sales volumes. For example, when Kroger purchased Fred Meyer, it increased its annual sales to $43 billion—or five times the sales earned by Nestlé USA. Such statistics indicate a new type of supplier–retailer negotiation in the grocery arena.[63]

Third, increased pressures on companies mean increased pressures on retail buyers. At one time, buyers focused primarily on purchasing and maintaining balanced inventories. Now, buying centers are also profit centers, responsible for capital management, service levels, turnover, retail margins and pricing, quality control, competitiveness and variety, operating costs, shelf space and position, and vendor float and terms. To help their companies make money, they look to suppliers for price breaks and merchandising support, and those suppliers that fail to provide them may find themselves without a sale.

Fourth, retailers can threaten not to buy most manufacturers' products, because they have so many other alternatives. Approximately 100,000 grocery products exist in the U.S. market, with thousands introduced every year (though most new products do not succeed, with estimated failure rates ranging from 25 to 80 percent[64]). The typical supermarket carries about 40,000 of them. Retailers therefore can choose products that benefit their own, not the manufacturers', profits. Of course, not all product categories are like groceries. Apparel markets, for example, are characterized by a strong preference for new products each season, so total turnover is not uncommon from season to season. However, the fundamental issue, in which many products seek to appear in a fixed amount of shelf space, persists in any brick-and-mortar retail context.

Fifth, suppliers themselves are partly to blame for their weakened position relative to retailers. Not only do they introduce thousands of new products every year, but they also have long engaged in product, price, and promotional allowances to "bribe" their way onto retailers' shelves. These activities have played into the hands of already powerful buyers. Figure 6.4 describes the types and objectives of various trade deals.

Buyers who receive promotional deals grow to expect and insist on them as a price of doing business. Yet manufacturers and retailers take very different views on the sufficiency of such promotions: manufacturers generally consider the value they receive for their trade promotions as relatively poor, at the same time that retailers largely report that the share of promotion dollars they receive is "not enough."[65] When asked about the effect of trade promotions on brand loyalty, 21 percent of retailers said trade promotion spending "definitely helps" brand loyalty, but only 12 percent of manufacturers said the same. These attitudes clearly indicate that even as manufacturers spend more on promotion (as demanded by powerful retailers), they perceive its value as lower. In the following sections, we detail the effects of several types of deals offered by manufacturers to retailers:

- Forward buying on deals.

- Slotting allowances.

- Failure fees.

- Private labeling.

Effects of Forward Buying

Consumer packaged goods manufacturers can experience wide swings in demand for their products from retailers when they use trade promotions heavily. Temporary wholesale price cuts cause the retailer to engage in **forward buying**; that is, buying significantly more product than it needs, and stockpiling it until stocks run down again. In the past, companies such as Campbell Soup Co. sometimes sold as much as 40 percent of their annual chicken noodle soup production to wholesalers and retailers in just six weeks, due to their trade dealing practices. This strategy increases the quantity sold to the retail trade, and requires the retailer to bear inventory costs, but it also plays havoc with the manufacturer's costs and marketing plans. If a manufacturer marks down a product by 10 percent, retailers might stock up with a 10- to 12-week supply. After the promotion ends, they purchase fewer products at list price, such that the manufacturer might not achieve greater profitability.

To some extent, these problems can be alleviated by technologies such as **continuous replenishment programs (CRP)**. The manufacturer and retailer maintain an electronic link that informs the manufacturer when the retailer's stocks are running low, triggering a reorder. If manufacturers and retailers enjoy this level of cooperation, forward buying is less of a problem, though manufacturers' pricing practices still can provoke it.

A related problem is **diverting**. When manufacturers offer a regional trade promotion, perhaps on the West Coast of the United States, some retailers and wholesalers buy large volumes and then distribute some cases to stores in the Midwest, where the discount is not available. This practice upsets manufacturers' efforts to tailor marketing efforts to regions or neighborhoods, but it is unquestionably legal,

FIGURE 6.4
Trade Deals for Consumer Nondurable Goods

1. *Off-invoice.* The purpose of an off-invoice promotion is to discount the product to the dealer for a fixed period of time. It consists of a temporary price cut, and when the time period elapses, the price goes back to its normal level. The specific terms of the discount usually require performance, and the discount lasts for a specified period (e.g., 1 month). Sometimes the trade can buy multiple times and sometimes only once.

2. *Bill-back.* Bill-backs are similar to off-invoice except that the retailer computes the discount per unit for all units bought during the promotional period and then bills the manufacturer for the units sold and any other promotional allowances that are owed after the promotional period is complete. The advantage from the manufacturer's perspective is the control it gives, guaranteeing that the retailer performs as the contract indicates before payment is issued. Generally, retailers do not like bill-backs because of the time and effort required.

3. *Free goods.* Usually free goods take the form of extra cases at the same price. For example, "buy 3 get 1 free" is a free goods offer.

4. *Cooperative advertising allowances.* Paying for part of the dealers' advertising is called cooperative advertising, which is often abbreviated as co-op advertising. The manufacturer either offers the dealer a fixed dollar amount per unit sold or offers to pay a percentage of the advertising costs. The percentage varies depending on the type of advertising run. If the dealer is prominent in the advertisement, then the manufacturer often pays less, but if the manufacturer is prominent, then it pays more.

5. *Display allowances.* A display allowance is similar to cooperative advertising allowances. The manufacturer wants the retailer to display a given item when a price promotion is being run. To induce the retailer to do this and help defray the costs, a display allowance is offered. Display allowances are usually a fixed amount per case, such as 50 cents.

6. *Sales drives.* For manufacturers selling through brokers or wholesalers, it is necessary to offer incentives. Sales drives are intended to offer the brokers and wholesalers incentives to push the trade deal to the retailer. For every unit sold during the promotional period, the broker and wholesaler receive a percentage or fixed payment per case sold to the retailer. It works as an additional commission for an independent sales organization or additional margin for a wholesaler.

7. *Terms or inventory financing.* The manufacturer may not require payment for 90 days, thus increasing the profitability to the retailer that does not need to borrow to finance inventories.

8. *Count-recount.* Rather than paying retailers on the number of units ordered, the manufacturer does it on the number of units sold, by determining the number of units on hand at the beginning of the promotional period (count) and then determining the number of units on hand at the end of the period (recount). Then, by tracking orders, the manufacturer knows the quantity sold during the promotional period. (This differs from a bill-back because the manufacturer verifies the actual sales in count-recount

9. *Slotting allowances.* Manufacturers pay retailers funds known as slotting allowances to receive space for new products. When a new product is introduced the manufacturer pays the retailer X dollars for a "slot" for the new product. Slotting allowances offer a fixed payment to the retailer for accepting and testing a new product.

10. *Street money.* Manufacturers have begun to pay retailers lump sums to run promotions. The lump sum, not per case sold, is based on the amount of support (feature advertising, price reduction, and display space) offered by the retailer. The name comes from the manufacturer's need to offer independent retailers a fixed fund to promote the product because the trade deal goes to the wholesaler.

unlike **gray marketing**, the distribution of authorized, branded goods through unauthorized channels overseas.

Effects of Slotting Allowances

Slotting allowances originated in the 1970s, as a way to compensate the grocery trade for the costs of integrating a new product into its systems, such as creating space in the warehouse, revising computerized inventory systems, resetting the shelves to create space in the store, and stocking and restocking the new item. Because of the scarcity of shelf space, slotting allowances have grown significantly. They reportedly cost manufacturers up to $16 billion in 2001, though the total amount spent is not known for certain.[66]

In 1999, the U.S. Congress held hearings on slotting allowances, in which small manufacturers testified that high slotting allowances prevented their reasonable access to store shelf space, whereas retailers countered that manufacturers should share in the risk of failure of new products. The Federal Trade Commission thus far continues to find no violation of antitrust law, and the continued complaints from manufacturers illustrate that slotting allowances, as an expression of retail power, have not gone anywhere.[67] Studies of slotting allowances continue, but no clear consensus exists about the net effect of these fees on retail performance or prices.

Effects of Failure Fees

Starting in 1989, J. M. Jones Co., a wholesaling unit of Super Valu Stores Inc., began imposing a fee when it had to pull a failing product from its warehouses. If a new product failed to reach a minimum sales target within three months, Jones withdrew it and charged $2,000 for the effort.[68] **Failure fees**, like slotting allowances, were a focus in a 2000 U.S. Federal Trade Commission conference: some argued for failure fees, to represent a credible commitment by the manufacturer that its product was good enough to sell. Unlike slotting fees, failure fees are not paid upfront, so even small manufacturers seeking product placement in grocery stores could pay them. But their effectiveness also seems questionable, because a product could fail not due to its inferiority or lack of appeal but as a result of poor retailer support (which creates a so-called moral hazard problem). Collecting failure fees also may be more difficult than collecting slotting allowances upfront.[69] Regardless of their efficacy, the continued use of failure fees is another indication of the degree of retailer control.

Effects of Private Branding

Private labels (or **store brands**) have been, and continue to be, very popular in Europe; their sales account for about 40–50 percent of all supermarket sales in Britain.[70] Yet when a group of U.S. retailers—notably, Sears, JCPenney, Montgomery Ward, and A&P—committed to private labels to generate loyalty to their stores (rather than to manufacturers' brands) and earn extra profits, the generic packaging and varieties they offered failed to give consumers sufficient value. In other words, they were money-saving but unexciting alternatives to national, heavily advertised brands.

Instead, modern retailers increasingly upgrade their private-label programs, to offer closer substitutes for branded products. In this context, we can identify five basic categories of private brands: (1) store-name brands, such that the products bear the retailer's store name or logo (e.g., The Gap, Ace, NAPA, Benetton); (2) the retailer's owned brand name, in which case the brand image is independent of the store name, but the products are available only in that particular company's stores (e.g., Kenmore [Sears], True-Value and Tru-Test [Cotter & Co.]); (3) designer-exclusive programs that feature merchandise designed and sold under a designer's name in an exclusive arrangement with the retailer (e.g., Martha Stewart [Kmart]; (4) exclusive licensed names, usually celebrity-endorsed or signature lines, developed in exclusive arrangements with the retailer (e.g., Michael Graves [Target]); and (5) generic programs with essentially unbranded goods (e.g., Yellow pack no name [Loblaws], Cost Cutter [Kroger]).[71]

Retailers thus must decide whether to affiliate their private-label brand with the store very clearly or use a hands-off strategy, such that the private-label brand stands on its own, and its affiliation with the store is understated. In the case of premium private-label brands, a store branding often is more prominent if the store follows a high-low pricing strategy and achieves strong brand equity.[72] For example, the Canadian grocery chain Loblaws pioneered its President's Choice store brand as an upscale offering, selling everything from chocolate chip cookies to olive oil. The brand has been so successful that Loblaws sells it in several chains in the United States as well, where it is positioned as a credible alternative to national brands. Grocery retailers such as Kroger and Trader Joe's in the United States also are starting to adopt European tactics by expanding their private-label-branded products. Sidebar 6.3 focuses on Kroger's successful brand, Simple Truth.

SIDEBAR 6.3

Kroger's Simple Truth: Bringing Organic Products to the Masses

Kroger is the second largest retailer in the United States, behind Walmart, and the largest grocery store chain. Established in 1883 in Cincinnati, it maintains more than 2,800 stores under various banners in 35 states, and it boasts more than $115 billion in sales. Nearly 10 percent of Kroger's sales come from natural and organic brands.

When Kroger launched Simple Truth in 2012, as a natural and organic line, it was responding to a market opportunity for an affordable, easily accessible private-label brand that offered the benefits of organic options. The blockbuster brand grew quickly to become the largest natural and organic brand in the United States, garnering more than $1.5 billion in sales. Its success largely stems from the retailer's ability to convert mainstream shoppers into purchasers of premium but affordable organic products.[73] Coupled with its existing distribution network and marketing muscle, Kroger made Simple Truth into one of the most storied successes among private-label brands.

Simple Truth also has diversified into more categories, including both food and non-food housing essentials and personal care items. It promises to offer more fair trade-certified products than other private-label grocery brands. It thus continues to grow exponentially and accounts for a big chunk of Kroger's sales.[74]

Supermarkets and discount stores have clear incentives for pushing their private-label offerings: private-label goods typically cost consumers 10–30 percent less than other manufacturer brands, but their gross margins are usually around 50 percent higher.[75] Private brands also enhance a retailer's channel power, by granting it more responsibility for fashion directions, trend setting, innovation, and so forth, as well as for communicating with consumers. Manufacturers thus may focus their marketing strategies on important retailers, as opposed to the end-users of their product. Consider that U.S. supermarkets earn 15 percent of their sales from private labels and make an average pretax profit of 2 percent on these sales. European grocery chains, with their heavier focus on store brands, earn 7 percent pretax profits on average. Of course, the European grocery industry also is much more concentrated, leading to less price competition than in the United States (e.g., the top four U.S. supermarket chains accounted for 68 percent of grocery sales in 2009; the top four in the United Kingdom accounted for 79 percent).[76]

Yet private-label programs could go too far; retailers need strong national brands to make the value comparison between offerings salient to consumers. When store brands soared to 35 percent of A&P's sales mix in the 1960s, shoppers perceived a lack of choice and defected to competitors. In the late 1980s, Sears added more brand-name goods to appeal to a broader base of customers. Competition from competent, stylish specialty retailers also weakened the position of formerly strong private-label goods retailers, such as Marks & Spencer, in the late 1990s.[77]

On balance, retailers can use private-label products to target consumers who seek value for the money they spend in the store. When done well, these private labels are formidable competitors to national (or international) brands. However, when done poorly, or if the environment changes to make a private-label program obsolete, the retailer may suffer. Thus, the threat to name brand manufacturers lies not with private labels *in general* but more specifically with upscale private labels that their retailers manage well.

RETAILING STRUCTURES AND STRATEGIES

Retailing is an enormously complex and varied enterprise the world over. As the key channel member in direct contact with the end-user, the retailer's actions are critical to the success of the marketing channel. A retailer's position is defined by the demand-side and cost-side characteristics of its operations. These characteristics map onto the service outputs provided to consumers who shop with the retailer. Because markets are made up of distinct consumer segments, each of which demands different levels of service outputs, a retailer can successfully differentiate itself from competitors on both demand and cost sides, even if it sells comparable or identical products to those offered by its competitors. Without a distinct value offering on the service output side, or a distinct cost advantage, a retailer of competitive products risks failure in the marketplace. Different types of retailers can be categorized by the levels of service outputs they provide and their cost positions.

Some of the most important developments on the consumer side have been the increasing importance of omni-channel retailing and the potential transformation available to retail management, due to the arrival and advancing technologies associated with big data.

Power and coordination issues still affect retail channel management. Retailers use their leverage to engage in forward buying and to demand concessions from their suppliers. Retailers in grocery and apparel industries have also developed strong private-label branding programs that pose a competitive threat to nationally branded goods supplied by manufacturers. Manufacturers respond by building and maintaining strong brands and by bearing the cost of more channel flows. They also seek to change the basis for their pricing and use multiple-channel strategies to limit their dependence on any one retailer.

Take-Aways

- Retailing is the set of activities involved in selling goods and services to end-users for personal consumption.

- Retailers can be classified by size, ownership arrangements, breadth and depth of assortments, and service levels.

- A retail positioning strategy involves both cost-side and demand-side decisions.

  - On the cost side, the retailer must decide in general whether to emphasize *high margin* or *high merchandise turnover* more; both are financially beneficial, but it is extremely difficult to achieve both together.

- On the demand side, the retailer must choose which service outputs to provide to the target consumer segment(s).

- Together, the cost-side and demand-side decisions the retailer makes constitute its *retail position*.

- Retailing strategically involves:

  - Managing a multi-channel shopping experience that is increasingly demanded by consumers.

    - The Internet is a well-established and growing retail channel, as well as an enabler of shopping through other outlets.

    - Direct selling provides an alternative method of going to market when close interpersonal ties are crucial to building and maintaining consumer relationships.

    - In hybrid shopping, consumers use more than one retail outlet to complete their shopping experience, which requires special skill to avoid channel conflict.

  - Recognition at the manufacturer level of the continued power of retailers in market. Powerful retailers use many tools to further their interests, including:

    - Forward buying on deals.

    - Slotting allowances.

    - Failure fees.

    - Private branding.

APPENDIX 6.1: A GLOSSARY OF PRICING AND BUYING TERMS COMMONLY USED BY RETAILERS

Cash Datings: Cash datings include C.O.D. (cash on delivery), C.W.O. (cash with order), R.O.G. (receipt of goods), and S.D.-B.L. (sight draft-bill of lading). The S.D.-B.L. means that a sight draft is attached to the bill of lading and must be honored before the buyer takes possession of the shipment.

Cash Discount: Vendors selling on credit offer a cash discount for payment within a specified period. The cash discount is usually expressed in the following format: "2/10, net 30." This means that the seller extends credit for 30 days. If payment is made within 10 days, a 2% discount is offered to the buyer. The 2% interest rate for 10 days is equivalent to a 36% effective interest rate per year. Therefore, passing up cash discounts can be very costly. Some middlemen who operate on slim margins simply cannot realize a profit on a merchandise shipment unless they take advantage of the cash discount. Channel intermediaries usually maintain a line of credit at low interest rates to pay their bills within the cash discount period.

Delivered Sale: The seller pays all freight charges to the buyer's destination and retains title to the goods until they are received by the buyer.

F.O.B.: The seller places the merchandise "free on board" the carrier at the point of shipment or other predesignated place. The buyer assumes title to the merchandise and pays all freight charges from this point.

Freight Allowances: F.O.B. terms can be used with freight allowances to transfer the title to the buyer at the point of shipping, whereas the seller absorbs the transportation cost. The seller ships F.O.B., and the buyer deducts freight costs from the invoice payment.

Future Datings: Future datings include:

1. Ordinary dating, such as "2/10, net 30."

2. End-of-month dating, such as "2/10, net 30, E.O.M.," where the cash discount and the net credit periods begin on the first day of the following month rather than on the invoice date.

3. Proximo dating, such as "2%, 10th proximo, net 60," which specifies a date in the following month on which payment must be made in order to take the cash discount.

4. Extra dating, such as "2/10–30 days extra," which means that the buyer has 70 days from the invoice date to pay his bill and benefit from the discount.

5. Advance or season dating, such as "2/10, net 30 as of May 1," which means that the discount and net periods are calculated from May 1. Sometimes extra

dating is accompanied by an anticipation allowance. For example, if the buyer is quoted "2/10, 60 days extra," and it pays in 10 days, or 60 days ahead, an additional discount is made available.

Gross Margin of Profit: The dollar difference between the *total* cost of goods and net sales.

Gross Margin Return on Inventory (GMROI): Total gross margin dollars divided by average inventory (at cost). GMROI is used most appropriately for measuring the performance of products within a single merchandise category. The measure permits the buyer to look at products with different gross margin percentages and different rates of inventory turnover and make a relatively quick evaluation as to which are the best performers. The components of GMROI are as follows:

Gross Margin Percentage	**Sales-to-Inventory Ratio**		**GMROI**
(gross margin)/(net sales)	× (net sales)/(average inventory at cost)	=	(gross margin)/ (average inventory at cost)

Initial Markup or Mark-On: The difference between merchandise cost and the original retail value.

Maintained Markup or Margin: The difference between the *gross* cost of goods sold and net sales.

Markdown: A reduction in the original or previous retail price of merchandise. The *markdown percentage* is the ratio of the dollar markdown during a period to the net sales for the same period.

Markup: The difference between merchandise cost and the retail price.

Merchandise Cost: The billed cost of merchandise less any applicable trade or quantity discounts plus inbound transportation costs, if paid by the buyer. Cash discounts are not deducted to arrive at merchandise cost. Usually, they are either deducted from "aggregate cost of goods sold" at the end of an accounting period or added to net operating profits. If cash discounts are added to net operating profit, the amount added is treated as financial income with no effect on gross margins.

Off-Retail: Designates specific reductions off the original retail price. Retailers can express markups in terms of retail prices or costs. Large retailers and progressive small retailers express markups in terms of retail prices for several reasons. First, other operating ratios are expressed in terms of the percentage of net sales. Second, net sales figures are available more often than cost figures. Third, most trade statistics are expressed in terms of sales. The markup on retail can be converted to a cost basis using the following formula:

markup% on cost = (markup% on retail)/(100% – markup% on retail).

On the flip side,

markup% on retail = (markup% on cost)/(100% + markup% on cost).

Original Retail: The first price at which the merchandise is offered for sale.

Quantity Discounts: Vendors offer two types of quantity discounts: noncumulative and cumulative. Whereas noncumulative discounts are offered on the volume of each order, cumulative discounts pertain to the total volume for a specified period. Quantity discounts are offered to encourage volume buying. Legally, they should not exceed production and distribution cost savings to the seller.

Sale Retail: The final selling price.

Seasonal Discounts: Discounts offered to buyers of seasonal products who place their order before the season's buying period, because such purchases enable the manufacturer to use its equipment more efficiently by spreading production throughout the year.

Total Cost: Total cost of goods sold – gross cost of goods sold + workroom costs – cash discounts.

Trade Discount: Vendors usually quote a list price and offer a trade discount to provide the purchaser a reasonable margin to cover its operating expenses and provide for net profit margin. Trade discounts are sometimes labeled *functional discounts*. They are usually quoted in a series of percentages, such as "list price less 33%, 15%, 5%," for different channel functions performed by different intermediaries. Therefore, if a list price of $100 is assumed, the discount for different channel members would be:

List Price $100.00
Less 33% $ 33.00 (retailer-performed flow)
$ 67.00
Less 15% $ 10.05 (wholesaler-performed flow)
$ 56.95
Less 5% $ 2.85 (manufacturers' representative-performed flow)
$ 54.10

APPENDIX 6.2: MERCHANDISE PLANNING AND CONTROL

Merchandise planning and control start with decisions about merchandise variety and assortment. Variety decisions involve determining the different kinds of goods to be carried or services offered. For example, a department store carries a wide variety of merchandise ranging from men's clothing and women's fashions to sports equipment and appliances. Assortment decisions instead involve determination of the range of choices (e.g., brands, styles or models, colors, sizes, prices) offered to the customer within a variety classification. The more carefully and wisely decisions on variety and assortment are made, the more likely the retailer is to achieve a satisfactory rate of stockturn.

The rate of **stockturn** (stock turnover) is the number of times during a given period in which the average amount of stock on hand is sold. It is most commonly determined by dividing the average inventory at cost into the cost of the merchandise sold. It is also computed by dividing average inventory at retail into the net sales figure or by dividing average inventory in physical units into sales in physical units. To achieve a high rate of stockturn, retailers frequently attempt to limit their investment in inventory, which reduces storage space, as well as such expenses as interest, taxes, and insurance on merchandise. "Fresher" merchandise will be on hand, thereby generating more sales. Thus, a rapid stockturn can lead to greater returns on invested capital.

Although the retailing firms with the highest rates of turnover tend to realize the greatest profit-to-sales ratios, significant problems may be encountered by adopting high-turnover goals. For example, higher sales volume can be generated through lower margins, which in turn reduce profitability; lower inventory levels may result in additional ordering (clerical) costs and the loss of quantity discounts; and greater expense may be involved in receiving, checking, and marking merchandise. Merchandise budget planning provides the means by which the appropriate balance can be achieved between retail stock and sales volume.

Merchandise Budgeting

The merchandise budget plan is a forecast of specified merchandise-related activities for a definite period. Although the usual period is one season of 6 months, in practice it is often broken down into monthly or even shorter periods. Merchandise budgeting requires the retail decision maker to make forecasts and plans relative to five basic variables: sales, stock levels, reductions, purchases, and gross margin and operating profit. Each of these variables will be addressed briefly.

Planned sales and stock levels. The first step in budget determination is the preparation of the *sales forecast* for the season and for each month in the season for which the budget is being prepared. The second step involves the determination of the *beginning-of-the-month* (B.O.M.) *inventory* (stock on hand), which necessitates specification of a desired rate of stockturn for each month of the season. If, for example, the desired stock-sales ratio for the month of June is 4 and forecasted (planned) sales during June are $10,000, then the planned B.O.M. stock would be $40,000. It is also important, for budgeting purposes, to calculate stock available at the end of the month (E.O.M. stock). This figure is identical to the B.O.M. stock for the following month. Thus, in our example, May's E.O.M. stock is $40,000 (or June's B.O.M. stock).

Planned reductions. This third step in budget preparation involves accounting for markdowns, shortages, and employee discounts. Reduction planning is critical because any amount of reductions has exactly the same effect on the value of stock as an equal amount of sales. Markdowns vary from month to month, depending on special and sales events. In addition, shortages are a serious problem for retailers. Shortages result from shoplifting, employee pilferage, miscounting, and pricing and checkout mistakes. Generally, merchandise managers can rely on past data to forecast both shortages and employee discounts.

Planned purchases. When figures for sales, opening (B.O.M.) and closing (E.O.M.) stocks, and reductions have been forecast, the fourth step, the *planning of purchases* in dollars, becomes merely a mechanical mathematical operation. Thus, planned purchases are equal to planned stock at the end of the month (E.O.M.) + planned sales + planned reductions – stock at the beginning of the month (B.O.M.). Suppose, for example, that the planned E.O.M. stock for June was $67,500 and that reductions for June were forecast to be $2,500. Then,

Planned E.O.M. stock (June 30)	$67,500
Planned sales (June 1–June 30)	10,000
Planned reductions	2,500
Total:	$80,000
Less	
Planned B.O.M. stock (June 1)	40,000
Planned purchases	$40,000

However, the planned purchases figure is based on *retail prices*. To determine the financial resources needed to acquire the merchandise, it is necessary to determine planned purchases at *cost*. The difference between planned purchases at retail and at cost represents the initial markup goal for the merchandise in question. This goal is established by determining the amount of operating expenses necessary to achieve the forecasted sales volume, as well as the profits desired from the specific operation, and combining this information with the data on reductions. Thus,

initial markup goal = (expenses + profit + reductions)/(net sales + reductions).

A term frequently used in retailing is *open-to-buy*. It refers to the amount, in terms of retail prices or at cost, that a buyer can receive into stock during a certain period on the basis of the plans formulated. Thus, planned purchases and open-to-buy may be synonymous if forecasts coincide with actual results. However, adjustments in inventories, fluctuations in sales volume, unplanned markdowns, and goods ordered but not received all complicate the determination of the amount that a buyer may spend.

Planned gross margin and operating profit. The *gross margin* is the initial markup adjusted for price changes, stock shortages, and other reductions. The difference between gross margin and expenses required to generate sales will yield either a contribution to profit or a *net operating profit* (before taxes), depending on the sophistication of a retailer's accounting system and the narrowness of its merchandise budgeting.

NOTES

1 See www.merriam-webster.com/dictionary/retailing.

2 eMarketer (2015), "US retail sales to near $5 trillion in 2016," www.emarketer.com/Article/US-Retail-Sales-Near-5-Trillion-2016/1013368, December 21.

3 Hu, Krystal (2018), "Amazon and Whole Foods disagree on products like Coca-Cola," *Yahoo Finance*, February 28.

4 Leamy, Elisabeth (2011), "Save big: Limited-assortment grocery stores offer fewer choices, bigger savings," http://abcnews.go.com/Business/ConsumerNews/limited-assortment-grocery-stores-consumers-save-big/story?id=12808224.

5 Mclinden, Steve (2016), "Top of the world," *SCT*, October, 30.

6 Turner, Zeke (2017), "How grocery giant Aldi plans to conquer America: Limit choice," *The Wall Street Journal*, September 21.

7 Sanicola, Laura (2017), "America's malls are rotting away," http://money.cnn.com/2017/12/12/news/companies/mall-closing/index.html.

8 Shaw, Gary (2016), "Get up to speed with the motion of missions today: What are the key requirements necessary to bring shoppers into stores, and how are they likely to change?" *Convenience Store*, March 25, 8,10.

9 https://stores.org/stores-top-retailers-2017, date retrieved December 28, 2017.

10 www.vendhq.com/us/2018-retail-trends-predictions, date retrieved December 28, 2017.

11 Brynjolfsson, Erik, Yu Jeffrey Hu, and Mohammad S. Rahman (2013), "Competing in the age of omnichannel retailing," *MIT Sloan Management Review*, 54 (4), 23–29.

12 Trenz, Manuel (2015), "The blurring line between electronic and physical channels: Reconceptualising multichannel commerce," *Twenty-Third European Conference on Information Systems (ECIS)*, Munster, Germany, 2015.

13 Herhausen, Dennis, Jochen Binder, Marcus Schoegel, and Andreas Herrrman (2015), "Integrating bricks with clicks: Retailer-level and channel-level outcomes of online–offline channel integration," *Journal of Retailing*, 91 (2), 309–325.

14 Melis, Kristina, Katia Campo, Els Breguelmans, and Lien Lamey (2015), "The impact of the multichannel retail mix on online store choice: Does online experience matter?" *Journal of Retailing*, 91 (2), 272–288.

15 Hobbs, Thomas (2015), "How Aldi's move into ecommerce shows it is becoming a more 'conventional' grocer," *Money Marketing*, September 28, 24.

16 Trenz (2015), op. cit.

17 Pauwels, Koen and Scott A. Neslin (2015), "Building with bricks and mortar: The revenue impact of opening physical stores in a multichannel environment," *Journal of Retailing*, 91 (2), 182–197.

18 Darke, Peter R., Michael K. Brady, Ray L. Benedicktus, and Andrew E. Wilson (2016), "Feeling close from afar: The role of psychological distance in offsetting distrust in unfamiliar online retailers," *Journal of Retailing*, 92 (3), 287–299.

19 Rapp, Adam, Thomas L. Baker, Daniel G. Bachrach, Jessica Ogilvie, and Lauren Skinner Beitelspacher (2015), "Perceived customer showrooming behavior and the effect on retail salesperson self-efficacy and performance," *Journal of Retailing*, 91 (2), 358–369.

20 Wang, Rebecca Jen-Hui, Edward C. Malthouse, and Lakshman Krishnamurthi (2015), "On the go: How mobile shopping affects customer purchase behavior," *Journal of Retailing*, 91 (2), 217–234.

21 Bradlow, Eric T., Manish Gangwar, Praveen Kopalle, and Sudhir Voleti (2017), "The role of big data and predictive analytics in retailing," *Journal of Retailing*, 93 (1), 79–95.

22 Germann, Frank, Gary L. Lilien, Lars Fiedler, and Matthias Kraus (2014), "Do retailers benefit from deploying customer analytics?" *Journal of Retailing*, 90 (4), 587–593.

23 Baird, Nikki (2017), "Co-creation: The future of retail stores?" *Forbes*, www.forbes.com/sites/nikkibaird/2017/01/31/co-creation-the-future-of-retail-stores/#eba02443f451, date retrieved February 21, 2018.

24 Bughin, Jacques (2014), "Three ways companies can make co-creation pay off," www.mckinsey.com/industries/consumer-packaged-goods/our-insights/three-ways-companies-can-make-co-creation-pay-off, date retrieved February 20, 2018.

25 Camps, Chris (2017), "How six retailers are using chatbots to boost customer engagement (and why you should too)," www.clickz.com/how-six-retailers-are-using-chatbots-to-boost-customer-engagement-and-why-you-should-too/111350, date retrieved February 20, 2018.

26 Morrison, Kimberlee (2017), "How Instagram is growing its social shopping efforts," *Adweek*, April 7, www.adweek.com/digital/how-instagram-is-growing-its-social-shopping-efforts, date retrieved February 20, 2018.

27 Roof, Katie (2017), "Poshmark cash flow positive, on track for $100 million revenue," https://techcrunch.com/2017/04/26/poshmark-cash-flow-positive-on-track-for-100-million-revenue, date retrieved February 21, 2018.

28 https://poshmark.com/what_is_poshmark, date retrieved February 21, 2018.

29 Konrad, Alex (2017), "Poshmark raises $87.5 million to take its social clothes marketplace global," *Forbes*, November 14, www.forbes.com/sites/alexkonrad/2017/11/14/poshmark-raises-87-million-for-its-social-clothes-marketplace/#4ec7078c3246.

30 www.forbes.com/sites/quora/2018/02/02/the-difference-between-virtual-reality-augmented-reality-and-mixed-reality/#684aa6752d07, date retrieved February 3, 2018.

31 Morris, Chris (2016), "Ikea embraces virtual reality with virtual kitchen," *Fortune*, April 16, 20.

32 Groeber, Janet (2018), "Where online and personal shopping meet," *Stores* (January), 20–21.

33 Perez, Sarah (2016), "Boon+Gable closes on $2.5 million for its in-home stylist and shopping service," https://techcrunch.com/2016/06/27/boon-gable-closes-on-2-5-million-for-its-in-home-stylist-and-shopping-service, date retrieved February 23, 2018.

34 See www.zara.com.

35 See www.hm.com.

36 For a detailed discussion of financial strategies adopted by retailers, including the strategic profit model, see Levy, Michael and Barton A. Weitz (2012), *Retailing Management*, 8th edition, New York, NY: McGraw-Hill/Irwin.

37 See Coughlan, Anne T. (2004), *Michaels Craft Stores: Integrated Channel Management and Vendor-Retailer Relations Case*, Kellogg Case Clearing House Number 5-104-010.

38 Pashigian, B. Peter and Eric D. Gould (1998), "Internalizing externalities: The pricing of space in shopping malls," *Journal of Law and Economics*, 41 (April), 115–142.

39 Bloomberg News (2016), "Analysis: Mall owners won't miss anchor stores too much," September 14, www.digitalcommerce360.com/2016/09/14/analysis-mall-owners-wont-miss-anchor-stores-too-much, date retrieved September 28, 2018.

40 Berner, Robert (2002), "Has Target's food foray missed the mark?" *BusinessWeek*, November 25, 76.

41 Spurgeon, Devon (2000), "Walgreen takes aim at discount chains, supermarkets," *The Wall Street Journal*, June 29, B4.

42 Morse, Dan (2002), "Tennessee producer tries new tactic in sofas: Speed," *The Wall Street Journal*, November 19, A1.

43 Berner, Robert (2003), "Dark days in white goods for Sears," *BusinessWeek*, March 10, 78–79.

44 See www.janieandjack.com.

45 Cahill, Joseph B. (1999), "The secret weapon of big discounters: Lowly shopping cart," *The Wall Street Journal*, November 24, A1, A10.

46 Ganesan, Shankar, Morris George, Sandy Jap, Robert W. Palmatier, and Bart Weitz (2009), "Supply chain management and retailer performance: Emerging trends, issues, and implications for research and practice," *Journal of Retailing*, 85 (March), 84–94.

47 www.emarketer.com/Report/Worldwide-Retail-Ecommerce-Sales-eMarketers-Estimates-20162021/2002090, date retrieved March 1, 2018.

48 www.emarketer.com/Report/Worldwide-Retail-Ecommerce-Sales-eMarketers-Updated-Forecast-New-Mcommerce-Estimates-20162021/2002182, date retrieved February 14, 2018.

49 www.census.gov/retail/mrts/www/data/pdf/ec_current.pdf, date retrieved February 14, 2018.

50 Wyner, Gordon (2016), "A turning point for e-commerce," *Marketing News*, March, 20–21.

51 Verma, Varsha, Dheeraj Sharma, and Jagdish Sheth (2016), "Does relationship marketing matter in online retailing? A meta-analytic approach," *Journal of the Academy of Marketing Science*, 44, 206–217.

52 This definition is taken from the Direct Selling Association's website, www.dsa.org. The Direct Selling Association (DSA) is a United States trade association of direct selling organizations, including such well-known, multi-level marketing organizations as Amway, Mary Kay, Tupperware, and Discovery Toys. The DSA serves as the Secretariat for the World Federation of Direct Selling Organizations (WFDSA, www.wfdsa.org), which is the super-organization of all national DSAs around the world. The WFDSA has more than 50 national DSAs as members.

53 www.dsa.org/docs/default-source/research/growth-outlook/dsa_2016gandofactsheet.pdf?sfvrsn=6, date retrieved March 2, 2018.

54 The example is drawn from Anne T. Coughlan and Kent Grayson (1998), "Network marketing organizations: Compensation plans, retail network growth, and profitability," *International Journal of Research in Marketing*, 15, 401–426.

55 See Coughlan and Grayson (1998), op. cit., for a model showing these effects.

56 Washington, Ruby (2012), "Bernard L. Madoff," *The New York Times*, December 17.

57 Chandler, Susan (2002), "Retailers heed call of catalogs," *Chicago Tribune*, September 21, Section 2, 1–2.

58 See Godes, David B. (2002), *Avon.com Case*, Harvard Case Clearing House, Case number N9-503-016. For another company's challenge in this realm, see Coughlan, Anne T. (2004), *Mary Kay Corporation: Direct Selling and the Challenge of Online Channels Case*, Kellogg Case Clearing House, Case number 5-104-009.

59 Wang, Kitty and Avi Goldfarb (2017), "Can offline stores drive online sales?" *Journal of Marketing Research*, LIV (October), 706–719.

60 Bhargave, Rajesh, Antonia Manonakis, and Katherine White (2016), "The cue-of-the cloud effect: When reminders of online information availability increase purchase intentions and choice," *Journal of Marketing Research*, LIII (October), 699–711.

61 Brynjolfsson, Hu, and Rahman (2013), op. cit.

62 See www.census.gov/retail for annual retail sales data.

63 Aufreiter, Nora and Tim McGuire (1999), "Walking down the aisles," *Ivey Business Journal*, 63 (March/April), 49–54; Peltz, James F. (1998), "Food companies' fight spills into aisles," *Los Angeles Times*, October 28, Business Section, 1; "Loblaw's continues to strengthen position," *MMR/Business and Industry*, 16 (October 18, 1999), 20.

64 "Slotting allowances in the supermarket industry" (2002), *Food Marketing Institute Backgrounder*, www.fmi.org.

65 ACNielsen (2002), "Trade promotion practices study," *Consumer Insight*, available at www2.acnielsen.com/pubs/2003_q2_ci_tpp.shtml.

66 Desiraju, Ramarao (2001), "New product introductions, slotting allowances, and retailer discretion," *Journal of Retailing*, 77 (3), 336.

67 Toosi, Nahal (1999), "Congress looks at the selling of shelf space," *St. Louis Post-Dispatch*, September 15, Business Section, C1; Superville, Darlene (1999), "Are 'slotting fees' fair? Senate panel investigates; practice involves paying grocers for shelf space," *The San Diego Union-Tribune*, September 15, Business Section, C1.

68 Zwiebach, Elliott, (1989), "Super value division imposes failure fee," *Supermarket News*, May 8, 1.

69 Federal Trade Commission (2001), "Report on the Federal Trade Commission workshop on slotting allowances and other marketing practices in the grocery industry," February, available at www.ftc.gov.

70 Vasquez-Nicholson, Julie (2011), "G.A.I.N. report: United Kingdom, Retail Foods, 2010," U.S.D.A. Foreign Agricultural Service, February 3, 4.

71 Sweeney, Daniel J. (1987), *Product Development and Branding*, Dublin, OH: Management Horizons.

72 Keller, Kristopher O., Marnik Dekempe, and Inge Geyskens (2016), "Let your banner wave? Antecedents and performance implications of retailers' private-label branding strategies," *Journal of Marketing*, 80 (July), 1–19.

73 Gallagher, Julie (2016), "Cleaning house," *Supermarket News*, November, 64 (11), 57–59.

74 www.prnewswire.com/news-releases/exciting-new-items-fuel-growth-of-krogers-simple-truth-brand-300577066.html, date retrieved February 21, 2018.

75 Allawadi, Kusum L. and Bari A. Harlam (2004), "An empirical analysis of the determinants of retail margins: The role of store brand shares," *Journal of Marketing* (January), 159.

76 The Reinvestment Fund (2011), "Understanding the grocery industry," Community Development Financial Institutions Fund, September 30, 2; ACNielsen (2005), "The power of private label in Europe: An insight into consumer attitudes," The ACNielsen Global Online Consumer Opinion Survey, 2.

77 Beck, Ernest (1999), "Britain's Marks & Spencer struggles to revive its old luster in retailing," *The Wall Street Journal*, November 8, A34.

CHAPTER 7

Wholesaling Structures and Strategies

LEARNING OBJECTIVES

After reading this chapter, you will be able to:

- Distinguish broad categories of institutions that constitute the wholesaling sector.
- Define how an independent wholesaler-distributor adds value and explain the importance of this sector.
- Detail the mechanisms by which channel members join federations or alliances that offer exceptional services while cutting costs.
- Identify the major distinctions between a wholesaler voluntary group and a dealer cooperative, then relate this distinction to the value they provide members.
- Explain why consolidation is common in wholesaling.
- List a manufacturer's possible responses to a consolidation wave.
- Describe how wholesaling is being altered by omni-channel phenomena.
- Compare sales agents with wholesaler-distributors on the basis of aspects that matter to manufacturers.
- Explain why the future for wholesaler-distributors is optimistic.

INTRODUCTION

What Is a Wholesaler?

Wholesalers are the quintessential mediators. Historically, they acted as a go-between linking manufacturers that mass produced a few items with the much larger number of widely dispersed, smaller retailers that carried small quantities of a variety of items. Although their role has changed—especially in the more economically advanced societies—and continues to evolve, wholesalers still have a central role in marketing channels. Wholesalers in the United States generated more than $5.6 trillion in annual sales in 2014, much greater (+120 percent) than the $4.6 trillion in retail sales volume that same year.[1] The National Association of Wholesalers-Distributors also reports that 83 percent of wholesalers-distributors generate less than $10 million in annual revenues, indicating that this sector is populated by many smaller firms, along with a few billion-dollar firms.

EXAMPLE: GRAINGER (USA)

Grainger is a *Fortune* 500 distributor of industrial supplies, maintenance, repair, and operations tools and materials.[2] It mostly caters to larger and mid-sized businesses, offering more than 1.5 million items that it sources from more than 4,500 major suppliers. Grainger does not perform any manufacturing; it is strictly a distributor. It uses multiple channels to cater to its clients, including its famous catalog, website, app, telephone, and national network of branches. Grainger relies on its deep expertise to provide customers with consulting and turnkey solutions to important issues that affect their organizations, including safety, compliance, environmental sustainability, and emergency preparedness. It also partners with third-party providers to offer various customer services, such as inventory management and energy efficiency. Its online subsidiary Zoro targets smaller businesses and individual business owners in similar spaces.

Wholesaling refers to business establishments that do not sell many products to ultimate households or end-users. Instead, they sell products primarily to other businesses: retailers, merchants, contractors, industrial users, institutional users, and commercial users. *Wholesale businesses sell the physical inputs and products required by other businesses.* Thus, wholesaling is closely associated with tangible goods, yet the value created by wholesale entities stems from the value they add by providing services—or in the terms we use in this book, by performing channel functions. Although that value added is quite real, very little about wholesaling is tangible. In this sense, it is the epitome of a service industry. In a channel stretching from the manufacturer to the end-user, wholesaling is an intermediate step. This chapter pertains to the institutions that wholesale—that is, those that provide physical goods as inputs to other businesses. We investigate not just the nature of these institutions but also the strategies they employ.[3]

How Are Wholesalers Different from Distributors?

Many different institutions perform channel functions in business-to-business (B2B) marketing channels. **Wholesaler-distributors**, the largest and most significant of these institutions, are independently owned and operated firms that buy and sell products over which they claim **ownership**. Generally, they operate through one or more warehouses, in which they receive purchased goods that they hold in inventory for later reshipping. This industry exerts a vast, influential role in the U.S. economy.

Yet there is a distinction between wholesalers and distributors. The terms have different roots, and at one time they represented distinct sectors. Traditionally, "wholesaler" referred to a company that resold products to another intermediary such as a retailer, whereas a "distributor" implied that the company resold products to industrial customers that would use the product. Formally, then, a pharmaceutical *wholesaler* resells prescription drugs to a retail pharmacy, which resells the product to a household consumer. An industrial maintenance *distributor* like Grainger instead sells cutting tools to an industrial customer that uses those tools in its manufacturing facilities.

But this terminology also varies from industry to industry. For example, distributors of printing paper are called "merchants," and distributors of automotive aftermarket products are called "jobbers." This terminology even might vary from market to market within an industry. Because our critical point is that wholesaler-distributors have the **title** to the goods they resell—that is, they have the authority to set prices—we override these terminology distinctions. This chapter instead highlights the key functions and traits of wholesaler-distributors: they know the identity of the next buyer in the channel, which they may or may not share with the manufacturer. They are defined primarily by their performance of an ownership channel function.[4] In Sidebar 7.1, we outline the role of wholesalers in the U.S. pharmaceutical industry as an example.

SIDEBAR 7.1

Wholesalers in the U.S. Pharmaceutical Industry

The United States has a two-class drug system, composed of prescription and over-the-counter medicines, both of which are regulated by the U.S. Food and Drug Administration.[5] Prescription drugs may only be sold by licensed pharmacies, after being prescribed by a licensed medical practitioner. They are intended to be used only by the person to whom they have been prescribed. In contrast, over-the-counter drugs do not need a doctor's prescription and can be bought off the shelf, in both pharmacies and non-pharmacy outlets, including convenience stores and gas stations. Some countries extend this structure to a three-class drug system, and the third class is over-the-counter medicines sold only in pharmacies.

The U.S. pharmaceutical sector is dominated by three wholesalers (McKesson Corporation, Amerisource Bergen, and Cardinal Health) that together account for 90 percent of the more than $400 billion drug distribution sector.[6] Each wholesaler-distributor generates revenues in excess of $100 billion from its drug distribution activities. Some other large wholesalers, though dwarfed in size by these three giants, also generate annual drug distribution revenues of over $1 billion (e.g., Morris & Dickson, H.D. Smith, Cura Script Specialty Distribution), and then smaller and mid-sized distributors round out the sector.

Regardless of their size, these wholesalers can be classified into two types: *full-line wholesalers* that distribute the full line of a pharmaceutical manufacturer's products and *specialty distributors* that distribute specialty drugs (e.g., only oncology drugs).[7] The big three wholesalers maintain specialty divisions to distribute specialty drugs. As merchant middlemen, drug distributors purchase medications from their manufacturers and warehouse and distribute them. The customers for full-line wholesalers in particular are varied, ranging from traditional pharmacy retail outlets (e.g., CVS and Walgreens, mom-and-pop drug stores, discount stores, supermarkets with pharmacies, mail order pharmacies) to hospitals, clinics, and long-term care facilities. The latter group tends to be a key customer base for specialty pharmaceutical distributors.[8] Specialty pharmaceutical distributors also service specialty pharmacies such as Humana.

THE WHOLESALER-DISTRIBUTOR LANDSCAPE

The importance of wholesaler-distributors is striking in two main ways: in itself and because it is not particularly evident in the business press. Popular reports instead seem to focus invariably on the doom and death of the sector. Oddly enough, this pessimism may prevail because the sector is generally so well organized in active trade associations. These associations commission regular reports that suggest ways their members can improve operations and caution against complacency. But as we have already learned, such efforts to adjust, improve, and increase efficiency likely signal the *health* of this channel function, not its demise.

A more fundamental reason for the misplaced pessimism may be that the wholesale sector has been subject to a massive, decades-long wave of **consolidation**, industry by industry (which we examine subsequently in this chapter). For now, suffice it to say that, understandably, the disappearance of two-thirds of companies in an industry (as has happened in some sectors) creates an atmosphere of panic and dread. But the fear is unfounded. Most firms in a consolidation wave actually exit by being acquired, not by going bankrupt or shutting down. The acquirers are large, healthy businesses that have supported steady increases in the wholesale sector's share of the channel in recent decades. Consolidation strengthens wholesaler-distributors even as it reduces their number—and eliminates some inefficiencies in the industry.

Consolidation was largely sparked by IT. That is, actors performing the distribution function experience intense pressures to invest in IT. The customer-facing elements of the business in particular are increasingly expected to be Internet-enabled and sophisticated. Concurrently, operations benefit from IT system investments that allow the distributors to participate in the supply chain management revolution. (**Supply chain management** refers to the strategic coordination of traditional business functions systematically across the channel, with the goal of enhancing long-term performance for the channel, or supply chain, overall.) Then these new systems must interface seamlessly. Such competitive demands encourage wholesaler-distributors to consolidate so that they can achieve the scale economies that justify massive investments in automation.

Despite these consolidation trends, though, traditional measures of industry **concentration** remain low in comparison with manufacturing sectors. To some extent, low concentration reflects the geographically distinct markets that mark most competition among wholesaler-distributors. A single wholesaler-distributor might totally dominate one region of a country but account for a miniscule proportion of national sales. Thus, the apparent fragmentation of wholesale distribution does not reflect the true nature of concentration, as measured in any single region.

This discussion sets up an issue we addressed previously: *power is a property of a relationship, not of a business*. A very large and reputable manufacturer, such as Monsanto or DuPont, may not be any more powerful than a single wholesaler-distributor, *in a given market*. This supplier even may be less powerful, if customer loyalty prevents the big supplier from bypassing a downstream channel member to access a territory. Distributors of pesticides, herbicides, and farm equipment often enjoy excellent relations with the farmers in their markets, many of whom simply will not do business without going through their favored distributor.

Master Distributors

Observers often find themselves puzzled by **master distributors**, a sort of super wholesaler, as represented in Figure 7.1.

Consider RCI, a master distributor of electrical motors for the refrigeration industry. (Recall that we make no distinction between "wholesaler" and "distributor" in this chapter, so we use these terms interchangeably.) The customer, such as an air conditioning contractor, makes purchases from one of its 4,000 conveniently located branches, run by 1,250 independent wholesalers (i.e., distributors to B2B customers). These wholesalers do not deal with the manufacturer, though, but with another, single point of contact, namely the master distributor, which only distributes to other distributors. In other words, Figure 7.1 really features 1,251 wholesalers: 1 master distributor + its 1,250 wholesaler customers, all of which sell to other businesses rather than to consumers. However, for a given manufacturer's products, this master distributor does not compete with other wholesalers for contractors' business. Although on paper it looks like an extra layer (and hence prompts some confusion about its existence), the master distributor actually creates a stable, prosperous system that suits all parties. To understand its value, we have to ask: what functions would be pushed onto some other player in the channel if the master distributor were eliminated?

Distributors rely on many services provided by manufacturers. But master distributors also can provide those services, so they thrive when they can do so more effectively and/or efficiently than the manufacturer does. Contractors, which

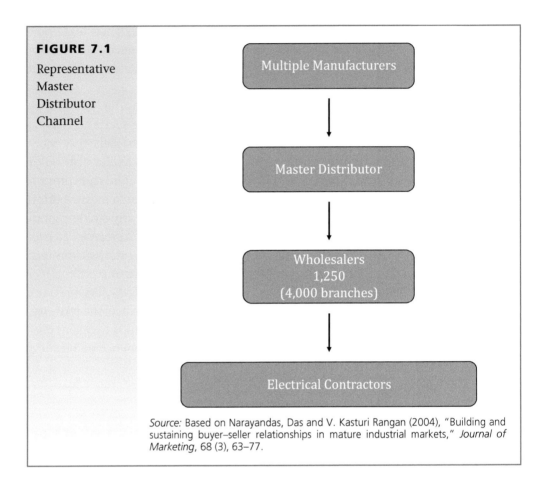

FIGURE 7.1

Representative Master Distributor Channel

Multiple Manufacturers

Master Distributor

Wholesalers
1,250
(4,000 branches)

Electrical Contractors

Source: Based on Narayandas, Das and V. Kasturi Rangan (2004), "Building and sustaining buyer–seller relationships in mature industrial markets," *Journal of Marketing*, 68 (3), 63–77.

represent the end-user in a B2B channel, demand enormous assortments (e.g., each specific replacement motor) and fast delivery (e.g., of refrigerated goods that spoil quickly). In Figure 7.1, the 4,000 branches of 1,250 wholesalers each would need to rush to provide one of the thousands of parts demanded, making the goal of keeping adequate stock close to the customer totally infeasible. Instead, distributors want to buy products as needed, using the master distributor as their "invisible warehouse." (Not surprisingly, the master distributor spends a lot on express delivery services!)

Master distributors also consolidate orders from all their manufacturers, so their customers avoid minimum-order requirements. Rather, these individual distributors can buy a variety of products from a multitude of vendors, while still enjoying the quantity discount and lower transportation costs obtained by the master distributor.

Finally, master distributors' roles sometimes mirror those of a franchisor (see Chapter 8). They help their customers (i.e., other distributors) improve their business processes, demonstrate best practices, and shoulder some of their channel functions, such as advertising.

Essentially, master distributors give distributors economies of scope and scale and help them resolve their logistic and support problems. Competitive pressures have driven their B2B customers to seek out such benefits, even as manufacturers rediscover that it often does not pay to provide individualized, direct services to all their distributors. In the United States in particular, master distributors have gained a lot of ground, often because manufacturers have adopted **balanced score-card methods** to evaluate their performance.[9] That is, rather than looking just at volume, manufacturers increasingly consider other performance criteria, such as marketing support, service levels, and next-day delivery. Master distributors fare well on such balanced scorecards, especially when they help manufacturers expand into new channels. Georgia-Pacific sells paper products and dispensing systems, but most distributors view these bulky, inexpensive products as a minor market. Master distributors solve the problem by helping the distributors meet their customers' needs without requiring them to devote warehouse space to products that offer them low value per cubic meter.

Many manufacturers in turn have grown far more sophisticated in their pricing for distributors, such that they offer functional discounts for:

* No minimum order size.

* Willingness to break case quantities down to small lots.

* Same-day shipping.

* Marketing support (e.g., customized catalogs, flyers, Internet ordering).

* Holding inventory.

* Taking responsibility for logistics.

This fine-grained approach favors master distributors because it offers more ways for them to get paid for what they already do. Why did this new flexibility arise? Because manufacturers increasingly focus on supply chain management and thus are interested in anything that can increase their coordination with downstream channel members.

Other Supply Chain Participants

Supply chains are complex and involve multiple participants, intermediaries, and service providers, all of which seek to facilitate the movement of goods and services from their source to their consumption location. Supply chain management focuses on various processes across purchasing, operations management, logistics, and marketing channels.[10] In a supply chain, the channel functions and activities that traditionally are the focus of wholesaler-distributors often get performed by other participants. For example, **manufacturers' sales branches** are captive wholesaling operations, owned and operated by manufacturers. Many manufacturers also maintain sales offices to perform specific selling and marketing functions. These locations rarely take physical possession of inventory, though, so they may continue to work with independent wholesaler-distributors. **Customers**, particularly large, multi-establishment retail firms, perform wholesale distribution functions, especially in vertically integrated channels, whether forward integrated by the manufacturer or backward integrated by the end-customer in a B2B sector.

Agents, **brokers**, and **commission agents** buy or sell products and earn commissions or fees, without ever taking ownership of the products they represent. These channels are critical in service industries, which have nothing to inventory and thus nothing to own. By convention, agents in service industries are not considered part of the wholesale trade, because there are no tangible goods involved. However, ignoring them would limit our view of wholesaling in practice.

The other examples of companies that perform supply chain activities in a B2B marketing channel are nearly innumerable. The transportation and warehousing industry provides logistics functions; increasingly, third-party logistics providers and value-added warehousing companies seek to perform some functions too. Unlike wholesaler-distributors, **third-party logistics providers (3PL)** do not take title to the products that they handle. Rather, they charge their customers an activity-based fee for services rendered, which replace traditional sell-side markup pricing by wholesaler-distributors. The emergence of large, sophisticated, end-to-end logistics providers remains a key challenge to wholesaler-distributors, because good 3PL providers can offer many services performed by wholesaler-distributors, including warehousing, transportation, and inventory management. Without sounding too pessimistic, we note that the number of manufacturer-owned distribution centers has declined sharply in the past decade or so, in part as manufacturers outsource more work to 3PLs.[11] The emergence of **4PL** providers involves firms that are not merely logistics providers but actually take over responsibility for the entire supply chain function for a manufacturer. They work closely with manufacturers to make the supply chain as cost-effective and efficient as possible.

WHOLESALING STRATEGIES

Wholesalers add value by performing nine generic channel functions (Chapter 1): they take physical possession of the goods, take title (ownership), promote the product to prospective customers, negotiate transactions, finance their operations, risk their capital (often by granting credit to both suppliers and customers), process orders, handle payments, and manage information. In general, they manage the flow of information both ways: upstream to the supplier and downstream to other channel members and prospective customers. In so doing, they provide utility upstream and downstream. Wholesaler-distributors survive and thrive if they perform these functions more effectively and efficiently than either manufacturers or customers.

This generalization varies from one economy to another, of course. Japan has long been noted for its very long channels, in which multiple wholesalers touch the goods several times between their emergence from the manufacturer and their final point of consumption. Historically, many wholesalers added margin but little value; thus in the 1990s, Japan's wholesale sector began to shrink steadily. Channels grew shorter; wholesalers were excluded, starting with secondary and tertiary wholesalers. But as Japanese consumers continued to express increasing price consciousness, retailers sought to purchase directly from manufacturers, which led to still shorter channels—and even greater pressures on wholesalers.[12]

A Historical Perspective on Wholesaling Strategy

The wholesaling sector is a funny scenario. It is critical and massive, and yet it remains largely invisible to the buyer, which takes the functions it performs for granted. Both manufacturers and customers have a troubling tendency to underestimate the three great challenges of wholesaling:

1. Doing the job **correctly** (no errors).

2. Doing the job **effectively** (maximum service).

3. Doing the job **efficiently** (low costs).

The history of the U.S. pharmaceutical wholesaling industry offers a good example.[13] The wholesale drug trade can be traced back to the mid-1700s. Europe already had retail pharmacies, but the American colonies did not. Instead, medical practitioners prescribed and dispensed medicine on their own. But wholesalers arose to meet demands for medicines imported from Europe. These wholesalers then integrated forward (e.g., opening retail apothecaries) and backward (e.g., manufacturing drugs from indigenous plants).

In the 19th century, new pharmacies arose, independent of physicians. These channel members grew in parallel with the growth of the hospital industry, which needed wholesalers to support its burgeoning demands. Drug wholesalers operated locally and in stiff competition with the vast numbers that operated in the same area. But instead of integrating forward or backward, these manifestations of the concept remained largely independent.

In the middle of the 20th century, the industry entered a new phase: larger wholesalers offered regional, or even national, coverage of pharmaceuticals but also expanded their product lines to include health and beauty aids. Two large national firms dominated in terms of name recognition, but most wholesalers were smaller, regional firms, operated by a founding family out of a single location.

From 1978 to 1996, this long-standing industry went through a period of dramatic consolidation. Drug wholesalers dropped from 147 firms down to 53, mostly through acquisitions. At the end of this period, only six firms accounted for 77 percent of the national market. Today, as outlined in Sidebar 7.1, just three firms account for 90 percent of the market.

Why did it take so long to discover such enormous economies of scale in the industry? The answer is the difficulty of doing the simple job of wholesaling drugs correctly, effectively, and efficiently. The heart of drug wholesaling (and actually, much of wholesaling in general) is the relatively banal task of **picking**—taking from a shelf the items that the customer needs and assembling them for shipment. Pharmacies typically order frequently, requesting a few units of many different items. The variety of the units is substantial, with many stock-keeping units (SKUs). Because the products are medicinal, doing the job correctly (i.e., picking exactly the right item in the right quantity, with no room for error) is critical. For generations, this job was done by people, picking from warehouse shelves. And there are simply few economies of scale to find in picking millions of items to move from a pallet to a warehouse loading dock to a storage shelf, and then picking those items from the shelves to put into a bottle for individual customers.

Beginning in the 1950s, though, firms began experimenting with different ways to do the picking better, faster, and accurately. But it was not until the task could be wholly restructured, using IT and automation, that the fundamentals of the industry shifted—and not in just one way. Many firms have experimented with IT and automation, and multiple methods continue to be in use, with no standard, best practice in place. Instead, a few tactics turned out to be clearly inappropriate, and firms that bet all their resources on one poor approach or another have since left the market.

But the winners changed so many operational aspects that they became nearly unrecognizable. On the operations side, they changed their picking technology, together with their order processing, billing, inventory control, delivery route scheduling, and inventory tracking through newly enormous warehouses. Electronic links with suppliers have replaced hundreds of clerks. On the demand side, wholesalers also profited from IT by turning to bar coding, scanning, and electronic order systems with direct data entry (which replaced salespeople who took handwritten notes about each pharmacist's order and clerks who entered in these orders into the system). The wholesale systems allow customers (i.e., pharmacies) to benefit from computerized accounts receivable and credit accounts, which they in turn offer to *their* customers. The pharmacies never could have been able to afford to provide such services otherwise. Then using the information obtained through these systems, wholesalers offer detailed advice about which inventory to hold and how to display it (planograms), while also updating their prices quickly.

In short, technology made it possible to change *everything*, and very rapidly. Acquiring firms rushed to achieve the size needed to amortize their huge investments. Firms being acquired sought to avoid making such investments. Through the free use of such mutually beneficial mergers and acquisitions, a few big firms emerged that had instituted an astonishing degree of organizational change. That is, the winners used technology to do the job right (fewer picking errors), effectively (swift and complete service to pharmacies), and efficiently (lower cost). This story recounts how it might take an industry 200 years to grow large—and then 20 years to consolidate.

Subsequently in this chapter, we present profiles of wholesalers that tend to dominate after the shakeout phase. We also suggest strategies for manufacturers that need to cope with a shrinking downstream (wholesale) channel.

Wholesaling Value-Added Strategies

Let's have a pop quiz: as quickly as you can, make a list of all the functions that wholesalers perform.[14] You might refer back to our generic channel functions. But often the first thing that pops to mind may be that wholesalers gather, process, and use **information** about buyers, suppliers, and products to facilitate transactions. Although this function traditionally has earned them substantial compensation, modern communication methods are likely to erode their information advantage for most forms, except perhaps the most complex, idiosyncratic transactions that demand substantial tacit knowledge.

In addition, as we noted briefly, wholesalers add value by creating an **efficient infrastructure** to exploit economies of scope (i.e., operating across brands and product categories) and scale (high volume). This advantage, which they may share with suppliers (upstream) and customers (downstream), reflects their specialization in channel functions and enables wholesalers to compete with manufacturers on price. Manufacturers frequently underestimate the magnitude of the wholesaler's efficiencies in terms of providing market coverage. Some of this advantage also stems from the wholesalers' ability to provide **time and place utility**, by putting the right product in the right place at the time the customer wants it.

Many customers also value the wholesaler's ability to **absorb risk**, in the sense that they guarantee everything they sell in some form. Risk declines further when the wholesalers **filter** the product offering, suggesting appropriate choices for each customer and reducing the customer's information overload. Thus the future for wholesalers might lie in *collaborative filtering* software, which uses information the wholesaler gathers about the preferences and choices of all its customers to suggest the best solutions for a prospect with particular characteristics or needs. Collaborative filtering likely is the key reason for Amazon's success: its early-introduced, proprietary, collaborative filtering algorithms have for years steered customers to the books and music considered or purchased by "other people who bought" the same product the focal customer is buying.

For B2B buyers, wholesalers also engage in many functions that traditionally constitute manufacturing functions, in the sense that they **transform the goods** they sell. Some wholesalers receive components and subassemblies and put them together at the last minute (*assemble to order*). In general, they support *customization* through *postponement* of the final manufacturing step; *"kitting"* combines various components into sets, often with instructions for finalizing their manufacture. They also might *add proprietary complements*, such as hardware and software. Wholesalers even *design* new products from unique combinations of components, or *program* semiconductors, or perform other actions in which they treat various elements as input to their channel functions. In this context, wholesalers enjoy an advantage because they can **unite knowledge** of the supplier base with information about the customer base and their specialized knowledge of customers' needs.

Consider Wesco, a distributor of electrical equipment and supplies. By distributing such products, Wesco enters everywhere in the B2B customer's facility; electricity touches all functions. Wesco then uses the knowledge it gains to help key accounts manage their facilities better. This management can have various, unexpected effects. When a hurricane destroyed a customer's oil refinery, Wesco's knowledge of how the electricity flowed through the facility helped the owner reconstruct its refinery in just six months.[15]

In the United States, attitudes toward wholesalers feature widespread skepticism about whether they add any genuine value, cover significant costs, or operate efficiently. We return to this theme later in the chapter, when we discuss how wholesalers generate revenue.

Alliance-Based Wholesaling Strategies

Wholesaler-distributors keep goods on hand that customers need immediately. Such availability often creates a situation in which the wholesaler-distributor backs up and extends the customer's own inventory system. In emergencies, unplanned repairs, or maintenance situations, distributors can supply products and minimize downtime; master distributors are an important provider of this function. Another wholesaling trend seeks other, innovative ways to respond to emergencies *while* cutting costs. The key to this extraordinary feat appears to be **federations** of wholesalers.

In federations, the goal is to enter into progressive, cooperative arrangements with other channel members, in which all elements—the nature of assistance, the procedures for providing it, and the appropriate compensation—have been defined *in advance*.[16] Such arrangements could cut costs substantially (often by 15–20 percent), improve service, and open new business opportunities. By cooperating, the members of the federation eliminate *redundant* inventory or service operations. These adaptive practices are being widely developed; here we describe some prototypes, led by either wholesalers or manufacturers.

Wholesaler-Led Initiatives

In new, adaptive channels that depend on alliance (or consortium) relationships, wholesaler-distributors pool their resources to create a new, separate organization for joint action.[17] These **alliances** exist in almost every industry and can grow quite large. For example, Affiliated Distributors is one of the largest distribution alliances in North America, with more than 370 independent wholesaler-distributors in approximately 3,000 locations and $25 billion in aggregate sales (www.indsupply.com/affiliated-distributors).

Another alliance, Intercore Resources, Inc., sells machine tools. Each of the four distributors that formed this **consortium** had faced difficulty providing timely, high-quality services to large customers with large contracts—the same ones that are most likely to confront emergency situations and demand exceptional service. Each distributor in the consortium therefore refers business that it has trouble handling to Intercore Resources, which is mainly an administrative operation staffed by personnel sent by each distributor. Intercore Resources draws on the resources of all four distributors (including their inventories, engineers, and other service personnel) to service each customer; it also can call on each distributor to demand the help it needs. Intercore Resources sends invoices and collects payments in its own name, then distributes profits to the owners (the four distributors), in the form of dividends.

Another method for creating an alliance is through a **holding company**. Otra N.V. is a Dutch company that comprises 70 wholesalers of electrical products. One of the firms, BLE, excels in service and training. Therefore, Otra N.V. relies on BLE to develop training programs and materials for all the other wholesalers in the group. In turn, BLE has become so proficient that it even offers its training to some of the group's suppliers. With its focus on the market, not on the producer, BLE's programs also are more thorough and less biased than the programs that suppliers usually develop themselves.

Manufacturer-Led Initiatives

Adaptive channels need at least one party to take the initiative. Wholesalers might create the preceding consortiums, holding companies, or divisions. Manufacturers that take the initiative instead organize distributors to pool their abilities and increase the efficiency of the supply chains overall, which benefits manufacturers, intermediaries, and end-users.[18] For example, Volvo Trucks North America Incorporated sells commercial trucks and repair parts in the United States, both through truck dealers and in its own regional warehouses. Dealers reported losses of lucrative repair business because they could not provide consistent, timely repairs when they were out of stock of the right parts. Yet the channel overall carried huge inventories. Volvo GM investigated and learned that dealers had trouble predicting the nature of demand for emergency roadside repairs and thus did not know what to stock. Yet truck downtime is so expensive that truck owners shop competing dealers to find substitute parts, rather than wait for an authorized Volvo GM dealer to get the right part.

To address the problem, Volvo GM assumed more of the inventory function and developed a delivery service, for which it bills dealers. Instead of maintaining three mid-sized supply warehouses, it built a massive new warehouse that stocks every part, locating it near Memphis, Tennessee. This choice of an obscure airport may seem odd, until we recall that Memphis is also the headquarters of FedEx. Thus, Volvo GM made a FedEx-specific investment and took on some risk, which enabled a mechanism by which dealers can call for the precise part they need and get it, via FedEx, the same day. Dealers still have to pay for this service, but they often pass it on to customers, who are price insensitive in the face of roadside emergencies. Furthermore, the result of this centralized solution is more business for the supplier and its dealers and a sharp drop in inventory costs, which offset the sharp rise in express delivery charges.

In contrast, we find a more **decentralized solution** in the warehouses of Okuma, a Japanese machine tool manufacturer. Okuma operates two of its own warehouses, electronically linked to 46 distributors. In addition, it links its distributors, encouraging them to draw on one another's inventories. The Okuma electronic system thus creates 48 possible sources (2 warehouses + 46 distributors) for any tool.

Retailer-Sponsored Cooperatives

A retailer-sponsored co-op may seem similar to wholesalers' voluntary groups, just initiated by the retailers. In practice, though, there are substantial differences. To coordinate, retail dealers are obliged to create an organization, such as a consortium. When they join, they agree to do a certain amount of business with the consortium and follow some of its procedures—so far, just like a wholesaler voluntary group. But the members also must buy shares in the co-op, such that *they are owners as well as members*. And as owners, they receive shares of the profits generated by their co-op (stock dividends) and end-of-year rebates on their purchases. Thus, the goals of the co-op and the interests of its members align closely.

Unlike wholesaler voluntary groups, retailer co-ops thus have a more formalized structure, run by dedicated professional managers whose jobs entail elaborate role descriptions. They also are better able to influence the marketing efforts of their owner/members, who must adhere to the co-op's advertising, signage, and brands if they hope to stay. In short, their marketing coordination is stronger. Sidebar 7.2 profiles Ace Hardware, the largest retail co-op in the U.S. hardware industry.

SIDEBAR 7.2
Ace Hardware Corporation

The roots of Ace Hardware go back to 1924, when Richard Hesse, owner of a Chicago hardware store, decided to circumvent wholesalers to reduce costs. Hesse formed a partnership with other small retailers to buy in bulk. The idea worked so well that, in 1928, Ace Hardware Stores incorporated. Today, Ace is a very profitable *Fortune* 500 firm (in size), counting sales in billions of dollars. Overall, Ace is the largest retailer-owned cooperative and a leader in the hardware industry in terms of wholesale and retail sales and brand strength. More than 5,000 Ace stores across all 50 states and more than 60 countries generate annual retail sales of over $5 billion.[19]

Becoming an Ace dealer requires an initial membership fee of $5000, an initial purchase of $5000 in voting stock, and substantial sums to remodel stores and convert operations to meet the Ace standard. Then there is the real commitment: a minimum annual level of merchandise purchased from Ace. Much of it is private-label merchandise, brightly trademarked in red and difficult to sell if the dealer is no longer an Ace affiliate. These sums represent a substantial commitment, because most members are small, family-owned operations (mom-and-pop stores). At the end of each year, the dealer-owners receive a cash rebate and more stock, based on how much they bought from Ace. This incentive draws members further into the profitable Ace system and gives them a reason not to leave. Should they do so, Ace buys back their stock immediately—unless they join a competing co-op. In the latter case, Ace still will buy back its stock, but very slowly. Defection is one thing; joining the enemy is another.

The real enemy, however, has ceased to be other dealer cooperatives and instead has grown from vertically integrated retail chain stores, such as Home Depot. Although independent hardware stores' business is growing, the chains' business is growing faster. These chain retailers operate enormous, impersonal stores (big boxes), featuring massive selections and low prices, though less personalized service. Their soaring popularity has driven more small hardware independents to join co-ops such as Ace.

Over time, Ace thus has shifted its focus, from signing up new outlets to helping its existing members compete against the big boxes. How can it do so?[20] In this summary (with the benefits to the dealer in italics), we address a key way: franchising. (For a further discussion of franchising, see Chapter 8.)

By managing the wholesale side of its business carefully, Ace uses its buying power to obtain low prices from suppliers. It achieves high inventory turns, despite carrying many thousands of SKUs. This scenario keeps *procurement costs down* for its members while still providing them with an appealing *assortment*. Yet independent hardware dealers often suffer from negative consumer perceptions of Ace—as little corner stores with great service but without competitive pricing. To counter this view, Ace mounts advertising campaigns to project the *image* that the local "helpful hardware folks" are part of a larger organization, with great buying power and expertise.

Another problem is that Ace's members are heterogeneous. They serve local communities, adapting to local tastes. The result is that their offerings vary so much that it can be difficult to figure out how to help them. To overcome this problem, Ace has studied its members' businesses intensively, using point-of-sale (POS) data from dealers with scanners to determine the best assortments. Ace also sends hundreds of *retail consultants* to work closely with dealers to develop and implement new business plans, store by store.

Through this research, Ace has come to categorize its members' businesses into five classes: (1) home centers, (2) lumber, (3) farm, (4) general store, and (5) hardware. Hardware is further subdivided into three formats: convenience, neighborhood focus, and superstore. By studying its members, Ace has been able to distinguish *best practices* and turn its knowledge into elaborate format manuals for different store types. Thus, Ace offers *detailed, proven operational recommendations* for each membership category. The retail consultants *customize* these recommendations for each member and assist in their *implementation*.

To further its learning, Ace also operates some of its own stores. Thus it gains an appreciation of dealers' *daily management problems* and seeks to devise solutions by experimenting, at its own risk. Such solutions go well beyond traditional inventory questions, to address issues such as how to recruit, motivate, and retain good retail personnel. The stores also provide a good place for Ace to experiment with items its dealers won't carry, such as water heaters and lawn tractors (Ace dealers tend to specialize in small, inexpensive items). Ace then can *demonstrate* that some stores could profitably step up to these complex, high-margin product lines.

In short, Ace binds its members to the system but delivers value in return for their compliance and participation. Members make commitments to the system, erecting barriers to their own exit. Thus motivated, they are more willing to work with Ace, accept Ace's suggestions, and funnel their purchases through Ace. The system is surprisingly close to a franchise, whereby Ace acts as a franchisor. The difference is that the profits go not to the franchisor (Ace would play the "franchisor" role) but to the dealers (*they* are the owners of Ace). We thus have a proposal for a new name: should Ace be called a model of "self-franchising"?

Despite a common impression, a co-op is not limited to dealers. There can be many types; in principle, the only thing required to define a co-op is that the members set up an organization to serve them and own shares in it. Cooperatives are becoming particularly popular in Japan, in response to the pressures of shortening marketing channels. Small- and medium-sized wholesalers, seeing their roles overtaken by large wholesalers or manufacturers, have created their own cooperatives to gain economies of scale. The Cooperative Association Yokohama Merchandising Center (MDC), for example, is owned by 75 wholesalers, which use it to gain scale. The wholesalers supply MDC, which warehouses the goods in a huge distribution center. By serving from this center, MDC minimizes separate deliveries (and their costs). In addition, MDC's wholesalers have sufficient scale to serve major retailers. They also have built a modern, online information center to manage orders.

Another type of cooperative has played a major role in distribution in the United States: the **farm cooperative**. The story of the emergence and growth of farm cooperatives could fill an entire textbook. Suffice it to say that organizations such as Sunkist, Ocean Spray, and Land O'Lakes have become extremely powerful forces, benefitting their members by organizing farm equipment and supply markets, as well as the markets into which farmers sell their produce. Although some farm co-ops have vertically integrated both backward and forward, they remain primarily wholesalers of goods and services, and they administer the channels that they control with the approval of the farmers who own them.

EXAMPLE: GUJARAT CO-OPERATIVE MILK MARKETING FEDERATION, OR AMUL (INDIA)

The Gujarat Co-Operative Milk Marketing Federation, better known as Amul, had humble beginnings: two village dairy cooperatives produced 247 liters (about 65 gallons) of milk in 1946 in the western Indian state of Gujarat.[21] Small farmers had no means to get their dairy products to the market, because they lacked refrigeration and transportation resources, leaving them exposed to exploitation by middlemen who paid them very little for the milk they produced.[22] Amul's successful co-op model was instrumental in making India the world's largest milk producer. Today Amul procures products from 3.2 million farmers, who belong to 16,794 village dairy cooperatives that collect the milk, then process it through 17 district cooperative unions. The organization's annual revenues in 2017 reached 270 billion rupees (US$4.1 billion), and it continued to expand to additional dairy-related product supply chains, including ice cream, cheese, and chocolates. In addition, Amul enjoys strong brand recognition in India. Although professionally managed, the co-op remains wholly owned by its 3.2 million members. This cooperative model has been successfully replicated in 21 other Indian states, such that nearly 15 million producers participate in co-ops, spanning various farm products.

Finally, **consumer cooperatives** have had impacts on distribution too. In the United States, consumer co-ops are not common; they tend to flourish in small, homogeneous, closed communities, such as college towns or rural communities. But they do better elsewhere, as Sidebar 7.3, regarding the direct selling movement in France, reveals.

SIDEBAR 7.3
Direct Selling in France

A large and growing phenomenon in France is direct selling from producers to consumers, entirely bypassing all intermediaries. Several French models are emerging, inspired by Japanese models established in the 1960s. These models vary in the service outputs they create and how they carry out channel functions. The constraints and obligations accepted by both sides also vary.

The primary success stories of this movement are in food sectors. In a representative model, consumers organized as a cooperative contract directly with a set of farmers. Farmers and consumers work together to decide what the farmer will plant and how it will be distributed (negotiation function). Consumers subscribe in advance, taking on risk and advancing money to the farmer (credit). They pay a price, and in return, they must take whatever the farmer succeeds in growing. Thus, buyers limit their assortments and assume the risk of crop failure. They must come get their food in a fixed way (e.g., pick up a pre-packed basket at the town social hall, from 4:00 to 5:00 on Friday afternoons). Then they bring their purchases home, discover what they have bought, and figure out how to cook it. Fruits and vegetables are commonly bought this way, but even meat and oysters can be distributed directly from farmer or fisher to consumer. In the process, consumers forgo third-party certification, taking it on faith that the meat is organic and freshly slaughtered, for example.

What's in it for these buyers? Many French shoppers prize regional foods and artisan-like variations in food. But the French distribution system for food also is heavily concentrated, standardized, closed, and rule driven. The startling success of direct selling thus might signal an expression of protest against a national, one-size-fits-all system. In some regions, up to 50 percent of the volume of oysters or wine moves directly. Up to two-thirds of people who regularly eat organic food meet some of their needs by direct-to-farmer co-ops. One grocery chain, System U, has taken heed of direct selling as a signal of frustration and thus relaxed its own rules in response, greatly increasing its sourcing of regional foods that do not meet national standards and can vary considerably from one day to the next.

Consumers who buy directly are not seeking price considerations (prices are not lower and often can be higher). Instead, they might be militantly opposed to conventional farming, with its intensive use of herbicides, pesticides, and animal crowding practices. They believe they are getting more authentic organic merchandise too. As one consumer put it, holding an apple full of insect marks and holes, "I know what the worm is eating." For many consumers, the motive also is political. They are suspicious of intermediaries, viewing them with suspicion and disdain. They buy directly to ensure farmers receive a fair share of channel revenues: by cutting out intermediaries, they send more of their retail euro straight to the farmer.

Farmers, for their part, agree to deal directly to find markets, gain financing, avoid certification procedures, and bypass intermediaries. Many share the consumers' political convictions and believe they are beating an oppressive system. Thus an aura of like-mindedness and solidarity surrounds many consumer–farmer encounters. But many farmers also have discovered that selling directly gives them newfound respect for the functions that intermediaries perform, in that:

- Dealing with the public can be quite frustrating, and many farmers discover they prefer rural solitude to the ambiance of a market or town hall.
- Consumers in the co-op get first priority at a semi-fixed price. When demand turns out to be high, that situation can be frustrating. For example, fish producers dock with their catch and must carry it past motivated prospects who are ready to pay a higher price than the co-op. The prospects often become angry, creating dockside scenes during high seasons.
- Farmers are expected to provide credit or take checks.
- They need to engage in promotion to build clientele.
- To locate where the customer wants to buy and be open when the customer wants to shop, some providers, such as vintners, must locate on well-traveled roads and open on weekends.
- It is difficult to find a match between what the soil can grow and the assortment that consumers want.

As a result, some farmers diversify, dealing with both co-ops *and* the much-reviled intermediaries. And some have renounced direct selling to the public altogether.

The identities of consumer cooperatives, their characteristics, and the reasons for their success (or lack thereof) are not well understood. They deserve further study, because they have great potential to improve consumer welfare. The Consumer Federation of America, founded in 1968, represents more than 100 different consumer cooperatives.[23]

Consolidation Strategies in Wholesaling

The popular image of small wholesalers often contrasts with the modern reality, in which wholesalers are large, sophisticated, capital-intensive corporations. This transformation occurred through consolidation, a phenomenon that has swept through many industries, in parallel with improvements in IT and changes in the wholesaler's customer base. In the United States, wholesaling remains an active merger-and-acquisition area, often funded by private buyout capital. Pressures to consolidate come from the wholesaler-distributor's larger downstream customers, including large manufacturers, multi-unit retailers, and sizeable purchasing groups. Such buyers value the ability to access multiple suppliers, spread over a vast geography, but pass through only a single source. This preference creates demand for huge wholesalers.

However, as they consolidate through acquisition, wholesalers also use their newfound scale to form partnerships with customers, which limits manufacturers' ability to access these same customers. The newly massive wholesalers often prune their supplier list, using their bargaining leverage to wring concessions from a shorter list of vendors. This move in turn sets off waves of consolidation upstream. That is, large customers provoke wholesaler consolidation, which stimulates manufacturer consolidation. The pace of consolidation can be startlingly fast: the number of U.S. periodical and magazine wholesalers dropped from more than 180 to fewer than 50 firms in just nine years, and the five largest wholesalers quickly gained control of 65 percent of the national market.

What can manufacturers do when they face a wholesale consolidation wave? They have four main options. First, they can attempt to predict which wholesalers will be left standing and build partnerships with them. This move is common in Europe, where economic unification has made national boundaries less relevant. But how can they identify likely **winners**? They look for four basic types:

1. "Catalyst firms" that trigger consolidation by moving rapidly to acquire.

2. Wholesalers that enter late, after consolidation has progressed, because such firms would not enter unless they had found defensible niches.

3. Extreme specialists, which tend to be attuned to the conditions likely to prevail after consolidation.

4. Extreme generalists, the opposite of specialists, which are large, full-line firms that can serve many environments well, such that their versatility is valuable once the market has consolidated.

Second, manufacturers facing wholesale consolidation can invest in **fragmentation**. They bet on and work with smaller, independent firms trying to survive the wave of consolidation. It represents an opposite strategy, compared with betting on a few winners. For example, manufacturers might seek out alliances of smaller wholesaler-distributors whose members bid for national or multiregional contracts, offering the same geographic reach as a larger company. The alliances also take advantage of volume purchasing opportunities from suppliers, yet each alliance member retains its operational autonomy and can continue to provide high service levels to local customers. Not only might manufacturers seek to work with these alliances, but they also can offer the alliance as a credible alternative to consolidators. In South Africa, financial services traditionally were sold through independent brokers. But in the face of changing societal and economic conditions, Old Mutual, a diversified provider of financial services, worried that consolidation would shift the distribution of financial services to banks and vertically integrated competitors. To keep its broker network alive and thriving, Old Mutual launched Masthead Broker Association, a division that sells distribution support services to brokers on highly favorable terms. The highly successful program has given Old Mutual (and its competitors) multiple routes to market that otherwise would have disappeared.

Third, a manufacturer facing wholesale consolidation can build a different, alternative route to market by **vertically integrating forward**.

Fourth, a manufacturer might **increase its own attractiveness** to remaining channels, usually by increasing its own ability to offer benefits (e.g., strong brand name). This strategy of becoming more attractive to channel members is a theme that permeates this book.

After wholesale consolidation, the balance of power in the channel changes. Industry sales mostly move through a handful of large, publicly traded, professionally managed companies. Entry barriers are high, and entrants must seek niche markets. The large wholesalers achieve lower gross margins than when the industry's wholesalers were fragmented, local, and privately held, but they also engage in more total business and operate more efficiently, such that their net margins are healthy, despite lower gross margins. These wholesalers put great pressures on suppliers, particularly in terms of pricing, and offer improved service to customers. The large surviving wholesalers also redesign supply chain management processes, often revolutionizing their current operating methods.

Wholesaler consolidation thus is a sea change in an industry. Once it begins, it usually progresses rapidly. Manufacturers must react quickly and be ready to change their marketing channels and methods. Wholesale consolidation is a force that cannot be overlooked.

ADAPTING TO TRENDS IN WHOLESALING

International Expansion

As we have noted, many wholesalers are smaller and tend to operate regionally or domestically within one country. A striking feature of wholesaler-distributors is that though they can become quite large, they seldom go global. Is this a historical artifact of the days of family-owned businesses? Will large firms that survive industry consolidation waves eventually expand abroad?

Many domestic wholesaler-distributors already *are* expanding internationally, often by acquiring foreign wholesaler-distributors, to meet the needs of their customers and suppliers. Global manufacturers and customers ask distribution partners to maintain a presence in all their major markets. The reduced costs of cross-border shipping and falling trade barriers also encourage expansion. For the same reasons, foreign wholesaler-distributors are making inroads into domestic markets. This trend of cross-border growth and acquisitions is particularly strong in Europe. Another interesting factor driving wholesalers into overseas markets is the global reach of e-commerce portals such as Alibaba.[24]

Yet, the very nature of wholesaling suggests that *most wholesalers will never be truly global*. Fundamentally, wholesaling entails meeting the needs of a local market, and these needs are so varied that it is exceedingly difficult to standardize marketing channels. Without standardization, it becomes very difficult for suppliers, customers, or wholesaler-distributors to pursue a truly global supply chain strategy. The few successful examples come from industries in which many participants in the channel are global, such as electronic components or computers.

Omni-Channels

Omni-channel distribution emerged among wholesalers much later than among retailers, through two key dimensions:[25] the number of channels a wholesaler makes available to prospective customers and the extent to which it allocates resources to each channel for use by buyers. We outline the various channels, their usability, and the required resource allocations in Figure 7.2.

When wholesaler-distributors extend the number of channels through which they operate, they tend to generate abnormally favorable stock returns. Merely adding distribution intensity without additional channels may not ensure favorable valuations for the company, though.[26] In particular, debate continues to rage about the impact of adding **e-commerce**. Doomsday predictions posit

FIGURE 7.2

Degrees of
Channel Usage

Distribution Channel	Channel Accessibility	Channel Usability
Company Sales Force	Number of sales reps, Number of offices	Training resources devoted
Telephone	Number of sales reps	Direct access to salesperson via telephone
Fax/Email	Number of sales reps	Direct access to salesperson via fax and email
Warehouses	Number of warehouses	Proportion of products available
Trade Fairs	Number of sales reps, Number of trade fairs	Proportion of products available, accessibility of trade fairs
E-Commerce	Availability of channel	Proportion of products available
Indirect Channels	Number of sales partners	Proportion of products available
Outsourced Sales	Number of sales reps	Training resources devoted
External Web Portals	Number of portals	Proportion of products available

Source: Based on Kauferle, Monika and Werner Reinartz (2015), "Distributing through multiple channels in industrial wholesaling: How many and how much?" *Journal of the Academy of Marketing Science*, 43 (6), 746–767.

that intermediaries will disappear, crushed by the ruthless efficiency of Internet search engines, but eliminating wholesalers does not eliminate their functions, and the Internet cannot provide all the channel functions they fulfill.

We argue that a more likely scenario is that e-commerce will continue to change but not replace wholesaler-distributors. All channel intermediaries, including wholesalers, need to gain customer knowledge and combine it with their knowledge of producers to resolve problems on both ends.[27] The Internet creates new problems (e.g., heightened risk of defective goods, fraudulent "merchants," credit card theft, release of private information). It also creates new ways to solve problems (e.g., collaborative filtering to help customers spend less time but still make better choices). Consequently, the Internet might not eliminate intermediaries, but it may demand careful reconsideration of the fundamental ways in which they create value.

Furthermore, some early indications suggest that wholesalers are benefitting from e-commerce, which they co-opt for their own uses, such as gaining new business and improving their work practices. Many wholesaler-distributors are racing to find new ways to use these tools to create even more value, including the use of artificial intelligence to provide service. In turn, the personnel roles and hiring by wholesalers have slowed dramatically, and existing salespeople are expected to provide enhanced levels of service, including consultative selling—a role for which many of them are not fully prepared.[28] Such challenges of e-commerce are clear in the following example too.

EXAMPLE: BURKHART DENTAL SUPPLY (USA)

More than 135,000 dental practices exist in the United States.[29] Along with a few corporate dental chains, most providers are single-unit practices, run by a single or a small group of dentists. Rarely do they staff dedicated purchasing personnel or maintain sophisticated purchasing departments; instead, purchasing tends to be done by the dentist, an assistant, or an office staff member. These service providers also require hundreds of products to maintain their practice: dental chairs, amalgamators, implants, crowns, fillings, numbing agents, dental floss, and x-ray accessories, just to name a few. The potential for inefficiencies (e.g., ordering too much or not enough), the demand for express orders, and the vast assortment of required products mean that dentists often seek the help of distributors. Burkhart Dental Supply offers both consultative practice solutions and one-stop shopping options, such that they can order everything from routine supplies to state-of-the-art software solutions to equipment repair and maintenance services. Burkhart even helps the practices with their office design and floor plans.[30] In turn, it enables dentists to optimize their order size (according to utilization rates), advises them on ways to cut costs by substituting equally effective but lower-priced products, and provides training. However, many dental products also are commodities, so some practices are turning to e-commerce channels to procure them, creating a threat to dental suppliers such as Burkhart. This disruption of the healthcare marketplace appears inevitable; reportedly 34 percent of dental and health care providers already use Amazon to purchase supplies.[31]

The key challenge for wholesaler-distributors seeking to create an omni-channel experience for customers thus is to ensure the integration of their online channels with their personal selling and other channels, such that the service quality offered through the e-commerce channel is commensurable with that in face-to-face, high-touch channels. As long as the quality remains comparable, the online channel can generate significant cost savings for the wholesaler-distributor by reducing employee costs and increasing order accuracy.[32]

In another implication of the growth of e-commerce, omni-channel initiatives of retailers also are affecting wholesaler-distributors profoundly. For most e-tailers, it is not cost efficient to build an infrastructure to hold slow-selling items, so they rely on wholesaler-distributors to ship these items directly to customers. That is, e-tailers are asking wholesaler-distributors to take over more of the inventory function and directly fulfill customer orders.[33] Traditionally, wholesaler-distributors have used central distribution systems, such that from the central distribution center, they could ship directly to a store or regional distribution center that would complete the order. In the omni-channel era, they instead need to adopt regional and local distribution center structures, because it is easier and more cost-effective to fill orders in closer proximities.[34]

In a related development, the omni-channel landscape motivates retailers to support same-day customer pickup in stores, which means wholesaler-distributors must reconfigure their operations to help retailers make this service possible. Because of the growth of omni-channels, even business customers expect deliveries in shorter time frames. Thus wholesaler-distributors need to develop order capturing systems that can track both small and big orders, across multiple channels, then complete them in a rapid and cost-efficient manner. Such demands imply better integration across wholesale and retail channels, and wholesaler-distributors may need to invest in IT and process improvements to achieve this integration.

The need to maximize data sharing and minimize errors also suggests the adoption of **blockchain** technologies. This technology allows companies to link points of data, without any central control point, such that no single party can modify or add to the record without the consent of other parties. They also can share verifiable information in real time. In a distribution context, blockchain technology can track a product throughout the supply chain, even if it undergoes multiple manufacturing steps, increasing both transparency and efficiency.[35] It also helps prevent counterfeit products from entering the supply chain, because of its provision of full tracing capabilities.[36] Figure 7.3 presents some of these drivers of blockchain adoption.

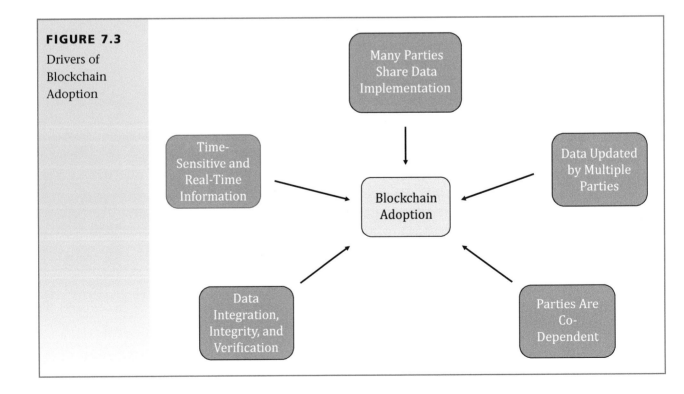

FIGURE 7.3

Drivers of Blockchain Adoption

B2B Online Exchanges

Independent electronic exchanges operate as online brokers in a given industry. These exchanges popped up notably in the late 1990s as companies offered aggregation services for online supplier catalogs, enabling buyers of similar products to source and purchase items from multiple suppliers from a single location. To widespread surprise, though, these exchanges did not exert devastating impacts on wholesalers, as predicted, but instead have failed themselves at high rates. Where they made inroads, it was often in already commoditized industries, such as personal computers. Why? As you should have guessed by now, the predictions of doom for wholesalers ignored the **basic value added** that wholesalers provide. Arrow Electronics is a large wholesaler of electronic components. In the 1990s, more than 50 Internet exchanges formed that could challenge Arrow's business model,[37] proposing to "cut out the middleman" by handling the information flows and letting the producer handle the product flows. Let's consider how Arrow beat back these exchanges by investigating the three classes of business in which Arrow competed:

- Book and ship: Commodity, standardized products that constitute 25 percent of its business are subject to competition from gray markets. The exchanges expected to win this business.

- Value-added orders: To rationalize the supply chain and lower total ordering costs, Arrow provides services such as kitting, programming, managing the customer's inventory on the customer's site, and guaranteeing inventory buffers. The customer thus benefits from the wholesaler's knowledge of its needs.

- Design wins: Complex sales to customers who are unsure of their requirements means providing brand-neutral advice that customers cannot get from the supplier.

In retrospect, the failure of the exchanges could have been predicted. Strong competition in the book-and-ship business had already dropped its margins drastically. The costs the exchanges proposed to reduce (for a 6 percent fee) were only 4 percent of the purchase price! Furthermore, the exchanges were unknown, whereas Arrow is known and trusted. In the design wins and value-added orders segments, the distributor clearly enjoyed advantages, and because customers benefit from one-stop shopping, the distributor could resist unbundling its book-and-ship business.

A story similar to Arrow's has repeated in various sectors. Wholesaling is brutally competitive. New entrants often have difficulty unseating incumbents, who benefit from their well-established, well-working routines and lean operations.[38] In particular, exchanges could not create new value that the existing wholesalers could not readily match, especially when they exploited the Web as a viable tool.

Nonetheless, exchanges should not be written off completely. They are gaining ground in sectors in which commodities can be separated from other parts of the business. The major obstacle appears to be **codification** of difficult-to-estimate parameters (e.g., quality of customer service). Exchanges flounder when customers discover they need something unexpected: emergency or rush service, design know-how, and so forth. Furthermore, just establishing a reliable relationship is costly. Expertise, credit worthiness, and general qualification to bid must be factored in, none of which is easy to do.[39]

Online Reverse Auctions

Perhaps a greater threat to wholesalers than online exchanges is **online bidding by reverse auction**.[40] In this real-time price competition, prequalified suppliers seek to win a customer's business. Using specialized software, bidders (whether distributors, producers, or both) submit progressively declining bids, and the winner submits the lowest bid before time runs out. Although only a small part of overall transactions, reverse auctions are gaining ground; many buyers perceive them as a fast, easy way to set aside "irrational" considerations (e.g., relationships, "soft" or subjective qualifications) and get straight to a low price. Estimates suggest that reverse auctions reduce the costs for buyers by 5–15 percent, but the experiences of firms tend to be mixed: sometimes cost savings fail to accrue, and the potential for damaging long-term relationships with suppliers is real, due to the transactional, price-oriented nature of reverse auctions.[41]

Wholesalers also tend to be suspicious of reverse auctions, because they seemingly reduce procurement decisions to price, without any consideration of capabilities—many of which reflect the wholesalers' supplier-specific investments. Especially when bids are open (revealed to all bidders) rather than sealed (only winning bids are known), wholesalers worry that open bidding may trick them into revealing their positions. Buyers can also manipulate the system by making artificial bids that reduce the final price.

Reverse auctions thus have real dangers: they may destroy excellent relationships, with the potential to generate performance breakthroughs and new ideas. Wholesalers (and other suppliers) hesitate to make investments specific to suppliers that run reverse auctions. And reverse auctions tend to focus on the lowest product prices, rather than the lowest procurement costs or lowest cost of ownership over the product's lifetime. These broader cost concepts involve intangible factors, but considerations of warranties, delivery time, switching costs, and capabilities tend to get lost in bidding wars. Efforts to incorporate such factors into the auction have not been successful, because they are so difficult to codify.

Ultimately, the long-run danger of reverse auctions is that suppliers use them to extract excessive concessions, driving suppliers (wholesalers and manufacturers) right out of business. This forced supply consolidation puts buyers into negotiations with just a few large wholesalers and producers. In the long run, this scenario may not be the route to sustainable competitive advantages for buyers.

Fee for Services

It has always been difficult for wholesalers to calculate the true **profitability** of a given product line or customer. Product lines compose a portfolio, and customers demand an assortment. Dropping an unprofitable product line can disrupt the appeal of the package. Dropping an unprofitable customer contradicts the basic notion of spreading costs over a large customer base. Thus wholesalers carry many customers that cost more than they bring in, usually because they demand multiple services along with their products. Traditionally, wholesalers charge for the product and include the service "for free." This **bundling** is based on the idea that customers will pay more for products from distributors that give them more service.

But over time, many customers have come to violate this convention, relentlessly wearing down distributors on price while training the distributors' personnel not to withhold services. Why do wholesalers tolerate such money-losing customers? Frequently, it is because they cannot identify who they are. It is no simple matter to assign costs to customers non-arbitrarily. One possible method is **activity-based costing (ABC)**, which assigns costs based on approximations of the activities needed to support each customer. An ABC analysis usually suggests that the distributor's portfolio of customers follows the **80/20 rule**: 80 percent of profits are generated by only 20 percent of customers, and the remaining 80 percent of customers actually drain profits away.[42]

A solution to this problem is rapidly gaining ground: **fee-for-service** models.[43] The idea is to break the traditional connection between the pricing model (gross margin on product) and the value model (providing superior service, which may be worth far more than the product and is more difficult to find elsewhere). By charging a product price and then a fee for each and every service the customer uses, the wholesaler unbundles products and services and makes its value proposition visible. For example, TMI is a cutting tools distributor that has introduced fees for inspecting, kitting, and tracking services associated with cutting tools. These services save the customer time and money in a demonstrable way, which is why TMI can collect fees on them rather than (trying to) charge more for its tools.

At the limit, distributors offer services for a fee *without* supplying the product (which is sourced elsewhere). The fee-for-service model represents a revolution in wholesaling, though like most revolutions, it has not been easy to introduce, particularly when customers are accustomed to thinking of services as "included" in gross margins. Wholesalers need to demonstrate that their services are valuable. They might do so by accepting more risk and agreeing to be paid only if the customer meets specific targets (e.g., cost savings, labor savings, performance improvements).

VERTICAL INTEGRATION OF MANUFACTURING INTO WHOLESALING

When manufacturers perform wholesaling activities, they operate sales branches and offices. At the retail level, huge "power retailers" even might bypass independent wholesaler-distributors by setting up their own branches to perform channel functions. This trend is gathering momentum in Europe (fueled by the EU) and Japan (fueled by rising price elasticity among consumers and questions about the length and operating methods of Japanese channels). In the United States, the trend already is well advanced.

Wholesaler-distributors are a small part of many traditional (physical) U.S. retail channels, due to the influence of **power retailers**[44] that dominate various sectors of retail activity. Power retailers typically buy in large quantities in select product categories (e.g., toys) and take a very prominent position in their channel. Because of this purchase volume, power retailers can adopt a **buy direct** approach. Retailers such as Walmart squeeze costs out of the channel by creating in-house distribution systems, in which wholesaler-distributors play small roles, then they further leverage their positions using tactics such as in-store media and advertising. For example, Walmart TV broadcasts on 100,000 screens in more than 2,650 stores, reaching approximately 336 million shoppers every month. In response, many of its suppliers, including Kraft Foods, Gillette, and Frito-Lay, began advertising on Walmart TV, which further strengthened their ties.[45]

Manufacturers must respond to the demands of dominant buyers, often at the expense of wholesaler-distributors. In addition, power retailers trigger industry consolidation among small- and medium-sized retailers—that is, the traditional consumers of wholesale distribution. Thus the role of wholesaler-distributors in retail channels has diminished or been eliminated in the past 25 years, leaving fewer, larger wholesaler-distributors among the survivors. This outcome provides another reason e-commerce is unlikely to have a devastating effect on independent wholesalers in most retail sectors: the devastation has already occurred. Power retailers have left few wholesaler-distributors standing for the Internet to affect.

At the same time, the hyper-efficient retail distribution systems used by power retailers are not well suited to "unit of one" sales, as required for online buying and shipping to a consumer's home. Thus many of these retailers partner with wholesaler-distributors or third-party fulfillment companies, such as Fingerhut, to enter e-commerce fields.[46] The Internet, curiously, may prove to be a way to bring independent wholesalers back into retail channels.

Take-Aways

- Wholesale businesses sell physical inputs and products to other businesses, retailers, merchants, contractors, industrial users, institutional users, and commercial users. Wholesaling is closely associated with tangible goods. Wholesalers also add value by providing services in channel functions.

- Buyers typically understate the difficulty of the three critical challenges of wholesaling:

  ○ Doing the job without errors.

  ○ Doing the job effectively (i.e., with a maximum of service).

  ○ Doing the job efficiently (i.e., at low costs).

- The challenges of wholesaling prompt firms to create economies of scope and scale, up and down the channel of distribution. The objective is to offer exceptional service at acceptable costs, such as through:

  ○ Master distributors, a type of super wholesaler.

  ○ Federations of wholesalers, which might be led by wholesalers themselves or by manufacturers.

  ○ Voluntary and cooperative groups of wholesalers, retailers, consumers, or producers.

- Consolidation is a common phenomenon in wholesaling, due in part to the economies of scale available through IT. Yet the wholesaling sector is typically less concentrated than the manufacturing sector.

- Four types of winners emerge when a wholesaling sector consolidates:

  ○ Catalyst firms (serial acquirers).

  ○ Late entrants that find defensible niches.

  ○ Extreme specialists attuned to post-consolidation conditions.

  ○ Extreme generalists that trade depth for breadth.

- Manufacturers can react to consolidation in wholesaling by:

  ○ Partnering with one of the four types of winners.

  ○ Investing in fragmentation (supporting small independents).

○ Vertically integrating forward.

○ Investing in becoming more attractive to survivors of the consolidation.

- E-commerce promises to change the wholesaling sector in many ways, some of which will benefit the sector. Online exchanges and reverse auctions are among these developments. In response, wholesalers are experimenting with new ways to add value and capture a fair share of it.

NOTES

1 www.naw.org/wp-content/uploads/2017/05/Wholesale-Distribution-Industry-Data-FINAL-AUG2016.pdf, date retrieved March 21, 2018.

2 www.grainger.com, date retrieved March 21, 2018.

3 Fein, Adam J. (2000), "Wholesaling," *U.S. Industry and Trade Outlook 2000*, New York: DRI/McGraw-Hill.

4 Lusch, Robert L. and Deborah Zizzo (1996), *Foundations of Wholesaling: A Strategic and Financial Chart Book*, Washington, DC: Distribution Research and Education Foundation.

5 www.chpa.org/DrugDistribution.aspx, date retrieved March 23, 2018.

6 Fein, Adam J. (2017), "MDM market leaders top pharmaceutical distributors," www.mdm.com/2017-top-pharmaceutical-distributors, date retrieved March 23, 2018.

7 Fein (2017), op. cit.

8 www.mckesson.com/about-mckesson/our-businesses, date retrieved March 23, 2018.

9 Palmatier, Robert W., Fred C. Miao, and Eric Fang (2007), "Sales channel integration after mergers and acquisitions: A methodological approach for avoiding common pitfalls," *Industrial Marketing Management*, 36 (5) (July), 589–603.

10 Kozlenkova, Irina V., G. Tomas M. Hult, Donald J. Lund, Jeannette A. Mena, and Pinar Kekec (2015), "The role of marketing channels in supply chain management," *Journal of Retailing*, 91 (4), 586–609.

11 Scott, Colin, Henriette Lundgren, and Paul Thompson (2011), *Guide to Supply Chain Management*, Berlin: Springer.

12 Anonymous (1997), "Ever-shorter channels: Wholesale industry restructures," *Focus Japan*, 24 (July/August), 3–4.

13 Fein, Adam J. (1998), "Understanding evolutionary processes in non-manufacturing industries: Empirical insights from the shakeout in pharmaceutical wholesaling," *Journal of Evolutionary Economics*, 8 (1), 231–270.

14 Anderson, Philip and Erin Anderson (2002), "The new e-commerce intermediaries," *Sloan Management Review*, 43 (Summer), 53–62. This source provides the primary basis for this section.

15 These services are described on the Wesco corporate website and in the Harvard Business School case #9-598-021, "Wesco Distribution."

16 Narus, James A. and James C. Anderson (1996), "Rethinking distribution," *Harvard Business Review*, 96 (July–August), 112–120. The section on adaptive contracts and the examples are drawn from this article, which goes into much greater depth on the specifics of such arrangements.

17 Fein, Adam J. (1998), "The future of distributor alliances," *Modern Distribution Management*, September.

18 Granot, Daniel and Shuya Yin (2008), "Competition and cooperation in decentralized push and pull assembly systems," *Management Science*, 54 (April), 733–747.

19 See website, www.acehardware.com/category/index.jsp?categoryId=34453606, date retrieved March 24, 2018.

20 This Sidebar is based on research carried out (using public sources and Ace Hardware press releases) by William Weil, Edward Stumpf, Stuart Quin, and Ahmed Nasirwarraich.

21 www.amul.com/m/about-us, date retrieved March 21, 2018.

22 www.nytimes.com/2012/09/11/world/asia/verghese-kurien-90-who-led-indias-milk-cooperatives-dies.html, date retrieved March 21, 2018.

23 Based on 2012 website at www.consumerfed.org.

24 Deng, Ziliang and Zeyu Wang (2016), "Early-mover advantages at cross-border business-to-business e-commerce portals," *Journal of Business Research*, 69, 6002–6011.

25 Kauferle, Monika and Werner Reinhartz (2015), "Distributing through multiple channels in industrial wholesaling: How many and how much?" *Journal of the Academy of Marketing Science*, 43 (6), 746–767.

26 Homburg, Christian, Joseph Vollmayr, and Alexander Hahn (2014), "Firm value creation through major channel expansions: Evidence from an event study in the United States, Germany, and China," *Journal of Marketing*, 78 (May), 38–61.

27 Anderson and Anderson (2002), op. cit.

28 Pembroke Consulting and the National Association of Wholesaler-Distributors (2004), Facing the Forces of Change: The Road to Opportunity, http:www.nawpubs.org

29 Kroh, Eric (2017), "Dental supply co. escapes price-fixing claims in NY," *Law 360*, www.law360.com/articles/966240/dental-supply-co-escapes-price-fixing-claims-in-ny, date retrieved March 28, 2018.

30 www.burkhartdental.com/what-we-do, date retrieved March 28, 2018.

31 www.beckersasc.com/asc-transactions-and-valuation-issues/34-of-physicians-use-amazon-to-purchase-medical-dental-supplies.html, date retrieved March 28, 2018.

32 Brescka, Carolynn Pitcher (2016), "The omni-channel approach is transforming your industrial supply model," www.linkedin.com/pulse/omni-channel-approach-transforming-your-industrial-supply-brescka, date retrieved March 30, 2018.

33 Graves, Jeffrey and George Swartz (2016), "Omni-channel fulfillment and the changing dynamics of wholesale distribution," www.inddist.com/article/2016/08/omni-channel-fulfillment-and-changing-dynamics-wholesale-distribution, date retrieved March 30, 2018.

34 Graves and Swartz (2016), op. cit.

35 www.naw.org/virtual-reality-and-blockchain-wholesale-distribution-trends-14, date retrieved March 30, 2018.

36 https://blogs.sap.com/2017/06/29/how-blockchain-will-intersect-with-the-wholesale-distribution-industry, date retrieved March 30, 2018.

37 Narayandas, Das, Mary Caravella, and John Deighton (2002), "The impact of internet exchanges on business-to-business distribution," *Journal of the Academy of Marketing Sciences*, 30 (Fall), 500–505.

38 Day, George S., Adam J. Fein, and Gregg Ruppersberger (2003), "Shakeouts in digital markets: Lessons from B2B exchanges," *California Management Review*, 45 (Winter), 131–150.

39 Kleindorfer, Paul R. and D.J. Wu (2003), "Integrating long- and short-term contracting via business-to-business exchanges for capital-intensive products," *Management Science*, 49 (November), 1597–1615.

40 This discussion is based on NAW/DREF and Pembroke Consulting (2004), op. cit.; Jap, Sandy D. (2003), "An exploratory study of the introduction of online reverse auctions," *Journal of Marketing*, 67 (3), 96.

41 Sambhara, Chaitanya, Arun Rai, Mark Keil, and Vijay Kasi (2017), "Risks and controls in Internet-enabled reverse auctions: Perspectives from buyers and suppliers," *Journal of Management Information Systems*, 34 (4), 1113–1142.

42 Niraj, Rakesh, Mahendra Gupta, and Chakravarthi Narasimhan (2001), "Customer profitability in a supply chain," *Journal of Marketing*, 65 (3), 1.

43 This discussion is based on NAW/DREF and Pembroke Consulting (2004), op. cit.

44 Lusch, Robert F. and Deborah Zizzo (1995), *Competing for Customers: How Wholesaler-Distributors Can Meet the Power Retailer Challenge*, Washington, DC: Distribution Research and Education Foundation.

45 Dukes, Anthony and Yunchuan Liu (2009), "In-store media and distribution channel coordination," *Marketing Science*, 29 (1), 94–107.

46 See www.fingerhut.com.

Franchising Structures and Strategies

Franchising is a marketing channel structure intended to convince end-users that they are buying from a vertically integrated manufacturer, even if they are actually purchasing from a separately owned company. **Franchise systems** are often mistaken by consumers for company subsidiaries. In reality, they are a particular type of the classic, two-firm marketing channel structure, in which one entity supplies and the other performs downstream marketing channel functions.[1] **Franchisors**[2] such as Burger King, Marriott International, or Hertz are the upstream manufacturers of a product or originators of a service. They write contracts with **franchisees**, which are separate companies that provide the marketing channel functions downstream. End-users (customers of the franchisee) believe they are dealing with the franchisor's subsidiary, because the franchisee *assumes the identity* of the franchisor, projecting itself as though it were part of the franchisor's operation. This **deliberate loss of separate identity** is a hallmark of franchising.

To enable this masquerade, the franchisee awards the franchisor category exclusivity (it does not sell competing brands in the product category). Usually, it does not carry any other product categories either. Thus, franchising goes beyond granting a producer favored status in a single product category.

Franchising is often considered a post-World War II phenomenon. But its roots go back much farther, to ancient times in practice and to the Middle Ages in legal precedent. Its linguistic roots reflect ancient forms of both English and French, drawing from two terms: freedom and privilege. Franchising as we know it today can be traced to the late 19th century, when in the United States, soft drink companies awarded bottling contracts, and retailing franchises dominated the sales of gasoline, automobiles, and sewing machines.

In business-to-business (B2B) applications, the franchising concept was largely developed by the McCormick Harvesting Machine Company to sell directly to farmers, bypassing wholesalers. Automobiles, sewing machines, and harvesters each represented relatively new, complex, mass-produced products, which needed to be sold in huge volumes to gain economies of scale in manufacturing. Selling the massive machines at such a large scale required specialized marketing services that were unusual at the time, including the extension of credit, demonstration services, and post-sales repair. Because firms in these industries could not hire and train their own dealers fast enough, they turned to franchisees, functioning in a way that made them nearly subsidiaries, to grow quickly. After they achieved the necessary growth, firms often turned their franchising operations into company-owned and -managed outlets, in a trend that has repeated itself multiple times in history.

To further the projection of a franchisor-based identity, franchisees purchase the right to use and market the franchisor's brand. The franchisors, or sellers, induce franchisees, or dealers, to acquire some identity of the producer and concentrate on one product line. Fundamentally, dedicated dealers stock a product and resell it, adhering to certain guidelines about what to offer the market. The agreement involves a detailed contract, describing the necessary fees and allowing the franchisee to use the proven methods, trademarks, names, products, know-how, production techniques, and marketing techniques developed by the franchisor. Effectively, the franchisor develops an entire business system, or a

business format, and licenses it to the franchisee to use in a given market area. In other cases, the agreement stops short of licensing the entire business format. Yet across the board, the producer's aim is to sell its product. The manufacturer seeks to maintain some control over the presentation of its brand name, and the franchisee agrees to follow the franchisor's methods. By contract, the franchisee cedes substantial legitimate power to the franchisor. The cooperation by both parties seeks increasing profits from selling the product.

And yet, the franchisee remains a separate business, with its own balance sheet and income statement. From the standpoint of an accountant or a tax authority, a franchise is a business like any other. Franchisees invest their own capital, run the business, and keep the profits or assume the losses. They own the business; it is theirs to alter, sell, or terminate (though even this fundamental property right can be circumscribed by the franchise contract).

FRANCHISING FORMATS

The European Union provides a good definition of franchising: a **franchise** is a package of industrial or intellectual property rights, including trade names, trade-marks, shop signs, utility models, designs, copyrights, know-how, or patents. This package may be exploited to resell goods or provide services to end-users. The EU definition uses three features to distinguish franchising:[3]

1. The use of a common name or sign, with a uniform presentation of the premises.

2. Communication of know-how from franchisor to franchisee.

3. Continuing provision of commercial or technical assistance by the franchisor to the franchisee.

Such a detailed, careful definition is critical, because the EU exempts franchising from many regulations designed to encourage intra- and international competition. This exemption recognizes that franchise systems must project a common identity, which in turn requires contracts that may restrict competition. The exemption is justified from a consumer welfare standpoint because, according to the European Commission, franchising "combine[s] the advantages of a uniform and homogeneous network, which ensures a constant quality of the products and services, with the existence of traders personally interested in the efficient operation of their business."[4]

Product and Trade Name Franchising

In a traditional form of franchising, generally referred to as **product and trade name franchising**, or **authorized franchise systems**, dealers (also known as distributors, resellers, or agents) meet minimum criteria that the manufacturer establishes regarding their participation in different marketing functions. The franchisor thus authorizes distributors (wholesalers or retailers or both) to sell a product or product line while using its trade name for promotional purposes. Examples at the retail level include authorized tire, auto, computer, major appliance, television, and household furniture dealers whose suppliers have established strong brand names such as Goodyear and Toyota. Such authorization can also be granted at the wholesale level—for example, to soft drink bottlers and to distributors or dealers by manufacturers of electrical and electronics equipment. These producers make most of their profits on the margins they obtain by selling to their dealers, rather than on fees and royalties. These are essentially "supplier–dealer relationships."[5] Although an estimated 68,311 establishments operate according to a product and trade name franchise model, three lines of business dominate this sector: (1) automotive and truck dealerships, (2) gas stations without convenience stores, and (3) beverage bottlers.[6]

Business Format Franchising

In the franchising world, though, the business format is far more prevalent than the product and trade name format, accounting for 732,842 establishments.[7] When we refer generally to franchising, usually we mean **business format franchising**, which licenses an entire way to conduct business under a brand name such as Great Clips or McDonald's.

For a franchisor, the reward for licensing its approach is ongoing fees from its franchisees. That is, establishing such an authorized franchise system helps suppliers increase the probability that channel members provide appropriate types and levels of service outputs to end-users, without assuming financial ownership. The organizers of authorized franchise systems might specify or impose restrictions on how channel members can operate.

The term "authorized" also implies that the system is clearly demarcated, but that assumption does not always hold. In some areas, legal requirements oblige any so-called franchisor to follow disclosure and reporting rules, as listed in Figure 8.1—and they thus must pay significant legal costs. In other contexts, though, the distinctions between franchising and other channel methods are less clear. Beyond vertical integration, a gray area exists between franchising and other forms of distribution. It can be difficult to determine whether a channel is actually franchised or if it might be technically separable but still led (legally or illegally) by an influential, upstream channel member. For example, both retailer cooperative and wholesaler-sponsored voluntary groups resemble franchising, but regulators sometimes intervene to determine if franchising laws might apply to these groups. In 1999, 34 franchise owners whose franchises were canceled by Baskin-Robbins banded together and formed a co-op called KaleidoScoops.[8] They maintain a national brand but management decisions are vested in the membership and each store owner can operate the business according to their own preferences.

Contents of a Franchise Disclosure Document
Total number of franchises.
Number of franchise relationships that dissolved within the past year due to termination or non-renewal.
The cost of starting and operating a franchise.
Evidence that can back up claims about a franchisee's potential earnings or details of earnings of current franchisees and contact information of at least 10 franchisees who live in the area where the franchisee is thinking of setting up shop.
An audited financial statement of the franchisor.
The responsibilities and obligations the franchisee and franchisor have if a franchising agreement is in place.
Information about the franchisor's key executives including their professional background and information about any legal actions being taken against the franchisors and other promoters.
Information about legal actions taken by the franchisor against other franchisees within the past year.

Source: Federal Trade Commission, www.consumer.ftc.gov/articles/0067-buying- janitorial-service-franchise.

FIGURE 8.1

Contents of Most Franchise Disclosure Documents

THE FRANCHISING ARRANGEMENT

Franchising is an inherently contradictory marketing channel, yet it functions surprisingly well in many circumstances. Two independent businesses join forces to perform marketing functions to their mutual benefit. But in so doing, they attempt to convince end-users that they are one company, owned and operated under the same brand name. To convince end-users of the cohesiveness of the channel and the brand name, franchisees compromise their independence. They voluntarily cede an astonishing degree of power to the franchisor—and pay the franchisor for the privilege of doing so.

Why would any downstream entrepreneur accept (indeed, seek out and pay for) a franchise? For that matter, why would any manufacturer go to market through independent companies, when its real intention is to control the channel tightly enough that the end-user doesn't know the difference? Why not give customers what they think they are getting; that is, company-owned and -managed outlets?

Such questions make it seem as if franchising is a flawed concept that should be very rare. Yet franchising is booming. There were 801,543 franchised establishments, employing 9 million people and producing output worth $868.1 billion, in 2016.[9] In Europe, franchising was once dismissed as an aberrant form of organization, but it continues to thrive and grow since being introduced in the

1970s. Furthermore, franchising continues to dominate retail sectors, but it also is expanding in B2B markets, particularly in the sale of various services such as cleaning and printing services to businesses.

As an institution, franchising is so well established globally that it has come full circle. Many countries that first experienced franchising as a U.S. import thanks to U.S. dominance in sectors like fast food have spawned their own firms that offer business formats they have exported to other countries—including "back" to the United States. The franchising institution is so stable and so pervasive that it offers the single most common way to become an entrepreneur in North America, Europe, and Asia.[10] Sidebar 8.1 describes the world's most admired franchisor, whose operations touch every aspect of the franchising system. Can you name it without looking? We bet you can.

SIDEBAR 8.1
McDonald's

McDonald's is not only the world's largest retail organization, in terms of the number of outlets (more than 36,000 units located in over 100 countries); it also is the largest and most admired franchisor in the world, and 85 percent of its outlets are owned by franchisees. The scale of this success can be difficult to grasp. Consider (www.mcdonalds.com):

- On average, a new outlet opens somewhere in the world every five hours.
- With 1.7 million employees, McDonald's is the world's largest private employer.
- It is the world's largest holder of real estate.

McDonald's may seem ubiquitous now, but it also made some errors along the way. The format emerged from California, in the aftermath of World War II, when Ray Kroc stopped selling milkshake machines to license the hamburger chain concept from its founders (the MacDonald brothers). In 1955, Kroc opened his own McDonald's and began to build his empire. Growth remained steady until 1996, when franchisees suffered declining profitability, mainly because the U.S. market had become nearly saturated, yet McDonald's continued to add units at a rapid pace, cannibalizing its existing franchises. After an in-house revolt, the chain slowed its growth (in part, by closing one unit for every two it opened) and invested heavily to modernize kitchens and improve both its product and its profitability. This back-to-basics approach, focused on growing same-store sales, to the benefit of franchisees, led the firm back to growth.[11]

Today, McDonald's owns 8 percent of the outlets located in the United States. Approximately 6,300 outlets (mostly in Asia and the Middle East) are joint ventures with local shareholders, and the remainder are owned by 5,300 franchisees. These franchisees invest heavily to build their outlets, often selling all their possessions to raise the capital. Then they pay McDonald's up to 25 percent of their earned revenue in fees and rent (McDonald's is usually their landlord). In return, they share in the system.

Format

Method. The operating manual weighs 2 kilograms (more than 4 pounds) and specifies virtually every detail of how operations must be performed. For example, employees wear uniforms without pockets, to discourage them from accepting tips or putting their hands in their pockets. Leaving their hands free in turn encourages constant action ("if you've got time to lean, you've got time to clean"). Cooking and serving specifications are timed down to the second, and detailed role descriptions mandate the responsibilities of every member of the staff.

Setup Assistance. Months of on-site training lead to courses at Hamburger University, a literal campus in suburban Chicago that every year teaches approximately 7,000 new franchisees and managers how to run the business. McDonald's also agrees to secure a site and build the restaurant, which it then rents back to the new franchisee.

Norm Enforcement. Once operations are underway, the franchisee receives regular assistance from an army of regional consultants, who also perform frequent and detailed performance checks. McDonald's insists that franchisees abide by its intricate system. McDonald's terminated its relationship with a long-time master franchisee in India who operated 169 outlets, with each side leveling charges of financial irregularities and noncompliance at the other.[12]

Worldwide Supply. McDonald's has a network of favored suppliers that function almost as subsidiaries. When entering a new market, McDonald's seeks out local suppliers and asks them to adapt to its methods. But in most cases, the franchisor finds these local suppliers inadequate and induces its own suppliers to enter the market as replacements. These key suppliers process astonishing quantities of food and supplies, matched precisely to McDonald's exacting specifications. The result is immediate uniformity, combined with economies of scale that allow the franchisor to operate profitably while charging low prices.

Marketing Strategy and Communications. McDonald's targets families by providing fast, inexpensive meals that children enjoy. To draw the family into the stores, it focuses on pleasing children with in-store events too (e.g., birthday parties), Happy Meals, and Ronald McDonald. The menu remains extremely similar worldwide, with some limited adaptation to local tastes. This standardization enhances its ability to capture economies of scale—and not just in food. McDonald's also is one of the world's leading distributors of toys through its Happy Meals.

Furthermore, it assigns massive advertising budgets to marketing campaigns, particularly those backing sporting events. For example, McDonald's spends millions to advertise during international football (for Americans, soccer) events. In contrast with the rest of its strategy, McDonald's advertising is not standardized, such that different countries and regions have their own slogans and campaigns. Communication is partly financed by franchisees, which pay 4.5 percent of their revenue as an advertising fee. They also may run local campaigns, for which the franchisor assists them with ready-to-use kits.

Participation

To enter this system, a prospective franchisee must pass tests of its motivation and capability. Applicants include professionals from a range of fields, including doctors, lawyers, and executives, though these candidates frequently get screened out for their inadequate motivation and lack of customer service orientation. In France, successful candidates invest substantial upfront fees and sunk costs to outfit the interior and kitchen (though the franchisor pays most of the costs to build the restaurant and holds the lease).

Despite such high early costs, most McDonald's locations break even after several years (and often sooner) and become quite profitable. In France, one franchisee drew a salary comparable to an executive's, while also collecting substantial dividends and building wealth in the location (where resale values ran upward of several million euros). Satisfactory performance also means a franchisee can open more stores, though McDonald's discourages overly large operations, fearing the owner will become too far removed from day-to-day operations.

McDonald's draws criticism as well as admiration, though. Social critics charge that the franchisor is too heavy-handed and anti-union in its personnel practices. Suppliers complain of being exploited. The secretive chain is often accused of being a heartless multinational, seeking merely to create an unhealthy, Westernized, fast food culture wherever it goes by suppressing local businesses and displacing local customs.

Yet McDonald's earns praise for offering employment (and ultimately franchising opportunities) to young people and those who often face discrimination in traditional job markets (e.g., Latinos and African Americans in the United States, people of North African descent in France). The franchisees often operate in struggling neighborhoods, creating jobs and businesses that benefit residents. And the persistent popularity of the product suggests that its fast food culture is not totally unwelcome!

BENEFITS OF FRANCHISING

To Franchisees

Imagine you are a private entrepreneur with a certain amount of capital, perhaps due to an inheritance, severance pay, accumulated savings, or equity from a previous business. You could invest the money and collect the earnings, but you are more interested in starting a business. Owning your own business sounds great:

- It is intrinsically appealing for psychological reasons (e.g., you feel pride in the idea of ownership).

- Other opportunities in society seem closed off to you, perhaps because of your gender, race, or background.

- You have grown tired of working for someone else.

- You are willing to assume some risk to gain independence.

- You are confident that you can earn better returns in the long run if you put your own labor into your own company than if you invest your resources—whether financial or labor—in someone else's.

- By owning a business, you could help support family members or friends who also need employment (though evidence indicates that the performance of family-owned franchises lags behind that of non-family-owned franchises).[13]

All of these needs and benefits can be fulfilled by starting your own business from scratch or from franchising. But the risks involved with starting a business from the ground up imply some additional benefits of a franchise arrangement:

- Failure rates for new businesses are high.

- Setting up a business takes months, even years. In particular, it takes time and resources to build a clientele.

- There are literally thousands of decisions, big and small, to be made:

  o Where should the business be located?

  o Should it have a theme?

  o What size should it be?

  o What kind of products should it provide, and how should they be prepared, economically and efficiently?

- There are so many legal, financial, marketing, managerial, and operating decisions to be made that any entrepreneur can be overwhelmed.

- The business easily could fail, wiping out all your capital.

Contemplating these prospects has made plenty of people too nervous to pursue their entrepreneurial ambitions. You may have met them in the job market, still drawing designs for their great idea on napkins and dreaming of walking into the boss's office to quit. But for those who remain dedicated to the notion of running their own business, while also minimizing some risks, a franchising arrangement offers perhaps the perfect combination. In effect, franchisees sell some portion of their independence to the franchisor, and in return, they obtain a corporate backer, a coach, and a problem solver. The franchisor's support personnel step in with assistance, training franchisees and sharing a proven formula for success. This business format provides a prepackaged solution to startup issues and well-established decisions for most critical choices an entrepreneur might face. In return for paying a fee, the franchisee also purchases a license to operate and exploit this format in a particular market area.

Startup Package

When a franchisee buys the license for a business format, it acquires the brand name, together with a set of well-explained and detailed marketing and business decisions. Furthermore, it receives training and assistance to implement the already determined decisions, including:

- Market survey and site selection.

- Facility design and layout (architectural and building services).

- Lease negotiation advice.

- Financing advice.

- Operating manuals.

- Management training programs.

- Training for the franchisee's employees.

These initial services are highly valuable. Franchisors are very motivated to share not just their explicit knowledge but also their tacit knowledge with franchisees, to ensure the uniformity of the operations and system-wide success.[14]

In particular, **site selection** is critical to retail operations, because the market's potential determines any specific store's sales and productivity.[15] The amount of help a franchisor provides for this selection varies with the business and the contract. For example, McDonald's typically performs all site analysis and most land acquisition and development; Budget Rent-A-Car merely assigns a territory and allows the franchisee to build wherever he or she pleases, subject to franchisor review and advice.

Another critical benefit, available from the very moment the franchisee starts up, is the **brand name** itself. By using the brand equity already associated with this name, the franchisee can quickly build a clientele that is loyal to the brand offering.

These initial services also benefit from **economies of scale**, which the franchisor can capture and share with the franchisee. By providing the same services over and over, the franchisor acquires deep, detailed knowledge of the nuances of every single activity. The franchisor also pools demand for these services, which makes it economical to dedicate specific personnel to the setup tasks (e.g., statistical specialists to perform site analyses; company lawyers to deal with zoning authorities and draft documents; architects to draw plans and supervise construction; technicians to train, install, and test equipment). By leveraging the franchisor's scale, the franchisee also gains preferred customer status with service providers (e.g., contractors, bankers). All of these benefits suggest better results at lower costs.

Ongoing Benefits

Were this the end of the story, franchising would only be a system for *launching* a business. But it is primarily a system for *running* a business. Once started, what services might a franchisee expect its franchisor to keep providing?

- Field supervision of operations, including quality inspections.

- Management report feedback.

- Merchandising and promotional materials.

- Management and employee retraining.

- National advertising.

- Centralized planning.

- Market data and guidance.

- Auditing and record keeping.

- Group insurance plans.

Of this list, the first two items stand out, because of their potential to create conflict. Almost all franchisors have a continuous program of **field supervision**, including monitoring and correcting quality problems. Field representatives visit each outlet to aid its everyday operations, check product and service quality, and monitor performance. They serve as coaches and consultants for the franchisee. But they also are employees of the franchisor, so their first priority is to inspect, evaluate, and report on the franchisees' performance. These roles might conflict with coaching roles, requiring diplomacy and skill to balance them.

Many franchisees also must submit regular management reports about key elements of their operations, such as weekly sales, local advertising, employee turnover, profits, and so forth. These regular reports reflect the nearly subsidiary nature of franchising; they would be highly unusual in other contractual channels. By reporting on operations, the franchisee facilitates various financial, operating, and marketing control procedures throughout the franchise system. It also enables the franchisor to offer feedback to assist the franchisee. But this confidential information constitutes the very heart of the business; to provide feedback, the franchisor might demand that franchisees buy special electronic invoicing or reporting systems and open their books to constant oversight and review. Such tactics can create resentment, especially if the franchisee's initial goal was gaining independence from an overseeing boss.

Competitive Advantages of Franchising

Consider the list of services that an entrepreneur might use its capital to obtain from someone else—architecture, law advice, and so on. Why buy these services from a franchisor, rather than independent consultants?

First, franchisors act as **consolidators** in this specific type of channel. They bring together all necessary services—no more, no less—under one roof and consolidate them, achieving economies of scale (size) and scope (synergy). Second, franchisors focus on one product line (e.g., fast food restaurants, car repair). They develop expertise and related benefits from this specialization. Third, perhaps the most critical and distinguishing benefit of a franchisor is its ability to bring everything together and focus on a **branded concept**. Everything the franchisor does is dedicated to the needs of the brand and the implementation of its concept. Even its specialization benefits are tied to brand equity, which cannot accrue without a multitude of units. Thus a key reason to turn to a franchisor is to rent its brand equity and become part of a large network, not just contract for business services.

This discussion brings us to a crucial, often-misunderstood reason for why entrepreneurs might pay for a franchise: *they are hiring an enforcement agency.* The franchisor acts as a police officer, judge, and jury. The business format is a system, and the franchisor makes sure that all players (franchisees) observe its rules, without allowing any opportunism. Each franchisee hires the franchisor to police the system, to make sure that everyone else implements the concept too. It is in each franchisee's interest to have a police officer on hand to protect brand equity—and brand equity is the very basis of the franchising concept.

This role often gets described as the *prevention of free riding.* **Free riding** occurs when one party reaps benefits while another party bears all the costs. Dunkin' Donuts positions itself as a producer of premium, fresh bakery goods. To sustain this positioning, franchisees agree to throw out unsold product after a few hours and replace them with freshly produced goods. This promise is costly to keep, which creates a temptation to keep selling donuts for a few more hours, hoping that no one will notice they are a bit stale. A franchisee that sells stale donuts benefits from the Dunkin' Donuts image, but this practice hurts the brand's image, which hurts all franchisees. Ultimately, the franchisor's field representatives are likely to find out, and the punishment for the shirking franchisee is likely to be swift and painful.

If franchisees did not have a franchisor, they likely would invent one to provide the channel function of policing the system. Brand equity is utterly critical to franchising. Safeguarding brand equity is a key reason franchising has become associated with the production of all kinds of services. For sectors such as document handling, building, business aids and services, child care, hospitality, tourism, travel, weight control—even autopsies!—a constant challenge is ensuring consistent outcomes. By branding a service business, the franchisor guarantees consistency, which attracts customers and enhances brand equity, for itself and its franchisees.

To Franchisors

Now let's turn the lens around and change our perspective: you head a company with a concept and a brand. You have a business format. You desire tight control over the implementation of your concept. You want that control to uphold the brand's image and ensure the proper sale and servicing of your product. With this directive focus, the logical choice seemingly would be to set up a network of outlets that you can own, operate, and supervise, with the help of managers you hire to supervise the staff at each outlet. Each outlet remains to be set up, after you hire and train the manager and staff.

Such efforts take significant time, effort, and money. You are ultimately responsible for every decision and every staff move. Furthermore, you must remain constantly on guard to avoid agency conflicts. That is, managers likely have different incentives and goals, so you have to find a way to get them to perform in the way you desire. Such considerations constitute the two main categories of reasons that you might prefer a franchise system rather than an owned network to spread your ideas.

Financial and Managerial Capital for Growth

Most people with a great idea want to grow fast, motivated by far more than just entrepreneurial ego or impatience. A unique idea needs to be exploited and established as fast as possible, to gain a first-mover advantage before others have the chance to copy it. If an idea is trendy (e.g., American-style fast food in Southeast Asia), the franchisor must encourage its rapid spread, before the market becomes saturated. In a business market with fragmented competition and no strong brands, a quickly spreading idea is more likely to build a strong brand name before others. Conversely, if the market hosts a strong competitor, the franchisor may need to grow quickly, before the competitor really notices or tries to block it. Furthermore, reaching a minimum efficient scale quickly enables the firm to amortize its costs over a larger operation. For example, to justify national U.S. advertising, it would need to achieve national coverage of a market of several hundred million people.

Such speed to market demands massive amounts of financial capital, which may not be available through a public stock offering. The earliest explanations of franchising focused on the idea that franchisees can be a cheaper source of capital, in that they often are willing to invest for a lower rate of return than passive investors that lack a good understanding of the business. Although appealing, this idea fell into disfavor, because it appeared to contradict financial portfolio theory, which states that investors of any kind prefer less risk. Because the risk of any single location is greater than risk spread across the entire chain, prospective franchisees should prefer to buy a share in the chain, rather than the rights to one location. But the idea also is making a comeback, in part because of the evidence that it persists in practice.[16] Perhaps capital markets remain inefficient for prospective franchisors. And perhaps franchisees do not act as merely rational financial investors, indifferent between owning their own business and owning a piece of a company.[17]

Remember, from the previous perspective, that franchisees want to be their own boss. They will manage their own outlets, which implies that franchisees that buy in are confident in their ability to influence the risk-to-return ratio of their operations. By buying franchise rights to a location of their choice, they seek to demonstrate their ability to earn high profits at lower risk. Investors in the overall chain instead have minimal influence over day-to-day operations and can only earn returns on their investments; franchisees, after paying suppliers and the franchisor, get to keep all the profits earned from the store. Thus, franchisees are rarely indifferent between owning a franchise and owning a piece of the franchisor, and their willing investments offer the franchise system a ready way to grow quickly and with sufficient financial resources.

The idea that entrepreneurs value the returns from their own wholly controlled operations more than they value equal returns from owning a piece of a larger organization implies that we need to move beyond conventional measures of profit. *Entrepreneurs have other motives.* For example, they may have found what they consider the perfect location and just need help getting it up and running. Often entrepreneurs have specific technology innovations that they want to employ, but they need help with peripheral organizational support. Although they may not value the entire chain as highly as they value their location or innovation, it still would be relatively easy to persuade such franchisees to invest.[18] By getting them to invest in a franchise system, rather than some other option, franchisors enjoy a sort of test run of their ideas. (Many would-be franchisors never find any franchisees—or buyers for their stock.) By attracting franchisees' investments, the franchisor gains an endorsement of its operations.

Finding franchisees also provides another sort of resource, beyond financial input. That is, it can address the pressing need to overcome **personnel shortages** and find good managers. Even with plenty of capital, an entrepreneur often must spend an inordinate amount of time trying to solve the *managerial scarcity problem*.[19] But remember, this startup still aims to grow its business quickly, with plenty of other issues to occupy the founders' attention. Spending time reviewing resumes, interviewing managerial candidates, and calling references is inefficient, difficult, and often ineffective. Instead, franchising offers a preestablished way to "screen" managerial applicants *by asking them to become franchisees*. Unmotivated, uninterested, or incapable managers are unlikely to pay a lump-sum entry fee, put up the initial investment, accept payment of an ongoing royalty, or accept the risk of living off the uncertain profits of their efforts. In contrast, dedicated managers who are confident in their abilities and entrepreneurial in their attitudes likely jump at the chance to prove themselves and their capabilities.

These arguments for starting up through franchising are rationally defensible, but of course, reality is not always rational. Many founders of franchise organizations exhibit an underlying goal of controlling the enterprise as it grows, and they believe it is easier to influence (or dominate) each franchisee (and thus the entire operation) than to influence a board of directors. In this case, the decision to franchise is driven by a fear of losing control by selling shares, rather than the desire to raise financial capital or resolve a shortage of human capital. Ironically, these founders often find that they have underestimated the independent spirit of their franchisees.[20] Then the founders lose control anyway, because they must give up power to professional managers as their organization continues to grow.

Harnessing the Entrepreneurial Spirit

An effective, persistent franchise system recognizes that franchisees offer all the benefits and gains of a vast group of entrepreneurs—the driving force of successful economies throughout time. Consider a general theory from organizational behavior literature: there are two main ways a firm can motivate the staff who work for it. It can control and monitor them, in which case it seeks to supervise employees, then sanction or reward them as appropriate. Or it can incentivize them to align their own interests with the best interests of the company by making them

residual claimants of the firm's profits. A residual claimant needs less monitoring, because to earn profits, he or she works hard to make the business succeed. In this sense, franchising encourages work and reduces monitoring costs by transforming managers into owners and residual claimants.

Furthermore, franchisees may gain substantial "psychic income"—not just financial rewards—from owning their own business. They likely feel pride of ownership and a sense of loyalty toward "their" franchise system, and they may appreciate the benefits it offers them, such as the ability to hire relatives and friends who need work. Perhaps most important, running a business offers franchisees a way to maximize the returns on the knowledge and relationships that they bring to the business. Such **human capital** is often so specific that it works only within specific ventures. (This idea of maximizing the returns on specialized human capital reappears in our subsequent discussion in this chapter of multi-unit franchisees.)

The franchisees' more intrinsic (i.e., internal) motivation to exert effort to benefit both the specific outlet and the wider system likely helps explain why franchising is so prominent in retail sectors, for which *effort truly matters for success*. But if the margins earned are too low to pay supervisors well and ensure that all staff members put forth continuous effort, a basic monitoring system will fail. Such concerns are especially problematic in service industries, in which production and distribution are simultaneous, so it would be impossible for an owner to inspect all output before the customer sees it. Table 8.1 lists sectors in which franchising has a strong presence, all of which match these traits and characteristics. In Figure 8.2, we also showcase a sample financial disclosure form that franchisors might be required to share with their prospective franchisees.

Sectors				**TABLE 8.1**
Amusement	Automobiles	Business services	Rental: Service equipment	Sectors with Substantial Franchise Presence
Building products and services	Cleaning services and equipment	Children's products, including clothing	Shipping and packing	
Educational services	Employment agencies	Home furnishings/equipment	Lodging/hotels	
Maintenance	Miscellaneous services	Personal services and equipment	Pet services	
Photography and video	Printing	Quick services	Restaurants: Fast food traditional	
Real estate	Retail food	Health and beauty (includes hair styling and cosmetology)	Travel	

Source: See 2013 website (www.franchising.com).

FIGURE 8.2

Financial Performance Representation and Projection

Financial Performance Representation and Projection	
Franchisors are permitted under FTC's Franchise Rule to provide information about actual or potential financial performance of their franchised and/or company-owned outlets. However, such information should be included in the disclosure document and there should be actual basis for making these claims.	
Representation: 60 percent of existing Clean Clips Hair Salon franchisees in mid-sized metropolitan areas have had at least $300,000 in annual sales. Not all outlets have sold this amount. There is no guarantee you'll do so, therefore you must understand the risk of not doing as well.	Projection: Our estimate is that for your first 12 months of operation your income would be $60,000. There is no guarantee that you'll do as well; you must accept the risk of not doing as well.
Bases: These sales figures are based on the actual historical performance in calendar years 2015 and 2016 of Clean Clips franchisees in five mid-sized metropolitan areas: Cincinnati, Denver, Seattle, Portland, and St. Louis. There are 400 Clean Clips franchisees in the entire Clean Clips system, of which 250 are in the above-mentioned five cities. 150 of these 250 franchisees attained at least $300,000 in annual sales.	Bases: This projected income figure is derived from the actual historical performance of 55 first-year Clean Clips franchisees. There are 400 Clean Clips franchisees in the entire system, of which 55 began their first year in operation in calendar years 2015 or 2016.
Assumptions: Our study measured Clean Clips franchisees' performance in mid-sized metropolitan areas. If your store were to be located in a different area (demographically or population size), these results may not be typical. Also, all the franchisees studied have been in business for at least 3 years. Sales in the first year tend to be about half of what a store that has been operating for 3 or more years generates.	Assumptions: 45 of the franchisees included in our analyses are located in mid-sized metropolitan areas. If your store were to be located in a different area (demographically or population size), these results may not be typical. These estimates also assume no economic downturn as that affects frequency of hair cuts and no additional competition from national hair salons. More details on our analyses can be provided upon request.

Source: www.ftc.gov/system/files/documents/plain-language/bus70-franchise-rule-compliance-guide.pdf.

We also distinguish between a lack of effort and misdirected effort. A franchising contract is a good way to combat a lack of effort, but it is often unsuccessful in resolving misdirected effort. Instead, franchisees with their entrepreneurial spirits often battle franchisors over exactly how things should be done. A good franchisor takes franchisees seriously and considers their ideas, as if they were consultants, rather than rejecting contradictory ideas out of hand, as difficult as that might be. One franchisor offers a pithy summary of the key challenge: "You see, a manager will do what you want, but … won't work very hard. A franchisee will work hard, but … won't do what you want."[21]

A franchisee as a **consultant** works out implementation problems for the franchise system and generates new ideas, especially on the local level. That is, the franchise system establishes the general vision; to be implemented on a large scale, or even globally, that vision must be *adapted to local circumstances*, as well as to *changes in the marketplace* over time. A franchisor lacks access to local markets and end-users; the franchisee provides it.

Consider the example of Southeast Asia, where U.S.-style fast food has become quite popular. William Heinecke, an American raised in Thailand, approached Pizza Hut with the idea of opening a franchise in Bangkok, but Pizza Hut worried about Asians' well-documented dislike of cheese. Despite corporate misgivings, Heinecke paid the necessary fees and signed a contract to go ahead. Both parties are thrilled he did, because Pizza Hut now enjoys substantial business in Thailand, and Heinecke owns dozens of outlets.

Thus in many situations, the franchisor might not know best; sophisticated franchisees can solve problems that the national office might not even notice. Even in this seemingly inverted channel, though, the franchisor remains a necessary participant. The central corporate office collects the various, diverse ideas provided by all its franchisees, screens out those that appear unworkable, adapts them for application to the entire chain, and then spreads them to other franchisees. Some of the best-known images and product ideas that appear in every modern McDonald's were generated by franchisees but spread by the franchisor.[22] Like the Filet-O-Fish? Thank a franchisee located in a heavily Catholic neighborhood, whose customers avoided meat dishes on Fridays. The widely popular $5 foot-long sandwich at Subway was developed by a franchisee in Florida.

A key point to retain from this discussion is an understanding of how franchise systems evolve. The franchisor has the original vision for the business format. Over time, though, franchisees develop the vision *collectively*. In general, no single franchisee has a better format. Rather, the franchisor continually *gathers, adapts, and diffuses the best ideas* across the set of franchisees.

In developing franchise systems, many of the most creative contributors are franchisees that previously worked as managers for the company. A motivated, capable manager can be rewarded for his or her effort, and also encouraged to remain with the company, by awarding him or her a franchise contract. In France, many large retailers face slow growth in their home market, forcing them to consider secondary locations, such as small towns that cannot support a large, company-owned store. Instead, they give employees the opportunity to transform from managerial employees into self-employed franchisees. Employees get to own their own businesses; franchisors enjoy reduced risk and investment demands while also growing into new areas. Employees in this situation often lack the necessary capital, which requires the franchisors to provide additional support and "bet" on their former employees, to preserve their loyalty and know-how. French franchisors also often offer these one-time employees additional financial backing, assistance with the transition, and advanced training. As long as this additional assistance does not go so far as to quench their entrepreneurial spirit, it can be a happy outcome for everyone involved.[23]

In a sense, this development again brings us full circle. We began by describing franchising as a way to find good managers (without having to hire them) quickly, who were willing to provide the franchisor with ready capital. Now we find that franchising helps keep existing managers within the firm's fold, by granting them the necessary assistance and capital. Accordingly, this section reflects the constantly evolving role of franchising. Fast Retailing, the Japanese company that owns the casual clothing retailer Uniqlo, opened hundreds of Uniqlo outlets by converting proactive employees with at least 10 years' experience into franchisees, in line with the founder's belief that store managers must be independent and that franchising can establish win–win relationships.[24]

In short, franchising is more than a way to grow fast, obtain capital, or avoid monitoring costs. It offers a versatile, generalized system of management motivation in marketing channels. Yet for many, it remains easy to underestimate the power of franchising and overestimate the value of controlling the operation, as Sidebar 8.2 describes.

SIDEBAR 8.2
ADA Discovers the Benefits of Franchisees

ADA rents cars and trucks. Its discount strategy centers on advertising a very low price—though the total price often turns out to be much higher, once the extras get factored in. It also offers minimal service. Initially, the firm kept costs ultra-low by sticking to a niche (cars and light trucks in cities) and using franchising to grow fast. But this approach meant that it soon saturated its home market of France where it has a network of 480 car rental agencies (www.avidcarhire. com). In the belief that it was essential to keep growing, ADA began to open rental counters in airports and train stations, renting a broader assortment of cars and trucks. To run this new operation, management believed it needed to "professionalize" its retail operations, so it staffed these sites with company personnel.

The results were disappointing. City dwellers who went to ADA counters were already well informed and needed little help. Travelers who frequented airports and train stations instead demanded information and assistance. Furthermore, these locations were highly competitive, such that ADA had to add personnel, broaden its vehicle stock, and make its rental terms more flexible. Still, the counters suffered from a lack of referrals from travel agencies, with which ADA had no connections.

As the counters sank to ever lower performance levels, employees deserted, leaving ADA with only its weakest managers. To rectify the situation, ADA added another level of corporate oversight. Ultimately, though, it had to concede that it simply could not compensate for poor supervision at the rental site. Its solution? Sell those troubled, "professional" company-run sites—to franchisees.[25]

REASONS NOT TO FRANCHISE

Not everyone agrees with this rosy view, though. By any stretch of the imagination, Starbucks is a highly successful chain.[26] Its fast growth and massive coverage of seemingly every urban corner have led many people to assume it is a franchised chain. Instead, every store is a company outlet, managed by Starbucks employees. Howard Schultz, its founder, remains sharply critical of franchising, arguing that it leads firms to expand too quickly, without stopping to address problems as they arise. The errors (e.g., hiring the wrong people, losing control of operations, compromising on quality, picking bad locations) propagate through the system and become established. Starbucks maintains legendary consistency, in both its operations and its product output, and somehow manages to hire and retain enthusiastic, committed store management, largely by offering stock options to all full-time employees (a perk that consistently lands Starbucks on lists of the best places to work). Equity stakes in the overall business seemingly allow Starbucks to duplicate the enthusiasm and sense of ownership that franchisees bring to their business.

Regardless of the arguments in favor of a franchising system, Starbucks offers ongoing proof that there is nothing that says franchising is the only viable way to run the channels presented in Table 8.1. Furthermore, as noted in Chapter 1, Starbucks has relied on franchising in some international markets; in airports and supermarkets, it operates under licensed arrangements that, though technically exempt from the franchise definition and obligations, share some characteristics of franchises and clearly are not company-owned stores.

FRANCHISING STRATEGIES

Franchise Contracting Strategies

Franchising is tightly governed by elaborate, formal contracts that run on for pages, filled with intricate legal language. It is tempting for both franchisor and franchisee to leave the contracts to the lawyers and simply presume that the working arrangements that arise will govern the relationship anyway. This is a dangerous error. In franchising, the contract really matters. In particular, three sections of a franchise contract determine *who will enter* the arrangement and *how it will function*:[27]

1. The payment system, particularly the lump-sum fee to enter the system, royalty fees, and the initial investment. The calculation of these fees and their potential adjustment over the contract duration is critical.

2. Real estate, including who holds the lease and how it may be transferred. Although this detail appears to entail financing, it is actually distinct and important.

3. Termination. Franchise arrangements anticipate the possible end of the relationship and spell out how it would be conducted.

In the United States, where franchising has a long history, regulators and courts similarly consider its social benefits, out of concern that franchisors (typically regarded as large, powerful, and sophisticated) might exploit franchisees (typically seen as small, weak, and naive). A key reason for this concern is that franchise contracts typically contain clauses that, on their face, outrageously favor the franchisor (probably because franchisors have better lawyers and more bargaining power).

But are the contracts truly unfair?

To explain why they might not be, consider a parallel with international politics, in which, to safeguard an agreement, two parties engage in **hostage exchanges**. The party that is more likely to break its promise offers a hostage to the other side. If it reneges, the other party gets to keep the hostage. If both sides are equally tempted to break their promises, they exchange hostages.

Franchise contracts represent attempts by each side to post "hostages" to ensure the other side lives up to its promises.[28] Both the franchisor and franchisee are tempted to renege, but the franchisee is in a better position to renege, so it posts more hostages—that is, it accepts contracts that give seemingly greater power to the franchisor.

Payment Systems

The franchisee usually pays a fixed fee, or lump-sum payment, to join the franchise system. If the contract ended there, the franchisor would be sorely tempted to abscond with the fee and do nothing to help the franchisee. This fee is a hostage posted by the franchisee. It also offers its initial investments in acquiring inventory, obtaining and adapting the facility, purchasing tools and equipment, and advertising its store opening. If the store closed quickly, the franchisee would lose much of its investment, especially if its purchases included fixtures and equipment specialized to fit the franchisor's operations or decor (e.g., distinctive colors, patterns, emblazoned logos and slogans). The part of the initial investment that the franchisee can never recover is called a **sunk cost**. Thus, both the upfront fee and the sunk costs are hostages posted by the franchisee. If it fails to live up to its promises to work in accordance with the franchise system and the business fails, it loses its hostages.

Of course, the franchisor must post some hostages of its own. The optimal hostage in this case is a **royalty on sales** (variable fee). If the franchisor refuses to help the franchisee, sales suffer, and the franchisor shares in that suffering by collecting less royalty income. Therefore, royalties motivate the franchisor to assist the franchisee.[29] At this point, we need to explain the appeal of royalties on sales, rather than on profit. That is, the franchisor's function is to help the franchisee make money. So profit seemingly should be the best measure. But in most cases, sales can be readily observed and verified, whereas profit is easy to manipulate and difficult to check.

EXAMPLE: GREAT CLIPS (USA/CANADA)

Established in 1982, Great Clips is a chain of walk-in (no appointment needed) hair salons that cut men's, women's, and children's hair; the more than 4,000 franchised stores typically locate in strip malls.[30] The company charges franchisees $20,000 to sign up and then 6 percent of sales as an ongoing royalty,[31] usually requiring an initial term of 10 years. Franchisees also must contribute an additional 5 percent of their gross sales to a common advertising fund. Then Great Clips charges various fees for software, credit card and gift card processing, and so forth, which can reach several thousand dollars annually.[32] Accordingly, the initial investment needed to start a salon ranges from $137,000 to $258,000, depending on the chosen location. In turn, Great Clips requires potential franchisees to demonstrate net worth of at least $300,000 and liquid assets of $50,000. Although an approved salon can be up and running in just 9–12 months, the key challenge is to find an acceptable location. The company establishes a protected radius (i.e., area around which no other Great Clips locations may open), which ranges from one-tenth to three-quarters of a mile, depending on the local population density.[33] Unlike some franchises (e.g., McDonald's) that require franchisees to work the business full-time, Great Clips franchisees can use it as a semi-active investment and continue with their day jobs, while they monitor and manage the franchise on the side. Great Clips helps them do so by providing startup advice, ongoing training, and encouragement to open multiple units (after they master the system, franchisees own an average of five units).

Thus franchisors make money from both fees and royalties, and the key question becomes, *What is the best way to get the most money?* Put differently, what ratio of fixed fees and variable sales royalties should franchisors prefer? One argument holds that fixed and variable payments should correlate negatively.[34] The rationale is that a franchisor charging a high fixed fee sends two signals: my franchise is valuable, but also, I am extracting as much as I can from you upfront so that I can exploit you later (i.e., "take the money and run"). To emphasize the positive signal but mitigate the negative signal, franchisors reduce their upfront fee (sometimes to nothing, even for well-known franchises[35]) and seek to make money later with higher royalty rates. This move also creates a new hostage, in that they share more risk with their franchisees.

The threat at this point is whether they are sharing too much. By forgoing upfront money in favor of potential royalty payments, franchisors take on a risk that franchisees accept their assistance to set up the business, then try to renegotiate the contract to their advantage. Such **opportunistic holdup** by the franchisee can take various forms, such as negotiating for the deferment or reduction of royalties, extra assistance, rent relief, and so forth. Franchisors might agree to renegotiate to avoid losing the sunk costs they already have invested to set the franchisee up in business. Thus, fear of opportunistic holdup seemingly should drive the franchisor to ask for more upfront money, in lieu of royalties.

In practice, though, ultimately we find little relation between the fixed fee and the royalty.[36] In terms of the sheer amount of the fixed fee, franchisors tend to concede and take less upfront money than they would prefer; the franchisees appear to make concessions on other aspects of the contract, which we discuss subsequently. In addition, the franchisee agrees to make heavy initial investments—including sunk costs in things such as franchise-specific decor and equipment or merchandise that is difficult to return or resell—that can run much higher than the franchisor's fixed fee. By incurring this investment, the franchisee offers a valuable hostage to assure the franchisor that it will exert its best efforts to stay in business, rather than mistreating the franchisor by renegotiating the contract at every opportunity.

Furthermore, franchisors might want to reduce their upfront fixed fees to enlarge the pool of applicants. As we discussed previously, franchising offers a viable method to identify the sort of entrepreneurial profile (i.e., personality, background, management ability, and local knowledge) that makes for an ideal franchisee. If this list included the criterion of substantial personal wealth too, the pool of qualified candidates would shrink dramatically.

But franchisors do not just lower their demands for upfront fees. Real-world evidence indicates they also ask for a lower royalty rate than they might. McDonald's reportedly leaves several hundred thousand dollars on the table (that is, in the franchisee's bank account) each time it grants a franchise.[37] So we must ask: Why?!

The primary answer is to enhance the value of the business to each franchisee. By being generous, McDonald's ensures that the franchisee has a lot to lose—not least its sense of loyalty to the company that has treated it so well. In turn, the franchisee is more motivated to live up to its promises, which constitutes the foundation for effective franchising.

In this vein, consider **tied sales**. Some contracts include a clause obliging franchisees to buy their inputs (products, supplies) from a specific supplier; in the United Kingdom, Avis and Budget require franchisees to purchase the cars they rent from the national franchisor. Such tie-ins appear anticompetitive, in that if franchisees could buy the same car elsewhere for less, they seemingly should be allowed to do so. Regulators make similar arguments to question whether the tie-ins are actually just a disguised method to collect more ongoing fees. Furthermore, overcharging franchisees for supplies could prompt retaliation, if franchisees look to compensate for the informal fees by cheating in some other way. A restaurant forced to buy overpriced ingredients from the franchisor might cut portion sizes or reuse food, for example.

For franchisors, though, the threats may be worthwhile, because tied sales provide a means to ensure quality. Avis and Budget know the cars being rented are fully equipped (e.g., air conditioning, satellite radio), as promised to end-users. When input quality is difficult to measure continuously, franchisors become more likely to use tied sales clauses. But they also seek to price them fairly, to avoid resentment and allegations of profiteering. Moreover, if any product can serve as input, franchisors rarely write tied sales clauses. Alternatively, if a range of products will do, franchisors might oblige franchisees to buy from approved sources, even if not from the franchisor.

Leasing

Regarding rent collection on a franchisee's premises, some franchisors, such as McDonald's, take pains to ensure that they are the landlord, or at least hold the right to lease the property to the franchisee. That is, they might negotiate the lease with the property owner, then sublet to the franchisee. These leases generally protect the franchisor's rights, at the expense of the franchisee. However, owning land is a capital-intensive practice, and the leasing negotiations absorb much management attention while also creating frequent disputes.

The investments may be worth it for the franchisor, though, because retailing depends on **location**, and the best locations are difficult to secure. Owners of prime commercial locations might prefer to deal with franchisors, rather than individual franchisees. The franchisor also may negotiate better than can a smaller franchisee.

A clearer explanation for why franchisors might insist on holding the leases for *all* sites (even the lesser ones) instead focuses on the contract with the franchisee, in that lease control makes the franchisor's **termination threats** credible.[38] A noncompliant franchisee that is also a tenant is easy to eject from the system: the franchisor simply terminates the lease, simultaneous with terminating the franchisee. A franchisee tenant agrees to the lease, which favors the landlord, to offer another hostage to the franchisor. This hostage is particularly valuable if the franchisee makes improvements to the property, because such improvements often can be appropriated by the landlord.

Finally, being the landlord provides franchisors with a means to assist franchisees, by reducing their capital requirements. That is, franchisors might defer rents on franchises that are in trouble. But even as they exhibit this flexibility, franchisors that are landlords retain their potent ability to enforce the contract, in that they can evict the franchisee while retaining the site for operations by a new franchisee.

Termination

Losing a franchisee is difficult and costly. The franchisor needs to replace it (and in the absence of leasing clauses, it might need to replace the location too), take the time to train the new franchisee, and suffer opportunity costs related to lost business. The franchisee thus faces the temptation of holding up the franchisor by threatening to quit while negotiating a better deal. To a certain point, the franchisor likely concedes in these negotiations, to avoid having to replace the franchisee.

At the same time, franchisors make it expensive and difficult for franchisees to leave. As we noted, they offer lucrative business deals (low royalties, even on a good business) and demand early, franchise-specific investments (e.g., decor). In addition, franchisors have several contract devices at their disposal to make it even more difficult to quit. In the United Kingdom, many contracts require franchisees to find their replacements. Not only must the franchisee find a candidate quickly, but that candidate must be acceptable to the franchisor. If it fails to find a replacement, the franchisor imposes a **transfer fee**, to cover the costs of finding the replacement on its own.

Franchisors also may insert **right of first refusal** clauses, such that they have the right to contract with the franchisee if they can match any offer the franchisee receives, perhaps from a competitor. Although these options protect the franchisor against a franchisee that threatens to sell to an unsuitable buyer, they also create an opportunity for the franchisor to abuse the franchisee, by denying it the right to liquidate its business at a fair value. Many states in the United States regulate termination clauses to prevent such abuse. Regardless of the available regulations, though, a franchise investment often accounts for a substantial portion of a franchisee's financial portfolio, and there are minimal restrictions on a franchisor's ability to sell the franchise.[39] Thus, power ultimately resides with franchisors.

Contract Consistency

Even with the various options available, franchise contracts exhibit surprisingly little variance. No two franchisees face the same situation, yet franchisors generally apply a single contract (with perhaps minor variations) and a single price to all franchisees, offered on a take-it-or-leave-it basis.

Contracts also do not vary much over time. Adjustments may occur occasionally, particularly in the price, such that royalties and fixed fees tend to rise as the franchisor becomes better established (McDonald's remains the exception that proves the rule). But in truth, contracts are surprisingly stable.[40] They often are written for fairly long periods, such as 15 years. Furthermore, tailoring contracts too specifically can heighten legal fees, especially in jurisdictions with high disclosure requirements. Finally, franchisors want to be perceived as fair, such that they treat franchisees equitably. By offering the same contract across the board, the franchisor avoids any appearance of discrimination—a threat that seems to loom larger than the possible loss of flexibility or a reputation for arbitrariness.

Contract Enforcement

Beyond contracts, safeguarding a franchise relationship often relies on the influence of reputation. Franchisors that take a long-term view of their businesses worry, rightly, about creating an image of themselves as harsh, oppressive, greedy bullies. Such an image threatens them with the loss of current franchisees, poor cooperation, and an inability to attract new franchisees. More broadly, no franchisor wants to be classed as some fly-by-night operation, out to make money quickly through fees and lucrative tie-in sales and then abandon the franchisees. Thus, franchisors that are not swindlers and that seek to build their business also make a strong effort to treat their franchisees correctly. Their reputation is worth far more than any short-term gains they might extract by invoking harsh contract terms to "win" disputes with franchisees.

Theoretical Rationales for Enforcing Contracts/Punishing Transgressions	**TABLE 8.2**
Sourcing from a supplier other than those approved by the franchisor.	When Do Franchisors Enforce the Franchise Contract?
Failing to maintain the look and ambiance of the premises.	
Violating the franchisor's standards and procedures.	
Failing to pay advertising fees.	
Failing to pay the franchisor's royalty!	

Costly Enforcement Situations, Making Franchisors More Likely to Overlook Violations

Dense, tightly knit network of franchisees, such that the franchisor fears a solidarity reaction because other franchisees would side with the violator.

The violator is a central player in the franchisee's network.

Performance ambiguity prevents the franchisor from identifying the situation clearly or monitoring well, so it cannot be sure it has a strong case against the violator.

Strong relational governance allows the system to operate on the basis of norms of solidarity, flexibility, and information exchange.

Benefits of Enforcement Outweigh the Costs, with Punitive Actions More Likely

The violation is critical one, such as missing a large royalty payment or operating a very shabby facility in a highly visible location.

The franchisee is a central player in the network. Rather than avoiding enforcement to reduce system backlash, the franchisor senses the need to send a signal that rules are rules. Tolerating a major violation by a central player instead would signal to the other franchisees that the contract is just a piece of paper, with no real weight.

The violator is a master franchisee with multiple units, such that the violation will propagate across its units and become a large-scale problem.

The franchisor has invested in the franchise *system* (not the particular franchisee) and thus needs to protect its investment, even if strong relational governance is in place. The franchisor will risk upsetting a given relationship to protect its system investments.

The franchisor is large.

High mutual dependence in the franchisee–franchisor relationship suggests it can withstand the conflict that enforcement will create.

The franchisor is much more powerful than the franchisee and can coerce the franchisee to tolerate enforcement.

Source: Antia, Kersi D. and Gary L. Frazier (2001), "The severity of contract enforcement in interfirm channel relationships," *Journal of Marketing*, 65 (4), 67–81.

In turn, franchisors do not always enforce the contracts they have written so carefully. Instead, they weigh the costs and benefits of punishing each act of noncompliance and tolerate those that they can, as Table 8.2 implies. Essentially, franchisors need to be mindful of the joint effects of the enforcement and compliance clauses in a franchising contract, as well as the actual effort they would need to expend to engage in monitoring and enforcement.[41] Franchisees use the clauses in their franchising contracts as contextual cues to predict monitoring efforts. Furthermore, even seemingly compliant franchisees might just be going through the motions, because they have signed a contract over which they had little influence. In this case, they might not truly understand the need to comply with the contract. If the relationship between franchisees and the franchisor is good, they instead should be more likely to comply wholeheartedly, rather than just doing the minimum.[42]

Self-Enforcing Agreements

Because each side still has incentives to cheat, though, a contract seeks to create a **self-enforcing agreement**. In such an arrangement, neither side wants to engage in a violation, regardless of the levels of monitoring or threats, because the contract rearranges their incentives to ensure that cheating is not in their *own* best interest. Yet every clause that stops one side from cheating creates a new way for the *other* side to cheat. That is, *every effort to balance power creates a new possibility for imbalance.*

This assertion is true of most business arrangements. But if franchisors and franchisees rely solely on elaborate contracts to address this problem, they take a great risk. Both parties are agreeing to tie their fates together for years. The franchisor is providing access to its secrets and trademarks; the franchisee is sacrificing its autonomy. Their arrangement is elaborate and forward looking, and the resulting contracts become highly complex very quickly, as we show in Table 8.3, listing many aspects that need to be covered in some way in any franchise contract. But no contract can fully specify all contingencies and craft proper solutions for all problems in the future.

Company Store Strategies

Franchisee- and company-owned outlets are usually considered substitutes, such that one or the other seems more apt to fit the situation. Yet in practice, many franchisors also run company-owned stores.[43] Among U.S. firms that franchise,

TABLE 8.3 The Franchise Contract	International Franchise Guide (from the *International Herald Tribune*) suggests that any franchise contract should address the following topics:	
	Definition of terms	Organizational structure
	Term of initial agreement	Term of renewal
	Causes for termination or non-renewal	Territorial exclusivity
	Intellectual property protection	Assignment of responsibilities
	Ability to sub-franchise	Mutual agreement of pro forma cash flows
	Development schedule and associated penalties	Fees: front end, ongoing
	Currency and remittance restrictions	Remedies in case of disagreement

Source: Moulton, Susan L. (ed.) (1996), *International Franchise Guide*, Oakland, CA: Source Books Publications.

an average of 30 percent of their outlets are company owned.[44] As more franchise organizations have gone public in recent years, they have discovered the benefits of increasing their tangible assets, namely by increasing the number of company-owned outlets.[45] However, doing so might leave the firm with fewer resources available to invest in brand-building. In this way, an increased proportion of company-owned outlets typically is associated with lower stock returns for publicly traded franchises.[46] If that is the case, then why do franchises seek to own their own stores? We address several reasons next.

Market Differences

Markets differ. Company outlets and franchisee outlets might serve different types of markets. For example, some markets require monitoring by the franchisor, because repeat business for any one franchisee is minimal.[47] A fast food restaurant franchise on a superhighway draws heavily on the market of consumers passing through only once. This franchisee likely is tempted to cheat (e.g., cut costs by serving stale food), because it would not suffer the consequences of its poor quality. Travelers are drawn in by the franchisor's brand name, and their poor experience lessens brand equity. Yet they are unlikely to return to this exact location anyway, so the franchisee does not suffer the usual consequences (i.e., lost future sales). To protect its brand equity, the franchisor likely prefers to own this outlet (and other franchisees should welcome this decision).

Temporary Franchises and Company Outlets

Some stores are **temporary**. Circumstances, at some point in time, may create a need for one form of ownership or the other. Franchisors usually start with one and then a few outlets of their own, which they use to formulate the business format and develop the brand name. If they skip this step and start franchising early, they cannot attract many franchisees, because they have little to offer (e.g., brand equity, proven format). So franchisors start with company stores. Once they have achieved a certain level, they can add franchisees, usually at a high rate.

But once a business is underway, why add further company stores? Sometimes it is accidental: a franchisee has a problem, and the franchisor buys out the location, for system morale (or, in the United States, to avoid lawsuits) or because a profitable franchisee must exit quickly (e.g., for health reasons). In these cases, company ownership is temporary, and the franchisor seeks to sell that outlet to a new franchisee as soon as possible.

We find a variation on this idea in Italy, where opening a retail store in a particular sector (e.g., food) requires a sector-specific license from local authorities. These licenses are limited in supply and thus valuable, representing a big obstacle for Italian franchisors. If they wish to expand quickly, they may be obliged to accept an undesirable franchisee, simply because it holds one of the licenses to sell that product in the area.

They anticipate conflict with this license holder, so franchisors decline to franchise and use their corporate influence to obtain their own license. In turn, they are required to run a company outlet for some time. Thus a predominant pattern in Italian franchising reveals *system growth, by divesting of corporate assets*. The franchisor operates the outlet, learns from its experience, then divests itself of the outlet by selling to a suitable franchisee. This divestment costs the franchisor little, because the newly franchised store cooperates with management, often with better operating results.

Ultimately, though, the idea of temporary franchisees or company stores cannot explain why franchisors, as they grow, continue to add new company outlets, at a lower rate than they add franchisees.[48] Systems that grow the fastest do so by favoring franchisees over company units. (And these systems have lower failure rates.[49]) So there must be reasons to maintain both types permanently, in which is known as a plural form.

Plural Forms and Synergies

Simultaneously and deliberately maintaining *both* company and franchised outlets to perform the same functions constitutes a **plural form** strategy.[50] The underlying principle holds that franchisors manage organizational duality (vertically integrated and outsourced) by drawing on the strengths of each system to offset the other's weaknesses. In particular, a plural form enables franchisors to build a control system that creates functional rivalry between the two forms. The rivalry is effective because franchisors monitor their own units very closely, using:

1. Elaborate management information systems that generate detailed, daily reports about every aspect of their outlets' operations.

2. Frequent, elaborate, unannounced field audits, covering hundreds of items and requiring hours to complete.

3. Mystery shoppers, or paid professional auditors who pose as customers.

Such heavy, invasive control mechanisms are tolerated by company managers because they have little choice: they are paid a salary to observe the franchisor's rules. Top management tells them what to do, and they do it. They are not separately accountable for earning profits.

Franchisees instead reject such invasive, frequent, thorough monitoring efforts. Rather than telling franchisees what to do, franchisors must attempt to persuade them. The titles that appear in each form thus are telling: whereas company store managers report to district **managers**, franchisees work with (do not report to) franchise **consultants**. However, the information and experience gained from heavy control mechanisms in company stores help franchisors understand the day-to-day operations of the business it purports to master.

The two forms in plural systems also serve as **benchmarks** for the other. By comparing the performance of company and franchisee outlets, the franchisor can encourage each to do better. The company and franchisee outlets perform exactly the same roles—which, as we have noted, seems senseless—so direct comparisons are possible. In turn, **competition** within the system increases dramatically.

The connection between the two forms is not solely contested, though. In the plural form, each side engages in teaching the other, which can create a **mutual strategy**. That is, the company stores and franchisees both try out ideas, then seek to persuade their counterparts to adopt the ones that work. In this process, strategy emerges from rigorous debate. Plural forms create more options, which get reviewed more candidly and thoroughly than they would in unitary forms. Thus the ideas are well refined, and each side commits more strongly to the new initiatives that arise.

Another advantage of the plural form is that the franchisor can create **career paths** for personnel to move back and forth between the company side and the franchisee side. Not only does this freedom accommodate personnel needs, but it also helps socialize the members of both sides of the franchise "family." One member might prefer a career path through the company side, dealing with company outlets as a manager, then supervisor, then as a corporate executive. Another might want to focus only on the franchise side, by starting a unit, adding new ones, and growing into a mini-hierarchy. Yet another member of the franchise family might prefer to span both sides, in which case the following three career paths are noteworthy:

1. Company employees become franchisees. This path is common. Company employees like it because they can develop into entrepreneurs, often with less capital than an outsider would need. Franchisors like it because their franchisee community is seeded with people they know and trust.

2. Company unit managers become franchisee consultants. This shift entails moving from running a company store (being on salary, following the rules) to working with franchisees to persuade them. The jobs are very different (similar to a promotion from a factory supervisor to a diplomatic post), so the transition can be difficult, but the ex-company manager likely enjoys credibility with franchisees because of his or her previous hands-on experience.

3. Company managers become franchisee managers. In this move, the member shifts from one organization to another, from the franchisor's hierarchy to managing in a multi-unit franchise. It offers an important way in which mini-hierarchies mimic the franchisor's organization.

All three spanning career paths solidly **unite** the franchisor and franchisee too. They allow personnel exchanges, regularly and on a large scale.

Beyond trading ideas and human capital, company stores provide a unique resource: They are good **laboratories**, in which a company can test new ideas while absorbing the risk of failure. Dunkin' Donuts regularly experiments with new products and processes in its own stores, using them as a sort of test market. In this case, the company can confirm that the tests are conducted properly and that the feedback it receives is candid. Once a new product or process has been perfected, Dunkin' Donuts can point to the success in its company-owned stores to encourage franchisees to adopt the change themselves.

Of course, company store managers are less likely to generate the innovative ideas for testing, because they are hired to follow rules. Ideas instead tend to come from the franchisor's central database or the active involvement of motivated entrepreneurs, especially those coping with local circumstances, including competition, labor forces, and customers. The increasing popularity of Indian food in London has led McDonald's to add curry and spice to its British menus.[51] Ideas like this can be tested in company stores, but they likely originate from local franchisees, adapting to local competition and tastes.

In short, plural forms **complement** each other in ways that make the chain stronger, and both franchisors and franchisees benefit—as long as active management is in place. Maintaining company and franchisee units simultaneously is beneficial if all the parties work to make it so and appreciate the benefits of the franchise system's "dual personality."

Exploiting Franchisees with Company Outlets

Just like any split personality, though, there can be a malevolent side, and this explanation for plural forms has attracted substantial attention from regulators and scholars.[52] Franchisors might prefer to run company outlets, to control the operation closely and appropriate all the profits generated by the marketing channel (assuming that the company system would be equally profitable, which is a heroic assumption, as we hope we have shown already). Given this premise, a trademark owner might franchise merely to build the business. Once established, this franchisor would use its profits to buy back its franchises. If they refuse to sell, the franchisor might attempt to appropriate their property (e.g., by fabricating a reason to invoke a termination clause, ending the lease).

In this sinister scenario, franchisors increase the fraction of company-owned units, especially in the most lucrative locations (e.g., urban commercial districts). That is, franchisors use franchisees to build the system, then expropriate them, according to this **redirection of ownership** hypothesis. Although existing evidence suggests this development is rare, anecdotal reports and court cases suggest that it does happen.

For example, Zannier, a retailer that covers the children's clothing market in France, uses 13 different brand names and a variety of routes to market (e.g., hypermarkets, single-brand boutiques, multi-brand boutiques, company owned and franchisee owned). Zannier seeks to lock up the market by covering every viable

FIGURE 8.3
Franchises with High and Low Success Rates

Success Rate	Name	Description	Total Units	5-Year Continuity	5-Year Growth	Avg. Initial Investment
Investment Level: $500,000+						
Highest	Culver's ButterBurgers & Frozen Custard	ButterBurgers, frozen custard, and salad	558	100%	5%	$2,517,651
2nd Highest	Firehouse Subs	Firefighter founded; serves hot sub sandwiches	944	95%	18%	$769,830
Lowest	DirectBuy	Members pay entry fee to be able to buy direct from manufacturer	38	41%	−12%	$500,500
2nd Lowest	Century 21	Real estate broker	2,204	63%	−7%	$552,869
Investment Level: $500,000–$150,000						
Highest	Jimmy John's	Sandwiches	2,407	99%	17%	$433,500
2nd Highest	Marco's Pizza	Pizza	674	94%	24%	$384,092
Lowest	Cookies by Design	Cookie gift baskets	69	52%	−12%	$162,250
2nd Lowest	Dippin' Dots	Ice cream-based frozen dessert	120	53%	−10%	$244,577
Investment Level: Below $150,000						
Highest	Right at Home	In-home care for seniors and disabled	433	90%	13%	$104,900
2nd Highest	Weed Man	Lawn-care services	177	94%	9%	$76,983
Lowest	Help-U-Sell	Fee-for-sale real estate brokerage	91	22%	−25%	$90,250
2nd Lowest	Curves	Strength-training and weight-loss services for women	1,262	33%	−20%	$61,201

Source:www.forbes.com/forbes/welcome/?toURL=https://www.forbes.com/sites/amyfeldman/2016/06/22/ranking-americas-best-and-worst-franchises-which-are-the-best-investments/&refURL=&referrer=#7feef0075d1b.

position. To do so, it used franchisees to grow quickly. The franchisees later charged that once the franchisor had grown large and successful, it used pricing tactics and restrictive contract terms to squeeze out more than 200 franchisees, in favor of other channels, including its company-owned stores.[53] Zannier simply paid the damages to settle these legal claims.

ADAPTING TO CHALLENGES IN FRANCHISING

Franchisors suffer very high failure rates. Various estimates suggest that three-quarters of the franchisors launched in the United States survive less than a decade. In 2012 the Small Business Administration reported that the default rate for the 25 worst performing franchise brands ranged from 37 to 71 percent.[54] For every high-profile franchisor such as McDonald's and its wealthy franchisees, there are multiple business formats and brand names that have failed, partially or completely, stripping franchisees of their wealth in the process. Many brands grow substantially but then collapse, such as when Krispy Kreme went from a regional treat to a short-lived national phenomenon, before shrinking back again due to the failure of many of its franchisees. Some franchisors fail to spread despite their best efforts; others actually set out to defraud their franchisees, just as they would any other investor. The Malaysian and Thai governments even have set up departments to help citizens become franchisees, out of concern that their people might be cheated by unscrupulous, would-be franchisors.[55] In Figure 8.3, we present some of the franchises with low and higher rates of failure.

Survival Trends

Most evidence indicates that *success forecasts success*.[56] The older the system and the more units it has, the greater its odds of continuing to exist. For a prospective franchisee, established franchisors may be more expensive, but they also lower the risk of system failure. Four years offers an attractive threshold: franchise systems that are at least four years of age offer a sharply lower probability of failing than do younger systems.[57]

Survival is also more likely if the franchisor can attract a **favorable rating** from a third party. For example, the U.S. magazine *Entrepreneur* surveys franchisors and verifies much of the information it collects, before adding in subjective judgments to compile proprietary ratings of hundreds of franchisors. This rating is a good predictor of franchisor survival, though it actually may reflect a sort of bias, in that the ranking creates a self-fulfilling prophecy. The third-party certification of predicted success helps the franchisor gain an image as a **legitimate player** in its operating environment. With this reputation, it can more easily acquire the resources it needs to survive.

Yet many entrepreneurs continue to assign a relatively low priority to certification and incomprehensibly refuse to cooperate with certifying bodies. The odds of franchisor bankruptcy increase significantly if a lot of franchisees in the system are going under, so it is critical for every franchisor to pay attention to its franchisees' economic health.[58] In addition, many private equity firms are acquiring franchises, including Arby's, Buffalo Wild Wings, and Planet Fitness. The private equity firms appreciate the opportunity to buy into a business model that works, with transparent financial reporting and strong growth possibilities.[59]

Maintaining a Cooperative Atmosphere

To encourage success and survival, the franchisor also must ensure that franchisees perceive benefits of opening a new outlet, and then that they believe they continue to receive value in exchange for the royalties they pay. Such beliefs generally require a sense of cooperation, but many franchise systems instead impose a conflict between the desire to be one's own boss, with the associated risks, and function as nearly a subsidiary of a central organization. One franchisee summarizes the typical ambivalence associated with this attitude:[60]

> [The franchise name] does not bring in much business, and whatever business it does bring in, I suppose it helps people feel more secure. But right now, I feel it's my business—and that's my name on the front because the numbers would be the same.

But franchisees are more likely to cooperate when they identify a solid relationship between themselves and their franchisor. Several conditions encourage business partners to develop feelings of **commitment** and perceive higher levels of **trust** and **fairness**,[61] such as when each partner believes that:

1. Its partner encourages it to innovate.

2. A team spirit exists.

3. Good performance is recognized.

4. The partner is fair.

5. Communication is open.

6. The partner is competent and acts reliably.

Although franchising is inherently asymmetric, with franchisees highly dependent on the franchisor, franchisees remain entrepreneurs and feel the entrepreneurial need to be the boss.[62] Accordingly, franchise consultants need to find ways to exert influence without appearing to threaten any franchisee's autonomy—a difficult balancing act, requiring diplomacy and persuasive skills. Furthermore, franchisors must seek to resolve conflicts by searching for integrative, win–win solutions, featuring a mutually acceptable solution with franchisees. Franchisors might motivate partners and increase the size of their system by lowering royalty rates over time, promising low upfront franchise fees that only increase over time, owning a small and decreasing proportion of stores, keeping franchisees' initial investment low, and helping finance the franchisees.[63]

Managing Inherent Goal Conflict

Every franchise system features structural conflict, due to the clash of goals between franchisee and franchisor that arises from the differences in each side's contributions to the business and their resulting outcomes. For franchisors, higher sales are always better, because they lead to higher variable fees and more income. With greater income, they can engage in more promotion and build brand equity, which in turn allows them to increase the (fixed and variable) fees they charge and enlarges the pool of prospective store managers and franchisees. For a franchisee in a specific trading area, more sales means more profit too—up to a point.[64]

In short, franchisors seek to maximize sales; franchisees seek to maximize profits. This **goal incongruity** becomes more vivid as chains expand. In their effort to maximize system sales, franchisors saturate the market area by authorizing many new outlets, to the extent that new stores might encroach on existing outlets and **cannibalize** other franchisees. Even McDonald's has miscalculated the best growth rates; in Brazil, it was at one time the largest (indirect) private employer, because it had added hundreds of franchisees in what McDonald's viewed as a model operation. But franchisees soon began complaining, and even sued, that McDonald's had undermined them by opening too many stores and making it impossible for them to earn profits.[65] Generally speaking, when franchises of the same brand operate in close proximity, they face inter-brand competition. Although new franchisees enjoy a sales boost from locating near mature outlets, in that they can learn from their colleagues' experience, there is no benefit for mature outlets to open near other mature outlets; they have little left to learn but would confront a very crowded marketplace.[66]

Overcrowding and too much expansion also harm the franchisor's reputation with franchisees, though the financial gains from authorizing new outlets may tempt it to encroach anyway. Even company-owned stores often build too many stores too close to each other, which can undermine long-term profits (e.g., Starbucks). Systematic evidence suggests that few systems can resist this temptation: as the system grows, they locate new outlets close enough to existing outlets to diminish single-store revenues—but the new outlet still adds enough revenue to raise total system royalties. In contrast, vertically integrated firms carefully space out their company-owned outlets to avoid cannibalizing an existing revenue stream, because their focus remains on profits, not just sales.[67]

For franchisors that want to grow, even to the point of encroaching on their existing franchisees, the question becomes, how can we cover a market densely without alienating our franchisees? One solution is to offer new sites to existing franchisees, or to give them right of first refusal on a new location. If economies of scale arise from operating multiple sites, the franchisee may be in a position to gain from them. This idea leads to the paradox of multi-unit franchisees.

Multi-Unit Franchising

Does a franchisor prefer a manager (company owned) or an individual entrepreneur (franchisee) in each unit? Curiously, the answer may be, "Neither."[68] Rather than dealing with a multitude of different, individual responsible parties for each location, some franchisors interact with a single company that runs multiple locations, through **multi-unit franchising**. Although we note some variations on the idea, it is possible to establish a primary principle: the manager of a unit is not the owner but is employed by the owner, which owns more than one unit and must hire employees to run the various locations. This arrangement is common and growing.

On the face of it, the system is difficult to explain, though. If the purpose of franchising is to replace lackluster employee managers with motivated owner-managers, then multi-unit franchising should fail, because it just adds a layer of franchisee management between the franchisor and the person running the outlet. The master franchisee monitors the monitor (i.e., store manager), instead of just controlling the situation itself. Why? The answer is not totally clear, to be honest. Some evidence indicates that franchisors resort to multi-unit franchising to grow faster and deal with unfamiliar markets. For example, U.S. franchisors heavily favor multi-unit operators when they need to open operations in Africa and the Middle East.[69] However, doing so may simply postpone problems, such that franchisors that use multi-unit franchising appear to fail more frequently than those that insist that franchisees own and manage their stores. This demand slows growth, but it may make the system healthier.

McDonald's prefers (but does not require) single-unit franchising. Perhaps as a result, it has virtually no presence in Africa. In contrast, Burger King embraced multi-unit franchising early in its history and used it to grow fast. Eventually, the chain had to confront fundamental flaws in its market strategy and operations, which had been masked by its fast growth. The franchisor also became embroiled in battles with powerful multi-unit franchisees, creating a spiral of conflict that hardened into embittered, lasting mediocre relations. Ultimately, the chain suffered severely and continued to remain second fiddle to McDonald's.

Before dismissing multi-unit franchising, however, we should examine its positive side. A multi-unit franchisee can create an organizational structure that mimics the franchisor's structure and imitates its practices. These "mini-hierarchies" simplify matters enormously for the franchisor, enabling it to deal with one organization; that is, the multi-unit franchisee. Because the multi-unit operators already replicate the franchisor's management practices and policies, they reduce the enormous job of managing hundreds of relationships into a more tractable management problem. For example, KFC has more than 3,500 U.S. restaurants, more than half of which are owned by just 17 franchisees. If KFC can convince only these largest franchisees of the merits of an idea, it influences almost more than half of the restaurants in the country!

Of course, if mini-hierarchies are to help the franchisor, there needs to be substantial cooperation, such that the mini-hierarchies replicate the franchisor's system. Many large restaurant chains appear to have mastered this process, demonstrating that if prospective franchisees are carefully screened, given a trial period, and observed, multi-unit franchising can be a viable and valuable strategy. If a franchisee fails to meet the franchisor's requirements, it simply is not allowed to open more units.

Another benefit of multi-unit franchising stems from its ability to preserve knowledge. Again using fast food restaurants as an example, we note that small details (e.g., the fastest way to fold a pizza box) ultimately make a big difference in competitive businesses. Such know-how demands experience and gets transmitted by example, but in this industry, personnel turnover is very high. Thus, personnel enter the learning curve, learn, then leave, taking their knowledge with them. A new restaurant franchise starts without any such knowledge, and as soon as it gains it, the personnel who possess it are likely to leave. Multi-unit franchisees provide a means to preserve and spread such knowledge across their own stores, through holding meetings, making phone calls, and using other means of communication. The resulting personal ties across stores also help spread knowledge. That is, multi-unit franchises spread learning curves by actively lobbying to disseminate know-how across their own locations.[70]

They are particularly likely to spread tacit, idiosyncratic knowledge when it refers consistently to a local area. Even in standardized businesses, such as pizza restaurants, local experience matters and can mitigate franchise failure rates. Distant experience, whether gained by the franchisor or the multi-unit franchisee, is less helpful than local experience.[71] Therefore, when franchisors use multi-unit franchising, they often award new sites to the franchisee that owns the next closest unit to exploit the **power of contiguity** by ensuring units owned by one person are adjacent, without intermingling units owned by different people. This strategy is particularly effective if the new site to be developed is not only contiguous but also offers a demographic profile similar to that served by the rest of the multi-unit owner's stores. These franchisors allow franchisees to build up large networks of stores that appear on a map as a single, unbroken mass, uninterrupted by other franchisees or company-owned stores.[72] Owning clusters of stores also makes it easier for franchisees to monitor their monitors (store managers) and amortize human capital connected to an area. Finally, because the local customer base is likely being served by the same owner in various stores, free riding declines.

For franchisees, the key appeals of multi-unit franchising include the ability to leverage higher-performing units and absorb the costs of running underperforming units. In addition, saturation in the franchise outlets puts pressure on margins. To earn meaningful returns (i.e., make enough money), many franchisees believe they must operate multiple units; multi-unit franchisees also have an easier time raising the required capital to fund their expansion and growth,[73] as exemplified by the Dhanani Group in Sidebar 8.3.

SIDEBAR 8.3
Dhanani Group: Masters of Multi-Unit Franchising

Founded by U.S. immigrants from Pakistan, the Dhanani Group is the largest Popeye's franchisee and also a substantial Burger King franchisee, with annual revenues estimated to be in the $2 billion range.[74] In addition to its 502 Burger King restaurants, 170 Popeye's outlets, and 130 convenience stores, it has ventured into purchases of La Madeleine French Bakery & Cafe franchises.[75] This wholly family-owned and -operated enterprise is based in Houston, where it started operating convenience stores in the mid-1970s. It expanded nationally and into fast food restaurant franchises in the 1990s, noting the then-emerging trend of outlets featuring co-branded restaurants and convenience stores. Some of its growth has come from acquiring other, struggling restaurants from fellow franchisees,[76] which it remodels and updates, then staffs with new management. Looking to expand even further, such as into casual dining franchise sectors, it recently acquired the historic Cyclone Anaya restaurant in Houston.

FRANCHISING AND OMNI-CHANNELS

The franchise sector has avidly embraced digitization and e-commerce, moving quickly into the omni-channel era—despite some rough patches in the initial stages of this transition. Web-enabled transactions created two main concerns for franchisors and franchisees: first, they worried about channel conflict, if franchisees had to compete with e-commerce websites hosted by the franchisor, which might cannibalize their sales. The franchisors seemingly could encroach, virtually, on their territory, subverting the territorial exclusivity that franchise contracts typically grant franchisees. The e-commerce site seemingly would be a virtual store right in the franchisee's backyard.[77]

EXAMPLE: ALLSTATE INSURANCE (USA)

As the largest publicly held property and casualty insurance company in the United States,[78] Allstate primarily has distributed its products through franchised agents, whose role is to build the relationship between the company and consumers. Its slogan, "You're in good hands with Allstate," promises that an agent will be on the scene, should any calamity strike an insured customer. In recent years, though, it has faced competitive threats from companies that have developed a novel, direct model, such as Progressive Insurance, to deal directly with customers via Web or telephone. Customers appreciate this model, because it enables them to compare offerings easily, obtain price quotes, receive customer service or perform self-service (e.g., printing out proof of auto insurance), and file and monitor claims.[79] In response, many companies establish various channels to satisfy customers' needs for information and cater to their preferences. Even if insurance companies retain some salespeople, multi-channel insurers acquire a substantial portion of their customers through digital channels. Therefore, Allstate needed to devise an agent compensation model that could motivate agents to work with Allstate, even as it expanded its e-commerce strategy. It also ultimately acquired a pure online player, esurance, to cater to consumers who prefer to transact only online with their insurance company.

Second, as e-commerce spread, franchisees began to worry that it was not just the franchisor but also other franchisees that were encroaching on its territory (real or virtual). That is, e-commerce enables consumers to access services from franchisees who may be located further away. A consumer shopping for automobiles thus might test drive a particular model at a nearby dealership but then contact other dealerships online to find the best price or preferred configuration, even if those dealerships are located hundreds of miles away. Because the online channel has reduced the impact of geography, sales territory demarcation becomes harder to implement in practice. Furthermore, some franchise arrangements allow the franchisors to sell their products through third-party websites, such as Amazon and eBay, further demolishing territorial boundaries.

Yet omni-channel franchising represents opportunities for franchisors and franchisees alike. It creates an additional forum to obtain customer feedback (complaints, likes, referrals, online reviews) or promote offerings. Because of the spread of omni-channel ordering, franchisees have needed to update their operations, to be able to accept payment methods other than cash and credit cards, such as tap-and-go or preloaded QR code payments.[80] When they also integrate promotional tools such as couponing and sweepstakes into the available apps, it can increase customer participation. In many sectors, the franchisors invest substantial resources to develop the e-commerce or omni-channel infrastructure. For example, fast food omni-channel franchisors develop or purchase systems to support online ordering, allow consumers to see the progress of their orders, or facilitate deliveries.

Although such benefits likely appeal to customers, benefitting both sides of the franchise agreement, to recoup its investments, the franchisor may demand higher service charges from the franchisee, threatening increased coordination costs. Finally, in some franchise sectors (e.g., tutoring, test prep services), the possibilities for online delivery are vast. Accordingly, investments in omni-channel systems have generated positive financial returns, and they offer a significant source for customer acquisition and brand-building.[81]

Franchisees also might open their own e-commerce websites, though franchisors must be sure that their websites present a professional and uniform brand image and secure all private or personal consumer information. Some franchisors even provide links to franchisees' webpages. For example, automobile dealerships have been quick to embrace e-commerce opportunities, but considering the different incentives online versus offline salespeople, this experience seems more multi- than omni-channel in nature.

EXAMPLE: CAR BUYING ONLINE (USA)

Traditionally, people shopping for a new car had to visit a dealership, have a salesperson show them around, and test drive a car from among the available options in stock, before entering into aggressive pricing and financing negotiations. These negotiations started from the Manufacturers' Suggested Retail Price, displayed on each automobile's window. But the Internet provides an alternative channel, such that consumers click to third-party sites like Edmunds.com to research vehicle features and pricing, use comparison tools to get a better sense of the vehicle, and read vehicle reviews. Edmunds even can help the consumer negotiate a price for the vehicle from dealerships that partner with it. Even without this third party, consumers can visit dealer websites or contact the dealer's Internet sales team, to find out what is in stock, schedule test drives, or negotiate the terms of the deal. Yet because salespeople at dealerships often are rewarded for volume sales, online sales reps might offer a low price, immediately, much lower even than what shoppers might get by haggling in the dealership.[82] In a more promising development, auto dealerships use online tools to set service appointments and service reminders, which in turn enhance consumers' omni-channel ownership experience.

Finally, franchisors might adopt an omni-channel approach primarily to attract and acquire franchisees, whereas traditional recruitment methods often relied on presentations at trade shows. But franchisors also are encountering much better-informed prospective franchisees. They have done their research (likely online) prior to attending the franchisor's presentation, requiring these recruitment efforts to be more detailed, sophisticated, and substantive than ever before.[83]

Take-Aways

- Franchising is a marketing channel structure intended to convince end-users that they are buying from a vertically integrated manufacturer, when they may be buying from a separately owned company.

- Franchising a business format is a way to grow quickly while building brand equity.

  - For the franchisor, the system provides quick access to capital and management resources. It also enables the franchisor to harness the motivation and capability of entrepreneurs. For "programmable" businesses (i.e., that can be formatted and transmitted easily), franchising is an excellent solution to the problems of monitoring employee managers.

  - For the franchisee, the system offers assistance and reduces risk. By paying fees, entrepreneurs purchase a corporate backer, coaching, problem solutions, and brand enforcement.

- The codification of the formula includes writing a complex contract specifying the rights and duties of both sides, to encourage their compliance.

  - Contracts might price franchises lower than the market will bear to increase the applicant pool and give franchisees a profit motive to stay in business.

  - Contracts often bind franchisees with clauses that award control of the property to the franchisor and/or limit the franchisees' ability to terminate their business.

  - Contracts give the franchisor means to punish noncompliance, which protects brand equity but also reinforces the franchisee's dependence on the franchisor.

  - Franchisors cannot exploit the franchisees' dependence opportunistically, so they rarely enforce contracts every time franchisees violate them. Instead, they weigh the costs and benefits and select which battles they want to fight with which franchisees that fail to comply.

- Franchise systems typically mix company-owned and franchised outlets. This plural form gives the franchisor a laboratory and a classroom to train personnel, try out ideas, and refine the business format.

- Failure rates are very high but mitigated by growth, ages, and certification by third parties.

- Conflict is inevitable, in part because of the built-in clash of goals.

- Multi-unit franchising is surprisingly common and rather difficult to understand.

- Franchisors have to make considerable investments to facilitate omni-channel experiences and this may increase coordination costs with franchisees.

NOTES

1 We thank Rupinder Jindal and Rozenn Perrigot for helpful discussions during the preparation of this chapter.
2 Spelling note: "franchisor" is U.S. English, whereas "franchiser" is British English. This textbook adopts the U.S. convention, but many documents, particularly in Europe, use "franchiser."
3 www.eff-franchise.com/101/franchising-definition-description.html, date retrieved October 11, 2018.
4 European Commission (1997), Green Paper on Vertical Restraints in EU Competition Policy, Brussels, Directorate General for Competition, 44. Available at http://europa.eu.int/en/comm/dg04/dg04home.htm.
5 PWC (2016), "The economic impact of franchised businesses, Vol. IV," January 3, E1.
6 PWC (2016), op. cit.
7 PWC (2016), op. cit.
8 www.kalscoops.com/about-us, date retrieved October 11, 2018.
9 PWC (2016), op. cit.
10 *The Economist* (2000), "The tiger and the tech," February 5, 70–72.
11 This information is drawn from multiple sources: Kaufmann, Patrick J. and Francine Lafontaine (1994), "Costs of control: The source of economic rents for McDonald's franchisees," *Journal of Law and Economics*, 36 (October), 417–453, Love, John F. (1986), *McDonald's: Behind the Golden Arches*, New York: Bantam Books; Wattenz, Eric (1999), "La Machine McDonald's," *Capital*, 96 (September), 48–69; Piétralunga, Cédric (2004), "Les Recettes Qui Ont Fait Rebondir McDo," *Capital* (June), 28–32.
12 www.economist.com/business/2017/09/30/mcdonalds-wages-a-food-fight-in-india, date retrieved October 11, 2018.
13 Patel, Pankaj C., Kyoung Yong Kim, Srikant Devaraj, and Mingxiang Li (2017), "Family ties that b(l) ind: Do family-owned franchises have lower financial performance than nonfamily-owned franchises," *Journal of Retailing*, https://doi.org/10.1016/j.jretai.2017.12.001.
14 Jeon, Hyo Jin, Rajiv P. Dant, and Brent L. Baker (2016), "A knowledge-based explanation of franchise system resources and performance," *Journal of Marketing Channels*, 23, 97–113.
15 Reinartz, Werner J. and V. Kumar (1999), "Store-, market-, and consumer-characteristics: The drivers of store performance," *Marketing Letters*, 10 (1), 5–22.
16 Combs, James G. and David J. Ketchen (1999), "Can capital scarcity help agency theory explain franchising? Revisiting the capital scarcity hypothesis," *Academy of Management Journal*, 42 (2), 198–207.
17 Norton, Seth W. (1988), "An empirical look at franchising as an organizational form," *Journal of Business*, 61 (2), 197–218.
18 BarNir, Anat (2012), "Starting technologically innovative ventures: Reasons, human capitol and gender," *Management Decisions*, 50 (3), 399–419.

19 Shane, Scott A. (1996), "Hybrid organizational arrangements and their implications for firm growth and survival: A study of new franchisors," *Academy of Management Journal*, 39 (1), 216–234.

20 Dant, Rajiv P. (1995), "Motivation for franchising: Rhetoric versus reality," *International Small Business Journal*, 14 (Winter), 10–32.

21 Birkeland, Peter M. (2002), *Franchising Dreams*, Chicago, IL: The University of Chicago Press, pp. 157.

22 Minkler, Alanson P. (1992), "Why firms franchise: A search cost theory," *Journal of Institutional and Theoretical Economics*, 148 (1), 240–249.

23 Aoulou, Yves and Olivia Bassi (1999), "Une Opportunité de Cassière à Saisir," *LSA*, 42–47.

24 Reported with comment in the February 27, 2004, weekly newsletter of IF Consulting (www.i-f.com) and 2012 website content (www.uniqlo.com).

25 Michel, Caroline (2002), "Ada, le Dernier échec de Papy Rousselet," *Capital* (August), 32–33.

26 See 2013 website (www.starbucks.com).

27 Dnes, Anthony W. (1993), "A case-study analysis of franchise contracts," *Journal of Legal Studies*, 22 (June), 367–393. This source is the basis for much of this section and the comparative statements about franchising in the United Kingdom.

28 Klein, Benjamin (1995), "The economics of franchise contracts," *Journal of Corporate Finance*, 2 (1), 9–37.

29 Agrawal, Deepak and Rajiv Lal (1995), "Contractual arrangements in franchising: An empirical investigation," *Journal of Marketing Research*, 32 (May), 213–221.

30 www.entrepreneur.com/franchises/greatclips/282392, date retrieved April 5, 2018.

31 www.greatclipsfranchise.com/territories-and-investment, date retrieved April 5, 2018.

32 www.franchisedirect.com/healthbeautyfranchises/great-clips-franchise-07056/ufoc, date retrieved April 5, 2018.

33 www.franchisedirect.com/healthbeautyfranchises/great-clips-franchise-07056/ufoc, date retrieved April 5, 2018.

34 Lal, Rajiv (1990), "Improving channel coordination through franchising," *Marketing Science*, 9 (4), 299–318.

35 The Economist Intelligence Unit (1995), "Retail franchising in France," *EIU Marketing in Europe* (December), 86–104.

36 Lafontaine, Francine (1992), "Agency theory and franchising: Some empirical results," *Rand Journal of Economics*, 23 (2), 263–283.

37 Kaufmann and Lafontaine (1994), op. cit.

38 Klein, Benjamin (1980), "Transaction cost determinants of 'unfair' contractual arrangements," *Borderlines of Law and Economic Theory*, 70 (2), 356–362.

39 Grunhagen, Marko, Xu (Vivian) Zheng, and Jeff Jianfeng Wang (2017), "When the music stops playing: Post-litigation relationship dissolution in franchising," *Journal of Retailing*, 93 (2), 138–153.

40 Lafontaine, Francine and Kathryn L. Shaw (1998), "Franchising growth and franchisor entry and exit in the U.S. market: Myth and reality," *Journal of Business Venturing*, 13 (1), 95–112.

41 Kashyap, Vishal and Brian R. Murtha (2017), "The joint effects of ex ante contractual completeness and ex post governance on compliance in franchised marketing channels," *Journal of Marketing*, 81 (3), 130–153.

42 Ibid.

43 Lafontaine and Shaw (1998), op. cit.

44 Carney, Mick and Eric Gedajlovic (1991), "Vertical integration in franchise systems: Agency theory and resource explanations," *Strategic Management Journal*, 12 (1), 607–629.

45 Hsu, Liwu, Patrick Kaufmann, and Shuba Srinivasan (2017), "How do franchise ownership structure and strategic investment emphasis influence stock returns and risks?" *Journal of Retailing*, 93 (3), 350–368.

46 Ibid.

47 Brickley, James A. and Frederick H. Dark (1987), "The choice of organizational form: The case of franchising," *Journal of Financial Economics*, 18, 401–420.

48 Lafontaine, Francine and Patrick J. Kaufman (1994), "The evolution of ownership patterns in franchise systems," *Journal of Retailing*, 70 (2), 97–113.

49 Shane (1996), op. cit.

50 Bradach, Jeffrey L. (1997), "Using the plural form in the management of restaurant chains," *Administrative Science Quarterly*, 42 (June), 276–303. This source is the basis for this section and is an excellent guide to the working operations of large chain franchisors.

51 See 2013 website (www.mcdonalds.co.uk).

52 This discussion is based on Dant, Rajiv P., Audehesh K. Paswan, and Patrick J. Kaufman (1996), "What we know about ownership redirection in franchising: A meta-analysis," *Journal of Retailing*, 72 (4), 429–444.

53 Bouillin, Arnaud (2001), "Comment Zannier Verrouille Son Marche," *Management* (June), 28–30.

54 Small Business Administration. SBA 504 and 7(a) disbursed loans from 2001 to 2011 as reported at www.bluemaumau.org/story/2012/06/15/worst-25-franchises-buy-highest-failure-rates-2012.

55 Reported with comment in the April 2, 2004 weekly newsletter of IF Consulting (www.i-f.com).

56 Shane, Scott and Maw-Der Foo (1999), "New firm survival: Institutional explanations for new franchisor mortality," *Management Science*, 45 (February), 142–159.

57 Shane (1996), op. cit.

58 Antia, Kersi D., Sudha Mani, and Kenneth H. Wathne (2017), "Franchisor–Franchisee bankruptcy and the efficacy of franchisee governance," *Journal of Marketing Research*, LIV (December), 952–967.

59 Galleher, Patrick (2017), "Private equity power boost: Why private equity-owned franchises thrive," *Forbes*, December 28, www.forbes.com/sites/forbesfinancecouncil/2017/12/28/private-equity-power-boost-why-private-equity-owned-franchises-thrive/#29043a74507e, date retrieved April 13, 2018.

60 Birkeland (2002), op. cit. pp. 21.

61 Samaha, Stephen, Robert W. Palmatier, and Rajiv P. Dant (2011), "Poisoning relationships: Perceived unfairness in channels of distribution," *Journal of Marketing*, 75 (May), 99–117; and Palmatier, Robert W., Rajiv P. Dant, Dhruv Grewal, and Kenneth R. Evans (2006), "Factors influencing the effectiveness of relationship marketing: A meta-analysis," *Journal of Marketing*, 70 (October), 136–153.

62 Dant, Rajiv P. and Gregory T. Gundlach (1998), "The challenge of autonomy and dependence in franchised channels of distribution," *Journal of Business Venturing*, 14 (1), 35–67.

63 Shane, Scott, Venkatesh Shankar, and Ashwin Aravindakshan (2006), "The effects of new franchisor partnering strategies on franchise system size," *Management Science*, 52 (May), 773–787.

64 Carmen, James M. and Thomas A. Klein (1986), "Power, property, and performance in franchising," *Research in Marketing*, 8, 71–130.

65 Jordan, Miriam and Shirley Leung (2003), "McDonald's faces foreign franchisees' revolt," *Dow Jones Business News* (October 21), 6.

66 Butt, Moeeen Naseer, Kersi D. Antia, Brian R. Murtha, and Vishal Kashyap (2018), "Clustering, knowledge sharing, and intrabrand competition: A multiyear analysis of an evolving franchise system," *Journal of Marketing*, 82 (1), 74–92.

67 Kalnins, Arturs (2004), "An empirical analysis of territorial encroachment within franchised and company-owned branded chains," *Marketing Science*, 23 (4), 476–489.

68 Kaufmann, Patrick J. and Rajiv Dant (1996), "Multi-unit franchising: Growth and management issues," *Journal of Business Venturing*, 11 (1), 343–358.

69 Dant, Rajiv P. and Nada I. Nasr (1998), "Control techniques and upward flow of information in franchising in distant markets: Conceptualization and preliminary evidence," *Journal of Business Venturing*, 13 (1), 3–28.

70 Darr, Eric D., Linda Argote, and Dennis Epple (1995), "The acquisition, transfer, and depreciation of knowledge in service organizations: Productivity in franchises," *Management Science*, 41 (11), 1750–1762.

71 Kalnins, Arturs and Kyle J. Mayer (2004), "Franchising, ownership, and experience: A study of pizza restaurant survival," *Management Science*, 50 (12), 1716–1728.

72 Kalnins, Artur and Francine Lafontaine (2004), "Multi-unit ownership in franchising: Evidence from the fast-food industry in Texas," *Rand Journal of Economics*, 35 (4), 749–763.

73 Lawrence, Benjamin, Cyril Pietrafesa, and Patrick J. Kaufmann (2017), "Exploring the growth of multi-unit franchising," in Frank Hoy, Rozenn Perrigot, and Andrew Terry (eds.), *Handbook of Research on Franchising*, Northampton, MA: Edward Elgar Publishing, pp. 94–115.

74 Feldman, Amy (2016), "Entrepreneur Shoukat Dhanani runs one of America's largest private businesses—very, very quietly," *Forbes*, www.forbes.com/sites/amyfeldman/2016/08/28/entrepreneur-shoukat-dhanani-runs-one-of-americas-largest-private-businesses-very-very-quietly/#1dd9 a8f12dd0.

75 www.franchising.com/articles/2018_mega_99_ranking.html, date retrieved April 11, 2018.

76 www.franchising-today.com/sections/profiles/234-the-dhanani-group, date retrieved April 11, 2018.

77 Cliquet, Gerard and Ekaterina Voropanova (2016), "E-commerce and encroachment: Evidence from French franchise networks," *Journal of Marketing Channels*, 23, 114–128.

78 www.allstate.com/about/about.aspx, date retrieved April 9, 2018.

79 www.the-digital-insurer.com/wp-content/uploads/2015/01/Ninety-Consulting_white-paper_The-Omnichannel-Insurer_Part1of2.pdf, date retrieved April 9, 2018.

80 Poelma, Chris (2018), "The financial frontier: Frictionless orders and digital money payments," *Franchising World* (January), 42–45.

81 De Franco, Agnes L., Cristian Morosan, and Nan Hua (2017), "Moderating the impact of e-commerce expenses on financial performance in US upper upscale hotels: The role of property size," *Tourism Economics*, 23 (2), 429–447.

82 www.edmunds.com/car-buying/part-one-internet-vs-traditional-car-buying.html, date retrieved April 11, 2018.

83 Erich, John (2017), "Franchise businesses must prepare for trade shows in the age of the Internet," *Franchising World* (August), 41–42.

Channels and International Markets

INTRODUCTION

Less than 5 percent of the world's population resides in the United States. The other 95 percent of the globe has emerged as a fast-growing and attractive market for both consumer and industrial goods. A few decades ago, economic activity and trade mostly concentrated in what management guru Kenichi Ohmae called the *triad*:[1] North America (the United States and Canada), Western Europe, and Japan. The rest of the world—barring a few relatively sparsely populated, petro-rich, Middle Eastern states and small pockets of affluence in the developing world—was not much of a market.

Historically, there was a basis for such a view. In the post-World War II period, much of the world was emerging from the yoke of colonial policies, leaving leaders of post-colonial nations in the developing world wary of foreign commercial interests that threatened to function as agents of a colonial enterprise. Many countries pursued communist or socialist economic policies, marked by an inward-looking approach that prioritized self-sufficiency, aversion to trade, and suspicion of the multinational corporations that represented apparent agents of imperialism. The resulting trade barriers, coupled with low incomes and poor infrastructure (e.g., ports, airports, highways, telecommunications—the hardware of an efficient distribution system), made much of the world a less-than-attractive market for conventional sellers.

Another challenge was currency inconvertibility, such that currency could not be easily traded. This inconvertibility hindered already low consumer demand, because consumers and businesses in various countries could not easily access foreign currency to transact with suppliers from other countries, which preferred to be paid in their own currencies, or at least have the option of converting the local currency into their own denominations. This limitation also made it difficult for Western businesses to repatriate profits, even if they were successful in generating profits in another country.

However, a confluence of more recent events has led to the gradual erosion of these barriers. The fall of communism and inadequate economic growth experienced by countries that embraced a socialist economy have led to wider embraces of market-oriented economic policies and greater openness to trade. The great economic success of many of the "East Asian Tigers," such as South Korea and Taiwan, which focused on export-driven economic growth, also helped policy makers realize the constraints of a completely inward-looking economic policy. Such insights encouraged even greater market openness, throughout much of the developing world. Furthermore, as fertility rates in the developed triad continue to decline, the population balance continues to shift. That is, greater openness to trade, rapid economic growth, and large, young populations have made non-triad markets very attractive to marketers.

In particular, China currently ranks as the world's second largest economy, in terms of nominal gross domestic product (GDP), and the largest economy when measured by purchasing power parity (PPP).[2,3] Every country calculates the total value of its economic activity (GDP) in its own currency, but for comparisons, they convert it to some standard currency, like the U.S. dollar, using prevailing exchange rates, which may not reflect the true purchasing power of a currency. The PPP thus offers a measure of the true purchasing power of one currency, relative to that of another currency.[4] India is the third largest economy in terms of PPP.[5] Other large, emerging markets include Brazil, Russia, South Africa, and Indonesia. These countries have embraced modern marketing and retailing tactics to varying degrees, though most consumers still rely on traditional, "mom-and-pop" retail outlets to make their purchases. Furthermore, along with the growing segments of affluent consumers (and sizeable numbers of new billionaires and millionaires) and fast-growing middle classes, these nations are home to sizeable populations of consumers at the "base of the pyramid"—that is, those who subsist on less than $1–$2 per day. Making goods accessible to this segment remains a significant distribution challenge.

Finally, the international marketplace features specialist middlemen who do not appear in domestic channels of distribution. Accordingly, we begin by highlighting a few of these types of middlemen, with their significant role in go-to-market strategies in overseas and still developing markets, before we move on to take a broader view of international distribution issues.

KEY MIDDLEMEN IN INTERNATIONAL MARKETS

In preceding chapters we have focused on various intermediaries including distributors, franchisees, and retailers. The international marketplace has a few other types of intermediaries. These specialist intermediaries help companies distribute products and services in overseas markets. They provide a range of expertise from identifying which country to target, finding customers in the said country, ensuring that various regulations and requirements in both the home and customer's country are met, and handling the various logistics and paperwork involved. The choice of middlemen in international markets depends largely on the company's prior familiarity and expertise in international marketing, as well as its degree of commitment to expending time and resources to acquire such expertise. Fortunately, even companies with minimal in-house expertise and resources can find appropriate partners to whom they can outsource the responsibility of distributing their products internationally.

The simplest way to enter an overseas market is to remain located in the same country and export products overseas. Besides exporting, the other ways to enter foreign markets include actually having a presence in those markets by setting up shop there and finding or setting up a distribution infrastructure there. These more intensive and expensive methods would involve studying the distribution setup in those countries and identifying distributor and retailer partners. But even the simplest mode of entry, i.e., exporting, requires finding customers, establishing channels to get the products to those customers, following regulations in place in both the home and the export market, and receiving secure payments following the completion of the transaction. Companies can acquire the necessary expertise in-house by hiring experienced managers with a strong background in exporting, provided the company is willing to devote considerable resources to building export capabilities, or they can find specialized intermediaries to assist them in these efforts.

Export Management Companies

An export management company (EMC) specializes in export sales and acts on behalf of the seller, to the extent that customers likely believe they are dealing with the company itself rather than an external intermediary. It offers an appealing option for companies that seek to enter overseas markets but have insufficient experience in doing so, because it handles all the necessary tasks involved in exporting: marketing research, business development, promotions, logistics, credit and payment handling, customer service, promoting products at trade shows, ensuring regulatory compliance, and even training sales forces.[6]

The choice of an EMC generally involves two main experience-based qualifications: experience in the specific country being targeted (because rules, regulations, and conditions vary across countries) and experience handling the specific product being exported. By hiring experienced EMCs, the focal company shifts various tasks to this channel partner, freeing up its resources to invest in training or personnel to acquire new expertise. Hiring an EMC also can reduce the time required to build a strong export market.

However, EMCs are unlikely to invest huge sums in developing a substantial distribution network for a single company. Most EMCs take commissions on their sales (typically, 10–15 percent), though some take title to the goods they sell.[7] They tend to be small businesses that need to earn immediate returns on their efforts; with their commission models, they rely heavily on sales volume. A company that hires an EMC thus must monitor the EMC's efforts to present its brand in a suitable manner and its investments in customer development, to prevent paying order takers that simply chase the proverbial low-hanging fruit.

Export Trading Companies

Export trading companies typically operate on a global scale and acquire various products, from raw materials to finished goods (industrial and consumer), which they then distribute and resell to customers in other parts of the world. Japan has a rich tradition of trading companies, called *sogo shosha*, including such famous names as Mitsubishi, Mitsui, Sumitomo, Itochu, Marubeni, Toyota Tsusho, and Sojitz.[8] A producer interested in exporting its products to Japan thus could approach one of these trading companies to enter into a supply relationship. Many trading companies are vertically integrated, such that they possess extensive processing, manufacturing, and transportation operations as well, and in many cases, they specialize in commodities such as metals. However, as the following example reveals, trading companies also are valuable in a wide range of industries.

EXAMPLE: SOJITZ (JAPAN/GLOBAL)[9]

With a rich, nearly two-century history, Sojitz and its 400 subsidiaries cover most of the requirements associated with buying and selling goods and services. It engages in project financing; it conducts manufacturing operations in sectors as diverse as minerals, automobiles, chemicals, food, energy, and industrial parks.[10] For example, Sojitz has been Boeing's sales agent in Japan for more than 60 years, such that it essentially fulfills all the airplane-related demands that Japanese Airlines might make. It also is one of the largest providers of railway cars to India,[11] one of the largest owners of ships in the world, a leading exporter of cars, and a leading trader of the coal and iron ore used in steel-making operations. Beyond these conventional industries, Sojitz is developing a city of 250,000 residents (Deltamas) in Indonesia, is heavily involved in food distribution in Myanmar and Thailand, operates hospitals in Turkey, and has started an in-home water delivery business in Japan. From the salt fields it operates in India, it ships supplies all over the world. As a key actor in the food processing industry, it owns farms and fertilizer plants and exports and imports various food products, including wheat products imported into Indonesia and tuna imported and exported from its tuna farms. Even in the energy business, Sojitz operates solar farms in Germany, Peru, and Mexico.

Piggybacking

A firm that engages in piggybacking relies on a partner company's already developed distribution network. With this method, the newly internationalizing company gets to partake in an existing distribution network, saving considerable costs in terms of both monetary investments and the time required to build a network from scratch in an overseas market. The host company that owns the distribution network earns commission or service fees and also might benefit from offering its customers an extended, improved product line. For piggybacking to be effective, the host company ideally does not already compete in the same product markets as the piggybacking firm, so that they can minimize conflicts of interest. A good fit in a distribution network context implies that both companies target similar customers, with products typically purchased in similar retail outlets. For example, a candy manufacturer's existing distribution network likely would be a good fit for a producer of cookies looking to spread overseas. Kimberly-Clark added 200,000 retail outlets to its Huggies brand distribution network in India simply by piggybacking on its partner Unilever's well-developed channels.[12]

International Retailers

Producers might gain a global presence by inserting their products into the various stores maintained by an international retailer. This option is appealing because, for many retailers, spreading globally represents a strategic necessity, due to slow growth in their home markets and the great attractiveness of developing overseas markets. For example, retail sales in emerging markets tripled between 2000 and 2015—twice the rate of retail growth in developed markets.[13]

Retailers that successfully expand outside their local borders also benefit from a **virtuous cycle**: as they grow, they achieve ever greater economies of scale in purchasing and sourcing, as well as advertising, marketing research, financing, and IT management. Popular products in one market can be exported to another. Furthermore, successful expansions can vastly enhance the brand's worldwide equity. The drive to keep getting bigger thus strongly motivates the global expansion that characterizes much of the retailing sector today.

But gaining these advantages is far from easy. Retailers expanding internationally confront substantial challenges. In 1996, the top retailers earned approximately 12 percent of sales outside their home markets; by 2016, it had more than doubled, particularly for famous names and leading retailers (e.g., foreign sales accounted for 24 percent of total sales at Walmart, 27 percent at Costco, and 28 percent at Walgreens).[14] Yet even those higher rates lag beyond the average foreign sales earned by companies in other industries, largely due to the following unique requirements for expanding retail operations across national boundaries:

- Finding high-quality locations for stores.

- Establishing physical logistics operations that are comparable to those in the home country to source and distribute products, regardless of the available infrastructure in the target country.

- Developing parallel supplier relationships in new markets or else convincing home country suppliers to move across borders too.

- Accounting for differences in zoning, pricing, taxation, hours of operation, labor, and hiring in operational choices to reflect the unique regulations in each market.

- Developing locally attractive products, packaged and positioned in a culturally sensitive manner.

- Overcoming restrictions on foreign ownership and other barriers to entry.

As a result of such barriers, even well-known retailers such as Marks & Spencer, Tiffany's, and Costco failed in their initial international efforts; Home Depot closed its Chinese operations due to inadequate performance.[15,16]

So what makes for a successful entry into a foreign retail market? A key factor is finding a sensible balance between exporting the unique competencies that have led to the retailer's success in its home market while also acknowledging and accommodating local preferences. Walmart's failed initial entry into Argentina offers an example of what not to do: it tried to export its U.S. retailing style with no adaptations; its merchandise mix included appliances wired for 110-volt electric power

(Argentina operates on 220 volts) and U.S. cuts of beef; and stores featured narrow aisles and carpeting that quickly looked faded and dirty. Only after it revised its local strategy completely, to be more in keeping with local norms, did Walmart start to see some success.[17] Accordingly, retailers need to be ready to find producers that will provide different package sizes, flavors, and other options to appeal to local customers.[18]

Another consideration for these firms is finding a way to compete effectively with local, incumbent retailers. In many cases, these niche retailers offer superior service, more locally appealing products, and good existing locations. Thus when Carrefour and Walmart arrived in Brazil, the local retailer Pao de Azucar refocused on emphasizing its convenient locations and its willingness to provide credit—a popular local service that the global entrants did not offer.

In turn, in many emerging markets, modern, professionally managed, self-service retail chain stores coexist and compete with full-service, owner-operated, local, mom-and-pop stores. Even as the exported chain stores make headway, the bulk of sales still move through traditional retailers, which continue to seek growth themselves. Shopkeepers with personal familiarity and long-standing relationships with their customers exercise more influence over purchases; in self-service stores, those influences are left largely to merchandise displays.[19]

EXAMPLE: CARREFOUR (FRANCE/GLOBAL)[20]

Established in France in 1959, Carrefour Group operates 12,300 stores in 30 countries, in addition to its sophisticated e-commerce and m-commerce presence. Its annual revenues of more than 88 billion Euros make it among the world's largest retailers. Its signature hypermarkets combine grocery and discount stores, offering a wide range of items, but Carrefour also operates other retail formats (e.g., traditional supermarkets, convenience stores, cash-and-carry stores that target small businesses). To achieve its significant presence in Latin America, Asia, and Europe, Carrefour has had to customize its offerings and accommodate local cultures. For example, in China, Carrefour sells live fish; in France, the fish is dead and on ice, but it is presented whole instead of filleted, so consumers can inspect its quality.[21] Thus Carrefour might have made its name initially with big box retail, but it continues to revise its strategy to compete in the omni-channel age, including investing heavily in enhanced food quality and delivery operations, while also reducing the average size of its hypermarkets.[22]

Finally, an important insight to take away from this description of retail-based globalization is that international competition is the norm, not an exception. Even for local retailers, this trend is more than an observational curiosity. When multinational retailers enter many markets around the world, not just developed ones, all channel members must consider how the international retail competition is likely to affect them, as well as how to protect their businesses and thrive even in the face of competition from these entrants.

International Franchising

As we discussed in Chapter 8, international franchising is widely used and also rapidly growing, especially in developing markets. For example, more than 9,000 franchises operate in Russia;[23] Brazil's thriving franchise sector produced revenues of roughly US$38 billion in 2015, and these franchisors express their deep motivations to seek increased sales, greater brand recognition, and better economies of scale.[24]

The principles of franchising remain the same anywhere in the world, but there are a few noteworthy differences in different countries, particularly in terms of the legal ramifications and requirements.[25] All franchising contracts need to be enforced, to protect both franchisors and franchisees, but because franchising remains a somewhat less familiar business model in some parts of the world, existing legal and regulatory frameworks in various countries might not include considerations for franchise agreements and the unique conflicts they can create. Before using franchising as a way to enter foreign markets, companies thus should answer the questions identified in Figure 9.1.

In addition, they need to specify their international franchising strategy.[26] First, they might adopt direct franchising, similar to domestic markets, such that they vet and sign up individual franchisees themselves. Second, they could use an "area-development" franchise, such that a franchisee gains the rights and responsibilities for a large geographic area (e.g., city, state, country), which it must develop with multiple units in some specified time frame.[27] A franchisee that obtains an area-development franchise usually must operate all the units in that area itself, such that it becomes essentially a multi-unit franchisee in that geographic area. Third, another popular method relies on **master franchising**,

FIGURE 9.1

Questions to Consider Prior to Franchising Internationally

Questions to Consider Prior to Franchising Internationally
1. Are there differences in labor laws, legal restrictions on days and hours of operation, and other operating rules?
2. Is the legal system dependable and are intellectual property rights protected?
3. Can profits be repatriated to another country easily or are there restrictions on the same?
4. Are there restrictions on charging franchisees various franchise fees and interest?
5. Can non-compete clauses be enforced?
6. How is the sale, termination, or non-renewal of franchises regulated in that country?
7. What contract clauses and financial disclosures are permissible and not permitted?
8. Is there a robust and active national franchise association that can be of help to foreign franchisors?
9. Are there any linguistic, gender role, and trademark challenges that one needs to be aware of?

Source: Zwisler, Carl E., www.franchise.org/sites/default/files/ek-pdfs/html_page/Ten-Questions-U.S.-Franchisors-Need-to-Have-Answered_0.pdf.

in which case the franchisee granted the right to operate in a given geographic region can become a principal and sub-franchise units to other operators. This master franchisee thus becomes a franchisor on the local level, while still remaining a franchisee at the international level. Fourth, some companies enter into a joint venture direct franchising operation, such as Tata and Starbucks in India, as we describe in Sidebar 9.1.

SIDEBAR 9.1
Tata–Starbucks in India

The Indian Tata Group earns its more than $100 billion in annual revenues through a diversified portfolio of companies that span a variety of sectors: steel, chemicals, power, automobile manufacturing (e.g., Jaguar and Land Rover brands), hotels, and technology services, just to name a few,[28] but also coffee plantations and beverage brands.

Starbucks generated more than $22 billion in revenue in 2017, through 28,000 stores in 76 countries. Most of those stores are in the United States, and China is its second largest market.[29]

When it sought to enter the highly attractive Indian market, Starbucks took a vastly different approach than it had used previously, joining an unprecedented partnership with the Tata Group. India offers a fast-growing economy, rising per capita incomes, and a huge population, many of whom are younger than 25 years of age. Yet the barriers to doing business in India are extensive, including expensive real estate and restrictive labor laws that make it difficult to fire workers. Starbucks needed local knowledge and expertise to navigate the complex market; it simply would not have entered the Indian market without a partner that could help it gain such insights.[30]

The Tata–Starbucks venture now operates more than 100 stores in six Indian cities. Although early returns have been limited, such that the venture did not break even in 2017, Starbucks expects India to emerge to become one of its top five markets.[31] In addition, the expanded partnership reaches other markets, such that Starbucks stocks Tata's single-origin coffee in its U.S. stores and Tata's Himalayan water brand in its Singaporean stores.[32]

EXAMPLE: DOMINO'S MASTER FRANCHISE (USA/GLOBAL)

Domino's is the world's leading delivery pizza company.[33] The United States is its largest market: the 5,000 stores mostly are operated by 799 franchisees, though it also maintains 392 company-owned stores. Moreover, it operates in 85 countries around the world,[34] following its first international foray into Canada in 1983. Of the more than 8,000 restaurants outside the United States, India (1,106 stores) accounts for the largest share, followed by the United

(continued)

(continued)

Kingdom (947 stores) and Mexico (655 stores). In most of these markets, which the corporation identifies according to their growth potential and size, Domino's relies on a master franchise model. The master franchisee must invest substantially and also needs to demonstrate operational expertise and local market knowledge. It is responsible for establishing operations in that country, with the right to build stores, sub-franchise, and design the distribution system to best support local store operations. In return, the master franchisee must meet growth targets, conform to Domino's standards, and make royalty payments. These royalties average around 3 percent of sales, which are in addition to the one-time master franchise fee and the franchise fee for each new store opening.[35] Some of these master franchises even trade on their country's stock exchange (e.g., ALSEA in Mexico, DOM in the United Kingdom), reflecting Domino's careful effort to ensure the financial strength of its partners and their ability to invest before selecting master franchisees.

INTERNATIONAL DISTRIBUTION CHALLENGES

The Role of Wholesalers

Customers tend to take the services provided by a wholesaler for granted, blissfully unaware of the costs that they incur. In emerging markets, the low level of institutional trust further undermines the business trade, leaving wholesalers without the trust and credibility that represent their main methods for encouraging business transactions.[36] Effective and efficient wholesaling is a vital prerequisite of nearly any industry, and in developing economies, the need for effective distribution is both particularly acute and badly met.[37]

Consider Niger, a desperately poor nation in West Africa.[38] Its harsh natural climate prevents most value-added agricultural commodities from growing well there—with the exception of onions. A superior onion variety, the Violet de Galmi, is appealing enough to offer a viable export crop, and since the 1960s, onion-growing practices have taken off in Niger. Yet onions have not been nearly as successful as they should be, considering the agricultural situation and market demand. That is, farmers produce onions, and consumers want them. So what was blocking the channel? According to a team of aid agency analysts, it was the lack of a wholesaling sector.

In agriculture, wholesaling usually consists of brokers and wholesalers. Brokers move the crop from the field to the wholesaler, which involves the considerable physical operations of sorting, sacking, and moving. Wholesalers then transfer the onions to the distributors, which sell to retailers (in Niger, either street merchants or fixed stores). Some 50 to 75 percent of the retail price of each onion goes to the wholesaler (even after farmer co-ops use their countervailing power to reduce that level). On the surface, their profits appear to be **exploitation**, according to farmers, retailers, and government officials. Wholesalers thus are reviled by other members of the distribution channel, including end-users who believe the price they pay is too high. But all these members are ignoring the costs that the wholesalers incur. These onion wholesalers also are not getting rich. As one put it, "It's a lot like playing the national lottery." Consider the following costs that consume so much of the onion's final market value:

- Locating, assembling, and sorting produce from different farmers in many locations. Sorting is particularly important, because it provides a bulk-breaking function. Many consumers can afford only one onion. Bulk-breaking can even mean buying a smaller onion.

- Assume credit risks for all actors in the channel, including farmers and retailers. These actors regularly pay late, if at all, or want to use another currency, or ask if they may provide goods or future considerations (offsets) rather than currency.

- Absorb opportunism by retailers, which systematically make false claims, after taking delivery, that some percentage of the merchandise arrived spoiled, and simply switch wholesalers that challenge these claims.

- Build and maintain expensive storage facilities.

- Absorb the risk of improper pricing, which is considerable. Information about prices, supply, and demand is difficult to obtain in a timely way, due to Niger's poor national infrastructure.

- Meet transportation costs, both traditional and illicit. The greatest element of this cost is not the truck, though Niger suffers from poor roads that increase shipping costs. Rather, it is illicit rent seeking by government officials (e.g., customs, police), who erect multiple unnecessary checkpoints, even within Niger's borders, extort bribes, and hand out fictitious traffic tickets. Wholesalers that protest find their trucks held up until the onions spoil. Wholesalers that take their grievances to the government might find their entire truck fleet vandalized in the night.

- Absorb the risk of crop loss—not only the onion crop but also any merchandise they might have taken as payment in lieu of cash.

- Absorb the costs required to meet official regulations and observe informal arrangements of all kinds.

These broadly ranging costs are difficult to estimate. When the aid analysts attempted it, they were unpleasantly surprised by their vast magnitude. By far the greatest cost was illicit rent seeking; beyond its direct costs, this effect has indirect implications too. For example, onion production is subject to sharp seasonal swings, which could be smoothed out by holding onions in storage facilities. But wholesalers hesitate to build them because, like trucks, they are easy to see and vandalize. The vandals are likely to be disgruntled government employees who feel entitled to more bribe money than they are getting.

Why do officials behave this way? And why doesn't public pressure stop them? The single greatest reason is the wholesalers' poor reputation everywhere in Niger. They are viewed as greedy parasites that exploit hapless farmers and consumers without adding value. The public believes wholesalers are getting rich by engaging in speculative hoarding or oligopolistic, collusive behavior. Extorting them and vandalizing their property thus seems fair or justified. Officials even offer a positive spin, arguing that bribe money saves the taxpayer higher civil servant wages!

Risk thus is pervasive in onion wholesaling, and contracts are no solution, considering Niger's weak institutional infrastructure. Therefore, wholesalers tend to work with relatives, friends, and other in-group members, as a way to coordinate their responses and mobilize unsecured credit on short notice. (Relying on informal ties is a standard way to hedge high risks in any economy, including highly developed ones.[39]) Furthermore, women in Niger are limited in many sectors but flourish in wholesaling, though their low literacy rates demand that they employ literate people to read and write for them. The collection of illiterate women hiring relatives looks, on the surface, like strong evidence of nepotism and favoritism, rather than merit-based considerations (particularly among observers who do not see the wholesalers' costs from the start). Consumers simply take for granted the time and place utility these wholesalers create and assume they are making supernormal profits.

In contrast, wholesalers are not well compensated for their risks. Aid agency analysts concluded that they do a fairly good job under onerous conditions, but they could do more, particularly if they were willing to invest more. The Niger onions would be perfect sources for a Nestlé factory *in Niger* that makes dried onions. But the factory does not source locally, because the multinational requires its onions to be certified to meet strict standards. Certification requires wholesaler investment.

Ultimately, analysts concluded that the best way to help the Niger farmer would be to help the Niger wholesaler.[40] They recommended a program of public education to change attitudes and create social pressure to stop illicit rent seeking. But this example is not an isolated situation: recall our discussion in Chapter 1 (Sidebar 1.1) about tea middlemen. Negative public attitudes (again based on the mistaken impression that exploitative wholesalers added no value) encouraged Japanese colonial administrators in Taiwan to back farmers' cooperatives to compete with wholesalers. Yet even with a tax subsidy, the cooperatives could not match the wholesalers' efficiency in providing the services most consumers take for granted.[41]

Of course, none of this discussion should be taken as a guarantee that wholesalers are never exploitative. As might any other channel member, they will pursue their own interests to a dysfunctional level, unless checked by countervailing forces. In

Niger, those countervailing forces include farmers' co-ops and the preponderance of alternative wholesalers. In Taiwan, many wholesalers also competed vigorously among themselves—as it should be.

These examples also should not be taken to imply that the problem exists only in emerging economies. In the United States, attitudes toward wholesalers feature widespread skepticism about whether they add any genuine value, cover significant costs, or operate efficiently.

Marketing to the Base of the Pyramid

International channels can transform consumers' day-to-day lives for the better, by giving them access to necessities in a cost-effective manner.[42] The late C.K. Prahalad, and others, made the case that the poorest segments of the world's population can be a profitable group for multinational corporations to target, ethically, because access to much-needed goods and services would improve these consumers' lives.[43] Each individual consumer may have limited purchasing power, but collectively the group of consumers at the bottom of the income pyramid represents the majority of the world's population, in that their number may exceed 4 billion people.[44]

Defining the Market

Different definitions of this segment are available, but a common threshold indicates that the people in the bottom-of-the-pyramid (BOP) segment live on less than US$1 or $2 per day. Another definition cites annual incomes of less than $1500 per year.[45] Regardless of the criterion used, most of these consumers live in emerging markets, often in remote, rural areas, which makes distributing products and services to this group a serious challenge. Other members of the BOP represent urban underclasses, living in slums and shantytowns. Although most discussions of the BOP refer to emerging markets, a BOP market segment also exists in every developed nation.

There obviously are differences in BOP markets across countries, regions within countries, or urban versus rural areas within the same country, yet some commonalities span national boundaries to identify nearly all BOP markets. A typical BOP consumer earns extremely low incomes, often seasonal in nature, and lacks access to savings or credit. These consumers also tend to suffer from low literacy and low geographic mobility. They often exhibit strong resistance to change. Much of their disposable income is devoted to obtaining the bare necessities of life.[46] Accordingly, companies seeking to sell to BOP consumers must gain their trust and expend considerable effort to help educate consumers in the benefits of their offerings.

Ethical Considerations at the BOP

Mainstream marketers have failed to address the needs of this segment, leaving a space open for "fly-by-night" operators to fill. These unethical operators use unscrupulous methods to take advantage of the poorest populations. For example, payday lenders step into the void left by the mainstream banking sector's failure to cater to BOP customers, charging usurious interest rates. Some rent-to-own businesses make huge profits by taking advantage of poor consumers who suffer both income and credit limits and often are financially illiterate.[47]

For ethical providers, serving the BOP segment successfully requires new business models and frugal innovation efforts, to develop products that will be affordable to this sector. Companies also must seek ways to adjust consumers' behavior, which often involves creating new distribution methods or modifying products. In particular, consumers often resist trying new offerings, due to their misconceptions. Sumitomo Chemicals found it challenging to get consumers in sub-Saharan Africa to use mosquito nets that could protect them from being bitten by mosquitos and thereby prevent being infected with malaria, partly due to the hassle of putting up the nets daily and partly due to ignorance about the causes of malaria.[48]

With novel methods of distribution, companies can ensure that products at least get into consumers' homes. When SC Johnson wanted to sell its cleaning products in rural Kenya, it trained youth groups, already out collecting trash, to use its products and clean people's homes during their rounds. Despite the promised benefits—improving standards for hygiene and health in rural Kenya could vastly reduce the spread of communicable diseases—the program failed, because consumers refused to allow strangers into their homes to clean, a task that they had not been convinced was necessary anyway.[49] In Ghana, SC Johnson enjoyed more success with its insect control products, because it used a direct selling model. Salespeople were trained to educate consumers; to reduce the costs, the company also developed refillable containers.[50]

Essentially, when marketing to the BOP, channel members must take on the information and education functions to a greater degree, even for mundane consumer products. In India, Bajaj Allianz General Insurance partnered with a microfinance lender to sell life insurance products to the microfinance's female customers' husbands and was able to write 1.8 million life insurance policies that doubled up as a savings instrument in 10 months.[51] To cater to this market and provide consumers with a safety net meant educating consumers on the basics of life insurance as many in this group had no idea about or appreciation for the need for these products.

Even a commonly cited success in the BOP market reveals the ongoing challenges associated with serving the BOP. In Mexico, Cemex's Patrimonio Hoy program model sent representatives house to house, offering customers construction materials and training to help them build stronger structures or add on to their homes. Customers would receive training, credit, and materials; Cemex would generate additional sales by catering to this underserved market segment. But to achieve sufficient scale to make its operations sustainable, Cemex ultimately had to shift its strategy and include middle-class homeowners in its offerings too.[52]

Distribution to the BOP

From a distribution perspective, companies must overcome infrastructure challenges to get products to varied and remote locations, often without the benefits of a well-established infrastructure. Many members of the BOP have unpredictable income flows, so companies also may need to devise creative ways to finance their purchases. The amount of profit earned from each individual consumer may be limited, requiring sufficient volume overall to make the venture profitable. Consumers also tend to buy in small quantities (e.g., single-use shampoos rather than an entire bottle), and many retailers catering to them lack substantial storage facilities, so frequent deliveries of items in small batches are necessary.

The inadequate infrastructure (i.e., roads, highways, telecommunications, and electricity) adds to the costs and challenges of distribution. Such issues also may be compounded by the limited penetration of mass media, which means that the task of informing and educating BOP consumers without modern advertising and marketing channels remains a key consideration. In these settings, special events and innovative promotional methods may be required, such as traveling movie screens and mobile movie projection systems that educate rural consumers about various consumer products. Distribution challenges become especially daunting when consumers are located in far-flung regions or hostile terrains, marked by harsh weather conditions, often so sparsely populated that it is nearly impossible to generate economies of scale in distribution.[53]

Distributing to a rural BOP population also means building an adequate transportation and warehousing infrastructure to limit the costs and time required to transport goods. For example, ice cream distribution is impossible without sufficient availability of refrigerated trucks and storage facilities, or if retailers lack adequate refrigeration facilities in their stores. Sidebar 9.2 illustrates how Godrej sought to introduce an innovative refrigeration system, called Chotukool.

SIDEBAR 9.2
The Chotukool by Godrej (India)

The fourth largest refrigerator manufacturer in India also operates in multiple other sectors, such as aerospace, construction, personal care and food products, and furniture. But refrigeration is an important element of the Godrej Group's annual revenues of more than $4.1 billion,[54] considering that India represents one of the largest refrigerator markets in the world, with 15 million units sold in 2017.[55] It also is growing at an annual rate of 12 percent, such that unit sales are predicted to reach 23 million by 2022.[56] Yet despite this vast size, a large segment of India's population lacks any regular access to refrigeration, due to their low incomes, inadequate supply of electricity, cultural preferences for fresh food, and minimal appreciation for the benefits of refrigeration.

Noting these influences, the Godrej Group launched Chotukool (www.chotukool.com) to appeal explicitly to the underserved BOP market and provide these consumers with this modern convenience. A Western audience might characterize the Chotukool as a high-end cooler: it can be plugged into an electric outlet but also can rely on an external, rechargeable battery (incidentally, Godrej also manufactures batteries). It can keep things cool for up to 3 hours even without power, which is crucial considering the frequent power outages in India.

The Chotukool retails for US$70–$110. But even more than price considerations, Godrej had to address the challenges of getting its products to remote rural areas. To do so, it established a direct selling force of women who could educate other women on the benefits. Product demonstration and education were key value additions provided by the company to ensure the channel's effective functioning. Godrej also partnered with the Indian Postal Service and its network of 150,000 post offices to ship Chotukools.[57] Post offices even set up Chotukool kiosks to make the products more accessible to consumers. In turn, Chotukool increasingly has been embraced by small stores, which use the coolers to keep their food products fresh, and by vegetable vendors that mount Chotukools on their bicycles and go house to house to sell their produce.

In expanding beyond the original BOP segment, Godrej is seeking to promote Chotukools as an appealing cooler that middle-class consumers might like to own as well. Thus it is available through more conventional channels, such as e-commerce merchants (Flipkart, Amazon) and Godrej's extensive mainstream retail distribution network.

Figure 9.2 lists some distribution infrastructure requirements associated with various product categories. Physical handling and distribution is important for all products, though for services, the physical distribution demands are less pressing. Promotion is critical to consumer products, more so than agricultural products; credit and after-sales service play much larger roles for durable items. Channel partners also need to function as conduits for information across the channel in all contexts (other than in agricultural sectors). Manufacturers rely on channel partners to inform them about BOP consumers' needs; consumers can learn about the benefits of various products and services from the channel partners that identify appropriate target markets and persuade them to buy. Another value provided by channel partners involves bulk-breaking; in BOP markets, products may already be packaged in smaller sizes, but the channel member still must be willing to sell, for example, one cola instead of a case or one cigarette instead of a pack. When consumers lack the ability to transport a large product such as appliances or have insufficient literacy to read instruction manuals, a retailer may have to arrange delivery and installation services, then educate the consumer on how to use the item. Finally, channel members must take on some portion of the risk of unsold inventory or costs due to spoilage.

A common channel structure for BOP markets relies on direct channels, such that the company maintains its own retail stores or contracts with **village-level entrepreneurs** to act as a sales force. A village-level entrepreneur, in the strictest sense, is a small entrepreneur that buys goods from a manufacturer and then resells them, at a profit, to consumers, often going door to door. These entrepreneurs solve the "last-mile" problem of marketing to remote areas with undeveloped

FIGURE 9.2
Distribution Requirements by Product Types

Product Classification	Consumer Packaged Goods	Consumer Durables	Services	Agricultural Inputs (Small-ticket)	Agricultural Inputs (Durables)
Examples	Soap, toiletries	Television sets	Banking, telecom	Seeds, fertilizers	Tractors, generators
Distribution Capability Demands					
Physical possession & Ownership	High	High	Low	High	High
Promotion	High	High	High	Low	Low–Medium
Financing	Low	High	Low–Medium	Low–Medium	High
After-sales service	Low	High	Low–Medium	Low	High
Market research	High	High	High	Low	Low
Finding buyers	High	High	High	High	High
Ordering & Payment	Low	Medium–High	Medium–High	Low	High
Negotiation	Low	Medium–High	Low	Low	High
Risk taking	Low	Medium–High	Low	Low	Low

Source: Shukla, S. and S. Bairiganjan (2011), http://web.mit.edu/idi/idi/idi/India-%20The%20Base%20of%20Pyramid%20distribution%20Challenge-IFMR.pdf.

FIGURE 9.3

Distribution
Options:
Company,
NGOs,
Cooperatives,
and Rural Retail

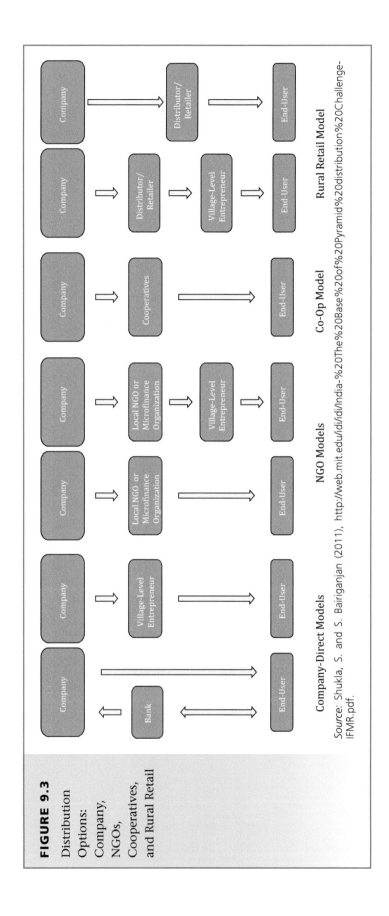

Source: Shukla, S. and S. Bairiganjan (2011), http://web.mit.edu/idi/idi/India-%20The%20Base%20of%20Pyramid%20distribution%20Challenge-IFMR.pdf.

channel structures. That is, international firms often can move their offerings efficiently through the distribution channel—up until the last few miles, when they need to get the products from a distribution center to individual households or small retailers in far-flung areas in a cost-effective manner. Unilever relies heavily on village-level entrepreneurs, namely local women in India who buy its soaps and shampoos, then resell them to their neighbors.[58] The model limits Unilever's risk, because its sales to the village-level entrepreneurs are cash-and-carry. But it also does not create too much risk for the entrepreneurs, who only need to supply enough working capital to purchase the goods, even while they enjoy the benefits provided by Unilever's extensive promotions and strong brand name recognition.[59] However, this model often fails if the village-level entrepreneurs must make large capital investments or the products being sold are less familiar or too expensive.[60] In such situations, it may be advisable to hire the entrepreneurs as employees or commissioned agents.[61]

Figure 9.3 depicts the various channel configurations that companies might use to reach BOP consumers. A company can market directly to end-consumers, sometimes with the aid of a financial intermediary like a bank that provides credit or supports installment payments. Another firm might rely on microfinance organizations, nongovernmental organizations (NGOs), or cooperatives (e.g., Gujarat Milk Marketing Federation from Chapter 7) to get products to end-consumers. Intermediaries such as NGOs often embrace a social purpose, motivated by a goal of improving the health and well-being of the BOP segment and ensuring consumers' access to offerings that can enhance their lives, such as education. Companies also can reach out to rural retailers or rely on distributors with distribution capabilities in rural areas. Many rural retailers are very small, such that they may need to be trained or incentivized to sell and promote any particular company's products.

EXAMPLE: DISTRIBUTING SANITARY PADS IN INDIA

India's vast and young population, with an average age of 28 years, obviously includes many women who menstruate.[62] However, a survey revealed that only 12 percent of Indian women used sanitary pads.[63] The reasons were varied: nearly two-thirds of Indians live in rural areas, which created issues of availability and affordability. A cultural stigma also discouraged discussions of menstruation, and many women were embarrassed to buy sanitary products from mostly male retailers in villages. A widespread falsehood that the use of sanitary pads caused blindness also contributed to the problem, such that women mostly use rags, rarely washed, that they are even too embarrassed to allow to dry in the sun.[64] These factors combined to create a major women's health challenge. An individual inventor named Murugunanthum sought to address this issue by developing a low-cost machine that women could use to manufacture their own sanitary pads, then sell them to other women in their communities.

(continued)

(continued)

In response, adoption of sanitary pads in India has grown exponentially. Murugunanthum traveled to a vast number of villages, including some of the poorest states in India, to gain permission from men to talk to their wives or daughters about the benefits of using sanitary pads, conduct educational sessions with these women, encourage acceptance of the business model involved in purchasing the machines, and finally deliver the machines themselves to women throughout India.[65]

As this example highlights, another solution to the last-mile problem is hyper-local production and distribution among peers. The women who bought the pad-producing machines took on the function of warehousing and distribution, and over time, they also have started to provide information (i.e., women educate other women about the benefits of sanitary pads and how to use them), promotion, and credit (e.g., accepting payment in trade for food instead of cash) functions. Because the distribution costs for low-priced products often account for a disproportionate percentage of the overall costs, even to the point that the products become unaffordable to BOP consumers, the BOP in a sense has become a hotbed for innovative distribution ideas.

OMNI-CHANNELS AND GLOBAL MARKETING

In Chapter 1, we introduced several omni-channel initiatives in large, emerging markets such as China and India. China even is leading the world in terms of mobile commerce and mobile payment systems. Emerging market consumers often leapfrog into the Internet age, and their first online access comes through smartphones. With their relatively low incomes and notorious price consciousness, these consumers rely heavily on smartphones to make efficient purchases, and emerging market retailers often appear at the forefront of the omni-channel revolution.

In India, large online retailers such as D'Mart and Flipkart (recently acquired by Walmart for $16 billion[66]) in turn have spread into physical channels. With its 5 percent stake in Shoppers Stop, Amazon gained a new channel, such that it has opened experience centers inside Shoppers Stop stores.[67] Yet modern retailing may be more likely to enter small-town India through the presence of online rather than physical stores. E-commerce and m-commerce likely will be the channels to provide most of the world's population with access to a wider array of consumer products. Because the low rate of credit card penetration (often less than 5 percent) has meant online vendors needed to accept cash on delivery, another form of leapfrogging has emerged in terms of the adoption of mobile payments. In contrast with consumers in developed markets, who rely on their credit cards, many emerging market consumers are directly moving into the cashless era by relying on mobile payment systems.

Although emerging markets feature cutting-edge omni-channel operations in modern retailing sectors, the bulk of their populations continue to patronize traditional, mom-and-pop retail outlets. Despite this sizeable market that operates outside of a modern, omni-channel retail sector, there are many reasons to be optimistic about its future. First, the rapid adoption of smartphones is bringing millions of people rapidly into the Internet age. These emerging market populations tend to be much younger than those in the mature Western markets, which implies a higher likelihood of adopting new, modern modes of shopping. Second, in a related point, leapfrogging advances and the growth of mobile payment systems imply that more consumers are gaining means to be able to partake in e-commerce transactions.

Third, famous retailers such as Walmart and Amazon actively are seeking entry into emerging markets, bringing with them the cutting-edge technologies and sophisticated retail operations know-how that have underlain their success thus far. Their presence also forces domestic retailers to adapt and embrace new commerce formats. Fourth, especially in urban centers, terrible traffic conditions force commuters to spend hours in traffic, or else rely on public transportation if available. In either case, people often commute long distances to work, which represents a boon for omni-channel shopping. Consumers can do their shopping while stuck in traffic and have items delivered to their homes rather than go out again, such that they can avoid traffic, as well as crowded stores or restaurants.

Fifth, countries with young populations often feature a large contingent of underemployed or unemployed youth, who constitute a ready labor market for delivery operations. The Chinese online food delivery market is now reported to be worth US$37 billion, such that nearly 350 million urban Chinese consumers use online food delivery services, obtained through mobile apps, to receive deliveries from drivers who ride bicycles or motor scooters to gather their dinner from local restaurants.[68]

Along with these promising trends, omni-channel efforts in emerging markets also must address some difficulties. Emerging markets often feature easily available knock-offs and relatively weak enforcement of intellectual property rights. Online marketplaces also are marked by a wealth of counterfeit products.[69] In combination, the widespread availability of knock-offs and counterfeit goods in these channels represents a source of concern.

Furthermore, the e-commerce age cannot guarantee that small merchants in remote corners of the world will find buyers elsewhere. A reported 27,000 Indian merchants signed up on Amazon to sell to U.S. consumers,[70] ranging from giants like the Tata Group to tiny boutique firms. For example, Rajlinen has sold more than 10,000 bed sets for recreational vehicles to U.S. consumers.[71] In Amazon's strategy, India provides a low-cost source for products that it can sell on its site, grabbing market share from competitors also targeting this consumer base, like Walmart.[72]

This collected evidence indicates that emerging markets are ripe for omni-channel efforts. They also provide compelling inducements for experimenting with channel innovations. But it is important to recognize that large swaths of populations in emerging markets continue to function outside the omni-channel realm, limited by their lack of access to advanced technology products and basic infrastructural support.

Take-Aways

- Less than 5 percent of the world's population resides in the United States and therefore it is essential to understand the distribution challenges faced when marketing products internationally. The need to understand channels in international markets has greatly increased due to the tremendous economic growth rates in emerging markets and their large and young population.

- Purchasing power parity (PPP) is an alternative measure of exchange between two currencies and one that captures the purchasing power equivalence of two currencies.

- The international marketplace is characterized by specialty middlemen not found in domestic marketing.

- Export management companies (EMCs) act on behalf of a seller and find customers and manage all export-related logistics for the seller such that the buyer may not even be aware that they are dealing with a third party.

- Export trading companies operate on a global scale and may produce or acquire products in one part of the world and distribute and resell them in other countries.

- Japan has a rich tradition of export trading companies who are called *sogo shosha*.

- Piggybacking is a distribution technique where one company latches on to the distribution network of another. The host company is motivated by a desire to have a more complete array of products to distribute and may agree to piggybacking as an additional revenue source.

- Retailers expanding internationally face many challenges finding suitable locations, establishing physical logistics operations, and developing parallel supplier relationships. Retailers have to be aware of differences across countries in zoning, labor, and operational practices.

- Master franchising is very popular in overseas markets. Master franchisees are given the right to operate in a whole geographic region and may in turn sub-franchise to other operators.

- Wholesalers play an important role in emerging markets but their role is not fully appreciated by consumers.

- The base of the pyramid comprises the world's poorest consumers who, because of their large numbers, can collectively make up a large market. But marketing to this group involves substantial challenges in distribution and raises ethical considerations. Companies have to come up with novel strategies to reach this consumer group and expend effort to solve the "last-mile" problem and engage in substantial consumer education.

NOTES

1   Ohmae, Kenichi (2002), *Triad Power: The Coming Shape of Global Competition*, New York, NY: Free Press.
2   World Bank (2018), http://databank.worldbank.org/data/download/GDP.pdf, date retrieved October 19, 2018.
3   www.cia.gov/library/publications/the-world-factbook/rankorder/2001rank.html, date retrieved October 19, 2018.
4   https://data.oecd.org/conversion/purchasing-power-parities-ppp.htm.
5   www.cia.gov/library/publications/the-world-factbook/rankorder/2001rank.html, date retrieved October 19, 2018.
6   www.powerlinx.com/blog/export-management-companies, date retrieved April 27, 2018.
7   Joyner, Nelson T., "How to find and use an export management company," http://fita.org/aotm/0499.html, date retrieved April 27, 2018.
8   www.japantimes.co.jp/news/2017/05/10/business/corporate-business/seven-top-japanese-trading-firms-enjoy-strong-earnings/#.WuTkIIjwbD4, date retrieved April 28, 2018.
9   http://sp.sojitz.com/switch/en.html, date retrieved April 28, 2018.
10 www.sojitz.com/en/corporate/profile, date retrieved April 28, 2018.
11 http://sp.sojitz.com/switch/en.html, date retrieved April 28, 2018.
12 Anonymous (2013), "Kirana stores will sell Huggies diapers piggybacking HUL's network," *FRPT-Retail Snapshot*, p. 9.
13 www.atkearney.com/documents/10192/8355530/Emerging+Market+Retailing+in+2030.pdf/54cb66fc-8aee-445f-bf55-b3aed2e0227b, date retrieved May 2, 2018.
14 Silverblatt, Howard (2017), https://us.spindices.com/indexology/djia-and-sp-500/sp-500-global-sales, date retrieved April 30, 2018.
15 Connor, Neil (2017), "Marks and Spencer pulls out of China's high street: The world's biggest retail market," *The Telegraph*, www.telegraph.co.uk/business/2017/03/14/marks-spencer-pulls-chinas-high-street-worlds-biggest-retail, date retrieved October 19, 2018.

16 Bhasin, Kim (2012), "Why IKEA took China by storm, while Home Depot failed miserably," www. businessinsider.com/ikea-home-depot-china-failed-2012-9, date retrieved October 19, 2018.

17 Krauss, Clifford (1999), "Selling to Argentina (as translated from the French)," *The New York Times*, December 5, Business World Section.

18 Ibid.

19 Venkatesan, Rajkumar, Paul Farris, Leandro A. Guissoni, and Marcos Fava Neves (2015), "Consumer brand marketing through full-and self-service channels in an emerging economy," *Journal of Retailing*, 91 (4), 644–659.

20 www.carrefour.com/content/group, date retrieved May 3, 2018.

21 Child, Peter N. (2006), "Lessons from a global retailer: An interview with the president of Carrefour China," *McKinsey Quarterly*, pp. 71–81.

22 Michelson, Marcel (2018), "French retailer Carrefour set to start fresh consumer revolution using bricks, clicks, and blockchain," *Forbes*, January 23, www.forbes.com/sites/marcelmichelson/2018/01/23/french-retailer-carrefour-set-to-start-fresh-consumer-revolution-using-bricks-clicks-and-blockchain/#170637ed6186, date retrieved May 3, 2018.

23 Hoffman, Richard C., Sharon Watson, and John F. Preble (2016), "International expansion of United States franchisors: A status report and propositions for future research," *Journal of Marketing Channels*, 23, 180–195.

24 Camargo, Maria Adriana A.P., Thelma Valeria Rocha, and Susana Costa e Silva (2016), "Marketing strategies in the internationalization processes of Brazilian franchises," *Review of Business Management*, 18 (Oct/Dec), 570–592.

25 Rosado-Serrano, Alexander, Justin Paul, and Desislava Dikova (2018), "International franchising: A literature review and research agenda," *Journal of Business Research*, 85, 238–257.

26 Ibid.

27 Jell-Ojobor, Maria and Josef Windsperger (2014), "The choice of governance modes of international franchise firms: Development of an integrative model," *Journal of International Management*, 20, 153–187.

28 www.tata.com/company/index/Tata-companies, date retrieved May 9, 2018.

29 Starbucks 2017 Annual Report, https://investor.starbucks.com/financial-data/annual-reports/default.aspx, date retrieved May 9, 2018.

30 Menon, Sangeeta (2016), "Starbucks would not be in India if it wasn't for Tata," www.tata.com/article/inside/sumitro-ghosh-starbucks-india-experience.

31 https://economictimes.indiatimes.com/industry/cons-products/food/starbucks-expects-india-to-be-among-its-top-5-markets-globally/articleshow/61206968.cms, date retrieved May 9, 2018.

32 Ibid.

33 https://biz.dominos.com/web/public/about, date retrieved May 7, 2018.

34 http://phx.corporate-ir.net/phoenix.zhtml?c=135383&p=irol-reportsannual, date retrieved May 7, 2018.

35 Ibid.

36 Zhang, Ran and Zabihollah Rezaee (2009), "Do credible firms perform better in emerging markets? Evidence from China," *Journal of Business Ethics*, 90 (2), 221–237.

37 Prahalad, C.K. and Allen Hammond (2002), "Serving the world's poor profitably," *Harvard Business Review*, 9, 49–57.

38 Arnould, Eric J. (2001), "Ethnography, export marketing policy, and economic development in Niger," *Journal of Public Policy & Marketing*, 20 (Fall), 151–169.

39 Palmatier, Robert W. (2008), *Relationship Marketing*, Cambridge, MA: Marketing Science Institute.

40 Bardy, Roland, Stephen Drew, and Tumenta F. Kennedy (2012), "Foreign investment and ethics: How to contribute to social responsibility by doing business in less-developed countries," *Journal of Business Ethics*, 106 (3), 267–282.

41 Koo, Hui-wen and Pei-yu Lo (2004), "Sorting: The function of tea middlemen in Taiwan during the Japanese colonial era," *Journal of Institutional and Theoretical Economics*, 160 (December), 607–626.

42 Hoppner, Jessica and David A. Griffith (2015), "Looking back to move forward: A review of the evolution of research in international marketing channels," *Journal of Retailing*, 91 (4), 610–626.

43 Agnihotri, Arpita (2013), "Doing good and doing business at the bottom of the pyramid," *Business Horizons*, 56, 591–599.

44 Kolk, Ans, Miguel Rivera-Santos, and Carols Rufin (2014), "Reviewing a decade of research on the 'base bottom of the pyramid' (BOP) concept," *Business and Society*, 53 (3), 338–377.

45 Simanis, Erik and Duncan Duke (2014), "Profits at the bottom of the pyramid," *Harvard Business Review*, October, 86–93.

46 Shukla, Sachin and Sreyasma Bairiganjan (2011), *The Base of the Pyramid Distribution Challenge: Evaluating Alternate Distribution Models of Energy Products for Rural Base of the Pyramid in India*, http://web.mit.edu/idi/idi/India-%20The%20Base%20of%20Pyramid%20distribution%20Challenge-IFMR.pdf, date retrieved May 16, 2018.

47 https://mic.com/articles/185592/is-rent-to-own-a-ripoff-rent-a-center-has-been-overcharging-customers-study-finds#.XfgN4KmK4, date retrieved October 19, 2018.

48 Ibid.

49 Ibid.

50 Ibid.

51 Ibid.

52 Palomarres-Aguirre, Itzel, Michael Barnett, Francisco Layrisse, and Bryan W. Husted (2018), "Built to scale? How sustainable business models can better serve the base of the pyramid," *Journal of Cleaner Production*, 172, 4506–4513.

53 Ibid.

54 www.godrej.com/who-we-are.html, date retrieved May 12, 2018.

55 www.portal.euromonitor.com.offcampus.lib.washington.edu/portal/analysis/tab, date retrieved May 14, 2018.

56 Ibid.

57 www.chotukool.com/buyoffline.aspx, date retrieved May 14, 2018.

58 www.inclusivebusinesshub.org/the-last-mile-challenge-need, date retrieved May 23, 2018.

59 Ibid.

60 Ibid.

61 Ibid.

62 www.cia.gov/library/publications/the-world-factbook/geos/in.html, date retrieved May 23, 2018.

63 Venema, Vibeke (2014), "The Indian sanitary pad revolution," www.bbc.com/news/magazine-26260978, date retrieved May 23, 2018.

64 Ibid.

65 Ibid.

66 Goel, Vindu (2018), "Walmart takes control of India's Flipkart in e-commerce gamble," *New York Times*, May 9.

67 www.businesstoday.in/current/economy-politics/retail-30-the-emergence-of-the-omni-channel-in-2017/story/267055.html, date retrieved May 16, 2018.

68 www.scmp.com/business/companies/article/2111163/dinner-your-door-inside-chinas-us37-billion-online-food-delivery, date retrieved May 25, 2018.

69 www.forbes.com/sites/ywang/2017/08/14/alibabas-struggle-for-e-commerce-legitimacy-is-undermined-by-fake-gucci-and-refugee-boats/#5def654f52d0, date retrieved May 25, 2018.

70 Goel, Vindu (2017), "Amazon in hunt for lower prices, recruits Indian merchants," *New York Times*, November 26.

71 Ibid.

72 Ibid.

CHAPTER 10

End-User Analysis
Segmentation and Targeting

LEARNING OBJECTIVES

After reading this chapter, you will be able to:

- Understand how end-users and their demands dictate the design of marketing channels.
- Define service outputs and know how to identify and analyze them.
- Distinguish between channel and market segmentation and recognize how to divide a market into channel segments for the purposes of marketing channel design or modification.
- Describe how to target channel segments to optimize sales and profits.
- Evaluate when and whether to try to meet all expressed service output demands in the short run in a particular market.
- Describe the relationship between service output demands and solutions to overall channel design problems.

INTRODUCTION: UNDERSTANDING THE IMPORTANCE OF CHANNEL SEGMENTATION

As you have learned throughout this book, the focus of any channel strategy should be to understand how people buy and then devise ways that make it easy, convenient, efficient, and cost-effective for them to do so, using their preferred mode. Developing a marketing channel strategy, similar to many other marketing activities, must start with the end-user—even for manufacturers that do not sell directly to those end-users. For example, a manufacturer selling through an intermediary may book a sale if that partner buys some inventory, but the ongoing demand from the intermediary only derives from the demand patterns of ultimate end-users. Therefore, a channel manager needs to understand the nature of end-users' demand to design an effective channel that meets or exceeds those demands throughout the channel. The most useful insights for channel design relate not to *what* end-users want to consume but rather *how* they want to buy and use the products or services they are purchasing. In this chapter, we assume that a viable product for the market exists, and therefore, we can focus more specifically on *how* to sell this offering, rather than on determining what to sell.

This chapter accordingly focuses on the **end-user**, or the demand side of a marketing channel strategy (i.e., downstream), and describes end-user behavior. In every market, end-users express varying preferences and demands for **service outputs** that can provide them with benefits, such as reducing their search efforts, waiting time, storage, or other costs. Grouping end-users by service output demands (rather than preferences for physical product attributes) helps us define potential target market segments and then design specific marketing channel solutions that appeal to them.

End-users (whether business-to-business buyers or individual consumers) purchase products and services of every sort. Yet in most cases, they consider more than just the product itself. A particular product or service can be purchased in various ways. The product may stay the same, but the method of buying and selling it and its associated services vary. In corporate technology purchases, for example, smaller corporate buyers might obtain electronic devices such as PCs, laptops, and tablets directly from a manufacturer or else rely on a corporate supplier such as CDW. Their choice likely depends on the customer services offered by CDW, which it tailors specifically to this segment of buyers. The service outputs offered through the CDW channel thus create a **product + service output bundle** that this targeted, small corporate customer really values. In Sidebar 10.1, we take a look at CDW's service outputs and how they provide value to end-users.

SIDEBAR 10.1

CDW and Purchases by Small- to Medium-Sized Business Buyers[1]

Personal computers virtually have become **commodity products**. The technology is well enough established that buyers know they can purchase a computer with a given combination of characteristics (e.g., memory space, weight, speed, monitor quality) from multiple manufacturers. In such a market, two questions immediately emerge:

1. How can any manufacturer differentiate itself from the competitive crowd to gain disproportionate market share and/or margins higher than purely competitive ones?
2. What role might an intermediary play when the product purchase appears to be a straight commodity one?

CDW (formerly known by its expanded name, Computer Discount Warehouse) has risen to the challenge by adopting an enduring role as a valued intermediary in specific market segments—particularly small and medium business buyers and government/educational markets. In this process, it also has attracted the attention and business of major computer makers. Thus in 2017, it achieved sales of $15 billion, by carrying more than 100,000 products representing thousands of brands.[2]

When serving these small- to medium-sized business buyers, CDW recognizes that it is not just a PC (or a set of PCs) being purchased but rather the products and the *ancillary valued services* accompanying them. The firm thus calls itself the chief technical officer of its small firm customers. What does that role mean, in terms of the demand for and supply of service outputs, along with the product purchased?

- CDW is a key provider of *advice and expertise* to buyers, involving everything from the appropriate configuration of products to buy to the setup of a local area network. CDW is also available after the purchase if any customer service problems arise.
- CDW prides itself on its *speed of delivery*; 99 percent of orders are shipped the day they are received. The company can make this promise because of its investment in a 400,000-square-foot warehouse, which permits it to hold significant speculative inventory and avoid stockouts.
- CDW offers different *customer service* options: a customer can buy online, without a great deal of sales help, but CDW also assigns a salesperson to every account, even small, online purchase accounts. This service output gives the buyer access to a person to talk to if any questions or problems arise, and it increases the buyer's flexibility in terms of how to shop. The salesperson has no incentive to be overly aggressive, because a sale results in the same commission, whether the customer orders online or through the salesperson. A CDW salesperson goes through four months of training before being allowed to serve customers, so his or her level of expertise and professionalism is high enough to serve the customer well.
- CDW offers its customers broad *assortment and variety*. A small business buyer can buy directly from a manufacturer, such as Dell or Hewlett-Packard, but that means restricting him- or herself to one manufacturer's product line. Buying through CDW gives the buyer access to many different brands, which can be useful when putting components together in the optimal computer systems. CDW enhances the effective assortment available by also refiguring products before shipping them out, to customize them to the demands of the business buyer.

How well does CDW compare to the competition? Offering high levels of service outputs is great, but the question always remains: How well did the channel perform against other routes to market through which a customer can buy? When CDW faced a strong challenge from Dell Computer, offering 0 percent financing for the first time, together with free shipping and rebate programs, how did CDW withstand the competitive attack? For an individual buyer, such questions take on a different perspective: how much are CDW's extra service outputs worth to my company? For the buyer that values quick delivery, assortment, and CDW's targeted customer service, the apparent price premium is well worth the money, because it saves the buyer the cost of acquiring those services in another way (or the cost of not getting the desired level of service). Ultimately, the appealing service outputs provided by CDW motivated Dell to enter into a partnership with the supplier, spanning Europe, Asia, and North America. Thus, Dell's servers, PCs, storage solutions, and networking services are available through CDW. For Dell, the combination of its product portfolio with CDW's sales and technical expertise proved optimal, leading to increased sales and customer satisfaction.[3]

Thus CDW's strategy of focusing on a particular subset of all computer buyers and providing valued service outputs to them, along with a wide assortment of quality products, has helped the company cement its relationships with these buyers, while also making it a preferred intermediary channel partner for key manufacturers.

In the omni-channel era, these examples are widespread; for example, contractors use e-commerce platforms in several ways. Some rely on e-commerce from start to finish and order items online; others leverage these tools to research technical specifications and then order over the phone or in person with their preferred distributors.[4]

Even when a product can be standardized across global markets, the user's preference in terms of how to buy the product likely is unique to each country. Researchers argue that among the four standard marketing mix variables (product, promotion, price, place), place, which defines the **channel strategy**, is the least amenable to global standardization.[5] Channel managers who seek to design channel strategies that can penetrate global markets need to segment end-users by their needs, even if standardized approaches might be sufficient for promotions or product designs.

EXAMPLE: GROCERY SHOPPING IN CHINA

In China in 2007, 80 percent of all food sold went through traditional "wet markets" that comprised countless numbers of small stalls, each selling a very narrow assortment of products, such as fresh fruit or fish. The remaining 20 percent of sales were split about evenly among 1,500 large and 20,000 small supermarkets.[6] The larger supermarkets were mostly located in major cities. That is, about a decade ago, well-to-do consumers in the biggest cities shopped like Western consumers in modern, state-of-the-art supermarkets, but the vast population of middle- and lower-income consumers, especially those who lived in smaller cities, towns, and rural areas, shopped in wet markets that looked much like the channels available throughout the developing world. In the past 10 years, though, massive expansion has increased the ranks of hypermarkets and supermarkets. By 2015, China hosted more than 33,000 supermarkets and 8,500 hypermarkets.[7] Major international players such as Walmart, Metro, and Carrefour compete with leading domestic chains such as Yonghui. These supermarkets and hypermarkets push sophisticated in-store promotions and complex, seamless omni-channel experiences. The stores often coexist in the same geographic areas as wet markets and convenience stores, which target end-users who may prefer to buy in small quantities on a daily basis from a familiar neighborhood retailer by paying cash; these consumers often find the posh settings of supermarkets too intimidating and unwelcoming.

These examples reiterate the need to identify *how* end-users want to buy, as well as *what* they hope to purchase. Different end-users have different needs; understanding and responding to their demands can create new business opportunities for manufacturers (and failing to understand them can short-circuit such opportunities). We thus turn to a discussion of the types of preferences that are most critical to evaluate when segmenting end-users, through a definition of the concept of service outputs.

END-USER SEGMENTATION CRITERIA: SERVICE OUTPUTS

An existing framework codifies and generalizes how end-users want to buy particular products, as a basis for determining channel structures.[8] We use this approach to discuss ways to segment markets for channel design purposes. According to this framework, channel systems exist and remain viable over time because they perform duties that reduce end-users' search, waiting time, storage, or other costs. These benefits represent the *service outputs* of the channel. All else being equal (e.g., price, physical product attributes), *end-users prefer a marketing channel that provides more service outputs*. These service outputs in turn can be classified into six general categories, as outlined in Figure 10.1:

1. Bulk-breaking.

2. Spatial convenience.

3. Waiting or delivery time.

4. Product variety.

5. Customer service.

6. Information sharing.

This generic list can be customized to different applications, but these six service outputs cover the main categories of needs that end-users demand from upstream channel partners.

Bulk-Breaking

Bulk-breaking refers to the end-user's ability to buy a desired (possibly small) number of units, even if the product or service originally was produced in large, batch-production lot sizes. When the channel system allows end-users to buy in small lots, these purchases more easily support consumption, reducing the need for end-users to carry unnecessary inventory. However, if end-users must purchase larger lots (i.e., benefit less from bulk-breaking), some disparity emerges between purchasing and consumption patterns, burdening end-users with product handling and storage costs. The more bulk-breaking the channel does, the smaller the lot size end-users can buy, and the higher the channel's service output level, which likely leads the end-user to be more willing to pay a higher price that covers the costs to the channel of providing small lot sizes.

The common practice of charging lower per unit prices for larger package sizes in frequently purchased consumer packaged goods categories is a well-known example of this phenomenon. Consider how a family might buy liquid laundry detergent at

FIGURE 10.1
Drivers of
Service Outputs
in Marketing
Channels

Extent of Bulk-Breaking	Ability to buy desired amount
Desired Spatial Convenience	Ease of access, distance
Waiting or Delivery Time	Time between order and delivery
Product Variety and Assortment	Breadth and depth of product lines
Customer Service	Ease of shopping
Information Sharing	Education and engagement

home versus when renting a vacation house. At home, the family likely buys the large, economy size of detergent, perhaps at a supermarket or hypermarket, because it is easy to store in the laundry room at home, and eventually, the family will use up that large bottle of detergent. The large bottle is comparatively inexpensive, per fluid ounce. But when on vacation for a week at a rental cottage, the family likely prefers a small bottle of detergent—despite its much higher price per fluid ounce—because they do not want to end the week with a large amount left over (which they will probably have to leave at the cottage). Most vacationers are neither surprised nor reluctant to pay a considerably higher price per ounce for the convenience of buying and using a smaller bottle of detergent when on vacation. Indeed, it is more common for the unit prices for such products to be much higher in resort town supermarkets than in supermarkets or hypermarkets that primarily serve permanent residents.[9]

In these examples, we assume that the more an end-user consumes, the more utility he or she attains. However, not all goods are "good." Consumers assess the pros and cons of each item they purchase; in the case of vice goods such as cookies or soda, they may want to purchase limited portions to help them stay healthy. Thus, firms can profit more from selling smaller packages when the general consumer finds a small portion more acceptable.[10] In bottom-of-the-pyramid (BOP) markets in emerging economies, some stores sell cigarettes individually, at a much higher unit cost, not necessarily because they are vice products but rather because consumers will pay higher costs to get their nicotine fix, without being able to afford an entire pack of cigarettes.

Spatial Convenience

The **spatial convenience** provided by market decentralization in wholesale and/or retail outlets increases consumers' satisfaction by reducing transportation requirements and search costs. Community shopping centers, neighborhood supermarkets, convenience stores, vending machines, and gas stations are but a few examples of the varied channel forms designed to satisfy consumers' demands for spatial convenience. Business buyers value spatial convenience too: the business PC buyer appreciates that CDW delivers PCs directly to the place of business, as well as coming to pick up computers that need service.

Waiting or Delivery Time[11]

Waiting time is the time that the end-user must wait between ordering and receiving the goods or post-sale service. The longer the waiting time, the more inconvenient it is for the end-user, who must plan or predict consumption levels far in advance. Usually, the longer end-users are willing to wait, the more compensation (i.e., lower prices) they receive, whereas quick delivery is associated with a higher price paid. This trade-off is evident in CDW's positioning for its small and medium business buyers, such that it has long focused more on ensuring faster delivery than its erstwhile competitors like Dell. However, in other situations, the benefits of longer wait times may not accrue to the customer.

EXAMPLE: APPS TO CUT WAIT TIMES (USA)

Fast food and fast casual restaurants are popular destinations and can get crowded at certain times of the day, such as during lunch hours. Many patrons stand in line at Chipotle and wait their turn to order, after which they can watch their food being prepared right in front of them. But like many restaurant chains, Chipotle also offers an app to enable consumers to order their food ahead. With these apps, users can reduce their wait times by preordering, then simply arriving at the restaurant to pick up their meal. In this sense, they cut in line, passing by those customers patiently waiting their turn.[12] This distinction clearly highlights two different types of end-users: those who enjoy the ritual of going to a restaurant, ordering, and seeing their food prepared fresh versus those who simply want their food quickly. The app caters to the needs of those who want to reduce their wait times; might it also end up alienating those who wait patiently in line, though? Walk-in, no appointment hair salon chains such as Great Clips similarly use online check-in apps to help patrons reduce their wait times.[13] When they go to register online, they are informed of the estimated wait times and then can check in online and arrive at the salon at the best estimated time of service.

The intensity of demand for quick delivery varies for the purchase of *original equipment* (for which it tends to be lower) versus the purchase of *post-sales service* (for which it is frequently very high). Consider a hospital purchasing an expensive ultrasound machine. Its original machine purchase is easy to plan, and the hospital is unlikely to be willing to pay a higher price for quick delivery of the machine itself. However, if the ultrasound machine breaks down, the demand for quick repair service may be very intense, and the hospital may be willing to pay a premium price for a service contract that promises speedy service. In such cases, a sophisticated channel manager must price the product versus post-sale service purchases very differently, to reflect the different concatenation and intensity of demand for these service outputs. Similarly, airline ticket prices change as the departure date approaches, to account for both the number of seats remaining and the lower price sensitivity of business travelers who need to reach a specific destination and do not want to wait.[14]

Another example combines demands for bulk-breaking, spatial convenience, and delivery time. In the beer market in Mexico, understanding market demand requires an understanding of the market's and consumers' environmental characteristics and constraints. A market with limited infrastructural development usually is characterized by consumers with high demands for service outputs, such as spatial convenience (i.e., consumers cannot travel easily to remote retail locations), minimal waiting time for goods, and extensive bulk-breaking (consumers lack sufficient disposable income to keep "backup stocks" of goods in their homes in case of retail stockouts). In the Mexican market, major beer manufacturers sell through grocery stores, liquor stores, and hypermarkets, as well as through restaurants. As an additional channel, though, they sell beer through very small local distributors—apartment residents who buy a small keg of beer and resell it by the bottle to neighborhood buyers who cannot afford a six pack. The end-users also usually provide their own (washed, used) beer bottles for the "local" distributor to fill. The manufacturer values this channel, because the other standard retail channels cannot meet the intense service output demands of these consumers.

Product Variety and Assortment

When the breadth of the variety or the depth of the product assortment available to end-users is greater, so are the outputs of the marketing channel system, but so too are the overall distribution costs, because offering greater assortment and variety means carrying more inventory. **Variety** describes generically different classes of goods that constitute the product offering, namely the *breadth* of product lines. The term **assortment** instead refers to the *depth* of product brands or models offered within each generic product category. Discount department stores, such as Kohl's or Walmart, have limited assortments of fast-moving, low-priced items across a wide variety of household goods, ready-to-wear apparel, cosmetics, sporting goods, electric appliances, auto accessories, and so forth. A specialty store dealing primarily in home audiovisual electronic goods instead offers a very large line of receivers, speakers, and high-fidelity equipment, offering the deepest assortment of models, styles, sizes, prices, and so on.

Not only is the extent of the product array important, but also critical is *which* assortment of goods is offered to each target consumer and where items are placed within a store. JCPenney, the U.S. mid-scale department store, had sought to change its image from "your grandmother's store"—and a relatively downscale one at that—to a trendy fashion boutique. It signed an exclusive distribution agreement with Michele Bohbot, the designer of the Bisou Bisou clothing line, previously only sold in boutiques and upscale department stores. It also hired David Hacker, a trend expert who looks for emerging fashion trends to attract the so-called Holy Grail of retail: 25- to 35-year-old women, who account for $15 billion in annual clothing revenue. This target market is a much younger, fashion-forward shopper than JCPenney's traditional, 46-year-old, female buyer. And indeed, at a Bisou Bisou fashion show in the Bronx, New York, JCPenney attracted almost 100 young women. One of them, laden with shopping bags, noted the difference: "I guess I'm going to have to start coming to JCPenney now. Wow!"[15]

Instead, the strategy failed, because JCPenney's core customer base, composed of suburban women making slightly above the national median income at an average of $63,412, sought a practical assortment of clothing and liked to use coupons when shopping, to feel as if they were getting a deal.[16] The retailer also had to fix a serious inventory management problem that led to massive stockouts during Black Friday. As it continued to experiment, JCPenney realized it had made some assortment errors too; sales of men's shoes rose when it placed them next to men's clothing, rather than next to women's shoes. Similarly, fashion jewelry located near Liz Claiborne brand options enhanced sales, because in both cases, female shoppers could see how the shoes and accessories would look with the main clothing items they were purchasing.[17]

The combination of the right assortment and quick delivery is a winning service output for Hot Topic, though. This chain of more than 600 stores targets teen girls; its CEO and directors often go to concerts to find popular new trends that can be turned into new store merchandise.[18] Hot Topic can roll out a new line (e.g., t-shirts with a popular band's logo) in just eight weeks, whereas its competitor The Gap often needs up to nine months to bring new products to store shelves. This speed is critical when the right assortment is fueled by fads, which flame and fade very quickly.

Customer Service

Customer service refers to all aspects that ease the shopping and purchase process for end-users during their interactions with commercial suppliers (for business-to-business purchases) or retailers (for business-to-consumer purchases).

The CDW Sidebar (10.1) outlines several types of customer service that are valued by small- to medium-sized business buyers, as encapsulated in the simple statement: "We're the chief technical officer for many smaller firms."

Excellent customer service can translate directly into sales and profit. But a U.S. industry that has long been plagued by poor customer service is cable and other pay television services. In American Customer Satisfaction Index (ACSI) surveys, cable TV operators often earn some of the lowest customer satisfaction scores of any company or industry.[19] Customer service is typically outsourced to third-party providers (another channel partner), which offer low pay and poor training to their employees. In contrast, DirecTV ranks at the top of its industry in customer satisfaction and enjoys high average monthly revenues from its customers, as well as a very low *churn rate* (i.e., the rate of turnover of end-users buying its service)—even though it uses the same outsourced customer service companies as some of its competitors. How does it accomplish this? It stations an employee at each of its outsourced call centers, to gain more control; it pays the call centers more for customer service, which translates into better service provision; it issues better information to customer service reps, through an overhauled information system; and it gives the customer service reps various non-monetary forms of compensation, such as free satellite TV.[20]

The type of customer service offered also must be sensitive to the targeted end-user. Cabela's, a small chain of stores catering to outdoorsy people, recognizes a key feature of its mostly male target market: these men hate to shop. To appeal to them, Cabela's makes its stores showcases of nature scenes, waterfalls, and stuffed animals, then staffs each department liberally with well-trained sales staff who must pass tests to demonstrate their knowledge of the products. Outside its rural stores, it offers kennels (for dogs) and corrals (for horses), to cater to customers who visit in the middle of a hunting trip. Cabela's augments this targeted customer service with a carefully determined product assortment. The depth of its assortment in most categories is six to ten times greater than that of competitors such as Walmart, and it stocks high-end items, not just low-priced, low-quality goods. To appeal to other members of the family, it also offers a relatively broad assortment that draws in women and children. Cabela's understands that rural shoppers want more than Walmart can provide; they care about service, fashion, and ambiance, not just price, so it can routinely draw shoppers who travel hours to reach its store (i.e., who are willing to trade off spatial convenience for superior customer service and assortment).[21]

Information Sharing

Finally, **information sharing** refers to education provided to end-users about product attributes or usage capabilities, as well as pre- and post-purchase services.

The business PC buyer values pre-sale information about what products to buy, in what combinations, with which peripheral computer devices and service packages, as well as post-sale information if and when components or systems fail.

For some manufacturers and retailers, such information sharing has been classified as *solutions retailing*, which appears crucial for generating new and upgrade sales from end-users. Home Depot offers do-it-yourself classes in all sorts of home improvement areas; computer and software companies like Hewlett-Packard (HP) and Microsoft have followed suit, setting up "experience centers" in retail stores to enhance sales of complicated products whose benefits consumers may not understand, such as Media Center PCs, digital cameras that print on computers, personal digital assistants, and the like. A collaboration between Microsoft and HP offered a series of educational programs at various retailers, designed to increase sales of HP Media Center PCs. One section of the display, called "Create," showed consumers how to use the Media Center PC as a digital photography center with Microsoft software. Other displays revealed how to use the PC for home office applications, as part of a home office network, and as a music center. The mini-classes were run by a third-party firm that staffed the retail store booths. For HP, consumers' purchase intentions increased by as much as 15 percent when they saw these product demonstrations, and further evidence indicated that the programs strengthened the products' brand image and brand equity. Such information dissemination is a costly proposition, though; Microsoft and HP bear the costs, not the retailers themselves. They also view such efforts as crucial in the short run but redundant in the longer run, because the relevant information eventually diffuses into the broader consumer population.[22] The trend is continuing as Microsoft adds retail stores to provide a two-way communication link with its end-users.

Note that price has not been listed as a service output. **Price** is what the customer pays to *consume* the bundle of product + service outputs; it is not a service that gets consumed itself. However, it is significant in the sense that end-users routinely make trade-offs among service outputs, product attributes, and price, weighing which product/service bundle (at a specific price) provides the greatest overall utility or satisfaction. Because of this trade-off, marketing researchers often investigate the relative importance of price, together with service outputs and physical product attributes, in statistical investigations (e.g., conjoint analysis, cluster analysis), consistent with our conceptual view of price as something different from a service output, just as a physical product attribute is not a service output yet still affects an end-user's overall utility.

The six service outputs we have discussed here are wide ranging but still may not be exhaustive. That is, it is risky to adopt an inflexible definition of service outputs, because different product and geographic markets naturally may demand different service outputs.[23]

SEGMENTING END-USERS BY SERVICE OUTPUT

Service outputs clearly differentiate the offerings of various marketing channels, and the success and persistence of multiple marketing channels at any one time suggests that different groups of end-users value service outputs differently. Thus, we must consider how to group end-users according to their **service output needs**, by segmenting the market into groups of end-users who differ *not in the product(s) they want to buy*, but in *how they want to buy*.

For example, at the very high end of service valuation in any market, there is a (usually small) segment of buyers who are both very service-sensitive and very price-*in*sensitive and who can be profitably served through a specialized channel. Consider men's clothing. Albert Karoll, a custom tailor in the Chicago area, sells fine custom men's clothing by visiting his customers, rather than making them visit him, as most fine clothiers do. He takes fabric, buttons, and all the makings to the customers, helps them choose the clothing they want, fits them, and then has the clothing made up before personally returning it, to deliver the finished goods and offer any final alterations. His target buyer segment clearly has a very high demand for *spatial convenience*, as stated by one of his loyal suburban customers: "For me to travel downtown is very hard to do. I'd much rather have him come here. It saves me time and money, and I get the same quality that I'd get going downtown to his store." The target customer also values custom clothing made to order—the ultimate in assortment and variety. Karoll provides quick service and delivery, both pre- and post-sale; he once flew from Chicago to Birmingham, Alabama, to alter some clothing sent to a client there, just two days after the client received the clothes and found they needed alterations. Ultimately, Karoll's target customer is a man whose most scarce asset is *time* and who thus has extremely high service output demands with little price sensitivity. Karoll does not seek to serve every man who would like to buy a suit; instead, he has carefully crafted a business centered around the delivery of service, rather than just the sale of a high-end piece of business clothing, and he knows who is in his target segment . . . and who is *not*. In this sense, the targeting decision, when applied to channel design, entails a choice of whom *not* to pursue, just as much as which segments *to* pursue.[24]

EXAMPLE: KIRANA STORES IN INDIA[25]

There are an estimated 10–12 million Kirana stores in India. These neighborhood grocers account for 96 percent of grocery sales,[26] whereas modern, air-conditioned supermarkets have failed to make headway in India, for several reasons. The Kirana stores have intimate knowledge of their customers and know to stock items preferred by individual households, sometimes bought regularly only by a single family or two. They are willing to take orders over the telephone, then deliver the selected items for free and nearly immediately. For regular customers, they often offer credit services.[27] Many Kirana stores cluster near other stores that offer different wares, so together they create a convenient shopping site for multiple items, even if it is not officially one-stop shopping. Shoppers do not have to drive on India's notoriously potholed, congested roads, as they would to access the supermarkets that tend to be more distant. Furthermore, many consumers prefer to shop for produce and dairy daily or every few days. Supermarkets are also stymied by India's laws, which favor the small Kirana stores, and by the high cost of real estate and air conditioning, which make it challenging to operate large supermarkets cost-effectively.[28] In contrast, Kirana stores use their wholesalers like warehouse services and seek to turn over all their merchandise quickly. The supermarket chains have not been able to change Indian shoppers' preferences; e-commerce also has proven difficult. Finally, without the influence to demand better deals from manufacturers, Indian supermarket chains cannot pass on deep savings to end-customers, which is often the basis of supermarkets' appeal in other nations.

From a **process perspective**, there are three general steps to segmenting end-users by service outputs. First, it is essential to generate a comprehensive list of all the potential service outputs desired by each end-user for the products being offered. This list can be derived from qualitative focus groups or exploratory interviews, designed to generate unbiased summaries of all the service outputs that apply to the particular product and market in question.[29] Such research provides a set of service outputs that might be demanded by some or all groups of end-users in the market.

Second, using this list of possible service outputs, the actual segmentation of the market can proceed in multiple ways. The market might be divided into *a priori* segments (e.g., those often used in product or advertising decisions), then analyzed to determine whether those segments share common purchasing preferences. Alternatively, research might be designed and conducted to define channel segments that best describe end-users' service output needs and purchasing patterns. This latter path is preferable, because end-users' preferred shopping and buying habits rarely correlate with their preferences for product features, media habits, lifestyles, or other traits that management and advertising agencies usually employ in their segmentation strategies. In general, channel segmentation should be designed to produce groups of buyers who (1) are maximally similar *within* a group; (2) are maximally different *between* groups; and (3) differ on dimensions that *matter* for building a distribution system. Traditional marketing research techniques such as cluster analysis and constant-sum scales can identify groups of end-users with similar service output needs. It is not enough to ask respondents about their preferences for various service outputs though. With completely free choices, most people naturally prefer more of *all* the service outputs. To obtain information that is ultimately useful for designing marketing channels that can meet the key needs of target segments, it is essential to understand how end-users actually behave in the marketplace, by asking respondents to trade off one attribute of the channel for another (e.g., locational convenience versus low price; extensive product variety versus expert sales assistance). In Sidebar 10.2, we look at the end-user needs of the customer base of a true omni-channel pioneer, 1-800-Flowers.

SIDEBAR 10.2
1-800-Flowers, an Omni-Channel Pioneer

Jim McCann opened a flower shop in 1976 on the Upper East Side of New York City,[30] but more notably, he has been a true pioneer of multi-channel shopping. Quick to spot the potential of telephone-based commerce, he plunged into the market for telephone orders of floral arrangements with 1-800-Flowers, investing heavily in call centers and staff who could provide excellent service and support. Through partnerships with independent brick-and-mortar florists, the company also could promise same-day delivery of floral arrangements nationwide.

Next, McCann realized the promise of e-commerce before nearly anyone else. The company launched its first online store (on compuserve) in 1991, had a presence on AOL, and debuted on the Web in 1995.[31] Continuing the tradition, it embraced social media immediately, becoming the first company to sell physical products via Facebook. Largely as a result of these market-sensing moves, 1-800-Flowers enjoys a 30.2 percent market share of the online floral business.[32] This positioning bodes well for the future, because even as brick-and-mortar floral shops struggle, floral sales are increasing in general, mainly through online options.[33]

An implicit element of this success story is the company's recognition that different end-users buy differently. Some need same-day delivery; others have specific assortment preferences and will wait for the particular flowers to be ready, shipped straight from growers. In addition, their preferences might extend beyond flowers, so 1-800-Flowers includes a variety of plants, gift baskets, and edible treats in its assortment, in collaboration with sibling companies such as Harry & David, Simply Chocolate, and the Popcorn Factory. In the modern global world, people send flowers to loved ones in other countries, so a florist that operates internationally is critical. If they don't quite know what to send, consumers might prefer to solicit advice from a friendly, sympathetic service representative, who will talk to them over the telephone about the best options. If they have a clear sense of their needs, they might instead order through a mobile app, and they likely want one-click capacities so they can quickly send off flowers (and receive reminders) each year in time for Mother's Day or Valentine's Day.[34]

Third, when the overall market has been segmented into similar groups of end-users, according to their preferred channel service outputs, price sensitivity, or other product-specific factors, the channel manager should name each segment to capture its identifying characteristics. Naming each segment facilitates internal communication and organizational alignment, which is helpful in executing an effective channel strategy.

Table 10.1 shows how constant-sum scales can be used to segment end-users in the business marketplace for a new high-technology product. The service outputs (references and credentials, financial stability and longevity, product demonstrations and trials), along with price sensitivity, are listed along the left-hand side; the columns represent the segments (lowest total cost, responsive support, full-service, and references and credentials) that emerge according to respondents' preferences. The names assigned to the segments derive from the strength of their preferences for specific service outputs. For example, the lowest total cost segment assigned 32 out of 100 points to the service output "lowest price" but only 8 points to "responsive problem solving after sale" output; in contrast, the responsive support segment flipped its allocations (29 points to responsive problem solving after sale, but 8 points to lowest price). Finally, the percentage of respondents in each segment appears at the bottom of each column; the majority of respondents (and thus of the population of customers at large, assuming the sample is representative) are in

Service Output Priorities	Lowest Total Cost/ Pre-Sales Info Segment	Responsive Support/ Post-Sales Segment	Full-Service Relationship Segment	References and Credentials Segment
References and credentials	5	4	6	25
Financial stability and longevity	4	4	5	16
Product demonstrations and trials	11	10	8	20
Proactive advice and consulting	10	9	8	10
Responsive assistance during decision process	14	9	10	6
One-stop solution	4	1	18	3
Lowest price	32	8	8	6
Installation and training support	10	15	12	10
Responsive problem solving after sale	8	29	10	3
Ongoing relationship with a supplier	2	11	15	1
Total	100	100	100	100
Percentage of Respondents	16%	13%	61%	10%

TABLE 10.1

Business-to-Business Channel Segments for a New High-Technology Product

Respondents allocate 100 points among the following supplier-provided service outputs, according to their importance to the company:

= *Greatest Discriminating Attributes*

= *Additional Important Attributes*

Source: Reprinted with permission of Rick Wilson, Chicago Strategy Associates, © 2000.

the full-service segment. This study supports a trade-off between price and service outputs, recognizing that a segment's demand for service outputs really reflects its willingness to pay for them—and highlights the need to include sensitivity to pricing levels in any such analysis.

Some interesting insights arise from Table 10.1. First, marketing channels serving any of the specific segments need to deliver more of some service outputs than others. Thus, it is unlikely that any one-channel strategy can satisfy the needs of all segments. For example, the lowest price is highly valued in only one segment (i.e., lowest total cost segment, representing only 16 percent of respondents). The majority of the market simply is not driven primarily by price considerations. This information is invaluable for designing channel strategies that respond to the service output needs of customers, even if doing so implies higher prices than a no-frills solution might entail. In contrast, all the segments value installation and training support at least moderately; therefore, this support capability must be designed into every single channel solution. Similar insights stem from the rows of Table 10.1, which reveal the contrasts among segments in terms of other specific service output demands. In Figure 10.2, we provide an overview of the steps involved in developing a service output segmentation template.

Appendix 10.1 outlines the process in Figure 10.2 in greater detail, with prototypical examples for completing a service output segmentation template, which is a tool for segmenting end-users to facilitate targeting by specific channel structures. Accompanying Appendix 10.1 is a blank service output segmentation template in Table 10.2, which can assist channel managers conducting end-user segmentation analyses.

TARGETING END-USER SEGMENTS

After segmenting the market and identifying each end-user segment's distinct service output needs, the channel manager can integrate these insights into an overall

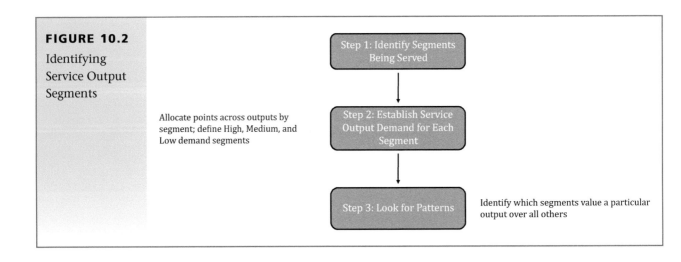

FIGURE 10.2

Identifying Service Output Segments

marketing channel design and management plan. In particular, this information should be used to:

- Assess segment attractiveness.

- Target a subset of the segments identified.

- Customize the marketing channel system solution to sell to each targeted segment.

Targeting a channel segment means choosing to focus on that segment, with the goal of achieving significant sales and profits from selling to it, just as Albert Karoll, the custom men's suit seller, has done. He recognizes that his target end-users "are business executives, men who are short on time, who work their brains out."[35] Note that this description *excludes* most buyers, as well as most buyers of business suits. Furthermore, Karoll's segmentation definition hinges not on the product being purchased but rather on the services that accompany it. Therefore, Karoll's high-service (and high-price) offering fails to meet the demands of most suit buyers, but it is ideal for Karoll's identified target buyers.

More generally, if the channel segmentation process has proceeded appropriately, targeting multiple channel segments for channel system design purposes implies the need to build different marketing channels for each segment. Because doing so can be a costly, hard-to-manage activity, channel managers likely choose an "attractive" subset of all the identified segments to target. We thus suggest a corollary to the targeting concept: *targeting means choosing which segments **not** to target*. Such choices represent difficult challenges for channel management teams, because all segments seemingly offer the potential for revenue dollars (though not always profits). Segmented service output demand information can help the channel manager choose which segments offer the greatest relative growth and profit opportunities for targeting. Even though other segments also offer some potential, only the best should be chosen for targeting. "Best" has different meanings for different companies, but it should include the size and sales potential of the targeted segment, the cost to serve them, the fit with the selling firm's competencies, and the intensity of competition for their business, among other factors.

Information on the targeted segments then can be used to design new marketing channels to meet needs or to modify existing marketing channels to better respond to demands for service outputs. A service output demand analysis can identify a new market opportunity that leads to the development of entirely new ways to sell to a particular segment. For example, fandango.com is a business formed by seven of the ten largest movie exhibitors in the United States, to sell movie tickets online (or by phone).[36] Instead of going to a movie theater the evening one wants to see a particular movie, standing in line, and perhaps finding out that the showing of that movie is sold out, fandango.com allows moviegoers to go online and purchase a ticket for a particular showing of a particular movie at a particular movie theater in advance, for a small fee per ticket. Tickets can be printed at home or picked up at the theater at convenient kiosks, saving time and lessening uncertainty for the consumer. This purchase channel provides consumers with a shorter waiting/delivery time (because there is no wait at the theater), higher spatial convenience (because they can search for and buy theater tickets online), and a very broad assortment and variety (fandango.com sells tickets to nearly 70 percent of all theaters in the United States that are enabled for remote ticketing). Clearly, fandango.com is not for every moviegoer, though, not least because of the extra charge per ticket it imposes. But fandango.com allows theaters to compete effectively against non-fandango theaters among a target segment of time-constrained moviegoers. It also might expand the total market for in-theater movie watching, because of the greater convenience it offers.

Ideally, the end-user analysis performed on service outputs supports segmenting, targeting, and positioning (channel design). Pursuing a channel strategy without this information is risky, because it is impossible to be sure that it has been executed properly, without knowing what the marketplace wants in its marketing channel. Considering the expense of setting up or modifying a marketing channel, it is prudent to perform the end-user analysis before proceeding to upstream channel decisions, which are also critical to any successful channel strategy. Performed correctly, an analysis of target segments' service output needs can be the foundation for higher profits, due to the achievement of high-margin sales with intensely loyal end-users.

OMNI-CHANNELS AND END-USER SEGMENTS

Omni-channel markets grant consumers many more and varied ways to interact with a firm; however, firms face a greater challenge to track offline interactions compared with the ease of doing so online.[37] Moreover, the proliferation of multi- and omni-channel strategies implies substantial increases in the number of end-user segments, each of which prefers and incorporates online or alternative purchasing options and interactions to varying degrees. For example, for customer service, some end-users prefer to place a call to a company; others embrace email or chat functions. Similarly, some customers prefer to browse through a paper catalog and then call a sales representative to place an order, but clearly, many others complete the entire purchase process online. Even if they adopt similar behaviors, some end-users may be webroomers while others are showroomers, so the channel strategy needs to accommodate both groups.

The greater variety of channels available, along with firms' efforts to integrate all of them into a seamless experience, also appears to have given rise to increased consumer tendencies to engage in "research shopping": research the purchase in one channel, buy in another. Such behaviors create further distinct end-user segments, each with varying degrees of knowledge and uses of online and offline channels.[38] Each channel's unique characteristics lead it to appeal distinctly to a certain segment of end-users. Thus, a key challenge of channel integration is finding ways to ensure that the unique features of a channel, which appeal to a certain group of end-users (e.g., attentive salespeople and social interactions), do not get lost (e.g., if the firm deploys self-service technologies in stores to facilitate integration of online and offline channels).[39] Technologies such as virtual and augmented reality and artificial intelligence are quickly and dramatically changing both distribution and retailing practices.[40] Their adoption by retailers and end-users suggests the notable potential to alter existing end-user channel segments even further, because technology tools can readily shift consumer channel preferences.

In the beginning of this chapter, we clarified the difference between channel segmentation and customer segmentation based on product preferences. We also caution that the two forms also could be interrelated, in that channel preferences could affect brand choice.[41] For example, an end-user who prefers shopping online might buy only those items that are available through that channel, so brands without an online presence would never even enter the consideration set. On the flipside, an end-user who strongly prefers a particular brand and likes to visit its stores still might search across many channels to gain access to that brand; if the local store suffers a stockout for example, this shopper likely goes online to make a purchase.

Take-Aways

- An end-user's decision about where or from whom to purchase a product (or service) depends not just on *what* the end-user is buying but also on *how* the end-user wants to buy.

- The elements that describe *how* the product or service can be bought are called *service outputs*. Formally, service outputs are the productive outputs of the marketing channel, over which end-users exert demand and preference influences.

- A general list of service outputs, customizable to particular marketplace contexts, is:

  ○ Bulk-breaking.
  ○ Spatial convenience.
  ○ Waiting time (or quick delivery).
  ○ Variety and assortment.
  ○ Customer service.
  ○ Information sharing.

- End-users make trade-offs among different combinations of (a) product attributes, (b) price, and (c) service outputs offered by different sellers to make final purchase decisions.

- Segmenting the market by service output demands is a useful tool for channel design, because the resulting groups of end-users are similar (within each group) in terms of the channel that best serves their needs.

- The ultimate purpose of a service output-based end-user analysis and design is to identify and assess end-user segments, target a subset of the segments identified, and customize the marketing channel system solution used to sell to each targeted segment.

- Omni-channel strategies and new technologies influence and shape end-user segments.

APPENDIX 10.1: SERVICE OUTPUT SEGMENTATION TEMPLATE—TOOLS FOR ANALYSIS

Table 10.1 shows a completed end-user segmentation analysis in the market for telecommunications equipment and services. This analysis rests on the collection of sophisticated marketing research data. Marketing channel managers generally are well advised to conduct marketing research to determine what end-users really want in the way of service outputs, because the cost of guessing incorrectly is very high in a channel context.

This Appendix describes how to complete the service output segmentation template in Table 10.2 (an empty and generic version of Table 10.1). With the assumption that the channel manager lacks detailed, quantitative marketing research data, we seek to provide an intuitive sense of how to perform such an analysis and what to do with codified information. The segmentation template is designed to help users segment the market, in ways that *matter* for distribution channel design, as well as to report on the segments' distinct demands for service outputs.

The first task is to identify the segments in the market being served. Standard segmentation measures may or may not be appropriate in a channel management context, though. A key criterion to determine whether the existing segmentation is appropriate is whether the resulting groups of buyers require different sets of service outputs. For example, we might identify two segments for buyers of laptop computers: men and women. It is likely a valid segmentation criterion for some purposes (e.g., choosing advertising media to send promotional messages) but unlikely to be useful in a channel design and management context, because there is no discernible difference in the service outputs demanded by men and women. A better segmentation thus might be business buyers, personal use buyers, and student buyers.

The next step is to fill in information about the service output demands of each identified segment on the segmentation template. More information is always better, but in the absence of detailed marketing research data, it can be useful simply to identify demands as "Low," "Medium," or "High." Then the manager can address precisely how they express their service output demands. Consider a few prototypical examples:

- A business buying laptop computers wants to buy more units than does a personal use or a student buyer. *Breaking bulk* (i.e., providing a smaller lot size) is effortful, so the business segment has LOW demand for the bulk-breaking service output, whereas the personal use buyer and student have HIGH demands for this output (i.e., they want to buy only one computer at a time).

- *Spatial convenience* may be important to all three segments, but for different reasons. For example, the "sale" of a laptop computer is not over when the unit is purchased; post-sale service is a critical factor that affects initial purchase decisions, as well as the subsequent satisfaction of end-users. We then might argue that personal use and student buyers have a relatively LOW demand for spatial convenience at the point of initial purchase, but they might express a HIGH demand for spatial convenience when it comes to getting a faulty unit fixed or obtaining technical service. Conversely, the business buyer may have a HIGH demand for spatial convenience at the initial point of purchase (e.g., require a sales rep to visit the company rather than having a company representative go to a retail store); a large enough company also may have in-house computer repair and consulting facilities and thus exhibit LOW demand for spatial convenience for post-sale service.

- The demand for *delivery/waiting time* is high if the end-user is unwilling to wait to receive the product or service. Impulse purchases are a classic product category for which almost all segments have HIGH demand for this service output. For our laptop computers, we again can differentiate between initial purchase versus post-sale service step demands. At the initial purchase, the personal use buyer probably has a LOW demand for delivery/waiting time, though a student may have a very HIGH demand for quick delivery, particularly if the unit is purchased just in time for the beginning of the school year! Finally, a business buyer may have a very HIGH demand for this service output, if the lack of the laptops means lower sales or affects employees' productivity.

  At the post-sale service stage, the personal use buyer may have a LOW demand for the delivery/waiting time service output, because he or she likely is willing to wait a few days to receive service or repairs, considering that personal uses of a computer often are not life-or-death concerns. The student instead has a very HIGH demand for the delivery/waiting time service output on the post-sale service side, because the cost of downtime for this user is very high (cannot get homework done without the unit). The business buyer also may have a LOW demand for this service output, though: its internal service facilities could make it less dependent on the manufacturer's technical service or repair facilities, and it could have excess units in inventory that can be "swapped out" for a faulty unit until it is fixed.

- *Assortment/variety* demands refer to segments' preferences for a deep assortment in a given category and for a wide variety of product category choices. In our laptop example, we might ask, how intense is each segment's demand for an assortment of computer brands, and how intense are their demands for a variety of computers, peripherals, software, and so forth? The business buyer probably has very precise brand demands (HIGH demand), because it wants conformity across the units in use in the company. This end-user has a LOW demand for assortment. Aggregated across the entire population of business buyers, though, our laptop marketer may observe considerable diversity in brand preferences. Thus, we must consider the different types of variety demands when studying markets from a micro (customer-specific) versus a macro (market-wide perspective) perspective. The business buyer may have a MEDIUM to HIGH demand for variety (e.g., software to do word processing, spreadsheets, and database management; printer ports and PC cards as peripherals), depending on the variety of tasks this buyer wants the laptops to perform. Among personal use buyers, the demand for variety is probably very LOW, because they tend to be the least sophisticated users and may demand only the most basic word processing or gaming software. However, their assortment (brand choice) demands may be HIGH; unsophisticated consumers often want to see a broad selection of models and brands before making a purchase decision. Student buyers probably fall in between, at a MEDIUM level, in their demand for assortment/variety: they may have more applications or uses for the laptop, and thus demand more peripherals and software programs, but they may not need to see a wide assortment of brands before making the purchase (the relevant brand set may be small if a school has dictated "acceptable" brands).

- Demands for *customer service* differ widely among the business, personal use, and student buyers in terms of not just levels but also *types* of customer service. The student buyer probably values home delivery very highly, as few students have cars to carry large items back from the store; the personal use buyer may not care about home delivery but value in-home installation services; and the business buyer likely cares little about either of these benefits but demands trade-in options on older machines.

- Finally, *information-sharing* demands can be separated into pre- and post-sale information elements. Before purchase, a buyer may need information about differences in physical product attributes, how components fit together in a system, and how to use the new, state-of-the-art features. After purchase, the buyer instead may have questions about which add-on peripheral devices can be used with the computer and how or what software programs versions to install onto the machine. The personal use buyer likely places the highest value on both pre- and post-sale information sharing, because she or he is unlikely to have a "support group" in place to provide key information about what, how, and where to buy. A student buyer may have more post-purchase informational needs than pre-purchase ones, particularly if the school recommends a certain subset of laptops for use. The business buyer probably has relatively low informational demands, both pre- and post-purchase, particularly if the company is large enough to identify and specify approved laptop models, then support them after purchase. However, a procurement specialist at the company may have significant pre-sale informational needs at the time decisions are made about which laptop models to select and support.

When completed with codified information, the service output segmentation template supports several strategic uses:

1. It can reveal why sales tend to cluster in one segment, to the exclusion of others. If post-sale service is poor, it will be difficult to sell to personal use and student buyers.

2. It may suggest a new channel opportunity for building sales among an underserved segment. Perhaps a channel structure can be designed that is ideally suited to the needs of student buyers. Competitors that otherwise fight solely on the basis of price for these sales then would be locked out of the sales channel.

3. Commonalities between and across segments, previously thought to be totally distinct, might emerge. For example, personal use and student buyers may share enough similarities that both can be served with only minor variations on a single channel theme.

4. The template can suggest what channel form would be best suited for serving each segment. Thus, it provides inputs to match segments to channels.

This list of service output demands cannot completely and fully characterize every demand in a specific market. For example, the customer service demand likely requires distinctions into pre- and post-sale service elements, as does the information-sharing service output demand. However, this framework provides an initial means to understand the types of service outputs firms must provide to appeal to end-users.

<table>
<tr><td rowspan="2">**TABLE 10.2**

Service Output
Segmentation
Template</td><td colspan="7">SERVICE OUTPUT DEMAND</td></tr>
</table>

Segment Name / Descriptor	Bulk-Breaking	Spatial Convenience	Delivery/ Waiting Time	Assortment / Variety	Customer Service	Information Sharing
1.						
2.						
3.						
4.						
5.						

Instructions: If quantitative market research data are available, enter numerical ratings in each cell. If not, adopt an intuitive ranking system, noting for each segment whether demand for the given service output is *High*, *Medium*, or *Low*.

NOTES

1 The sources for this Sidebar include Campbell, Scott (2003), "CDW-G calls on VARs," *Computer Reseller News*, November 17 (No. 1071), 162; Campbell, Scott (2004), "CDW snags companywide Cisco premier status: Relationship advances reseller's bid to build services business," *Computer Reseller News*, 12, April 12; Gallagher, Kathleen (2002), "CDW computer remains afloat despite market's choppy waters," *Milwaukee Journal Sentinel*, September 29, 4D; Jones, Sandra (2004), "Challenges ahead for CDW: Dell deals make inroads in already difficult market," *Crain's Chicago Business*, June 28, 4; Kaiser, Rob (2000), "Vernon Hills, Ill., computer products reseller has an approach to win business," *Chicago Tribune*, August 16; McCafferty, Dennis (2002), "Growing like gangbusters: Sales at Chicago-area CDW-government shot up 63 percent from 2000 to 2001," *VAR Business*, July 8; Moltzen, Edward (2003), "Looking for SMB traction, Gateway inks reseller pact with CDW," *CRN*, May 26, 55; O'Heir, Jeff (2003), "CDW teams with small VARs to access government biz," *Computer Reseller News*, August 25 (No. 1059), 6; O'Heir, Jeff (2003), "Time to move on," *Computer Reseller News*, October 20 (No. 1067), 98; Schmeltzer, John (2003), "CDW pulls out the stops to reach small business," *Chicago Tribune*, September 8; Zarley, Craig and Jeff O'Heir (2003), "Seeking solutions: CDW, Gateway and Dell come calling on solution providers for services expertise," *Computer Reseller News*, Vol. 16, September 1.

2 http://investor.cdw.com, date retrieved June 12, 2018.

3 www.dell.com/learn/us/en/uscorp1/press-releases/2015-10-12-dell-and-cdw-expand-partnership, date retrieved June 15, 2018.

4 Lucy, Jim (2018), "31 flavors," *Electrical Wholesaling*, March, 4.

5 Boryana, Dimitrova and Bert Rosenbloom (2010), "Standardization versus adaption in global markets: Is channel strategy different?" *Journal of Marketing Channels*, 17 (2), 157–176.

6 Diamond, David (2007), "Wall of values," *Progressive Grocer*, 86 (15), November 1.

7 USDA Gain Report, Report Number: CH0001, 1/26/2017.

8 Bucklin, Louis P. (1966), *A Theory of Distribution Channel Structure*, Berkeley, CA: IBER Special Publications; Bucklin, Louis P. (1972), *Competition and Evolution in the Distributive Trades*, Englewood Cliffs, NJ: Prentice Hall; Bucklin, Louis P. (1978), *Productivity in Marketing*, Chicago, IL: American Marketing Association; see pp. 90–94.

9 Sailor, Matt, "10 things you should buy in bulk," *HowStuffWorks*, www.money.howstuffworks.com.

10 Jain, Sanjay (2012), "Marketing of vice goods: A strategic analysis of the package size decision," *Marketing Science*, January, 36–51.

11 Ibid.
12 https://venturebeat.com/2017/02/26/mobile-ordering-lets-customers-cut-in-line-and-thats-a-problem, date retrieved June 20, 2018.
13 www.greatclips.com, date retrieved June 20, 2018.
14 "Price of elasticity of demand," *Convention Center Task Force*, San Diego County Tax Payer Association, July 31, 2009, www.conventioncentertaskforce.org.
15 Daniels, Cora (2003), "J.C. Penney dresses up," *Fortune*, 147 (11, June 9), 127–130.
16 Wahba, Phil (2016), "The man who's re-[re-re] inventing JC Penney," *Fortune*, March 1, 77–86.
17 Ibid.
18 "Hot Topic, Inc. reports 1st quarter financial results," *Hot Topic Inc.*, May 18, 2011, www.investor relations.hottopic.com.
19 www.theacsi.org/index.php?option=com_content&view=article&id=147&catid=&Itemid=212&i=Subscription+Television+Service, date retrieved June 20, 2018.
20 Moran, Francis (2012), "Don't wait until your customers say goodbye to tell . . ." *Francis Moran and Associates*, September 20. http://bx.businessweek.com.
21 Helliker, Kevin (2002), "Retailer scores by luring men who hate to shop," *The Wall Street Journal Online*, December 17.
22 Saranow, Jennifer (2004), "Show, don't tell," *The Wall Street Journal Online*, March 22.
23 Kasturi Rangan, V., Melvyn A.J. Menezes, and E.P. Maier (1992), "Channel selection for new industrial products: A framework, method, and application," *Journal of Marketing*, 56, 72–73. These authors define five service outputs in their study of industrial goods: product information, product customization, product quality assurance, after-sales service, and logistics. Some outputs are specific examples of the generic service outputs defined by Bucklin (e.g., logistics refers to spatial convenience and waiting/delivery time), yet their work also highlights the value of being aware of the specific application.
24 Stanek, Steve (2003), "Custom tailor finds house calls often worth the trip," *Chicago Tribune Online Edition*, July 13.
25 Mediratta, Arvind (2018), "The Kirana store will remain evergreen," *Hindu Business Line*, www.the hindubusinessline.com/opinion/columns/the-kirana-store-will-remain-evergreen/article24016592. ece, date retrieved June 19, 2018.
26 Ibid.
27 Anonymous (2014), "A long way from the supermarket," *Economist*, October 18.
28 Ibid.
29 Such data sometimes already exist. For example, in the computer industry, data on service outputs valued by end-users are collected by firms like IntelliQuest, Inc. and International Data Group.
30 Forte, Daniela (2015), "How 1-800-Flowers rode the wave of change," http://multichannel merchant.com/must-reads/1-800-flowers-rode-wave-change, date retrieved June 19, 2018.
31 Ibid.
32 Shropshire, Corilyn (2018), "Amid sagging sales and a shrinking stock, FTD sees way forward in new HQ, tech investments," *Chicago Tribune*, May 29.
33 Ibid.
34 www.1800flowers.com/about-us-company-overview, date retrieved June 19, 2018.
35 Stanek (2003), op. cit.
36 See www.fandango.com for more details.
37 Ailawadi, Kusum L. and Paul W. Farris (2017), "Managing multi-and omni-channel distribution: Metrics and research directions," *Journal of Retailing*, 93 (1), 120–135.
38 Herhausen, Dennis, Jochen Binder, Marcus Schoegel, and Andreas Herrmann (2015), "Integrating bricks with clicks: Retailer-level and channel-level outcomes of online–offline channel integration," *Journal of Retailing*, 91 (2), 309–325.

39 Cao, Lanlan and Li Li (2015), "The impact of cross-channel integration on retailers' sales growth," *Journal of Retailing*, 91 (2), 198–216.

40 Grewal, Dhruv, Anne Roggeveen, and Jens Nordfalt (2017), "The future of retailing," *Journal of Retailing*, 93 (1), 1–6.

41 Neslin, Scott A., Kinshuk Jerath, Anand Bodapati, Eric T. Bradlow, John Deighton, Sonja Gesler, Leonard Lee, Elisa Montaguti, Rahul Telang, Raj Venkatesan, Peter C. Verhoef, and Z. John Zhang (2014), "The interrelationships between brand and channel choice," *Marketing Letters*, 25, 319–330.

CHAPTER 11

Omni-Channel Strategy

LEARNING OBJECTIVES

After reading this chapter, you will be able to:

- Understand the challenges involved in creating a successful omni-channel strategy.
- Define the four pillars on which a successful omni-channel strategy rests.
- Recognize the role of technology in creating successful omni-channel strategies.
- Outline the tasks involved in assessing omni-channel performance.
- Describe the need for seamlessness in an omni-channel context.

INTRODUCTION

As we have outlined throughout this book, not just manufacturers but all channel members need an omni-channel strategy, as a key element of their branding and channel strategy, to remain relevant for consumers. In the omni-channel era, consumers can avoid or escape firm-dictated or prescribed decision processes for their information search, product evaluation, or purchase or post-purchase efforts.[1] Along with our definition of *omni-channel* as the integration of customers' ability to research, purchase, communicate, engage with, and consume a brand through a seamless customer experience across online, physical, mobile, social, and communication channels (Chapter 1), we have emphasized the challenges that manufacturers, retailers, and other sellers face in the omni-channel era, especially with regard to cross-channel coordination, cooperation, and relationship management.

EXAMPLE: A PROTOTYPICAL OMNI-CHANNEL SHOPPER (USA)[2]

Neal is a 19-year-old college student, shopping for a moderately priced, sporty-looking, but dressy watch. On Amazon Prime Day, he searched the site and found a nice Bulova watch at a fabulous price that he ordered promptly. But when he received it, Neal found the watch too heavy on his wrist, so he returned it. The experience left him hesitant to buy another watch online without trying it on first, so he visited a local Costco store, but nothing in its limited range of offerings appealed to him. Recalling that his family has long been loyal to Macy's, he took a trip to the mall and found a Seiko watch at the department store that he liked. While still in the store, he brought up the Amazon app on his smartphone and found the same watch, but for $120 less. He turned to the Macy's salesperson and asked if the store would offer a price match, but the counter staffer indicated it would not and advised him to buy the watch from Amazon. He did so.

Even if both manufacturers and retailers recognize the importance of distributing through multiple channels, to add to their value proposition and expand their ability to reach customers, they often grow by adding channels in a disjointed fashion, without any consideration of creating a seamless customer experience.[3] Consider T-Mobile, for example: it offers phones and service plans through its website, company-owned stores, and third-party retailers. At T-Mobile company stores, customers must pay a $20 service fee to purchase a phone, a charge not levied on customers visiting T-Mobile's website.[4] Such a multi-channel organization encourages each channel to focus on optimizing its own efficiencies, rather than the overall results, which creates mismatches in the data, pricing, and inventory available across channels.[5]

The apparel maker Levi-Strauss generates one-third of its sales through its own website and company-owned retail stores, but two-thirds come from its partnerships with leading department store chains including JC Penney, Macy's, and Kohl's.[6] Therefore, Levi's must manage its relationship with channel partners, which account for the bulk of its sales, but at the same time, it must make it easy for consumers to find and purchase its products directly from Levi's company-owned channels. To manage these dual demands, Levi's focuses strategically on creating consistent omni-channel experiences in any channel that customers might choose to access. Of course, each customer experience comprises many phases (e.g., information acquisition, research, purchase, payment, delivery or pickup, returns),[7] and Levi's can exert more control over the customer experience on its own website and company-owned retail stores. But it also seeks to build strong partnerships with its retail partners to encourage them to support and help it create consistent omni-channel experiences. It does this by investing in sophisticated information systems that can track the customer journey, inventory, and returns, and enable it to work closely with retailers to forecast in-store demand and leverage offline and online data to provide them with an integrated view of the customer.[8]

A successful omni-channel experience also means that the company starts with and continues to gather deep, rich data to understand what consumers want, supports meaningful engagement modes with consumers, designs effective and efficient retailing and e-commerce capabilities, and maintains successful partnerships with channel partners. Ultimately, a successful omni-channel strategy means consumers can buy easily, in the mode and manner they prefer.

EXAMPLE: STARBUCKS (CHINA)[9]

Starbucks counts China as its second largest market, behind the United States, where more than 3,400 restaurants dot the landscape in approximately 140 Chinese cities. In 2017, the largest Starbucks in the world opened in Shanghai. Unlike the nearly saturated U.S. market, China promises substantial room to grow, such that Starbucks plans to double the number of stores. The effort will not be without hurdles, though; Starbucks faces tough competition from the Chinese startup Luckin Coffee. Launched in 2017, Luckin offers beverage delivery services, ordered via mobile apps, from its 660 stores throughout China. It took Starbucks nearly 12 years to open that many stores.[10] Many Luckin stores only offer delivery and solely accept mobile payments,[11] but its app allows customers to watch a livestream of their drink being prepared. In addition, its drinks cost approximately half of what Starbucks charges.[12] Without a well-developed delivery system, Starbucks had to collaborate with the retail giant Alibaba to deliver beverages to Chinese consumers, though this partnership also has created a new potential channel, such that Hema supermarkets, run by Alibaba, may soon start hosting Starbucks delivery kiosks.

KEY CHALLENGES OF THE OMNI-CHANNEL APPROACH

The challenges associated with delivering a seamless omni-channel experience to customers vary somewhat across the different types of sellers attempting to establish it. For example, for **online-only** stores, the cost of customer acquisition remains rather high; they have to battle to achieve customer awareness, attention, and share of wallet.[13] In response, some e-tailers have opened physical, offline stores, which they must integrate into their omni-channel strategy. Real Real, the luxury consignment site, maintains physical locations mainly as fulfillment centers for online orders. When a customer tries on an item in the physical store, the website automatically puts it on hold, to ensure that the same item does not get sold simultaneously to two people. The fulfillment centers also provide repair and valuation services for items sold through a consignment arrangement, and staffers help customers learn about the potential resale value of items they are considering purchasing.[14]

Brick-and-mortar stores have a different problem: customers tend to view them solely as physical locations and ignore their e-commerce websites or offerings. Such a situation restricts the e-commerce operations from reaching their full potential,[15] including their ability to help consumers purchase anywhere and anytime, in support of an effective, seamless experience.

EXAMPLE: WALMART (USA/GLOBAL)

Walmart sells more than 67 million items in its stores and online.[16] Yet its online portfolio of approximately 19 million items is dwarfed by the 365 million items available on Amazon.[17] Still, even as same-store sales have fallen flat, Walmart has achieved a significant boost in its e-commerce sales,[18] prompting the retail giant to embrace its omni-channel future—and compete even harder against Amazon—through several notable moves. It acquired an Amazon competitor, Jet.com.[19] It introduced a scan-and-go app that allows consumers to scan items as they place them in physical shopping carts, provide a mobile payment, and then simply show their receipts as they exit the store.[20] To enhance the synergy between in-store and online shopping, Walmart requires its suppliers to deal with a single buyer, responsible for making purchase decisions for both e-commerce and in-store merchandise. Anticipating drastic changes to the overall shopping environment in the next few decades, Walmart aims to allow its mobile site to evolve into a personal shopping assistant that helps consumers make informed choices, wherever they might be.[21] Then the brick-and-mortar stores can emerge as desirable, go-to locations, attracting shoppers by featuring compelling experience goods, such as restaurants, hair salons, healthcare services, demonstrations, and sampling. Taking the omni-channel even further, Walmart seeks to integrate consumers into the supply chain, by encouraging them to create original content and serve as beneficial influencers. Accordingly, Walmart's omni-channel strategy highlights the ongoing need to develop better consumer analytics, especially those that can attribute sales to specific channels.

For both types of retailers, a key question revolves around whether they should target the same customer base, both online and offline. Brick-and-mortar retailers can overcome their shelf space and **trade area** (i.e., the proximal geographic region from which the store draws the bulk of its customers) constraints when they move online. Accordingly, they could carry a much wider array of products online and cater to a wider customer base, including segments that differ substantially from the members of its core, store-based customer group. Expanding the base has clear appeal for retailers, but different merchandise assortments, catering to different customers, also could create a completely different type of store online, one whose image might not match the retailer's conventional, offline image.

Such expanded assortments also might increase the level of competition that the retailer faces. For example, if the well-known retailers Walmart, Costco, and Best Buy all carry televisions on their websites, they become direct competitors online. If a consumer browsing online finds a low price for their desired television on Walmart.com, she or he might be willing to buy it, even if this consumer rarely visits a physical Walmart store. At the same time, Walmart can stock more, and perhaps more high-end, televisions in its online store, which might appeal to a customer demographic that is far more affluent than its typical shopper profile. This would result in Walmart becoming a direct competitor of Best Buy and invading their space. Walmart has invested heavily in e-commerce to compete effectively against Amazon and is also going after a more affluent audience through its acquisition of Jet.com.[22]

Another category of sellers challenged to create omni-channel strategies is **manufacturers**, which must find ways to maintain and manage healthy partnerships while also expanding their direct-to-consumer sales. Doing so demands acquiring necessary retailing expertise, especially if they set up their own retail stores. For example, to build brand awareness and offer a unique customer experience, retailers might design dedicated stores, or they might insert dedicated, clearly demarcated stores-within-a-store in existing retail locations. In the omni-channel age, manufacturers are increasingly held responsible for understanding and contributing to the consumer journey. Consumers can easily visit a manufacturer's website, where they expect to find detailed product information, even before they go to a store to interact with the product or obtain recommendations from a salesperson. For manufacturers, a key objective is to manage channel conflict, which likely means making sure they do not undercut the price position of their retail partners, but still ensure a well-designed channel strategy that meets customers' needs.

THE FOUR PILLARS OF AN OMNI-CHANNEL STRATEGY

Even as we emphasize the benefits and appeal of an effective omni-channel strategy, we also must recognize that not all companies plan to adopt omni-channel strategies, and not all consumers want to be omni-channel consumers. A consumer who does not use a smartphone will never shop the mobile channel; someone who prefers to use cash might shop online occasionally but is not truly an omni-channel consumer. Although modern sellers likely cannot avoid adding channels, if they hope to remain in business, they might exhibit a multi-channel, instead of a truly omni-channel, strategy. For example, automobile manufacturers establish channel arrangements that heavily emphasize offline channels to interact with customers and rely on their online operations mainly for branding or informational purposes.[23] At the other extreme, industries that have been radically altered by digitalization trends (e.g., publishing, music) have shifted most of their focus to online channels, with less attention and resources devoted to their "legacy" offline channels.[24]

But for those companies and consumers who understand the benefits and actively pursue seamless omni-channel interactions, it becomes necessary to integrate retail, social, mobile, and mass communication channels, with the goal of

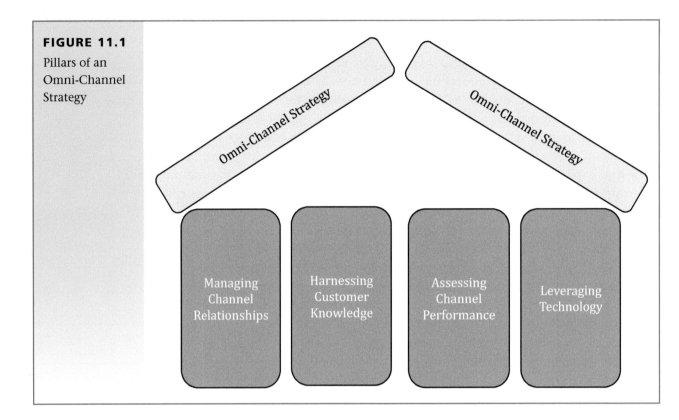

FIGURE 11.1

Pillars of an Omni-Channel Strategy

Managing Channel Relationships

Harnessing Customer Knowledge

Assessing Channel Performance

Leveraging Technology

maximizing customers' experiences and total brand sales across all channels.[25] We argue that such a strategy is metaphorically a canopy, held up by four pillars, as we depict in Figure 11.1:

1. Harnessing customer knowledge.

2. Leveraging technology.

3. Managing channel relationships.

4. Assessing channel performance.

Harnessing Customer Knowledge

The first pillar is deep, data-driven understanding and appreciation of the customer. An omni-channel environment is data rich, so firms have means and opportunity to gain intimate insights into consumer needs, preferences, and behaviors. An omni-channel marketer should leverage data from multiple sources: in-store visits, calls to customer service, loyalty program data, web and mobile visits, and social media. With these combined data, omni-channel marketers can design the best, most efficient, individualized customer experiences. In turn, customers can move among channels, depending on the specific characteristics of the product, the service, and the channel, as well as their own preferences and goals.[26] For example, even on its Instagram page, Nordstrom lists "shoppable" posts that consumers can click to obtain product details and make a purchase, without ever leaving the social media site.[27]

Because an omni-channel shopper moves across channels to complete the purchase process, a key goal is to understand what drives a consumer to choose a particular channel at each specific stage and for various reasons, such as seeking sources of information or wanting to complete the actual purchase.[28] That is, the importance that consumers assign to each channel depends on their purchase stage and the purchase situation.[29] Consumers who use more channels tend to shop more frequently, offer greater lifetime value, and increase firm revenues more than customers who only patronize a single channel.[30] We previously discussed (see Chapter 1) the practices of webrooming (to research online and buy in store) and showrooming (to research in store and buy online); in these clear examples, omni-channel consumers use the different channels distinctly for their information versus purchase needs. Omni-channel integration thus involves integration across not just channel types but also purchase stages.[31] For example, incentivizing online shoppers to visit offline physical stores increases profits, but incentivizing store shoppers to go online decreases them,[32] mainly because consumers tend to engage in impulse shopping in-store, where experiential products such as clothing can catch their eye. This scenario also means they tend to compare prices less when they are in the store rather than shopping online.[33] Online shoppers within "reasonable" distance to a store thus might be encouraged to visit physical stores through tactics such as supporting in-store pickup or sending coupons that are only redeemable in stores.

In addition, each customer may take a different path through the purchase process, so marketers need to identify, recognize, and minimize any potential or perceived hurdles along the way.[34] According to a recent study, to do so, marketers must address a prominent and persistent challenge, namely being able to recognize and access customer information across multiple channels and devices.[35] In practice, firms may access less data about a consumer than is available, due to the fragmentation of their interactions. Without comprehensive insights, though, the firm cannot appeal optimally to customers, nor can it educate them about all its omni-channel capabilities. With a focus on the customer interaction with a brand (manufacturer brand or private label), the variety of communication (traditional media, online, sales force) and marketing channels is vast.[36]

Because not all customers want the same thing, the degree of heterogeneity or homogeneity of customer segments becomes a matter of great import. Even if marketers know that consumers rely on both brick-and-mortar stores and online stores, the extent to which they visit each channel varies. For example, banks have made significant investments in information technology, and more than one-quarter of bank customers only use digital channels. But even if these consumers are less costly to serve, because they are not using more expensive, in-person branch services, they seem less satisfied and less connected with their banks.[37] Marketers need to manage relationships with each customer segment, but even when they enter the same segment, due to their similar channel usage patterns, different consumers value different attributes more or less. Some consumers demand next-day delivery; others are more focused on obtaining the lowest price and willing to wait longer to receive the product.

Combining these notions, we argue that the task before today's omni-channel marketers is to find ways to integrate customer data from multiple touchpoints to identify an effective segmentation strategy that enables the firm to deliver what each consumer segment wants, without wasting resources on offers that specific segments do not value or are unwilling to pay to obtain, while also identifying any future customer-related challenges and opportunities by mining their data.[38] As the Luckin Coffee example showed, Starbucks missed an opportunity to meet Chinese consumers' latent need for delivery-only coffee stores.

Moreover, strong omni-channel operations (just like any form of sales and marketing) require effective store retailing, e-commerce, and merchandising capabilities.[39] Online customers express deeper connections to a brand when they visit a showroom, and retail salespeople can get a better sense of their needs by interacting with customers in person.[40] Yet in the future, stores might continue shrinking in size, increasingly functioning as showrooms and experience centers rather than fulfillment centers.[41] As these developments arise, it would be difficult to integrate across channels without a clear mastery of the operational elements and strong ability to keep up with the changes in the landscape of each channel.

Leveraging Technology

With regard to the second pillar that holds up the canopy of an omni-channel strategy, it is worth noting that technology essentially initiated and has enabled the omni-channel age. Thus mastery of technology clearly is necessary to integrate across channels; existing tools enable firms to perform cost-efficient inventory management, synchronize inventory availability across channels, and establish in-store pickup or delivery to get their offerings into consumers' hands in the shortest, most cost-effective way. Technology also can be leveraged to enable customers to make better, more informed choices or facilitate their shopping experience. Finally, as a communication tool, technology is invaluable, allowing interactions that provide customers with detailed product information, product comparison tools, or customized promotions.

With the proliferation of smartphones worldwide, omni-channel marketers in particular must ensure their websites are mobile friendly and that their brands can be found through mobile searches.[42] To remain competitive, brands must support mobile payments, invest in cybersecurity, and guarantee that they can protect consumer privacy and secure transactions.[43] Mobile channels also can serve to update customers on promotions, send them real-time targeted promotions, and keep them informed at each stage of the delivery process. In a related effort, companies should develop a social media strategy and enable interactive consumer experiences through social media, allowing consumers to engage with firms and learn about the latest offerings, various product features, uses of various product features, installations, and troubleshooting. In parallel, firms might develop apps or incorporate gaming into their omni-channel strategy.

Consider the healthcare industry as an interesting example. It is fragmented and has been relatively slow to embrace online experiences,[44] though that status is changing, as consumers increasingly turn to reviews to find the best physicians or queue up a video chat with a medical professional to receive a diagnosis of easily treatable illnesses. They can access their medical records electronically and order prescription refills through mobile apps, as well as have those prescriptions delivered to their door. As wearable technology devices become more sophisticated and widely adopted, these technologies also could help monitor patient health, giving physicians detailed, real-time information about their health status. As this example shows, leveraging technology means vastly expanding the omni-channel possibilities.[45]

The use of technologies also should span every stage in the purchase process, wherever they take place.[46] For example, retailers might develop apps that consumers can use in their physical stores, to accept mobile payments and allow shoppers to bypass checkout lines, or else to provide them with e-coupons that reflect location-based promotions. Alternatively, technology tools can facilitate more seamless integration across channels, as in arrangements such as click-and-collect, showrooming, and ordering a home delivery of heavy products while in the store. Other technologies are more devoted to the decision-making stage, including examples we have noted previously in this book, such as virtual mirrors in fitting rooms, online comparison tools, and self-service kiosks that help consumers scan QR codes and access pricing information, product reviews, and so forth.[47,48] By leveraging technology to understand the customer's **journey**, sellers make it easy for customers to complete the purchase, often without ever being tempted to compare offers from other sellers.[49] This concept of a customer journey refers to combinations of steps and interactions between the consumer and brand, such that people follow different paths and journeys. For marketers, the goal is to make these journeys efficient and easy, by predicting and removing any hurdles along the way.[50] Ambitious companies even might try proactively to redesign consumer journeys, by altering their organizational structure to reflect the stages of the journey, rather than products, brands, or other commonly used elements. As Sidebar 11.1 details, L'Oreal created a Make-Up Genius app—an excellent example of how technology can move consumers along in their journey to purchase the right cosmetics for them.

Cosmetic consumers can find their favorite products in various channels, including direct selling consultants such as Mary Kay or Avon representatives, drugstores, discount stores, and department stores. A popular, traditional sales model involves higher-end make-up products being sold by dedicated beauty consultants who staff the counters in department stores. These experts in the field can spend extended time with luxury shoppers and recommend products that work best with the customer's skin tone or style.

But not all consumers have the patience, ability, or desire to spend an hour with a beauty consultant in a store. In-store purchases of cosmetics declined by about 17 percent between 2011 and 2016.[51] L'Oreal, as the world's largest cosmetics company, with its offerings of lipstick, lip gloss, eye shadow, mascara, make-up foundation, concealers, and blush,[52] has responded to these trends by creating a make-up app that enables consumers to use their smartphones to access a virtual beauty consultant.[53]

The Make-Up Genius app relies on users' phone cameras and proprietary image capture technology to reflect back to consumers how they would look if they put on specific make-up products, from various angles.[54] Once consumers devise their favorite look, they can share the image and get instant feedback from friends. The app also allows consumers to scan various products while they are in stores, apply them to their faces virtually, and check how they look, even before they open a bottle.

Technology-enabled data analytics support advanced personalization, price optimization, and delivery efforts too.[55] Data analytics might lead to unique product or product bundle ideas. The insights also might prompt sellers to organize their product lines more efficiently, in accordance with consumers' actual purchase paths and search habits.[56] For example, old-fashioned, centralized distribution centers that ship items in bulk to stores are no longer optimal, because this model struggles to deliver individual items to residences efficiently. Data analytics also can specify which items omni-channel sellers should limit only to certain channels, rather than allowing their online channel to become an **endless aisle** that sells virtually everything. Some items that the retailer carries in-store, such as those with high weight-to-value ratios, including bags of cement or large packages of rice, may not be worth the shipping costs and should be designated for only in-store or click-and-collect channels.

As this example suggests, a good omni-channel seller integrates inventory and pricing information across channels, to avoid cross-channel competition or confusion among consumers. Firms might designate and clearly mark certain items as only available online; if they charge different prices across channels, they should offer a clear description and explanation for why. When Walmart acquired Jet.com, it also gained access to Jet's proprietary smart cart technology that relies on real-time dynamic pricing mechanisms and adjusts the prices customers pay for the items in their electronic shopping basket, according to the number of items they order, where in the supply chain the items are located, and whether a customer is willing to forgo return privileges.[57]

With regard to their inventory management, the best solution matches sellers' wider strategy. Retailers operating just a few locations might be better served by a centralized inventory management system, but such a design could be risky if the central location experiences bad weather or other disasters, such that it cannot react with sufficient speed to shifts in demand in other geographical locations.[58] Larger operations thus tend to adopt hub-and-spoke models, with larger stores acting as hubs that ship orders to both smaller stores and to customers who have ordered online.[59] In this setup, the sellers need a sophisticated order management system to synchronize inventory across hubs, spokes, and distribution centers, in an effort to find the least expensive means to get products to consumers quickly, while also avoiding stockouts anywhere in the supply chain. In essence, technology can get customers the products they want, at a time and place of their choosing, according to what they are willing to pay. Retailers increasingly rely on artificial intelligence (AI) tools to make this a reality.

Obviously, the use of technology is not limited to product markets. It can motivate consumers to sign up for **subscription services** and automatic replenishment. Through the use of advanced technologies, the service providers can "kick up" the service by several notches, such as by applying predictive analytics to time when various offerings should be shipped, right before the consumer runs out of supply. Such technology uses can create loyal customers, closely tied to the firm or retailer. For example, the Vitamin Shoppe's Spark Autodelivery service is integrated with the retailer's loyalty program, for which customers can sign up while visiting one of the chain's 775 stores, online, or in its mobile app.[60]

Managing Channel Relationships

The third pillar of an effective omni-channel strategy is managing relationships with channel partners—be it distributors, retailers, or franchise partners—and breaking down organizational silos so that different units work together and with the same purpose (i.e., to deliver the best possible customer experience). We have dealt with this pillar at length in previous chapters, with the consistent reminder that the focus is on the whole, which is greater than the sum of its parts. A team effort and team-oriented approach are critical. A retailer, at an organizational level, must define and incentivize actions that overcome organizational silos and optimize the success of the entire system. Doing so also means carefully managing the interests of each individual member and element of the supply chain, whether it be individual store managers or the design of e-commerce operations, to ensure they do not conflict with one another or the goals of the organization as a whole.

As we outlined in detail in Chapter 2, retailers and manufacturers should conduct a careful audit of the contributions of each channel, their incentive systems, and how they assign credit for achievements to each channel. Along with these audit systems, they need training programs to educate employees about the role that each channel plays in generating customer leads or sales, contributing to customer satisfaction and loyalty, and helping other channels. When e-commerce was still brand new, store managers often complained about the risk of possible cannibalization of their store sales, creating a new form of channel conflict. The companies that dealt best with this new concern made sure to train managers about the potential benefits of a collaborative e-commerce channel, but they also protected those managers' interests, often by crediting stores for online sales that took place within their trade area. Once managers got more familiar, they could more easily recognize the synergies across channels, such as when click-and-collect services help get more consumers into the store, to pick up their already ordered items, but also potentially to purchase additional items that the store promotes to them. Thus, for example, a grocery retailer might have a preordered dinner ready for customers to pick up on their way home and could send them a coupon for a special bakery item to encourage them to grab something for dessert too. In Sidebar 11.2, we take a closer look at some of the possibilities and challenges associated with managing multiple channels in the automobile industry.

SIDEBAR 11.2
Omni-Channels and Car Buying

Automobiles are a high-involvement purchase for most consumers. In the United States, most manufacturers sell vehicles through franchised dealerships, and prior to the Internet age, buyers would go from dealership to dealership to learn about car models in their consideration set, inspect and test drive the vehicles, and receive offers from the seller. Both the manufacturers and the dealerships relied heavily on television and newspaper advertising to inform consumers about brands and promotional offers. Even though a sticker on each car listed the manufacturer's suggested retail price, buyers and car salespeople usually engaged in intense haggling to arrive at the terms of the deal—a process that many consumers found stressful and unpleasant. To arm themselves and overcome some of their information disadvantages, buyers might consult industry sources, such as the Kelley Blue Book or *Consumer Reports*, to gather expert evaluations and reasonable prices to pay for additional features.

As it has in so many industries, the arrival of the Internet age changed the entire market. For example, a new partner entered the channel, in the form of infomediaries or information aggregators. Consumers could visit sites such as Edmunds.com to get even more detailed information, often specific to their geographic locations, about vehicle specifications such as pricing, fuel economy, mileage, and various available features. Many sites also incorporated comparison tools to help shoppers review different models head-to-head. In response, car dealership and manufacturer websites added more detailed information, videos, and photographs of their vehicles. Dealerships also have hired Internet sales agents to conduct the purchase interaction completely online, engaging in email exchanges and chat features to answer questions and complete the sale.

As a result, the car-buying consumer journey has changed. Whereas once dealerships' territories were clearly demarcated, today consumers who have settled on a make and model might contact multiple dealerships to find the best deal. Distance to a particular dealership is less of a hindrance. In addition, according to a Bain and Co. study, today consumers start researching their car purchase about nine weeks before they complete it, and 60 percent of buyers already have decided on the price, make, and model before they ever visit a dealership. Then the average number of dealerships they visit is smaller, down to just 2.4.[61]

Yet auto manufacturers and dealerships generally have been slow to keep up with these trends. Showrooming (rather than vast lots with thousands of cars) and virtual reality test drives are likely to become the norm. Some consumers still might want to visit a dealership to iron out the final details for the vehicle configurations and financing, but an increasing number of them are happy to get these negotiations done online. Therefore, to deliver a seamless omni-channel experience, the manufacturers and dealerships will have to figure out ways to share data and gather much more complete information about each potential buyer, so that they can interact and engage with customers in the research stage, before they have made up their minds.[62] It is up to marketers to develop means to capture customer contacts made through touchpoints across all channels. Traditional dealer lots are very expensive to maintain, so virtual showrooms represent a key opportunity,[63] such that a dealership could encourage consumers to visit their virtual showrooms to select a car of interest, then perhaps offer test drives by bringing the car to the consumer's home or office, as an advanced service offering.

Turning upstream, another element of managing omni-channel relationships involves channel partners such as franchisors, which need to provide their franchisees with the tools and "expert power" to cater effectively to customers. The franchisors likely need to establish an overall IT infrastructure and real-time data, so the franchisees can achieve operational efficiencies and sufficient customer knowledge. At the same time, such systems enable franchisors to monitor franchisee performance and provide feedback. Some franchisees may resent such close monitoring, though, which could become a source of conflict as franchisees who signed up to run their "own" businesses may resent what they perceive as excessive and suffocating oversight. Franchisors could reduce such conflict by demonstrating the clear benefits to franchisees in terms of additional profits and sales.

The key to a successful omni-channel strategy is that the digital experiences have to be integrated with the in-store experiences. Essentially, there should be no breakdown when consumers "travel" between the online and offline worlds. Such breakdowns would happen, say, if a consumer ordered merchandise only and then called the store to ask some questions and the store had no idea or was unable to pull up the customer's order. We have raised the issue of consumers ordering food via an app and then "cutting in line" to go pick it up in the restaurant, while those not using the app find the lines are even longer than they had anticipated because the "invisible" online orders were being prepared.

It should be clear by now that the nature of the omni-channel strategy varies by industry as some products are easier to consume digitally (e.g., movies, music, computer software, and e-books) and the online purchase rate varies significantly by product category (e.g., airline tickets versus groceries versus automobiles).

Assessing Channel Performance

In Chapter 2 we provided an overview of various omni-channel metrics. In Figure 11.2, we provide a snapshot of omni-channel performance assessments as the fourth pillar holding up the overall omni-channel canopy. We propose three main categories of assessment. The first centers on the touchpoints that customers use, whether the store, the website, telephone, a mobile app, or social media. Sellers need an effective mechanism to assess the relative **utilization** and cross-utilization of each channel or touchpoint, as well as traffic flows across these channels (e.g., percentage who start on social media and then visit a store). With these analyses, they also can determine the breadth and depth of the company's omni-channel presence.

The next component, **engagement**,[64] refers to both store-driven and customer-led forms. First, store-driven engagement pertains to recommendations made by agents, created on the basis of purchase and behavioral algorithms. For example, in-store salespeople in an omni-channel context should be able to offer personalized recommendations to customers that reflect their prior purchase habits and preferences, so sellers must measure the extent to which salespeople have easy access to these data. Second, marketers need to harness data that reflect customer-led engagement, including customers' activity on social media, word-of-mouth recommendations, product or store reviews, and time spent on the firm's website or app. This latter metric remains challenging; most firms trying to assess this type of engagement struggle with missing and incomplete information that is still difficult to capture entirely.

Finally, assessing performance demands quantifying the **conversion rates** (percent of visitors who buy), both within (e.g., visit a website and buy from a website) and across (e.g., visit a website but buy from a store) channels. In parallel, firms should measure customer patronage of the store, according to customer lifetime value and RFM analysis (how Recently the customer purchased, the Frequency of purchasing, and the Monetary amount of purchases).

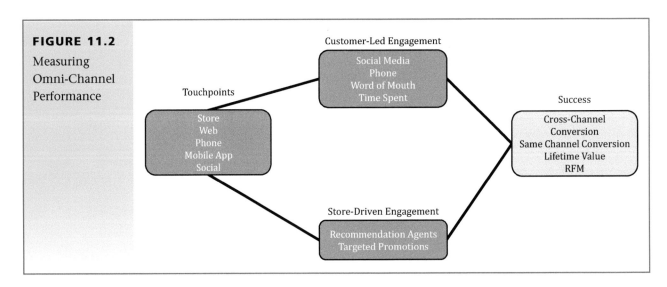

FIGURE 11.2

Measuring Omni-Channel Performance

As a reflection of the four pillars of an omni-channel strategy, we close with an example of Home Depot's impressive omni-channel initiatives.

EXAMPLE: HOME DEPOT (USA/GLOBAL)

Home Depot has embarked on an ambitious omni-channel strategy, investing upward of $5 billion in its initiatives.[65,66] Notably, it plans to leverage the 1.7 trillion data points it has collected, then integrate them with weather and consumer location data, to gain the capacity to target consumers by highlighting products that they are likely to find relevant and that are in proximity to where the consumer is located at each moment.[67] By installing lockers outside stores, it hopes to improve its ability to cater to click-and-collect customers. With new showroom locations and fulfillment centers, Home Depot also plans to reconfigure its delivery services. Using data that indicate 45 percent of online orders get picked up in store, and 85 percent of online order returns get processed inside stores,[68] Home Depot also has designed the interaction to require customers to check in with a store associate, so that it can provide more guidance and potentially increase their satisfaction—but also gain an opportunity to engage in some cross-selling. For products rarely bought online, such as lawn mowers, Home Depot has located them right outside the store entrance, so even online shoppers can observe and investigate them when they come to collect their online purchases.[69]

Take-Aways

- An omni-channel strategy involves the successful delivery of a seamless experience across channels, including the ability to synchronize the strengths of each channel to support all other channels that in turn share their strengths.

- A successful omni-channel strategy also demands a deep understanding of the consumer journey—the path consumers take from information search to purchase.

- Imagining an omni-channel strategy as a canopy, marketers should work to establish four strong pillars to hold it up: harnessing customer knowledge, leveraging technology, managing channel relationships, and assessing channel performance.

- Consumer insights, including the recognition that not all consumers are the same and that different consumers value different things, must be integrated with a deep understanding and mastery of retail operations, along with advanced applications of novel technology.

> - An omni-channel strategy necessitates realigning the incentives of individual channels to make the channels work for the good of the whole.
>
> - Companies need metrics that acknowledge the holistic and cross-channel nature of the omni-channel experience.

NOTES

1 Hosseini, Sabiolla, Marieluise Merz, Maximilian Roglinger, and Annette Wenninger (2018), "Mindfully going omni-channel: An economic decision model for evaluating omni-channel strategies," *Decision Support Systems*, 109, 74–88.

2 Author personal experience, July–August 3, 2018.

3 Saghiri, Soorosh, Richard Wilding, Carlos Mena, and Michael Bourlakis (2017), "Toward a three-dimensional framework for omni-channel," *Journal of Business Research*, 77, 53–67.

4 Author personal experience, July 22, 2018.

5 Saghiri, Wilding, Mena, and Bourlakis (2017), op. cit.

6 Bergh, Chip (2018), "The CEO of Levi Strauss on leading an iconic brand back to growth," *Harvard Business Review*, 96 (4), 33–39.

7 Saghiri, Wilding, Mena, and Bourlakis (2017), op. cit.

8 Thomas, Winston (2018), "Levi Strauss stitches omnichannel with DX," *CDO Trends*, www.cdotrends.com/story/13843/levi-strauss-stitches-omnichannel-dx?refresh=auto, date retrieved October 23, 2018.

9 Anonymous (2018), "As competition mounts, Starbucks tie-up with Alibaba," *The New Indian Express*, August 3.

10 Pei, Li and Adam Jordan (2018), "China's caffeine war: Fast-growing Luckin brews up a threat to Starbucks," www.reuters.com/article/us-china-coffee-focus/chinas-caffeine-war-fast-growing-luckin-brews-up-a-threat-to-starbucks-idUSKBN1KE1C2, date retrieved July 24, 2018.

11 Horowitz, Josh (2018), "A startup challenging Starbucks in China is now worth $1 billion," July 11, https://qz.com/1325403/luckin-coffee-startup-challenging-starbucks-in-china-worth-1-billion, date retrieved August 9, 2018.

12 Ibid.

13 TEDx (2017), "Omnichannel retail (r)evolution, Killian Wagner, TEDxHSG," www.youtube.com/watch?v=5SAtdSM0Trk.

14 Edelson, Sharon (2018), "The Real Real's Rati Levesque talks omnichannel and brick-and-mortar," *Women's Wear Daily*, June 27, p. 19.

15 Whosay (2018), "What are omnichannel customers and why Walmart thinks they are the future," January 24, www.youtube.com/watch?v=AeUKqWME1CQ.

16 Ibid.

17 "Walmart refocuses on Omnichannel," *Business Insider*, February 16, 2017, www.businessinsider.com/walmart-refocuses-on-omnichannel-2017-2, date retrieved July 18, 2018.

18 Ibid.

19 Samuely, Alex (2018), "Will Walmart become the world's largest omnichannel retailer with Jet.com deal?" www.retaildive.com/ex/mobilecommercedaily/walmart-could-become-worlds-largest-omnichannel-retailer-with-jet-com-deal, date retrieved July 18, 2018.

20 "Walmart refocuses on Omnichannel," *Business Insider*, February 16, 2017, www.businessinsider.com/walmart-refocuses-on-omnichannel-2017-2, date retrieved July 18, 2018.

21 Whosay (2018), op. cit.

22 Jones, Charisse (2018), "Now who's on top? Walmart gains on Amazon as more shoppers click and buy online," *USA Today*, May 17, www.usatoday.com/story/money/2018/05/17/walmart-gains-amazon-more-people-shop-online/599488002, date retrieved October 23, 2018.

23 Kim, Jae-Cheol and Se-Hak Chun (2018), "Cannibalization and competition effects on a manufacturer's retail channels strategies: Implications on an omni-channel business model," *Decision Support Systems*, 109 (May), 5–18.

24 Ibid.

25 Verhoef, Peter C., P.K. Kannan, and J. Jeffrey Inman (2015), "From multi-channel retailing to omni-channel retailing: Introduction to the Special Issue on multi-channel retailing," *Journal of Retailing*, 91 (2), 174–181.

26 Sousa, Rui and Chris Voss (2012), "The impacts of e-service quality on customer behaviour in multichannel e-services," *Total Quality Management and Business Excellence*, 23 (7–8), 789–806.

27 Barker, Shane (2018), "How to create your omnichannel retail strategy," *Forbes*, www.forbes.com/sites/forbescoachescouncil/2018/08/03/how-to-create-your-omnichannel-retail-strategy/#4ac109526561, date retrieved August 31, 2018.

28 Nakano, Satoshi and Fumiyo N. Kondo (2018), "Customer segmentation with purchase channels and media touchpoints using single source panel data," *Journal of Retailing and Consumer Services*, 41, 142–152.

29 Saghiri, Wilding, Mena, and Bourlakis (2017), op. cit.

30 Kumar, V. and R. Venkatesan (2005), "Who are the multichannel shoppers and how do they perform? Correlates of multichannel shopping behavior," *Journal of Interactive Marketing*, 19 (2), 44–62.

31 Emrich, Oliver, Michael Paul, and Thomas Rudolph (2015), "Shopping benefits of multi-channel assortment integration and the moderating role of retailer type," *Journal of Retailing*, 91 (2), 326–342.

32 Zeng, Fue, Xiaomeng Liu, and Yuchi Zhang (2016), "How to make the most of omnichannel retailing," *Harvard Business Review*, July/August, 22.

33 Ibid.

34 Bianchi, Raffaela, Michal Cermak, and Ondrej Dusek (2016), "More than digital plus traditional: A truly omnichannel customer experience," *McKinsey Quarterly*, July, www.mckinsey.com/business-functions/operations/our-insights/more-than-digital-plus-traditional-a-truly-omnichannel-customer#0, date retrieved August 22, 2018.

35 www.targetmarketingmag.com/article/new-research-omnichannel-marketing-the-key-customer-experience/all, date retrieved August 22, 2018.

36 Payne, Liz Manser, Victor Barger, and James Peltier (2017), "Omni-channel marketing, integrated marketing communications, and consumer engagement: A research agenda," *Journal of Research in Interactive Marketing*, 11 (2), 185–197.

37 Rodriguez, Bernardo (2018), "Putting customer experience at the center of digital transformation," *MIT Sloan Management Review*, July 3.

38 Kumar, Raj, Tim Lange, and Patrik Silen (2017), "Building omnichannel excellence," *McKinsey Quarterly*, April.

39 Columbia Business School (2015), "The future of omni-channel retail: Emily Culp of Rebecca Minkoff," May 15, www.youtube.com/watch?v=IR6wGM_WAvk.

40 Bell, David R., Santiago Gallino, and Antonio Moreno (2018), "The store is dead: Long live the store," *MIT Sloan Management Review*, 59 (3), 59–66.

41 Ibid.

42 www.mytotalretail.com/article/must-have-strategies-and-technologies-for-omnichannel-retailers, date retrieved August 23, 2018.

43 Ibid.

44 www.beckershospitalreview.com/healthcare-information-technology/how-to-provide-an-omnichannel-patient-experience.html, date retrieved August 31, 2018.

45 Ibid.

46 Piotrowicz, Wojciech and Richard Cuthbertson (2014), "Introduction to the Special Issue: Information technology in retail: Toward omnichannel retailing," *International Journal of Electronic Commerce*, 18 (4), 5–16.

47 Ibid.

48 Brynjolfsson, Erik, Yu Jeffrey Hu, and Mohammad S. Rahman (2013), "Competing in the age of omnichannel retailing," *MIT Sloan Management Review*, 54 (4), 23–29.

49 Edelman, David C. and Marc Singer (2015), "Competing on customer journeys," *Harvard Business Review*, 93 (11), 88–100.

50 Ibid.

51 Packaged Facts (2017), "Amazon strategies and the Amazon shopper," *marketresearch.com academic*, date retrieved August 29, 2018.

52 www.lorealparisusa.com/products/makeup/shop-all-products.aspx?size=21&page=6, date retrieved August 28, 2018.

53 Edelman and Singer (2015), op. cit.

54 www.lorealparisusa.com/beauty-magazine/makeup/makeup-looks/makeupgenius-changes-makeup-application-forever.aspx, date retrieved August 29, 2018.

55 Piotrowicz and Cuthbertson (2014), op. cit.

56 Brynjolfsson, Hu, and Rahman (2013), op. cit.

57 Harpaz, Joe (2015), "Will Jet.com's 'smart cart' disrupt ecommerce?" *Forbes*, www.forbes.com/sites/joeharpaz/2015/08/05/will-jet-coms-smart-cart-disrupt-ecommerce/#4134eb8c34d0, date retrieved August 29, 2018.

58 Sheehan, Alexandra (2018), "How to centralize your inventory and 3 benefits for making the switch," www.shopify.com/retail/how-to-centralize-your-inventory, date retrieved August 24, 2018.

59 Ibid.

60 https://risnews.com/vitamin-shoppe-adds-omnichannel-subscription-services, date retrieved August 29, 2018.

61 Morrissey, Ryan, Klaus Stricker, Raymond Tsang, and Eric Zayer (2017), "The future of car sales is omnichannel," www.bain.com/insights/the-future-of-car-sales-is-omnichannel, date retrieved August 30, 2018.

62 www2.deloitte.com/us/en/pages/manufacturing/articles/foundation-of-future-automotive-retail-omni-channel-customer-engagement.html, date retrieved August 30, 2018.

63 www.whisbi.com/info/omnichannel/solution/customer/seamless/car, date retrieved August 30, 2018.

64 www.magestore.com/omnichannel-kpis, date retrieved September 4, 2018.

65 www.digitalcommerce360.com/2017/12/08/home-depot-spend-5-4-billion-sharpen-omnichannel-strategy, date retrieved September 4, 2018.

66 www.businessinsider.com/home-depot-ups-omnichannel-strategy-2017-12, date retrieved September 4, 2018.

67 Ibid.

68 Ibid.

69 https://channelsignal.com/blog/home-depot-took-omni-channel-retailing-straight-to-the-bank-in-2016, date retrieved September 4, 2018.

Index

Locators in *italics* refer to figures and those in **bold** to tables.

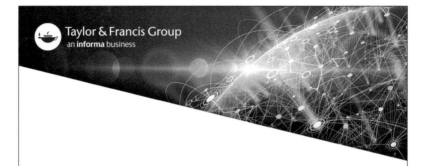